BATTLE LINES - FROM BEACHHEAD TO BERLIN D-DAY TO THE DEFEAT

PROGRESS OF INVASION: D-Day success depended on Allied deception, German error in plan and response, great sacrifice on beaches and bluffs. It nearly failed. Especially at Omaha Beach, poor planning by Gen. Bradley, bad weather, naval transport errors, and inadequate gunnery until late led to horrific losses. The bulk of the 51st landed 3 weeks later, after the historic June 18-22 storm which did more damage than all the earlier German firepower. As materiel poured ashore, the buildup was unexpectedly bottled up by extremely defensible, fiercely defended hedgerows. Even so, a million troops landed by July & German Gen. Rommel knew the invasion was unstoppable. He planned surrender but was seriously injured July 17. In Berlin, a July 20 assassination attempt on Hitler failed. Four days later, at Patton's suggestion, concentrated breakout at St. Lo loosed the Allies to chase the Germans to Germany (Dec.15 line). On June 22, the battle-hardened Soviets attacked, destroying 25 German divisions in 12 days. By contrast, Allied higher command wasted time and possibly war-ending opportunities, letting trapped Germans escape, to the distress of Patton, whom the Germans most feared. Especially costly were the pointless Brittany invasion, failure to close the "Falaise Pocket", slowness to block escape across the Seine. Later, suffering supply shortages and unaware the West Wall was nearly wide open into mid-October, the Allies slowed and attacked into strength with generally very negative results, as toward Arnhem in the Netherlands (by Montgomery, with his bad planning and delays), at Metz (by Patton), and worst of all from September to December in the Hürtgen Forest (S. of Aachen), where 70,000 Americans and Germans died for a few worthless miles of foggy, icy, shattered landscape. Otherwise, on the North Sea-to-Switzerland line most energies at the end of 1944 were directed to supply, recovery and preparation for invasion of Germany.

BATTLE OF THE BULGE: That this was the largest single battle in US Army history, with over a million combatants, shows the importance of containing the powerful German surprise attack (**darkened bulge** out to Dec. 26 line), deceptively small compared to the sweep of Allied movements earlier. Recent history emphasizes this was a soldier's victory. Not until January '45 did the full chain of command start providing excellent leadership, finally doing justice to these valiant American citizen soldiers. [A lesser German diversion near Strasbourg developed Jan. 1-30 (**darkened**)]

ALLIED COUNTERATTACK: The Allies slowly attacked in January-mid-March bitter winter fighting. Once the Rhine was crossed in force, they sped through Germany in six weeks. Even so, fanatics held to the end: Allied deaths in April neared June '44 and exceeded February '45 levels. To the east, on Jaan. 12 the Soviets began a brutally rapacious but brilliant attack with 4 million men and 10,000 tanks, culminating in 360,000 casualties in taking Berlin. Hitler committed suicide April 26. On May 7, Allied and Soviet troops met and the great invasion was done.

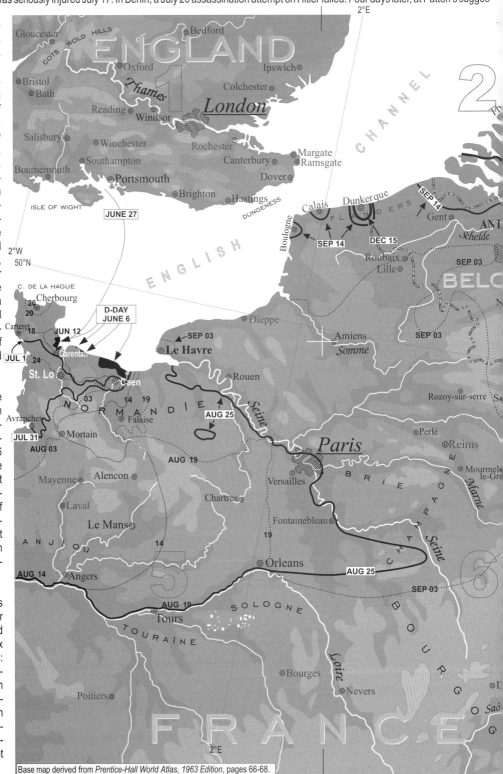

Base map derived from *Prentice-Hall World Atlas, 1963 Edition*, pages 66-68.

BATTLE LINES: on indicated dates, the edge of Allied advance is shown, based on 23 maps in *The West Point Atlas for the Second World War*. Boxed dates are about a month apart. The Battle of the Bulge line (Dec 26) shows maximum German penetrations and is not a front line. Movement from D-Day onward was into German positions excepting an August drive to Mortain toward Avranches, the Bulge, and January 1-30. Pockets (light encirclements) were the "Ruhr Pocket" (April 4), and others near Halle and Stuttgart. The complexity of this map perhaps hints at infinitely greater complexity on the ground.

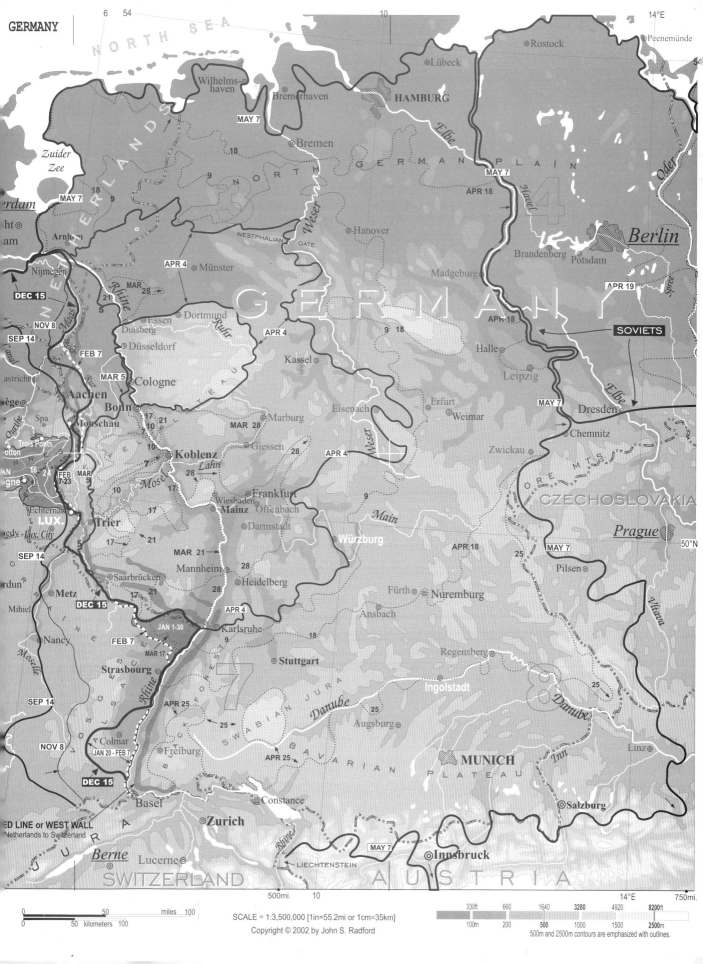

UNBROKEN LINE

THE 51ST ENGINEER COMBAT BATTALION
From Normandy to Munich

Under the command of Lt. Colonel Harvey R. Fraser, recipient of the 1999 George S. Patton Award, the 51st Engineer Combat Battalion earned the highest honors given to entire units: the American *Presidential Unit Citation* and the French *Croix de Guerre with Silver Star*, given for "extraordinary heroism and outstanding performance of duty" in the Battle of the Bulge.

For his superior military leadership from 14 December 1944 to 7 July 1945
This book is dedicated to Lieutenant Colonel (later Brigadier General) Harvey R. Fraser

Lt. Col. Fraser at an awards ceremony, Heister, Germany (map page 136) *Corps Files - 23 March 1945*

At first, Lt. Colonel Fraser was unhappy assigned to the rearmost engineer combat battalion in the First Army Area. But later, he stated: "I'd like to congratulate General Carter on his enlightened decision to send Harvey Fraser to the rearmost battalion. The 51st was a superbly trained, experienced combat outfit and it was my great privilege to cast my lot with them. We didn't save the First Army Front, but we sure as hell helped save it's rear." [Ft. Belvoir, 1984]

UNBROKEN LINE

THE 51ST ENGINEER COMBAT BATTALION
From Normandy to Munich

Albert E. Radford and *Laurie S. Radford*
John S. Radford, Editor

With contributions by
Brigadier General Harvey R. Fraser, PhD
Major General John W. Barnes
Colonel Floyd D. Wright
Captain Sam C. Scheuber
First Lieutenant Joseph B. Milgram, Jr.
First Lieutenant Fred L. Nabors
First Sergeant Raymond Millard
T/5 Wilson Roberts
Sergeant Thomas Banks
Corporal Frank H. Lee

Woodside, California

Copyright © 2002 by Albert E. Radford and Laurie S. Radford

Maps copyright © 2002 by John S. Radford

Book design and maps created by John S. Radford.

Battle lines taken from *A Time for Trumpets* are used by permission of HarperCollins Publishers Inc. *Times Atlas of the World* maps are adapted by permission of HarperCollins Publishers and are copyrighted © 2002 by Bartholomew Map Data Limited, Glasgow, Scotland.

All rights reserved. Except for brief quotations of several hundred words or less, no part of this book may be reproduced or utilized in any form or by any means, electronic or mechanical, including photocopying, recording, or by any information storage or retrieval system, without permission in writing from the Publisher. Inquiries should be addressed to Cross Mountain Publishing, PO Box 3760, Half Moon Bay, CA 94019.

ISBN 0-9717638-0-1

Printed by Professional Graphics Printing Co., Laurel, MD; binding by United Book Press, Baltimore, MD.

For Comrades, Family and Friends
Too soon they will be gone. Let us not soon forget.

Overview

Late into the second night of the great German offensive, in full-overcast darkness, forbidden the use of blackout lights, the 51st Engineer Combat Battalion headed *towards* the front. In what became the great "Battle of the Bulge", a half million German Infantry and Panzer troops were pouring across the Ardennes frontier to the total shock of isolated and overwhelmed American forces. Many of these units fought with desperate tenacity, some nearly to the point of annihilation. Others fled in panic or strategic retreat along dark Ardennes back-roads to regroup to the west. In the midst of this chaos, fear and uncertainty, the men of the 51st calmly, confidently elbowed their way eastward against the flow, to prepare strategic defenses in the Ourthe River Valley and at Trois Ponts and ... to take their place in military history.

A providential, some say "miraculous", chain of events found the 51st Engineers to be superbly trained; to be diverted at the last moment from Asia to Europe; *to gain solidly competent, true leaders less than two days before the German attack*; to have critical weapons appear by chance at exactly the right time; to be sent to Trois Ponts barely in time to stop and deflect Kampfgruppe Peiper's powerful armored column that had been chosen by Hitler to spearhead the German breakthrough; and finally, to be sent to defend against the center of the last best German hope of a push to the Meuse River and beyond towards Antwerp.

Also miraculously, out of proportion to their critical role, their losses were few. For every 1300 American soldiers killed in the Battle of the Bulge (3.2% rate), 1 died from the 51st (1%). Reasons for this include excellent training and leadership, determined courage, wise use of terrain and of opportunities for deception, and luck. Though not infantry or paratroopers, they were trained well for combat; and in this hour of greatest need, they readily accepted their challenge, proving themselves heroic both as fighters and as engineers. Their outstanding performance placed them in the ranks of an elite few units receiving the highest honors bestowed upon entire units by the United States and by France.

These honors insist we remember what might have been if not for the men of the 51st and others like them. For despite mounting defeats and setbacks, such as German "wonder weapons" proving ineffective, a 60% casualty rate, devastating losses to the Soviets, and a severely battered and strained production, the Germans threatened with this last desperate blitzkrieg to cut through the Allies. Failure to stop them could have led to worse than Dunkirk and perhaps only conditional surrender or even truce, with Nazi leadership contained yet undefeated, with time to complete and erase the evidence of monstrous crimes of genocide. Or perhaps Allied bombing, which took over a million killed and seriously wounded, might have been far more devastating to a German heritage, much of it our own, and to a German people, generally a good friend in decades since. Or had the Allies in the West been stopped or split, their leverage may have been lessened with the seemingly unstoppable, rampaging Soviets, who may well have forced a German surrender single-handedly in the summer of 1945, resulting in perhaps no post-war "West Germany" to speak of.

Forcing unconditional surrender was essential for all concerned. The 51st Engineer Combat Battalion, from Normandy to Munich, but most especially in the Battle of the Bulge, did more than its share to bring that about. The lines of defense established by the men of the 51st in the Battle of the Bulge held and did not break; and, afterwards, their bridges and close support for infantry and armor forged an unbroken line of advance, stopping only with the defeat of the Nazi regime.

John S. Radford

BATTLE OF THE BULGE: DECEMBER 16-26, 1944
Hitler's Plans for Breakthrough.   **Containment by the Allied Forces.**

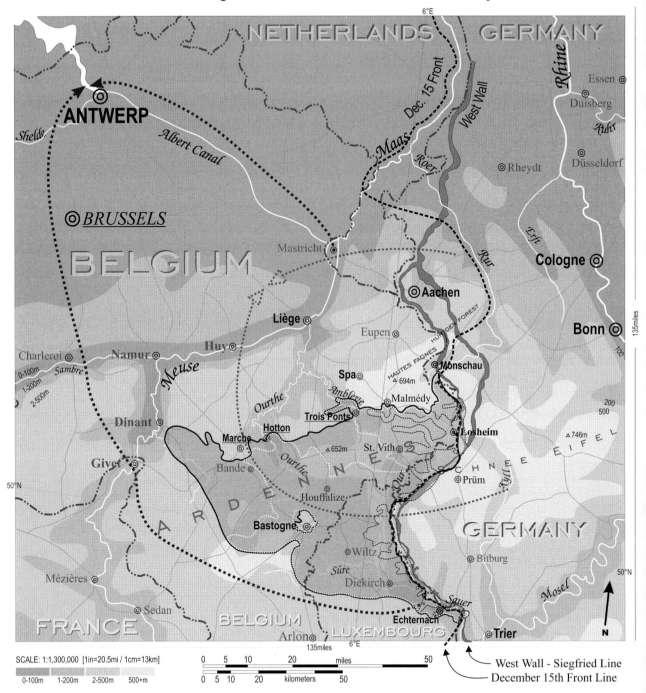

Hitler's Plan was to capture Antwerp(━▶), split Allied Forces, force a "Dunkirk" or worse, gain time for victory or truce. Almost none of his generals believed this possible and secretly hoped only to encircle Liège (⋯⋯). The **Marche-Hotton-Trois Ponts** defensive line, including the 51st ECB, stood dead center, opposed to this great offensive. It's containment, the "Battle of the Bulge", engaged over a million troops in the greatest single battle of U.S. Army history. The map bulge (darkened) outlines maximum penetrations. The breakthrough by the end of the 17th (2 days) is shown as a superimposed lighter shading. By the end of the 22nd (7 days), the Germans had pushed about to the dashed white boundary. By December 26 (10 days), they had run out of time.

Source maps are mostly in *A Time for trumpets*: pages 30 and 31 and derivatives of many other smaller maps. Outline of the "bulge" is deduced from maps and descriptions in *A Time for Trumpets* plus the December 16-25 map in *West Point Atlas for the Second World War: Europe and the Mediterranean*. Contours and main streams are derived from *The Prentice-Hall World Atlas, Second Edition*, page 68. NOTE: The West Wall is more accurately mapped next to the bulge, using the more detailed maps in *A Time for Trumpets*. North of the Bulge and east of Losheim, West Wall mapping relied on *West Point Atlas* maps, which are often more boldly drawn, perhaps to highlight the feature.

The Battle of the Bulge

The greatest single victory in US Army History
[excerpts from *A Time for Trumpets*]

On 16 December 1944 the vanguard of three German armies totaling 500,000 men attacked suddenly out of the mists and snow cloaking the eastern edge of the rugged Ardennes region of northern Central Europe. A bold and brilliant stroke by Adolph Hitler himself, it precipitated an unprecedented crisis for the Allied forces. In the most dismal failure of battlefield intelligence in the history of the U.S. Army, the Germans achieved total surprise. Ultimately, six hundred thousand Americans fought back in what came to be known as the Battle of the Bulge -- the most decisive battle on the Western Front during World War II, and America's greatest single victory of the war.

"Among 600,000 Americans eventually involved in the fighting - including 29 divisions, 6 mechanized cavalry groups, and the equivalent of 3 separate regiments - casualties totaled 81,000, of which 15,000 were captured and 19,000 were killed. Among 55,000 British -- 2 divisions and 3 brigades -- casualties totaled 1,400, of which just over 200 were killed. The Germans, employing close to 500,000 men -- including 28 divisions and 3 brigades -- lost at least 100,000 killed, wounded, and captured.

"Both sides lost heavily in weapons and equipment, probably as many as 800 tanks on each side, and the Germans a thousand planes." p. 618

The Distinguished 51st Engineer Combat Battalion
[excerpts from ***Dark December***]

"Here was a case where the fate of divisions and armies rested for a few brief moments on the shoulders of a handful of men; first at the town of Trois Ponts [primarily 51st ECB], and then, only hours later, with another, smaller, handful of men [291st ECB] at the bridge just east of Werbomont." p. 147

"One German column which attempted to seize the vital Ourthe River Bridge at a little town called Hotton, was turned back by another of the unheralded small handfuls of men [primarily 51st ECB] so important in the ultimate Allied victory." p. 165

Place Names Mentioned in the Text

F - FRONT: Battle Lines (8 sections)	page **6** Bulge	**46** Normandy	**78**-80-204 Trois Ponts	**88**-92-94 Hotton	**124** Roer (Rur)	**132** to Rhine	**136** Rhine	**148** Germany (4 sections)	**B** - BACK Ardennes Offensives (8 sections)

Easily found locales aren't listed as are names not mentioned in text and used in only one picture caption.

Aachen   F2, 6, 124
Ahr River   136
Aisomont   78, B3
Andler   B4
Arlon   6
Arnhem   F2
Attenkirchen   148-4
Aye   88, B2
Aywaille   B3
Bad Homburg   148-1
Bad Neuenahr   132, 136
Baillonville   88, B2
Barvaux   88, B2
Basse-Bodeux   78, B3
Bastogne   F6, 6, B7
Biebelried   148-4
Bigge   148
Bonn   F3, 6, 132, 136
Brilon   148-1
Brück   124, 132
Carentan   F5, 46
Celles   B1
Champlon (Crossroads)   88, B6
Champlon Famenne   88, B2
Cheneux   78, B3
Cherbourg   F1, 46
Chevron   78, 204, B3
Ciergnon   B1
Ciney   B1
Clavier   88, B2
Colmar   F7
Cologne   F3, 6
Dachau   148-4
Dainrode   148-4
Dattenberg   136
Desertines   46
Dinant   6, B1
Durbuy   88, B2
Erezée   B2
Erft River   132
Esch   132
Eupen   6, 124
Forrieres   88, B6
Fosse   78, B3
Froitzheim   132
Gaimersheim   148-4
Gas   46
Geisenfeld   148-4
Germeter   124
Givet   6, B1
Grand-Halleux   78, B3
Gullesheim   136, 148-1
Gunzenhausen   148-4
Hâbièmont   78, 204, B3
Hamoir   88, B2
Hampteau   88, 92, B2
Hargimont   88, B2

Harsin   88, B2
Haute Fagnes   6, B4
Hebert   46
Heister   136
Herresbach   B4
Hetzingen   124
Hogne   88, B2
Hotton   F6, 6, 88, 92, B2
Houffalize   6, B7
Humain   88, B2
Hürtgen   124
Hürtgen Forest   6, 124
Huy   B2, 6
Inde River   124
Ingolstadt   F8, 148-4
Jemelle   88, B2
Kalenborn   132, 136, 138
Kall River   124
Kirchasch   148-1
Klein (Vernich)   132
Kornelimünster   124
Kripp   132, 136
Küstelberge   148-1
La Chapelle-en-Juger   46
La Gleize   78, B3
La Levée   78, B3
La Roche   B2
La Tour   80
Lammersdorf   124
Langenhahn   148-1
Liège   F2, 6
Lienne Creek   78, 204
Linz   132, 136, 148-1
Lohrmannshof   148-4
Lommersum   132
Lorcé   78, B3
Ludendorff Bridge   136
Maffe   88, B2
Malmédy   6, B4
Manderfeld   B4
Manhay   78, B3
Marburg   F3, 148-1
Marche   6, 88, B2
Marcourt   88, B2
Martelange   B7
Medendorf   B4
Melreux   88, 92, B2
Metz   F6
Modave   B2
Monschau   F2, 6, 132, B4
Mont Rigi   B4
Montmedy   F6
Mortain   F5, 46
München   F8, 148-4
Namur   F2, 6, B1
Neufchatel-en-Saoanois   46
Neustadt (on Wied R.)   136

Neustadt (near Marburg)   148-1
Neustadt (near Main R.)   148-4
Niaster   78
Nideggen   124, 132
Noiseaux   88, B2
Nuremberg   F8, 148-4
Nuttlar   148
Ober Forstbach   124
Ochsenfurt   148-4
Ourtheville   88, B6
Perlé   F6
Pessoux   B1
Petersaurach   148-4
Petit Coo   78
Petit-Spai   80
Raeren   124
Reharmont   78
Remagen   132, 136
Rochefort   88, B2
Rodenhausen   148-1
Roetgen   124
Rollesbroich   124
Rothen-bacher Lay   148-1
Rozoy-sur-Serre   F6
Rur (Roer) R.   F3, 124
Saar [Saarbrücken]   F7
Salmchateau   78, B3
Schmidt   124
Schnee Eifel   F3-7, 148-1, B4
Schoenberg   B4
Schwammenauel   124, 132
Soy   88, 92, B2
Spa   F2, B3
St. Hubert   B6
St. Lo   F5, 46
St. Symphorien-les-Monts   46
St. Vith   6, B4
Stavelot   78, B3
Stoumont   78, B3
Tohogne   88
Trois Ponts   F2, 6, 78, 80, B3
Unkel   132, 136
Urft River   124
Vielsalm   78, B3
Vosges   F7
Wallau   148-1
Wanne   78, B3
Werbomont   78, B3
Wied River   136, 148-1
Wulkersdorf   148-4
Würzburg   F7, 148-2
Xhoris   B3
Zerkall   124
Zülpich   132
Zweifall   124

Table of Contents

Overview — 5
- The Battle of the Bulge — 7
- Chapter Summaries — 11
- Campaign Combat Summary — 12
- The Spirit of the 51st — 13

Preparing for the Worst — 17
- Activation and Basic Training — 19
  - Cadre and Cadre Training — 19
  - Plattsburg, New York — 22
  - Basic Training — 24
- Reorganization and Advanced Training — 28
  - The Weather and Training — 28
  - Unit Training — 30
  - Combined Training — 31
  - Maneuvers and Fort Belvoir — 32
- England by Way of North Africa — 34
  - In North Africa — 36
  - England — 38
  - Preparation for Crossing the Channel — 42

Into Battle: from Normandy to the West Wall — 45
- Normandy Campaign — 47
- Northern France Campaign — 57
- Ardennes Campaign (Belgium) — 59

A Place in History: The Battle of the Bulge — 71
- Introduction — 72
- The Patton Myth — 73
- Holding the Line — 76
  - Commanding Officers — 77
  - Defense at Trois Ponts — 79
  - The Battle of Hotton — 89
- Ardennes Campaign (Letters) — 102

Bridges to Victory: The Invasion of Germany — 107
- The American Counteroffensive — 108
  - Support to the Divisions — 109
  - Bridging at Grand-Halleux — 113
- Germany and the Roer (Rur) Crossing — 123
- Bridging the Rhine and Germany and the Ruhr Pocket — 137
  - Introduction — 137
  - Bridging the Rhine — 138

Germany and the Ruhr Pocket	146
The Sorbonne, Paris (France)	152
The Race South to the Danube and Munich	155
The Long March	155
Assault Crossing of the Danube at Ingolstadt	157

Post-War Occupation — 167

Biebelried	168
Würzburg	169

A Lifetime Later — 179

Brigadier General Harvey R. Fraser	180
Major General John W. Barnes	183
Colonel Floyd D. Wright	186
Captain Sam C. Scheuber	191
Captain Albert E. Radford	194
First Lieutenant Joseph B. Milgram, Jr.	195
First Lieutenant Fred Nabors	199
First Sergeant Raymond Millard	209
T/5 Wilson Roberts	211
Sergeant Thomas Banks	212
Corporal Frank Lee	215

Honors and Memorials — 221

Plaque Presentation	222
Distinctive Unit Plaque	224
Presidential Unit Citation	225
Croix de Guerre Avec Etoile d'Argent	226
Letter of Commendation - Major General Craig	227
Letter of Commendation - Colonel Ekman	228
Certificate of Appreciation	229
Trois Ponts Plaque	230
Hotton Plaque	231
Individual Awards	232
1999 General Patton Award	233
Purple Heart	234

Roll Call — 235

Appendices — 241

Bibliography	241
About the Maps and Photographs	243
Notes on Personnel Changes	244
Selected Weaponry	247

OVERVIEW

Chapter Summaries

This is a citizen-soldier account, vividly illustrated with over 90 photographs and 18 high quality, original maps. The text was selected or written, except where noted, by Albert E. Radford, H&S* Company Commander from March 1943 to August 1945. As such, it blends historical documents and first-hand impressions, with emphasis on the period under the command of Lt. Col. Harvey R. Fraser, 14 December 1944 to 7 July 1945. It affirms the American Way in World War II of selecting and training citizen-soldier officers and enlisted men combined with excellent, professional leaders like Lt. Col. Fraser and Capt. J.W. Barnes, provided by our military institutions such as West Point.

Overview highlights and outlines the book and summarizes the achievements and spirit of the battalion.

Preparing for the Worst (June 1942 - June 1944) is a soldier's account of 23 arduous months of training and traveling -- from blistering Texas to icy Plattsburg, North Africa, England, and Utah Beach. This account is based on the Official Military Record, the author's personal experiences and letters from Laurie Radford to her parents.

Into Battle: from Normandy to the West Wall (27 June 1944 - 15 December 1944) draws a first-hand, pup-tent level view of the unit's day-to-day life from Normandy to the eve of the German Counterattack into the Ardennes. This narrative uses excerpts, from many of the some 500 daily letters written by Captain Radford to his wife Laurie during five European Campaigns and the Occupation, to evoke images of the camaraderie, sense of duty, courage, initiative, and skills of the American Soldier in WWII.

A Place in History: the Battle of the Bulge (16 December 1944 - 3 January 1945) retells those crucial 10 days in December and thence into January, through extracts from: *Dark December* by Robert E. Merriam, 1947; *The 51st Engineer Combat Battalion and the Battle of the Bulge* by Ken Hechler, 1945 (1988); *The 51st Again!* by Barry W. Fowle & Floyd D. Wright, 1992.

Bridges to Victory: the Invasion of Germany (4 January 1945 - 8 May 1945) takes us to V-E Day: through combat in the worst Ardennes winter of 50 years, bridging under fire the Roer (Rur) and then the great Rhine River barriers, and the swift Danube, excerpting *The 51st Again!* and Captain Radford's letters.

Post-War Occupation (9 May 1945 - 8 July 1945) is composed of excerpts of Captain Radford's letters from the Würzburg area.

A Lifetime Later is a collection of recollections from the lives of some of the men in the 51st ECB, with colorful detail published nowhere else.

Honors and Memorials is a collection of the awards and honors bestowed on the 51st from 1945 to 1999 including a full list of Purple Heart awards.

Roll Call honors the sixteen soldiers who died in action and gives a full list of all members of the Battalion during the Northern Europe campaigns.

---

* H&S is the abbreviation for Headquarters & Services. Trained in all the skills of combat engineering, they specialized in administration and intelligence and the like. Captain Radford also specialized in mine detection.

Campaign Combat Summary

Conditions: The 51st Engineer Combat Battalion endured 10 months of continuous combat in Normandy, Northern France, the Ardennes, the Rhineland, and Central Europe. They were fired on by small arms, machine gun, and mortar; pounded by armored attacks and shelling; threatened underfoot by deadly minefields; assaulted from above by strafing, bombing, missiles, and buzz bombs. During the worst of these military assaults, the weather in Northern Europe was the most severe in fifty years.

Accomplishments: Amidst all this danger, they were called on to lay, remove and/or neutralize mines, booby traps, and demolitions. They constructed, repaired, and destroyed bridges. They cleared, maintained, and built roads. They captured enemy parachutists and retreating troops. They rescued captive G.I.'s. They secured command posts, water points, and supply depots. They extinguished a burning ammunition dump. In sum, they …

- stood their ground in the Ardennes, while many American units withdrew to the rear in great haste and disorder to avoid entrapment;

- defended their positions across the very center of the "Bulge", at Trois Ponts and along the Hotton-Marche-Rochefort barrier line, until relieved by elements of the 82nd Airborne, 2nd and 3rd Armored Divisions, 84th Infantry Division and the 53rd British Infantry Division;

- stopped advance Panzer units of the 1st SS Panzer Division, Sixth Panzer Army at Trois Ponts and 116th Panzer Division, Fifth Panzer Army, at Hotton;

- constructed under fire and air attack, across the swift Rhine River near Remagen, a 967 foot-long heavy pontoon bridge, the longest tactical bridge ever built;

- built under small-arms fire, a 400 foot treadway bridge across the Danube at Ingolstadt in Central Europe;

- provided effective support for the 82nd Airborne and the 75th and 9th Infantry Divisions in the Counter-Offensive in the Ardennes and Rhineland.

Casualties: Of the 630 men in the 51st Engineer Combat Battalion, 16 lost their lives in the line of duty and 96 received the Purple Heart.

Unit Awards: For extraordinary performance in the Battle of the Bulge, the unit was recognized with the Presidential Unit Citation and the French Croix de Guerre with Silver Star.

Individual Awards: Individuals were recognized with 1 Legion of Merit, 5 Silver Stars, 1 Bronze Star with Oakleaf Cluster, 25 Bronze Stars, 7 Soldier's Medals, and 5 Foreign Awards. Each Battalion member involved in the 5 Campaigns received 5 Battle Stars.

OVERVIEW

The Spirit of the 51st*

The spirit of the 51st which infused the whole Battalion, began with a sense of fitness and competence instilled by Colonel Anderson and was fully realized in battle by exemplary leaders such as Major Yates.

Major Yates

On **15 December** 1944, Major Yates returned to the 51st from hospital in England. According to a letter written by his wife Vera, to Laurie Radford on July 10, 1988:

> "The doctors wanted to amputate Robert's foot (while in an English Hospital following a serious accident). He said 'No'. Then they wanted to send him State Side, He said, 'No! I want to get back to my men. I came over here to help them win a war.' "

> "He once told me, 'Mama, I never gritted my teeth so hard and walked so straight as I did the day I walked out of the hospital.' [He went AWOL to return to the 51st.] The ankle remained stiff, the metatarsals were overlapped, the foot was an inch shorter than the other one, his toes were drawn up so that they never touched the floor."

Major Yates at Macomb Reservation near Plattsburg, NY.   *Corps Files - 1943*

> "After Robert came home, he had only one ear to hear with, one eye to see with, and only two lobes to breathe with. He fought a good fight."

On **16 December**, three German Armies attacked the Americans in the Ardennes. Two days later Major Yates found himself in Trois Ponts leading its defense with a mere 140 men against more than 4000 Panzers rolling by just yards away and probing his defenses day and night.

At 1300 "... on **18 December**, the bridge over the Salm River on Highway N23 was demolished. Shortly thereafter, Major Yates arrived in Trois Ponts, unaware of the situation and merely bound for the daily liaison meeting at the 1111th Engineer Combat Group. Colonel Anderson charged him with the defense of the city ...." p. 22

"Before the breakthrough, Major Yates had held various staff positions within the battalion for the preceding two years, having been its CO for several months in 1943. His 6-foot, 3-inch 200-pound figure towered over the scene at Trois Ponts. An affable Texan, easygoing in nature but determined in spirit, Major Yates held together his little company by prodding, cajoling, and encouraging them to resist long after they had reached reasonable limits of human endurance. 'I would find them asleep standing up after 94 hours on the

---

* This section was prepared by Albert Radford with quotes as attributed; un-attributed quotes are from *Holding the Line*.

job,' said Major Yates, 'but they were standing up.'" p.14

"Major Yates deployed his men in houses along the river, providing flank and rear guards and good fields of fire for machine guns and bazookas." ... "We kept sniping at them across the river for the next few days," said Major Yates, "but every shot of ours seemed to draw about a thousand in return. So we decided to deceive them as to how great a force we had available." ... "The company had about six 2½-ton trucks available, and they were kept running in and out of town. After dark, they were run out of Trois Ponts on Highway N23 toward Werbomont without lights and then run back on the same road with their lights on, simulating the arrival of reinforcements. Major Yates hit on the idea of simulating the presence and arrival of armor in Trois Ponts. This was done by putting chains on a single four-ton truck, and it was clanked back and forth repeatedly during the next few days. The closest facsimile to artillery or anti-tank guns that the company had were the bazookas, as Major Yates said, 'They made a pretty loud noise, so we used to shift them around from place to place after dark and it may have deceived the enemy into thinking we had a couple of light artillery pieces.' In addition, he moved small groups of riflemen from place to place and had them fire in such a way as to create the impression of considerable strengths in small arms." p. 22

"Colonel William E. Ekman, CO of the 505th Parachute Infantry Regiment, which entered Trois Ponts on **20 December**, paid high tribute to the spirit and courage of Company C of the 51st and singled out Major Yates for his leadership. 'He had everything under control,' said Colonel Ekman, 'and appeared ready and able to hold the town indefinitely. When the 82nd Airborne Division came in, we expected to find this unit decimated and discouraged. Instead, Major Yates approached me and uttered a classic phrase, 'Say, I'll bet you fellows are glad we're here.' " p. 14

"At 1100 on **21 December**, reports began coming in that the two companies of the 505th were having difficulties across the river. The enemy launched a strong counter-attack and started to surround elements that were defending on the hill overlooking Trois Ponts from the east. At 1500, Major Yates received a message from the 1111th Engineer Combat Group ordering Company C to withdraw. He brushed it aside and characteristically replied that it was impossible to disengage from the enemy, inasmuch as Company C was covering the withdrawal of the 82nd Airborne Division." p. 27

After leaving Trois Ponts, Major Yates joined the forces defending the Marche area where he was captured and quickly made a daring escape worthy of any war movie. "At 1500 on **22 December**, Company C, now returned from its defense of Trois Ponts, sent a reconnaissance party along Highway N4 to set up roadblocks. The party consisted of Major Yates, Captain Scheuber, Lieutenant Green, and Lieutenant Nabors. The men approached southeast of Marche and were fired on by the lead vehicles of an enemy armored column at [310805 - see map, p.88]. They stopped their jeep and advanced on foot and were soon cut off by five enemy tanks, two half-tracks filled with enemy personnel, and additional armor that was not actually seen. All officers but Major Yates escaped by taking off through fields and avoiding roads. Major Yates, who had only a few days before returned from the hospital where he had been confined with a foot injury, could not run and hence hid in a bush by the road. After two hours, he was discovered, disarmed, and taken prisoner. When the man guarding Yates relaxed his vigil for a moment, Major Yates dived into a stream beside which they stood, worked his way downstream, under about three feet of water, and escaped under a hail of small arms fire to return to friendly lines shortly before 2200 the same night. [almost frozen]" p.45*

---

* For more detail on Yates' escape story, see the colorful, first-hand account by 1st Lt. Fred Nabors on pp.207-208 in this book.

OVERVIEW

Colonel H. Wallis Anderson

Colonel H. Wallis Anderson, a veteran of the Mexican War, World War I and World War II, led the 51st ECB through rigorous training at Plattsburg, New York, through combat preparation at Highnam Court, England, and into action in the five European Campaigns. Having seen the awful loss of life in WWI due in good measure to poor training, Colonel Anderson became a firm believer in a sometimes unappreciated, severe regimen of training. He believed in "taking advantage of all inclement weather to toughen troops" and that "it is always better to train under adverse conditions and then accept more favorable circumstances as a bonus." This was the basis for a feeling of fitness and pride shared by many in the 51st: "we were maybe the best outfit in the Army". And the Colonel, able to do 50 one-handed pushups at age 50, himself embodied this fitness.

Assembling heavy pontoon units on the ice of Lake Champlain, building an H10-wooden trestle bridge over the Salmon River in the dark with a wind chill many degrees below zero that seemingly separated body from soul, camping out in pup tents on the "tundra" at Macomb Reservation near Plattsburg in 10 below zero weather, digging foxholes in solid frozen ground, running night compass courses through the deep snow of the forest and the icy bogs of the Reservation -- all this arduous training helped prepare the men of the 51st for their excellent performance of duty in the Battle of the Bulge and the American Counter-Offensive in the Ardennes and Rhineland.

Col. Anderson, 10 June 1944, England.
Collection of Joseph Milgram

In combat, Colonel Anderson always knew the deployment of his troops. Although his style was so low-key that his visits to the front were seldom seen, he nevertheless kept in close touch with his men and led the 1111th Engineer Combat Group with the 51st and the 291st, two of the best battalions in the First Army area.

The Men of the 51ST

The training and character of the men of the 51st Engineer Combat Battalion were severely challenged, by fierce combat and brutal weather, from 16 December 1944 to 8 May 1945. With ingenuity, deception, fortitude, and endurance, these men stopped advance elements of two lead Panzer Divisions during the Battle of the Bulge. There, facing overwhelming force alone or with scant support, they were finally relieved by five combat divisions.

During the American Counter-Offensive, from the Ardennes to the Rhine and beyond, they supported the 82nd Airborne and 75th and 9th Infantry Divisions with skill, determination, and tireless effort. In often brutal weather, they lived daily with the dangers of clearing mines, booby traps, demolitions, and obstacles and built, maintained, and guarded bridges, many while under fire.

From commander to private, the Battalion met these challenges ... in the spirit of the 51st.

Near Plattsburg, NY, 1943. The 51st was very mobile, here transporting pontoons. *Corps Files*

The first Bailey Bridge built by the 51st: Davis, West Virginia, August-September 1943. *Corps Files*

Preparing for the Worst*
Organization, Training, Transport

(June 1942 - June 1944)

ACTIVATION AND BASIC TRAINING
REORGANIZATION AND ADVANCED TRAINING
TO ENGLAND BY WAY OF NORTH AFRICA

Summary of the Pre-Invasion Camps and Movements of the 51st
Short transport by train or truck (1-2 days) not explicitly noted

Camp Bowie, Texas (for 124 days)	June 13, 1942 to October 15, 1942
Plattsburg Barracks, NY (321)	October 17, 1942 to September 3, 1943
West Virginia, XIII Corps maneuvers (10)	September 5-15, 1943
Fort Belvoir, Virginia (13)	September 17-30, 1943
Fort Dix, N.J. (35)	October 1 to November 5, 1943
Camp Patrick Henry, Virginia (6)	November 6-11, 1943
Hampton Roads, Virginia (2)	November 12-13, 1943
Liberty Ship (21)	November 14 to December 4, 1943
Port Oran, Algeria (1)	December 4, 1943
Fleurus, Algeria (31)	December 6, 1943 to January 5, 1944
Casablanca/Camp Don. B. Passage, Morocco (5)	January 8-12, 1944
HMS Andes transport (9)	January 12-20, 1944
Llanelly, Wales (23)	January 21 to February 13, 1944
Highnam Court, England (127)	February 14 to June 17, 1944
Bournemouth/Southampton, England (2)	June 18-19, 1944
Channel Liberty Ships at anchor (7)	June 20-26, 1944
Normandy - Utah Beach Landing	June 27, 1944

(About 105 men and officers followed the June 27 crossing, landing at Utah Beach July 4, 1944.)

---

* This chapter is based on the personal experiences of Albert Radford prior to and including his command of H&S Company, except where otherwise noted.

Unit Organization

Military organization can be quite variable. After a series of changes, the strength of the various components of the 51st ECB became the following by March of 1943:

Men / Unit	Unit	Composition	Officers	
14	**Squad**	= 12 Men	+ 1 "Buck" Sgt.	+ 1 Corporal
44	**Platoon**	= 3 Squads	+ 1 Staff Sgt.	+ 1 Lieutenant
175	**Company**	= 3 PL.+ HQ PL.	+ 1 1st Sergeant	+ 1 Captain
649	**Battalion**	= 4 Companies	+ 1 Lt. Colonel	+ 1 Major (XO)

Thus there were 1 Lt. Col. and Major + 4 Captains and 1st Sgts. + 12 Staff Sgts. and Lts. + 36 "Buck" Sgts. and Corporals + a remainder of 543 Privates, technicians and others.

"Unit History" below shows main *changes* for 1942-1944. For example, "H & S [Barnes]" means command of Headquarters & Services Company went to Barnes, August, 1942. Note: "CO" means "Commanding Officer"; "XO", "Executive Officer"; Co., "Company". (Dates based on *The 51st Again!*)

Unit History: 1942-44

1942	June 13	(Camp Bowie) *51st Engineers* Regiment activated ...	[CO - **Massoglia**]
		subdivided into H&S Co. (Headquarters & Services) / 1st Battalion (Co. A, B, C) / 2nd Battalion (Co. D, E, F) / "Medical Detachment"	
	late June	H & S [Pederson] C [Schroff]	[CO - **Ketchum**]
	August	H & S [Barnes]	
	September	A [Wittwer] B [Spurrier]	[CO - **Anderson**]
	October 17	(Plattsburg) Regiment *assigned to VI Corps*	
	November	1st Battalion [Yates] 2nd Batt.[Massoglia] A[Pederson]	[XO - **Kirkland**]
1943	January	Regiment *assigned to XIII Corps* B[Hodges]	
	March 18	*51st* Regiment renamed **1111 Combat Group**	[CO **Anderson**]
	comprised of	**238th** Engineer Combat Battalion (old 2nd Battalion)	[CO **Massoglia**]
	... and	**51st** Engineer Combat Battalion (old 1st Battalion)	[CO **Yates**]
		[51st consists of Companies H&S and A, B, and C]	
	June 4	**51st** Engineer Combat Battalion [XO - Yates]	[CO **Reafsnyder**]
	December 7	(Algeria) C[Schroff]	
1944	January 21	(England) Battalion *assigned to First Army*, under Gen. Omar Bradley	
	December 14	(Ardennes) First day for new CO	[CO **Fraser**]
	December 15	First day for returned XO	[XO **Yates**]

(During the Bulge, Company CO's were: H & S[Radford] / A[Wright] / B[Hodges] / C[Scheuber])

PREPARING FOR THE WORST

Activation and Basic Training
(13 June 1942 - 18 March 1943)

The 51st Engineer Combat Regiment (ECR) was activated on 13 June 1942, at Camp Bowie, Texas, and assigned to VIII Corps [-917]*. The First Battalion of this Regiment was the forerunner of the 51st Engineer Combat Battalion (ECB). The Commanding Officer of the Regiment was First Lieutenant Martin F. Massoglia. According to the initial morning report, the regimental strength totaled one -- Massoglia. Shortly afterwards a few others arrived, mostly second lieutenants.[1]

Colonel E. F. Ketchum replaced Massoglia on 20 June 1942. On 5 September 1942, Colonel H. Wallis Anderson assumed command following the transfer of Ketchum and the temporary command of approximately three days by Captain Albert B. McCollam.[1]

Colonel Anderson, the ongoing regimental commander, was a professional engineer with combat duty overseas during World War I. Afterwards, he served for many years in the Pennsylvania National Guard, mostly as Division Engineer, 28th Infantry Division.

Cadre and Cadre Training

By the end of June 1942, the officer complement of the regiment consisted of one colonel, one captain, one first lieutenant, and fifty-two second lieutenants. The noncommissioned officers (NCOs) were outnumbered by the latter. The first unit commanders included Second Lieutenant John W. Barnes, H & S Company; Second Lieutenant Glade S. Wittwer, Company A; Second Lieutenant Edward J. Matish, Company B; and Second Lieutenant Clifford P. Schroff, Company C. On 25 September 1942 Matish was succeeded by Second Lieutenant James D. Spurrier. By September the organization also had a medical officer, a dental officer, and a chaplain on the official roster, along with twelve more second lieutenants.[1]

On the whole, the second lieutenants, the nucleus of the new regiment, had a common background of limited military experience -- basic combat engineer training as enlisted men and three months of officer indoctrination and development at Officer Candidate School (OCS), Fort Belvoir, Virginia. Many were recent college or high school graduates. Their work experience represented a variety of occupations: banking, farming, clerking, teaching, accounting, construction, architecture, and others. Only a few had any formal professional engineer training. They came from across America: California, Texas, New Jersey, Iowa, Washington, Utah, North Carolina, Illinois, Alabama, and Virginia.

The cadre of enlisted men assigned to the new regiment was fewer than normally authorized. The total number of troops in the regiment was so limited -- less than one hundred -- that as an expedient, the personnel available for duty, excluding the kitchen crew, skeleton guard, and motor pool detail, were organized into an enlisted platoon and an officer platoon with each carrying out an improvised schedule.[2]

The officer and enlisted contingent spent much of the summer learning administrative procedures for the handling of incoming equipment and the processing of future enlisted fillers -- amid recurring rumors of "they're coming, they're coming." Training during that time involved calisthenics in the early mornings,

*[-917] Bracketed numbers are the days remaining to Saturday morning, 16 December 1944.

Military Organization*

Some 16.4 million Americans served in WWII. In the US Army, they were organized into about 10 hierarchical levels, outlined in this format below: **GROUP** Commander / typical troop strength < subunits. Below that there are Commissioned and Non-Com. officers in descending order, and a Glossary of terms used here.

ARMY GROUP	General/100s of thousands	**ARMY**	Gen. of Army/60-100,000<several Corps
CORPS	General/40-60,000<various Divisions	**DIVISION**	Maj. Gen./10-20,000<~10 Battalions
BRIGADE	Brig. General/5-7000<1-sev. Reg.	**REGIMENT**	Colonel / 2-6000 < ~3 battalions
BATTALION	Maj./500-1000<~3-4 companies	**COMPANY**	Captain/100-200<~3-4 platoons
PLATOON	Lt./usually 25-50<~3 squads	**SQUAD**	NCO type officer/10-20

(Battalion C.O. was "field grade officer", e.g., Major)

COMMISSIONED: General of the Army...... General .... Lt. General ....
Maj.General................ Brig. General .... Colonel .... Lt. Colonel ....
Major .... Captain .... 1st Lieutenant .... 2nd Lieutenant ....

NCOs: Sgt. Maj. of the Army.... Command Sgt............. Major...................
Sgt. Major .... First Sergeant .... Master Sgt. .... Sgt. First Class ...
Staff Sergeant .... Sergeant .... Corporal .... Specialist ....
Priv. First Class .... Private ....

GLOSSARY

L - Latin / Fr. - French / Ital. - Italian / M.E. - Middle English / Med. - Medieval

Army	<M.E. & Old Fr. *armee* <Med. L. *armata* (army,fleet) <L. *armatus* (armed) <L. *arma* (arms)
Battalion	<Old Fr. *battaillon* <Old Ital. <<*battaglia* (troop) <<L. *battuere* (batter)
Brigadier	<Fr. *brigade* <Old Ital. *brigata* (troop) <*briga* (strife) <perhaps Celtic root
Captain	<Middle Eng. *captein* <Old Fr. *capitaine* <Late L. *capitaneus* (chief) <L. *caput* (head)
Colonel	<Old Ital. *colonnello* (commander of a column) <L. *columna* (column)
Company	smallest unit w/full admin. function<Med. *Company* - group accompanying knight or lord
Corporal	<Obsolete Fr. variant of *caporal* <Ital.*caporale* <*capo* (head,chief) <L. *caput* (head); perhaps influenced by L. *corpus* (body)
Corps	body of persons acting together <L. *corpus* (body)
Division	smallest balanced team with all arms & services for extended independent operations
General	<L. *generalis* (belonging to a kind /relating to all) <L. *genus* (race, kind)
Infantry	<Fr. *infanterie* <Ital. *infante* (youth, foot soldier) <L. *infans* (infant)
Lieutenant	<Old Fr. *lieu* (in place of) <L. *locus* (place) + Fr. *tenant* (holding): acts in place of superior
Platoon	<17th Cent. term for musketeers firing volley / term for the volley <L. *pila* (little ball; pill)
Private	<M.E. *privat* <L. *privatus* (not public) <L. *privare* (to deprive, release) <L. *privus* (single, individual)
Regiment	=M.E.= Old Fr. <Late L. *regimentum* (organization, systematization) <L. *regere* (to rule)
Sergeant	<M.E. *sergant* <Old Fr. *sergent* <L. *servire* (serve) <L. *servus* (slave)

* Unit descriptions from **www.britannica.com**. Glossary derivations from *The American Heritage Dictionary of the English Language*, William Morris, Ed. 1969 . American Heritage Publishing Co, Inc., New York, N.Y.   ** Symbol "<" means *derived from*".

either athletics or jujitsu or both in the late afternoons, and an occasional midday march in the Texas heat. The study of military manuals occupied much of the late mornings and early afternoons. The new second lieutenants became all too familiar with the Officer of the Day routine, particularly on weekends.

The summer was a tremendous adjustment-integration period for the mix of "ninety-day wonders" from Officer Candidate School (OCS), one National Guard Officer, two graduates from the Reserve Officers' Training Corps (ROTC), and three graduates from the United States Military Academy at West Point. Those from OCS had to make a difficult transition from enlisted man to officer with the attending problems associated with their new military responsibilities and "niceties."

One of the latter was the awesome prospect of calling on the Colonel and his wife at home for the first time. The new second lieutenants wondered: "Where do I get a calling card and what do I do with it? Who is supposed to introduce me? Suppose he forgets my name? What should I say to the Colonel? How do I know when to leave and how do I get out of here properly?" ... and on and on. The Officers' Guide was of little help to most of the 64 new lieutenants in that situation.

Even saluting was a problem. One new officer, Lieutenant Radford, disliked going down town after supper because the place was "lousy with soldiers." He wore out his arm returning salutes. His solution was to take "the back alleys and less busy streets." Apparently a form of weekend recreation for the Camp Bowie draftees was walking the streets of Brownwood in groups, then dropping back in single file to properly salute any approaching new second lieutenant.[3]

Wives, too, had their own adjustments to make to this new army life. According to the Officers' Guide, an officer was not supposed to carry any large or ungainly parcel in public. Yet his wife was perfectly free to do so. Obviously there had to be some restrictions, for an officer in dress uniform would be "neither glamorous nor awe-inspiring" nor free to return salutes if loaded down with bundles, say a watermelon for example. One of the lieutenants decided it was not beneath the dignity of an officer to carry a small weekend bag to which he could transfer his watermelon in some dark street, as long as he didn't "get arrested on suspicion of melon-stealing." Most of the young married lieutenants lived off base and their wives had to shop by taxi or bus.[4]

Many years later, Martin Massoglia, the first regimental commander, had difficulty recalling much of military significance that had occurred during our stay in Texas. But he vividly remembered the off-duty hours spent in the Officers' Club with its bar and dance floor.[5] Converting an old mess hall into a respectable club took some doing on the part of the officers and their wives. Curtains at the windows, wax on the floor, and fresh paint on the walls turned the room into quite a pleasant place.

The men worked hard and played hard during the summer of 1942. Many highly competitive second lieutenants did begin the development of a camaraderie and respect necessary for a real esprit de corps in the combat battalion of the future. All in all, much of the experience at Camp Bowie was marked by trivia and the pursuit of more trivia. On the whole, there was little to indicate that the raw, inexperienced second lieutenants and inadequately trained NCO cadre would ever become the nucleus of a first class unit.

Who would have ever believed that the 51st Engineer Combat Regiment could produce a battalion of 650 men with the military skills and leadership that would stop and slow salients of the German Army along a 40-mile barrier line in the Ardennes in late 1944 -- until the 82nd Airborne, the 2nd and 3rd Armored and the 84th Infantry Divisions and the British 53rd Infantry Division could move into position?

Who could have ever foreseen that from this regiment, with the addition of some quality fillers, would come a distinguished Engineer Combat Battalion in the European Theater of Operations -- the product of the excellent training initiative and discipline of Colonel H. Wallis Anderson and the outstanding combat leadership of Lieutenant Colonel Harvey R. Fraser?

Plattsburg, New York

In October 1942 [-791], the 51st Engineer Combat Regiment was ordered to move its equipment and supplies by rail to Plattsburg, New York. Packing was hectic. Never had so many new lieutenants filled in and signed so many forms -- OCS never prepared them for that. The officers got plenty of hands-on experience loading equipment onto the railroad flat cars. The 51st left the hot dry plains of Texas on 15 October 1942, arriving four days later in the cool environs of Plattsburg with the snow flying -- an omen of things to come.

The tree-lined streets, the paved sidewalks, the brick buildings, and the parade grounds of the fence-enclosed base in New York contrasted strongly with the endless dry landscape and wooden barracks of Camp Bowie, Texas. There the 51st was a small group of men among many thousands; at Plattsburg the regiment would become nearly the full complement of troops on the post. This was a most welcome change. An added attraction was the availability of housing on the post for married officers and NCOs. Training would now proceed with fewer distractions than had faced the cadre at Camp Bowie. The post staff, however, seemed to resent the intrusion of the 51st Combat Engineer Regiment into their domain.

Colonel Anderson described Plattsburg Barracks as a really comfortable little post with the station personnel operating it very much like a private country club. "The gaggle of rooky troops counting cadence in their reveille exercises in the dark of a winter morning" disturbed the slumbers of the permanent establishment.[2] The continuation of the country club atmosphere, however, was not the objective of the 51st Engineer Combat Regiment's presence in Plattsburg.

One small incident during the unloading of equipment at the railroad siding at Plattsburg Barracks highlighted the fundamental difference between the command of the 51st and the post personnel. "All of the officers were in fatigues unloading equipment when Colonel Chapin, the Post Commander, resplendent in his boots and breeches and accompanied by his staff in their pinks and greens," came by to visit the unit. He asked one of the men, diligently engaged in removing the wire tie-downs on a truck, where the commanding officer was. The man in fatigues replied, "I am he. I am Colonel Anderson."[5]

The next two months in the campus-like surroundings were spent in preparation for the arrival of the new troops. During November and December the cadre had time for adjusting to their new environment.

Colonel Anderson thought that the "post was a very nice residence area but with very limited and inappropriate field training terrain for combat troops."[2] Some twelve miles away was a rugged, uninhabited place, called Macomb Reservation. This was an ancillary facility well suited to many phases of military engineering. Here were ridges, hills, bogs, streams, lakes, forests, scrub, open flats, relief (about 1,000 feet), and space for maneuvers. All could be used effectively for combat engineer training. November 25, 1942, was the date of the first of many regimental marches to and from Macomb Reservation and the beginning of innumerable experiences associated with that rugged area.

At last, after more than five months, the first contingent of the newly drafted and long awaited recruits arrived on 25 December 1942. Colonel Anderson wrote:

"Our faith was finally rewarded -- about 0500 Xmas morning. By some odd chance we were aroused by the fact that a train had stopped on the main track of the D & H (Delaware & Hudson) just east of the barracks. Investigation developed that it was a load of chilled and rather bewildered young men, mostly from the deep south. Only a few had been far from home, many had never seen snow ... and at Plattsburg we had a couple of feet of it and it was then 30^0 below zero.

"We later learned the train crew for many miles had been 'briefing' the lads as to the rigors of the weather they could anticipate in their prospective 'home' along Lake Champlain - and of course they did not have to exaggerate very much. When our own children came up just a few days previously to spend Christmas with us, we met them at the station in a horse drawn sleigh, which we found quite appropriate for the existing conditions.

"We fed the new arrivals, gave them a brief orientation, staged an impromptu Christmas, movie, etc., for them, bedded them down and on the following day 'processed' and assigned them to companies, and so on -- in the absence of any modern classification records and procedures".[2]

Through 10 January 1943, the fillers came, and came -- mechanics, carpenters, salesmen, clerks, school teachers, farmers, truckers, bookkeepers, and construction workers, mostly from the southern and middle Atlantic states, with a high percentage from North Carolina and Pennsylvania. What a mixture of speech and ethnic richness: Louisiana Cajun, Brooklyn Irish brogue, New England twang, southern drawl, Bronx Yiddish, Texas Mexican-Spanish, Southern Appalachian Anglo-Saxon, and on and on, including a few who could speak only broken English. They represented a good cross-section of America. Most of the men seemed to have come with a solid work ethic and one or more skills. They were well past the age of high school graduates, yet adaptable to the new life. Generally they were family and small town oriented. Regimental numbers increased from approximately one hundred officers and enlisted men to authorized table of organization (T/O) strength of 1,600.

The men were brand new inductees who had not yet been through basic training. Many were not prepared for Plattsburg weather. Some had been swimming off the coast of Florida just before leaving for New York. Most of the southerners were not familiar with long johns, and some would not wear them. Only a few men had ever seen a fur hat. Shortly after the arrival of the fillers, a near epidemic of "strep" throat broke out. Colds, flu, and pneumonia were rampant.

The sleeping quarters and hallways of the barracks resembled hospital wardrooms with the sick isolated by sheets hung between and around their beds. Part of the sickness was due to the resistance to pill-taking by some of the southerners. That problem was neatly resolved by lining up the men with their mouths open and their hands behind their backs, while a medic went down the line popping a sulfa tablet into each open mouth. A second medic followed with a paper cup of water for washing down the pill, watching sharply to make certain it was swallowed, not spit up or out.[6]

So many inductees were ill that the cadre began to wonder if there would be any men physically fit for training. Officially, individual and basic training was to be conducted between 11 January and 18 March 1943.

Basic Training

Basic training of the new men in the rugged Plattsburg climate was a real challenge to the inexperienced officers and limited NCO cadre. During the 1943 training period the fillers received the standard army individual soldier and combat engineer instruction. The inductees were the manpower for their own housekeeping, security, and food preparation chores. They also had to obtain specialist training in messenger, clerk, driver, maintenance, and supply procedure for normal battalion operations. All of the men were supposed to have nearly equivalent time on duties, details and instruction such as guard, kitchen police (k.p.), bridge construction, demolitions, and marksmanship.

Combat engineers are soldiers with basic engineer duties who are prepared to fight as infantrymen. Traditional soldier instruction includes: military discipline, courtesy, and organization; close and extended order drill; ceremonies and inspections; physical fitness; care and maintenance of clothing and equipment; and personal hygiene and first aid. Basic combat engineer duties embrace: tools and rigging; road repair and maintenance; mines and demolitions; obstacles and traps; and fixed and floating bridge construction. Standard infantry training covers: marching and bivouacking; map reading, compass exercises, and reconnaissance; and the use of infantry weapons. All of these subjects are integral components of Basic Training for Combat Engineers.

For a better perspective on the development of the 51st ECB, an enlisted man's point of view is presented here, followed by the officers' assessment of basic training.

An Enlisted Man's Comments on Basic Training*

> [Ed. Note: Prior to Basic Training, preparations included the standard physical, mental, and aptitude tests, shots, and personal interviews. Besides that, recruits had very little other preparation beyond learning simple drill commands and "policing", Army style.]

The First Week: "Our day starts at 5 A.M. that is Reveille, then roll call, chow, about two hours of drilling in the snow, then a two or three hour march through the woods with a light pack and rifle ... weighs about 20 lbs., then back to camp for Retreat at 5 P.M. or 1700 army time. All in between we have to shovel snow and ice from the sidewalks, mop the barracks, latrines, and orderly rooms."

"One day I stood K.P., an honorary position on this post (not punishment for dereliction of duty) a sum total of 14 hours washing pots, pans, dishes, scrubbing, cutting wood, hauling coal, serving meals .... I finished up about 7:30 P.M. or 1930. Then I had to report to headquarters to type until eleven that night -- next day a regular day of drill. Then Saturday, the payoff. I was Charge of Quarters (CQ) -- nothing to do but answer the phone, go after the mail, and do other little jobs -- kind of soft after those other days. (Also) during the week we had (to run) an obstacle course and had to build a tank trap, lay mines, and

---

* This section excepts letters of Private Frank H. Lee to his mother, Alice, and sister, Elinor, from 29 December 1942 to 31 March 1943. Lee was inducted into the U. S. Army in Louisiana on 21 December and boarded the train to Plattsburg on 26 December 1942.

everything!" (1/10/43)

Early Weapons Training: "Yesterday we were issued our rifles, which gives us one more job to do, that is keeping it clean. 1/01/1943. Today we had bayonet practice and I did fairly well but that is one phase of training I must admit I did not enjoy, don't think I ever will unless I get a chance to play the game for keeps. It may be fun then. I am learning to shoot the rifle from the right shoulder (Lee was left-handed). I haven't fired any actual shots but the Lieutenant complimented me on my form and posture." (1/20/43)

Bridge Construction and Demolitions: "We spent all day Thursday in the woods building a bridge, a real large one for tanks and convoys to cross over on. Did a pretty good job for rookies, too. We had chow right in the open served from a truck. It was delicious but if you didn't eat it fast, it would freeze to the mess kit and you couldn't get it out. It was a pretty nice experience, though one I won't forget for a long time." (1/24/1943) "This week we have been learning how to use demolition charges -- Dynamite, Nitro-starch, Nitro-glycerine, and Nitro-mone, all very good explosives. We have blown up bridges, trees, roads, and stumps, even cut trees down with them. They are very useful and harmless to the extent of your respect for them." (2/14/43)

Rough Days: "I pulled K.P. again, worked 15 hours …. Tuesday I drilled all day and Tuesday night about 11:30 or 2330 army time, we had to fall out with full field packs (with rifle, total about 62 lbs.), march about two miles out into the woods and build another bridge in total darkness. Well about one hour and 15 minutes after we started on the bridge it could have been used for light traffic such as jeeps, light trucks, and cars -- in two hours and 40 minutes it was completed for any traffic …. Anyway we were back at the barracks at 3:30 A.M. We were served coffee in the kitchen and then went to bed, had to fall out again at 5:45 A.M. for Reveille, had breakfast and then were allowed to sleep until noon. Wednesday evening (afternoon) we went out and tore the bridge down." (1/28/43)

Classroom Training: "The medics sure do all they can to help a fellow out. Here is an pamphlet they gave us to read. It is the plainest and most thorough explanation I have ever seen on the subject of Venereal Diseases. They also show a film of actual cases and how they are contracted. Makes a fellow with any amount of common sense sit up and take notice." (1/14/43) "Some nights we have special classes in the day room for all sorts of different jobs. Sometimes they show movies or training films and everyone has to attend so we are kept right on the ball." (1/28/43)

Hazards of Training: "A terrible thing happened here a day or so ago. One of the boys from another company who was going to a motorcycle school learning how to be a messenger had an accident. There is an obstacle course which they have to go over in a certain length of time. Well this boy was going through his paces when the vehicle slipped on ice and ran into the side of one of those brick buildings …. He had a broken jaw, some of his teeth knocked out … and possible internal injuries …. And there was a Lieutenant … who had his fingers (badly damaged) by a dynamite cap which exploded as he was crimping the fuse into the cap." (3/31/43)

Driver Training: "I took my driver's test today and if I pass I will be a licensed army driver. We had a test on convoy driving and drove out about 15 miles south of here …. By the way I led the convoy or set the pace. We stood inspection on our trucks, that is, the one we drove this past week and made it alright." (3/13/43)

Chow: "We are eating regular and plenty but the northern cooking is different from the south, hardly no salt and very little seasoning of any kind. By the way, I haven't had red beans and rice since I left home." (12/29/42) "The food here is excellent." (Several menus were itemized). (1/24/43)

Weather: "Everything here is covered with real snow -- it is a beautiful sight, just like the Christmas scenes we used to see on cards." (12/29/42) "Aunt Bess wrote that it was freezing and at 20° above zero there, well up here at that temperature the ice and snow melts. It has been around 10° above. Last week the weather hit a new low (36° below zero)." (2/14/43)

Dressing for the Cold: "We received a pair of "Arctics"; those are overshoes that come about three fourths the way to your knees. We have a regular winter cap which covers your head, ears, and neck and it is wool-lined and ties beneath the chin. We are going to be issued long handled drawers tomorrow." (12/29/42) "Just two days before (36° below morning) we had issued to us a woolen headpiece which slips over the head and drapes down on the back and chest like a diver's helmet, with a small slit for you to see out of. Also a pair of wristlets, they are a complete glove minus the thumb, you wear them under your gloves. So you see we were well protected." (2/14/43)

Rigors of Training: "We have been busy, busy as the proverbial cat, not hardly time to catch a breath, but we manage somehow." (1/20/43) "The exercise is really fine, makes a man want to eat, and really enjoy life." (1/24/43) "They weren't kidding when they said you belong to Uncle Sam 24 hours a day. But we can take it and we are going to take it and like it. Still drilling." (2/14/43) "We are still on routine here, drill, drill, drill, and study. It isn't the type of routine one gets used to. It is very interesting and useful too." (3/03/43) "... but it takes every minute of that 13 weeks (basic training) for us to learn what we have to ...." (3/31/43)

Rest and Recreation (R&R): Private Lee mentioned day room activities; post movies; passes into town to the USO for shows, ping pong, pool, dances; and visits to the American Legion Hall, the "Fife and Drum," and similar watering places.

Officers' Assessment of Basic Training

After the initial sickness, acclimation to the weather and military life was rapid. The men knew they had a job to do and that many opportunities were available in the regiment. There were still a number of NCO positions to be filled. Everyone found close order drill, calisthenics, map-reading, first aid, use and care of equipment, and so forth, challenging in sub-freezing to sub-zero weather. Forced marches on ice and snow, and running the obstacle course were making men of them in a hurry.

The obstacle course was a narrow snow and ice covered trail that ran first along the railroad bank high above the lake, then plunged suddenly down through bushes and brush toward the lake, then to the top of the bank again, jumping ditches and weaving in and out. Next it descended abruptly by widely spaced "steps" to a platform that jutted out of the bank about 10 or 12 feet above the flat shore level. Here a long heavy rope hung from a high limb. The runner was supposed to grab the end of the rope, swing out over a pile of brush and let go on the other side at a height of about 12 feet, landing on hard packed ice or snow. Surviving that, he had to rush along the beach to a frozen rope that was hanging from a limb about 15 feet high - "you can't climb with your gloves on because your hands will slip, and you can't climb with your gloves off because your hands will freeze"- he had to climb the rope, touch the limb, drop down, and grabbing another rope pull himself up an icy cliff. Then it was suddenly down again over even rougher terrain. So the course continued, in and out, and finally back to the starting point.[7]

By the end of the individual and basic training, the recruits had been made aware of the need for personal hygiene, the use of a helmet for shaving and bathing, the dangers of communicable diseases, the necessity for proper clothing and footwear under adverse weather conditions, and the importance of careful maintenance of equipment. They were exercising self-discipline, learning military protocol and responsibility, and becoming more mature individuals. Physically they were now much stronger and tougher than only a few short weeks before.

Morale of the troops and officers was high despite the extreme cold, frost-bitten noses and toes, and great distances from home. This was the first group to be trained by the mass of second lieutenants who had come to the 51st as brand new officers barely six months earlier. With the many opportunities for exhibiting leadership and organizational skills, they were gaining experience and exercising their training abilities. Some promotions were now in order. In January 1943, Second Lieutenants John W. Barnes, Karl G. Pedersen, and Clifford P. Schroff were promoted to first lieutenant. In February, Captain Parke O. Yingst was appointed battalion commander in place of Captain Robert B. Yates who was placed on detached service.[1]

At the end of this period the officers felt that the majority of the draftees had the makings of good soldiers. There were few misfits or overaged in the group. Officers, NCOs and recruits were shaping up as well-disciplined individuals who were beginning to realize their military potential. Much of their basic training and most of their combat engineering were yet to come.

Reorganization and Advanced Training
(18 March 1943 - 30 September 1943)

On 18 March 1943 [-639], the 51st Engineer Combat Regiment was reorganized as the 1111th Engineer Combat Group under the command of Colonel H. Wallis Anderson. The first battalion of the regiment was designated the 51st Engineer Combat Battalion with Captain Robert B. Yates in command and the second battalion as the 238th Engineer Combat Battalion with Captain Martin F. Massoglia commanding.[1] (See Appendix for 51st ECB assignments.)

Colonel Anderson, the new group commander, was a quiet, confident, thoughtful military man, keenly aware of what was going on around him. He understood the mix of officers in his command, particularly his second lieutenants. He knew how to utilize their talents and how to develop their potential. He knew when to crack down and when to ease up. It was apparent that he was a strong believer in self and military discipline, personal and military fitness, and sound combat and engineer training. By his actions he exemplified his beliefs. For instance, he slept in a pup tent in sub-zero weather just like everyone else and he did his push-ups every morning also (50 at age 50). Philosophically, the Colonel was convinced that "it is always better to train under adverse conditions, and then accept more favorable circumstances as a bonus."[2]

The Weather and Training

For basic and unit training, Colonel Anderson directed the officers to "take advantage of all inclement weather to toughen troops." He did and his officers did.

It seemed that all weather at Plattsburg that winter was "inclement." Many times temperatures fell 20 or more degrees below zero during the night, followed by a rise of only a few degrees during the day. On several occasions thermometers registered 30 degrees below zero. Wind was also a factor to be reckoned with, producing a chill that made temperatures of 15 or 20 degrees F seem colder than several degrees below zero on a calm day. Moisture in the wind made the cold even more bitter. Sometimes heavy snow driven by a fierce northwest wind almost turned day into dusk. Then there was ice, which made walking or any other outdoor activity extremely hazardous. On one such occasion it was so bad that the adjutant did not have the men fall out for reveille.[8]

The Official Record for that period of training indicated that in no way had the battalion been "barracks-bound" during the extremely adverse Plattsburg weather. Anyone experienced with engineer combat troops knows that proper training can take place only outdoors. The Colonel's edict was being carried out and every man in the outfit was convinced that inclement weather was being fully used to toughen troops.

The men assembled pontoon bridge units on frozen Lake Champlain. This was a novel introduction to floating bridge construction. They ran five miles daily before breakfast, no matter what the weather. They learned to survive snowstorms and to sleep in pup tents at 10 degrees below zero. One night in the back of a truck convinced some men that it was warmer to sleep on the ground. They had to use open-air latrines in sub-zero weather. This was cruel and punishing torture that would have delighted the sadistic heart of a

Spanish Inquisitor. They dug foxholes in the frozen north woods, rather shallow ones because the entrenching tool was not the best instrument for excavating ice. Some members of the motor pool did become very familiar with the entrenching tool after they were caught using a jack-hammer. Soldier initiative was commendable, but it had to be quiet. They sprouted horns of ice as sweat pouring from their headgear froze, on a 42-minute four-mile forced march with full field gear. They built a steel H-10 wooden trestle bridge over the frozen Salmon River, under blackout conditions and with a severe wind chill factor. All of these exercises toughened the men of the 51st mentally and physically.

Constructing the H-10 wooden trestle bridge was such a traumatic and memorable experience for the trainees, such a superb lesson for the officers in the necessity for proper preparation and organization and coordination in a simulated tactical exercise, and such excellent training for bridge building at night under the most adverse conditions, that it warrants a more detailed description.

> On a bitter cold and moonless night in early March, two platoons were each assigned to construct one half of a wooden trestle bridge while a third was to put up the steel H-10 on which the trestle bridge would stand. Lieutenant Radford, in charge of the first platoon, described that night as the "most horrible" he had ever spent. His men hand-carried over a hundred timbers each weighing 150 pounds from the water's edge up a steep ice-covered bank. The men slipped and slid and fell repeatedly, but finally got all the timbers to the top. In about an hour or so they finished their half. In the wind his men waited, huddled together like a "bunch of baby rabbits behind a woodpile" trying to keep from freezing, while the lieutenant waited to see that no one fell asleep.
>
> Meanwhile, the third platoon was in trouble. Their light truck could not swing the steel girder into place, so they had to wait for the arrival of a 4-ton wrecker. There was barely room on top of the narrow bridgehead for the driver to operate. Everyone expected to hear him plunge into the river 30 feet below. In the pitch darkness, he couldn't see how far to back or go forward, but luckily he drove not too far either way.
>
> Finally, everything was ready to lower into place when the steel cable snapped and the H-10 fell with a crash -- five more hours to recover the thing only to have it happen again! At last toward dawn the H-10 was in place, and after a few more hours the bridge was completed and ready for testing. Around 11:30 a.m. the truck driver went across "very gingerly," not sure the bridge would hold up his vehicle, and since there was no place on the other side to turn around, he had to back across.
>
> Then with perfect coordination, the whole company fell to and within an hour and a half had the bridge taken down, all parts neatly stacked in proper piles, nails salvaged, area policed, and all ready to leave by 1:00 o'clock .... "The water froze in their canteens and they had none to drink and the hot food had ice on it almost before they could get it into their mouths."[9]

Activities during the first two weeks of March demonstrated the rigor of the training program: the combination wooden trestle-H-10 construction on Monday night and Tuesday, with troop recovery on Wednesday; Thursday, preparation for a pontoon bridge exercise with assembly of pontoon units that night on frozen Lake Champlain; Friday, time for recovery and attention to miscellaneous details; Saturday morning, the usual inspection-physical fitness period, and that afternoon a critique of the work of the week; Saturday evening and Sunday, time off. On the second Monday, preparation-organization was begun for the construction of a 30 foot high wooden trestle bridge (minus the H-10). This exercise was scheduled for later in the week at the same Salmon River site under the same tactical conditions but with greater security.[10]

These exercises in a limited time frame under adverse conditions proved to be vital training for the Battle of the Bulge, and the Roer, Rhine, and Danube crossings in 1944/45.

To ensure sufficient outdoor training, the battalion was moved to Macomb Reservation in early April. A tent city was constructed with the troops sleeping on the ground in pup tents under all weather conditions. Command, staff and service functions were based in pyramidals. The troops stayed at Macomb for the rest of their training in Plattsburg, commuting on foot to and from the post on most weekends.

Unit Training

Basic and Unit training overlapped in time. Although the weather did not have the organization "barracks-bound," it did influence the scheduling of events. Firing on the range, an integral part of basic training, is not very productive in sub-zero weather, so it actually started in late March. On the other hand, fixed bridge training at the company level can be done over frozen streams, so was begun during the basic training period in February. Basic training, scheduled to end on 18 March, was extended to 24 April, and unit training, although begun earlier, officially began on 25 April and lasted through July 1943.[1]

Most of the unit training revolved around bridge construction. Training funds were spent for materials needed such as timber and hardware, and used in conjunction with Bailey and H-10 equipment to construct, demount and reconstruct various types of fixed expedient bridges. Each company completed the project in turn, competing time-wise with each other. A nearby abandoned right of way for a railroad located southwest of the post afforded an excellent work area. The projects were usually done at night under simulated tactical conditions.[2]

Timber trestle bridge. Plattsburg. 1943. *Collection of Floyd Wright*

After the lakes thawed in April, the same training scheme was followed with the floating equipment provided by the light pontoon company attached to the group. Initial training in pontoon equipment as well as fixed bridging was done at the platoon level during daylight. Each company gained experience with log corduroy, wooden trestle, H-10 portable steel, Bailey fixed bridges, and pneumatic rubberized and aluminum pontoon floating equipment. The companies also built the standard footbridges and improvised others. Some of the units experimented with raft construction, using assault boats and pontoon floats.

All of the trainers and trainees were toughened during basic and unit training. All had learned much about their endurance and physical limitations. At the time most of the troops were convinced that the training officers were sadistic and that their physical conditioning was deteriorating. These outdoor activities and hardships, the twelve-mile march between the barracks and Macomb Reservation, and the training in general, were molding the battalion into a well-disciplined, well-conditioned and well-coordinated organization with a high esprit de corps. Steady progress had been made in most phases of basic training.

At the end of April the battalion took the mobilization Training Program Tests given by XIII Corps to determine the progress made by the battalion. The unit passed all of the tests with an 83 percent average, the highest of any similar organization in XIII Corps.[1]

On 11 June the results of the firing range were published. Overall the battalion performed well with over 85 percent with passing scores. There was a total of 29 experts and 184 sharpshooters in the battalion with Sergeant Ralph K. Middleton of Company B earning the highest score, a 206 out of a possible 210. Company C had the highest percentage of men qualifying with 90 percent. On 16 June XIII Corps conducted physical tests. Company C, selected to represent the battalion, passed the rigid tests with flying colors.[1]

While the battalion trained in New York, many personnel changes occurred. Overaged men, those physically unfit, and others were weeded out of the battalion. Many of the highly qualified new men were rapidly promoted into the higher grades called for in the table of organization. Second Lieutenants Carver, Henry, Radford, Hodges, and Wright became first lieutenants in late March; Green in May; and Harwood and Nabors in June 1943. Captain Yates was assigned command of the battalion on 10 April, but was replaced by Major Victor J. Reafsnyder on 4 June. Captain Yates then became executive officer of the battalion, and on 11 June was promoted to major.[1]

During May, four officers (Petrini, Garrity, Hulce, and Levitus) and sixty enlisted men were sent to the newly activated 163rd Engineer Combat Battalion at Camp Van Dorn, Mississippi. On 13 May, six lieutenants (Brucker, Kelso, Johnson, Fossett, Conklin, and Baugh) were transferred to overseas assignments. Second Lieutenants Jamison, Attardo, Senger, Pulawski, and First Lieutenant Scheuber joined the battalion in July 1943. Other changes were made in staff and headquarters assignments but the company commanders, primary platoon leaders, and NCOs remained steady, providing the basic continuity and stability necessary for excellence in training of the battalion.[1]

Combined Training

During July and August the battalion conducted combined training. This included platoon, company, and battalion exercises; squad and platoon combat firing; attack of a fortified area; combat in cities; mine laying and removal; intensive bridge and road construction; and review of basic and unit training. Officers armed with pistol and officers and men armed with carbines fired required familiarization and qualification courses. One hundred percent of those firing qualified.[1]

Every member of the organization successfully completed the infiltration course. Designed to test troop reaction to simulated battlefield conditions, it was a most harrowing and unforgettable experience, even for the most stout-hearted. The course at Macomb Reservation was about half the length and width of a football field. At one end an open seven foot trench crossed the width of the field and at the other were two emplaced .30 caliber machine guns. Between the trench and the guns were low barbed wire entanglements, craters, and trip wires attached to charges that would explode if the wires were touched. A platoon or similar sized group would be sent into the trench, then while the machine guns were sweeping the entire field with live ammunition about 30 inches above the ground, the men were ordered out. Crawling with their rifles cradled in their arms, they inched forward on their bellies, trying to avoid craters and trip wires, keeping their heads and butts down. When they reached barbed wire, they had to flip over on their backs and wriggle under while holding up the wire with their hands ... and finally on past the guns where they could rise safely up again above the 30 inch level.[11]

Various competitive exercises were held for the companies -- competition in bridge building, squad and platoon combat firing, and other phases of combined and unit training. Both squad and platoon combat firing records were set by Company C, as were the best times in both pontoon bridge and H-10 portable bridge construction. Company B set the best time in the construction of the footbridge. The battalion received valuable construction training in the building of ranges, roads, and various combat courses at Macomb Reservation.[1]

H & S Company participated in most of the line company training but did not enter into competition since it had approximately 100 fewer men than the other companies. Much of their training was done during off-duty hours. Most of the period the men were learning their headquarters and service duties: S-1, personnel and communications; S-2, intelligence and reconnaissance, S-3, operations, training, and planning; and S-4, supply and equipment, motor pool and the care, use, and maintenance of trucks and construction equipment. Many of the men became adept at Engineer technical jobs such as booby-trapping and the building of assault boat rafts and other bridge expedients.

On 8 July 1943, Company A was ordered to Aberdeen, Maryland for the purpose of constructing experimental bridges. The company constructed all of the types of fixed bridges used by the United States Army -- wooden trestle, H-10, Bailey, and trestle approaches to pontoon bridges -- with abutments of varying sizes for tank impact testing. Company A returned from Aberdeen on 24 July with a letter of commendation from the Commanding General, Aberdeen Proving Grounds, on the excellent services rendered. Company A missed about one week of combined training.[1]

In late July and early August 1943, Second Lieutenants Mueller, Coats, Baldwin, and O'Neill were promoted to first lieutenant, and First Lieutenant Schroff to captain on 4 August. Captain Richard F. Huxman joined the battalion and was assigned to Headquarters on 31 August 1943.[1]

The last of August marked the end of the battalion's stay in Plattsburg. In eight months the inductees had gone from raw recruits to tough, well-trained combat Engineers. The men as a battalion still had to put it all together. There had already been a shakedown of officers and enlisted men but there were more changes to come. The organization was now ready for engineer support tasks.

Maneuvers and Fort Belvoir

On 1-2 September 1943, the battalion prepared for a move by rail to the XIII Corps maneuver area in a rugged section of West Virginia, eight miles east of Elkins for a brief period known as "mountain training." The trip was made on 3-4 September with the unit moving into the bivouac area after dark. The transfer from Plattsburg to West Virginia was a permanent change of station in preparation for overseas movement. This caused a "shakedown" which led a number of families of married personnel to return to their homes for the duration.[2]

Fall comes early to the higher altitudes of the Alleghenies. But the men were not prepared either physically or psychologically for the uncomfortably cool nights on the damp earth in the mountainous maneuver area of West Virginia at that time of year. Neither were the cold water outdoor showers nor washing in the Monongahela River conducive to regular bathing. In the H & S Company area, taking a bath necessitated a walk of one mile to wash in the river where the unusually abundant water snakes were performing their fall mating rituals. Sergeant Lowery, H & S mess sergeant, told some of his men where to wash, and emphasized that all you had to do was put your hands in the water, brush aside the snakes, and dive in. Needless to say, personal cleanliness among the cooks was a continuing problem in West Virginia.[11]

The physical conditions, the psychological letdown with the "shakedown," and the anticipated overseas assignment cast a shadow over the Engineers during their construction support tasks. From 6 to 15 September 1943, the battalion performed Engineer missions for the other XIII Corps units. Company A was assigned to road construction in and around Elkins, West Virginia; Company B to an airplane landing strip and Bailey bridge construction near Davis, West Virginia; and Company C to the construction of a fixed target at a known distance range two miles from Davis. The missions accomplished by B and C companies were for the XIII Corps field artillery brigade. Its commanding general personally commended Lieutenant Hodges, Company B commander, for the work performed by both companies. At the end of this period the 51st ECB was detached from the 1111th Engineer Combat Group (ECG) and command of Col. Anderson.[1]

On 16 September 1943, the battalion left Davis, West Virginia, by motor convoy for assignment as demonstration troops at the Engineer School, Fort Belvoir, Virginia. After a two day trip, the 51st moved into the barracks in the First Battalion area of the Engineer Replacement Training Center. For the period 18-30 September, the battalion acted as demonstration troops for the trainees. As a result of their work, the 51st received several letters of commendation for individual officers and men, and for the battalion as a whole. These came from the commandants of the replacement training center and the engineer school.[1] Perhaps the most significant compliment of all came to Lt. Henry and his motor pool crew from the Post Ordinance Inspector who stated that the 51st Engineer Combat Battalion "had the best maintained trucks that have ever been on this post."[12]

The stay at Fort Belvoir, with its indoor flush toilets, hot and cold running water, and beds, was a great change from the past months tenting out in New York and West Virginia. Had the troops been able to foresee the unspeakable latrines of North Africa and the "honey buckets" of England, they would have appreciated these luxuries even more.

September had been marked by a decline in the morale of the battalion for the first time in its history. This was due in part to the realization that the unit would soon be going overseas. But primarily it was the lack of decisive leadership by the Battalion CO [Reafsnyder] that was becoming more and more disturbing to the staff and to the company commanders. However, the performance of the outfit in West Virginia and at Fort Belvoir did not seem to have been affected by low morale. Professional pride had prevailed.

"On 1 October 1943, the 51st Engineer Combat Battalion left Fort Belvoir for a one day motor trip to Fort Dix, New Jersey, to prepare for movement overseas."[1][-442]

England by Way of North Africa
(1 October 1943 - 19 June 1944)

The 51st Engineer Combat Battalion (ECB) motor convoy arrived at Fort Dix, New Jersey, on the evening of 1 October 1943, and the men moved into wooden barracks similar to those just vacated the night before at Fort Belvoir, Virginia. While at Fort Dix, the battalion prepared for movement overseas. Equipment was put into excellent condition, crated, waterproofed, and marked for shipment. Showdown inspections of personal and organizational equipment and of individual clothing were conducted. Shortages were filled and overages turned in. Personnel were also readied for movement. Medical and dental examinations were conducted. Physical training (PT) tests of several kinds were given, for example, a 25-mile march in eight hours with full field gear.[1]

Many new aches and pains surfaced and disciplinary problems multiplied as a result of the projected move overseas. In one company an enlisted man complained of a "busted" nose he had had for six months or more; another had a "hurting" in his chest; another could not sleep on the ground because of his bad back; another had a crooked spine; and another's overlapping toes were "killing" him. Some of the disciplinary problems included: a tech sergeant going over the hill to find his dog, Blackout; two master sergeants and two staff sergeants sleeping through three formations; and a mess sergeant gambling with privates.[13]

The aches, pains, and disciplinary problems of the battalion were resolved with the detachment of some misfits and the transfer of those men with real medical problems. Some good men, left behind in hospitals along the way, managed to join the unit at Fort Dix, eager to go overseas with the 51st ECB. Twenty-five men from the 22nd Armored Division joined the battalion in late October to bring the unit to approximate Table of Organization (T/O) strength.

A few personnel changes were made in the organization during its stay at Fort Dix from 2 October to 4 November 1943. Second Lieutenants Jack E. Boies and Raymond L. Trafford and Warrant Officer Junior Grade (WOJG) Julius J. Horecka joined the battalion. Second Lieutenant Pulawski and WOJG d'Antuono were transferred to different hospitals. First Lieutenants Radford, Hodges, Carver, and Barnes were promoted to Captain; Second Lieutenant Bailey to first lieutenant; and WOJG Morin and Keesing to chief warrant officer (CWO).[1]

The battalion left Fort Dix by rail on the morning of 5 November for final staging at Camp Patrick Henry, Virginia. There all the men were inoculated with a variety of shots and a final inspection of individual clothing and equipment was conducted. Transfers were made to bring the unit into conformity with staging T/O strength. Passenger lists were drawn up and completed.[1]

All officers and enlisted men, with their personal clothing and equipment, were now ready for movement to the Port of Embarkation (POE). The organizational equipment had been shipped from Fort Dix by rail to the Los Angeles POE, Wilmington, California, with CWO Keesing in charge of the supply detail.[1] CWO Keesing, the supply detail, and the organizational equipment were never seen again by the 51st ECB after leaving Fort Dix. (See Appendix for officer overseas assignments.)

PREPARING FOR THE WORST

To North Africa

On 12 November 1943 [-400], most of the battalion, under command of Major Reafsnyder, left Camp Patrick Henry by rail for the Hampton Roads POE. All of the men in the organization except Major Yates and the 2nd and 3rd platoons of Company C boarded the SS Calvin Coolidge. On the following day Major Yates and the two platoons went aboard the SS Richard Rush, along with Company A of the 49th ECB and Company C of the 237th ECB. Major Yates was designated troop commander.[1]

The Calvin Coolidge and the Richard Rush became part of a convoy of 74 Liberty Ships and 17 escort vessels. On 14 November, traveling at 8 to 9 knots, the ships left the United States for an unknown destination, unknown at least to the 51st ECB. From the deck of the Calvin Coolidge ships were visible nearly to the horizon in every direction. There was some comfort in not being on the periphery like an 8-knot sitting duck, vulnerable to prowling German U-boats.

The convoy first followed a southerly route nearly to Bermuda then headed North 85 degrees East almost to the Straits of Gibraltar. It entered the European - Middle Eastern - African Theater of Operations on 23 November while still on the high seas. About five days later the 51st ECB received orders to leave the convoy and proceed to the Mediterranean Base Section at Oran, Algeria, for transshipment to India. The Straits of Gibraltar were first sighted on 1 December 1943. On 4 December the SS Richard Rush and the SS Calvin Coolidge dropped anchor in the harbor of Oran. The troops were thankful for a safe voyage. The battalion was more than ready to set its collective feet on Algerian terra firma.[1]

The trip across the Atlantic had been uneventful except for three days of heavy seas. The ups and downs of the heaving ships caused some seasickness among the troops. Other than that, the only excitement was the appearance of a lone reconnaissance plane near the Straits that caused an alert for a few moments before it flew off to the east.

After three weeks of close togetherness the men knew which of their buddies were the best crap shooters, poker players, and cribbage nuts. Reading, letter-writing, bull-shooting, games of chance, and calisthenics filled most of the waking hours. Looking at flying fish and porpoises, enjoying the deep blue of the Gulf Stream, spotting a few whales in the colder waters, and watching the phosphorescent flecks on the ocean surface on starry nights provided the men some diversion while on deck.

Morale remained high even though the food was terrible, the space limited, and the troops stacked five high in the converted cargo compartments. Liberty ships were freighters, never designed for carrying troops. Powdered eggs in any shape, form, or mixture are distasteful. The battalion did have one good meal -- Thanksgiving dinner. The merchant marines let the cooks scrounge through the old food lockers so that the troops had "steak", kidney beans, potatoes, and cold chocolate or mincemeat pie for that meal.

Thanksgiving was also celebrated on the Calvin Coolidge with a successful variety show put on by the troops. The performance included songs, impersonations, jokes, and hula dancing. For grass skirts, the dancers wore new mops. The food scrounging and the show led Captain Radford to write, "I've got a wonderful bunch of men who can do anything from making moonshine to preaching. When we get away from civilization, we'll be able to take care of ourselves in every respect."[14] A combat engineer unit is of necessity a survivable, self-contained organization.

Some battalion business did take place on the voyage other than sleeping, eating, and whiling away the hours. Captain Huxman, Assistant Division Engineer, replaced Captain Schroff as S-3, who then became Assistant Division Engineer.[1]

In North Africa

On 5 December 1943, the troops of the battalion disembarked at Oran, Algeria, and were loaded onto trucks for a twelve mile ride to Staging Area 2 near Fleurus. The men bivouacked in pyramidal tents from 6 December to 5 January 1944, while awaiting transshipment to India.[1] The officers slept on cots, the enlisted men on straw ticks on the ground. Later, after nearly floating out of their pyramidals during several deluges, the enlisted men were also issued cots.

During the battalion's stay the climate was just plain disagreeable -- even though the temperature seldom fell below 40 degrees F. Instead of the expected hot, dry, sandy country, the outfit found itself in a cold, wet, muddy area. Many temporary ponds dotted the depressions in nearby citrus groves and vineyards. Occasionally some of the days were sunny, but many more were monsoon-like. On most days the men were hot one minute, cold the next, and oftentimes miserable all night. One officer wrote that he "finally managed to sleep warmly with four blankets, two shelter halves," and his bedding roll. Of course, he was also sleeping in his clothes. The dry cold of Plattsburg could numb one to death without much pain; the wet cold of West Virginia and Algeria, though not life-threatening, made everyone extremely uncomfortable.[15]

The food was about the best the battalion ever had, but the water was so heavily chlorinated that it was undrinkable. Even the boiled coffee tasted like chlorine. The men were permitted to barter for fresh eggs and citrus fruits for awhile, but sanitation in the countryside was such that soon nearly every man in the battalion had gastro-intestinal problems of some sort (GIs). Bartering ceased in a hurry.

Since all the equipment had been shipped west to the Los Angeles POE for the China - Burma - India Theater of Operations, the battalion could not conduct training while in North Africa. Most of the time was spent on care of clothing, maintenance of personal equipment (removal of mud), calisthenics, one long march of about 15 miles, climbing steep Lyon Hill, and inter-company athletics when the weather permitted. Fortunately, no one sustained any cracked or broken bones from the vigorous touch football games.

A provisional company for largely ceremonial purposes was formed with one platoon selected from each of the line companies. Captain Barnes was commander, and Lieutenants Wright, O'Neill, and Nolan were platoon leaders. This select unit participated in the daily retreat parade in Oran on 11 December with Major Reafsnyder as the reviewing officer, and was complimented on its showing by the G-3 Section, Mediterranean Base Section.[1]

During the Algerian stay, Lieutenant Boies was appointed Reconnaissance Officer, with Lieutenant Trafford replacing him in Company A and Captain Schroff appointed commander of Company C. Captain Barnes was assigned as Assistant Division Engineer. All officers were now eligible for the European-Middle Eastern-African Theater Campaign Medal and Ribbon on 23 December 1943.[1]

A diversity of activities kept the men from getting too bored. They bathed out of helmets in either

PREPARING FOR THE WORST

chlorinated or salt water; showered in either salt water, or fresh water that was always either too hot or too cold, no in between; laundered with same; ate good food; enjoyed Christmas caroling; and speculated on "what's next" for the battalion. The weather, the people, the landscape, and the local sanitation or lack of it were the subjects of many bull sessions. In spite of unpleasant physical conditions, restrictions to base, no equipment for training, and especially no mail since leaving Fort Dix, the morale of the organization was excellent.

On To England

The "what's next" for the battalion was resolved at the Teheran Conference then being held while the 51st ECB and four other engineer combat battalions awaited orders for transshipment to India. All five were subsequently ordered to England to prepare for the invasion of continental Europe.[1]

The 51st left the staging area near Fleurus on 6 January 1944, proceeded to Oran by truck, and entrained for Casablanca. The enlisted men were piled into cattle cars known as 40 and 8's (40 men or 8 horses), 30 men to a car, with their personal clothing and equipment. The officers were not much better off in the compartments of the pre-1900 passenger cars. But they at least had seats, the enlisted men did not.[1]

No man on that trip will ever forget the torturous 48-hour, 420-mile journey by rail, at about 9 miles per hour through the cold Atlas Mountains of western Algeria and eastern Morocco. That ride will remain forever etched in the memories of each and every man aboard that primitive transportation. There were neither toilets nor sleeping facilities, and the cars were unheated. The only food available was that which each man had brought along. Nearly all the men had the GIs to one degree or another. The train stopped fairly frequently so all could dash to the sides of the tracks to stretch and exercise providing they had nothing more serious to do. The engineer would then toot three times at appropriate intervals to alert the men to board the train again.

The battalion commander and his orderly were the only men ever left behind during the trip. This little incident happened when the French engineer halted on a down grade and let the men off as usual. Unexpectedly, he cut short the interval between the all-aboard toots and took off. The battalion commander and his orderly, having gone modestly to the rear as usual, were taken by surprise and couldn't make the train. Many hours later they were seen coming down the track, pumping away on a handcar, desperately trying to catch up with the battalion.

Forty-two years later the truth finally came out. A certain company commander had noticed that the slow-footed major and his orderly usually went to the rear of the train at these stops. So the CO and his buddy had bribed the French engineer with a 1000 franc note to stop on a grade, speed up the toots, and take off.[16]

The battalion arrived in Casablanca about 1800 hours on 8 January and moved by truck to Camp Don B. Passage about two miles away. During the next two days the organization prepared for its voyage to England. On 11 January the 51st ECB boarded the HMT Andes, a converted passenger liner with a troop capacity of about 10,000. The following day it set out for England, unaccompanied by any other troop ship or escort vessels. Supposedly the ship's speed of 28 knots was sufficient for eluding enemy submarines. The ship sailed west for 2 days, north almost to Iceland, then southeast to North Channel and into the Irish

37

Sea on 19 January, arriving in Liverpool, England, on the morning of the 20th. The troops left the ship about 2000 hours that night, glad to be on solid ground again.[1][-331]

The voyage had been exceedingly rough. The vertical motion of the V-keeled SS Calvin Coolidge during a tropical disturbance was in no way comparable to the wild rolling motions of the round-keeled HMT Andes in that North Atlantic storm encountered during the trip. Captain Weinstein set up a pendulum in his wardroom and estimated the roll of the ship to be more than 30 degrees on many occasions. (A member of the ship's crew reported one roll of 42 degrees.) On one roll, Weinstein, while prone in his bunk, was thrown against the wall on the other side of the room, some five feet away. Many of the "amateur sailors" estimated the distance from trough to crest of some of the waves to be at least 60 feet. The wild seas had nearly everyone seasick. The floor was slick with vomit and spilled food and drink much of the time. Very few of the men bothered to eat or had any desire to move around. There was not much space for moving around anyway. Troops were crammed into every nook and corner of the big boat. The sight of the raging sea through the hatch windows and the constant bouncing of the ship were reasons enough to keep most of the men inactive.

Shortly after disembarking from the HMT Andes, the troops boarded a train for Llanelly, Carmarthenshire, South Wales, arriving at 0400 hours on 21 January. From the train the men were trucked to billets around the city: H & S Company to the Exchange Drapery Building; Company A to Furniss Camp; Company B to the Richard Thomas Institute; and Company C to the Corona Works.[1]

On 21 January 1944, the battalion was assigned to the First United States Army (FUSA), then commanded by General Omar N. Bradley.[1] On 25 January the troops received their first mail from the States, three months after leaving Fort Dix. This was a real morale booster.

Training without organizational equipment was conducted in the outlying districts of Llanelly from 22 January to 10 February 1944. It consisted of physical conditioning, marching, and tactical exercises.[1] The troops had their first experience with British rain and fog at Llanelly. Frequently the officer leading calisthenics could not see his men beyond the first row, sometimes he could not see them at all. On marches he did not know how far his unit was strung out behind him, or even if the men were there. The Welsh habit of wearing hob-nailed boots eliminated many collisions with the troops on the walkways and streets in the dense fog and during the blackouts.

Changes in personnel during the Llanelly stay included the appointment of Captain Barnes as Adjutant and Lieutenant Attardo as Assistant S-3; and the transfer of Lieutenant Norton to Company C.[1]

England

On 5 February 1944, Captain Huxman and sixteen men were sent as an advance detail to prepare for the battalion's move to Highnam Court, two miles northwest of Gloucester, England. The individual companies left Llanelly for the new training area on successive days starting on 10 February with H & S Company. For the 51st Engineer Combat Battalion (ECB), Highnam Court was the training camp of final preparations for the invasion of Europe.[1]

From 11 February through the remainder of the month, the battalion was attached to the 1128th Engineer

Combat Group (ECG), commanded by Colonel G. C. Reinhardt. On 1 March the battalion was detached from the 1128th ECG and returned to the 1111th ECG under the command of Colonel H. Wallis Anderson. Except for a brief period with the 1159th ECG under Colonel Kenneth E. Fields at Remagen during March 1945, the 51st remained with the 1111th through most of five campaigns in the European Theater.[1]

As previously noted, the battalion's organizational equipment had been shipped to the China-Burma-India Theater. The 51st ECB was now confronted with a serious supply problem at Highnam Court. Requisitions were hand-carried to the nearest supply depot by Sergeant Paris Pugh. He returned empty-handed and downcast with the report that no such request would be honored because the "51st ECB" was not on any United Kingdom authorized supply list." Lieutenant Maurice Coats, 51st S-4, relayed this information to Major Yates. The Major's reply was swift and unmistakable: "Coats, take my jeep (borrowed from another unit) and go see Base Section Headquarters, and don't come back until you have approval to draw our equipment!" Next morning, in the pre-dawn darkness, Coats was on his way to Base Section Headquarters where he was told: no authorization because the "51st ECB" is not on our list of units scheduled to be in England." Undaunted, by mid-afternoon Coats finally contacted the Deputy CO, who gave him the same familiar turn down, but added "I'm going to send a cablegram to Washington and get this cleared up." He advised Coats to stay overnight -- Coats had no intention of facing Major Yates without the authorization. Next morning the answer came: "We are not sure why the 51st Engineer Combat Battalion is in England, but take immediate action to issue full allowance of organizational equipment."[17]

Refresher and combined training and specialist activities could now proceed. The battalion was more than ready for serious training with the proper tools and gear. Calisthenics, marches, tactical exercises, and little else day after day had become quite monotonous. The common elements of training from the middle of February through May were physical conditioning, Bailey and fixed bridge construction, laying of mines and minefields, explosives and demolitions, road construction and repair, chemical warfare, night operations related to bridge construction, combat tactics, and tactical motor marches. The troops also had some training with pneumatic floating bridges, flame throwers, and booby traps.[1]

In order to properly instruct these classes, members of the battalion were sent to various courses taught throughout England. On their return, they conducted classes for battalion personnel. Lieutenant Norton attended a 16-day course for instructors on aircraft recognition; Lieutenant O'Neill, the FUSA training program in minefields and booby traps; Lieutenant Attardo, the courses for unit gas and bomb disposal officers; Major Yates, the transport school; Lieutenants Trafford and Harwood, the Bailey bridging course; Lieutenant Wright, the camouflage school; Lieutenant Boies, the bomb reconnaissance course; and Captain Carver, a three day course for education program leaders.[1]

During the evenings, from 27 March to 10 April, specialist classes were held by the battalion for first sergeants, supply, motor, and platoon officers. Operator classes were conducted for water supply, radio, and air compressor workers. Company, battalion, and general clerks were trained in their fields as were squad leaders, auto mechanics, electricians, radio repairmen, and others.[1]

The companies had their own specialists for instruction in the most hazardous operations such as booby trapping, flame throwing, bomb handling, and the use of explosives.

The battalion commander, executive officer, key staff, and company commanders participated in Command Post Exercises at the end of March. This exercise included selection of bivouac areas, the establishment of

More than ready to do the job so long in preparation. Highnam Court, England, 1944. *Collection of Joseph Milgram*

Command Posts (CPs) and outposts, and the movement of CPs to new locations. Camouflage discipline, vehicle dispersal, column control, and battalion standard operating procedures were stressed. Later, on 24 April, the 1111th ECG scheduled a Command Post Exercise emphasizing reconnaissance and various phases of signal communications such as radio transmission, the laying and retrieving of land lines, and cryptography.[1]

Training with an immediate purpose, that is, knowing that those experiences would be used in the next few weeks or days, improved morale and increased combat preparedness. Comparatively pleasant weather and good eating, sleeping, bathing, and toilet arrangements at Highnam Court also helped morale considerably. However, "honey buckets" did take a little adjusting to. Company athletics, Armed Forces boxing events, many old motion pictures, friendly native company, a pleasant landscape with grass and flowers, church services on the country estate, and passes were all conducive to excellence in morale and effectiveness in combat training for troops preparing for battle with the Germans.

Some passes were contingent upon proficiency. H & S Company personnel had to successfully navigate a simulated ten by twenty yard minefield in order to get rest and recreation away from camp. Capt. Radford had set up the field with American antitank and German Teller and "S" mines, along with booby traps and trip wires. Burned fingers and ears ringing from exploding cherry bombs were the penalties paid for unsuccessful attempts to complete the course. The men finally became very adept at deactivating booby traps and finding antipersonnel and antitank mines.[17]

Many changes in personnel were made in England. On 23 March Lieutenant Mueller (upon returning from a hospital in North Africa) replaced Captain Barnes as adjutant who then returned to the Assistant Division Engineer assignment. Major Reafsnyder was promoted to Lieutenant Colonel on 1 May; First Lieutenants Poronsky and Coats to captain on 1 March; the following Second Lieutenants to first lieutenants: Trafford on 1 May, Jamison, Nolan, and Norton on 25 May; and S/Sgt. Paris Pugh to WOJG in supply on 2 June, replacing CWO Keesing who was dropped from battalion records on 20 May 1944.[1] (See Appendix for other personnel changes.)

Reviews, Awards and Commendations

Inspection reports and several highlights of the training period are presented here to illustrate the nature and quality of the organization. The commanding officer and staff of the 1111th ECG found inspections of the troops in ranks, staff operations and establishments, and general training to be satisfactory. The Official Military Record indicated satisfactory progress each month on the common elements of combat engineering training such as bridge construction, mines and minefields, explosives and demolitions, road construction and repair, night operations and tactics. On 1 May the 51st ECB received from inspectors an overall rating of satisfactory in combat efficiency.[1]

One of the major highlights for the entire battalion was the Activation Day program. On Saturday, 18 March 1944, the 51st Engineer Combat Battalion marked its first anniversary as a unit [-273]. The battalion commander set aside the day for commemoration and activities. These included sporting events, an awards and decoration ceremony, and pass in review ceremony involving the entire battalion. Major Reafsnyder, the battalion commander, issued a memorandum commemorating the Activation Day program in which he stated:

"To each and every member of this command I extend my heartiest congratulations on the excellent work you have performed during the year. You have made this battalion the best battalion in the Army. I am proud indeed to have been selected to command this organization. In the future I shall depend on the unquestionable loyalty you have shown to me in the past, and we shall by team effort work together in doing our part to bring this War to a successful conclusion.

"For each and everyone of you I ask God's blessing in the task which lies ahead of us. May he see fit to give us all the courage to give our lives willingly if necessary in our struggle to maintain the freedom to which our country has been dedicated. May He help us all in winning the War quickly that we may return home safely and speedily to the loved ones we have left behind."[1]

Company C won all of the athletic events of the day: football, volley ball, and softball. The Good Conduct Medal for exemplary behavior, efficiency, and fidelity was awarded to 238 enlisted men. The day ended with Major Reafsnyder reviewing the battalion.[1]

One of the outstanding performances during this period in England was given by Company B, 51st ECB. On detached service to give basic and engineer training to fillers for the period 22 February to 2 April 1944, their efforts so impressed Colonel Louis P. Leone, Commanding Officer, Field Force Replacement Depot #4, that he sent a letter through channels praising each man's work in the unit, but especially praising the company commander, Captain Preston Hodges, for his "untiring efforts and his outstanding and exemplary leadership." (See Appendix for complete letter.)

While awaiting the Channel crossing, at a ceremony on 10 June, in which the 51st, 291st, and 296th ECBs participated, Colonel H. Wallis Anderson, Commanding Officer, 1111th ECG presented T/5 Thomas G. Banks, 51st H & S Company, the Soldiers Medal. While working in the motor pool, the greasy and oil-soaked clothes of one of the men (T/5 James Spedden) in the unit caught fire. Banks' instructions to the soldier to lie down went unheeded, so he knocked the man down, threw himself on top of him, and smothered the flames. As a result of this quick thinking and his quick action, a man's life was saved.[1]

During this period of training, Staff Sergeant Russell B. Watson, Company B, devised a breakdown modification of the Standard Mine Marker and submitted it to FUSA. On 13 May S/Sgt Watson received a reply from FUSA, congratulating him and advising him that the idea had merit and was being published in Engineer Intelligence Memorandum No. 13.[1]

Preparation for Crossing the Channel

On 18 April 1944, the 51st ECB received alert orders for movement under the provisions of European Theater of Operations Preparation for Overseas Movement, Short Sea Voyage. Prescribed detailed instructions on administrative and supply procedures were instituted immediately. The battalion was divided into a forward echelon, assigned to the 12th phase of the overseas operation, and a rear echelon, assigned to the 18th phase. Captain Barnes drew up a detailed loading plan for impedimenta and personnel to avoid possible confusion at loading time.

Back home, in the pre-dawn darkness of 6 June 1944, came the first official announcement that the long-expected invasion of Europe had begun. The greatest amphibious assault in history was underway. D-Day was a fact. "From all reports there was quiet and calm anxiety over this land, as people gathered in small groups to listen to news flashes .... It seemed that for the first time in our nation's life most people were as humble as they knew how to be, and that most prayed in that spirit ... this must be a day of rejoicing for countless thousands of Europeans who have been so horribly tortured for so long."[18]

America and her European Allies prayerfully awaited the establishment of a firm foothold in Normandy. The 51st anxiously anticipated its action in the 12th and 18th phases of the channel crossing. During their stay in England the men had thoughts about home, family, loved ones, and their own futures, particularly on Activation Day (18 March), and again on D-Day when flight after flight of aircraft had winged over their camp in a southerly direction.

Waterproofing of all vehicles, radios, and other equipment was completed by 16 June and all organizational transportation was grounded on the same date.[1] The forward echelon of the battalion, under the command of Lieutenant Colonel Reafsnyder, was placed on a readiness alert on 17 June 1944. It completed its packing and loading on the 18th, and left Highnam Court at 1040 hours, arriving at the marshaling area at Bournemouth, England at approximately 1830 hours the same day. The vehicles were lined up and all personnel, except the drivers who stayed with their vehicles, were assigned to pyramidal tents for the night. Each soldier received one day's "K" and one day's "D" rations, blankets, a carton of cigarettes, halazone tablets, vomit bags, and one can of "canned heat". The troops' British currency was exchanged for French

"Invasion Money" and each man received a partial payment of four dollars. Vehicles were refueled and de-waterproofing kits were distributed. The forward echelon of 24 officers, 1 warrant officer, and 524 enlisted men was now ready for movement to the port of embarkation.[1] (See Appendix for a list of officers at the Channel Crossings, 18 June and 2 July 1944.) The rear echelon of five officers, two warrant officers, and 99 enlisted men stayed at Highnam Court under the command of Captain Radford. On 2 July 1944, the rear element went through the same procedures as the forward echelon.

After more than 17 months of training and traveling, the 51st Engineer Combat Battalion was ready to cross the English Channel. And now, with thoughts even more somber, they sat in their pyramidals with vomit bags and rations for two days, awaiting orders to embark.

The quality of the 51st Engineer Combat Battalion would soon be tested and the success of its training measured by performance on the battlefield. [-193]

NOTES

1. *Organizational History, 51st Engineer Combat Battalion, 13 June 1942 to 18 October 1944*, Modern Military Records Branch, National Archives, Suitland, Maryland, hereafter referred to as the Official Military Record.
2. From "Some Military Experiences", a narrative by Col. H. Wallis Anderson of his experiences in World War II.
3. Letters from Laurie S. Radford (LSR), to her parents, Mr. and Mrs. S. C. Stewart (SCS), dated 7/27/1942, hereafter referred to as LSR to SCS.
4. LSR to SCS, 9/14/1942.
5. Letter from Martin F. Massoglia to the first reunion of 51st Engineer Combat Battalion, April 1986.
6. Personal communication from Frank H. Lee, November 1987.
7. LSR to SCS, 1/04/1943.
8. LSR to SCS, 12/20/1942, 1/16/1943, 1/20/1943, 2/12/1943, 2/15/1943, and 2/26/1943.
9. LSR to SCS, 3/03/1943.
10. LSR to SCS, 3/03/1943, 3/04/1943, and 3/08/1943.
11. Based on a letter from Albert E. to Laurie S. Radford, 9/12/1943, hereafter referred to as AER to LSR
12. AER to LSR, 9/20/1943.
13. AER to LSR, 10/05/1943
14. AER to LSR, 11/28/1943.
15. AER to LSR, 12/10/1943 and 12/12/1943.
16. Personal communication from Preston Hodges, April 1986.
17. Personal experiences of Col. Charles J. Attardo, AUS, Retired, while a member of the 51st ECB from 1943 to 1945.
18. LSR to AER, 6/06/1944 and 6/28/1944.

The 51st in convoy across the Channel. *Corps Files - 27 June 1944*

Utah Beach landing site. The 51st came ashore June 27 and July 4. *National Archives - 12 June 1944*

Into Battle: from Normandy to the West Wall

(27 June 1944 - 15 December 1944)

EXCERPTS OF LETTERS WRITTEN FROM THE FIELD
by Captain Albert E. Radford to Laurie S. Radford
28 June 1944 to 21 December 1945

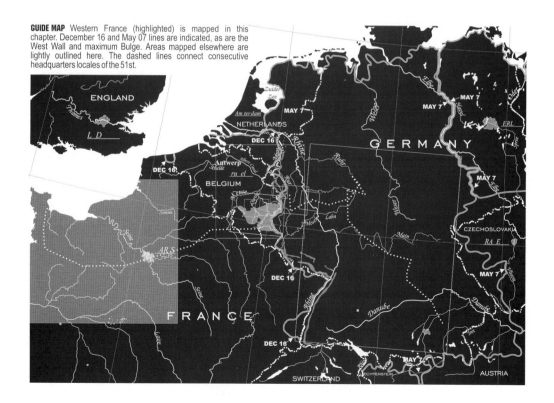

GUIDE MAP Western France (highlighted) is mapped in this chapter. December 16 and May 07 lines are indicated, as are the West Wall and maximum Bulge. Areas mapped elsewhere are lightly outlined here. The dashed lines connect consecutive headquarters locales of the 51st.

ALLIED INVASION: June-August 1944

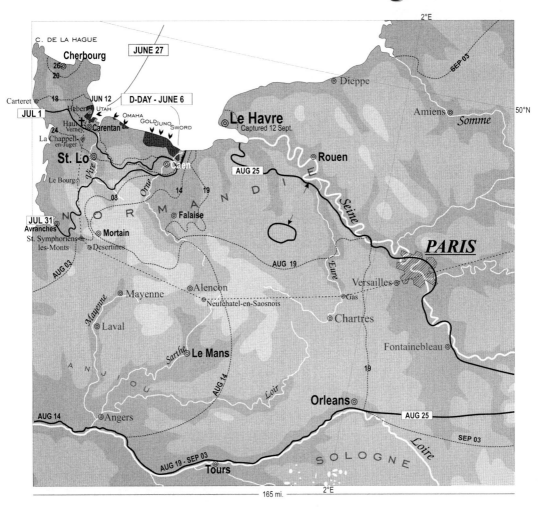

NORMANDY & NORTHERN FRANCE
Unit Headquarters - Dates of Arrival

- Utah Beach — 27 June
- Hebert — 28 June
- Haut Verney* — 17 July
- La Chappell-en-Juger — 29 July
- LeBourg* — 1 August
- Symphoriens-les-Monts — 15 August
- Desertines — 19 August
- Neufchatel-en-Saosnois — 26 August
- Gas — 30 August

*location not found on modern maps

Shanes killed (✝)

Background map derived from *The Prentice-Hall World Atlas*, p. 67. Invasion front lines are transposed from the *West Point Atlas for the Second World War: Europe and the Mediterranean*. Unit locations and dates are from *The 51st Again!*

From Normandy to the West Wall ... INTO BATTLE

Normandy Campaign*

Repairing and maintaining roads and bridges; Removing mines and deactivating booby traps; Digging in; Shelling in the hedgerows; Raining bombs on St. Lo; Break-out

Small arms and mortar fire, shelling, strafing, digging and diving into foxholes were not conducive to letter writing. Describing decaying paratroopers dangling from trees and befuddled soldiers looking for lost buddies, seeing mangled corpses in minefields, finding skull-less G.I. victims of booby-trapping, clearing strafed and bombed convoy wreckage from the roads, and removing from streams bodies and body parts - both human and bovine - before the water could be treated and pumped for the use of our troops ... these were not the scenes or subjects that would allay the fears a1nd anxieties of loved ones back home. All this, plus tight censorship, reduced most of our letters from Normandy to not much more than "I miss you, I love you, I'm still alive."

Hébert (28 June-16 July 1944) *

4 July - [-165 -- count-down to December 16]. Here I sit beneath the shade of an old apple tree in a foxhole writing .... Forget about the bursting artillery and the roar of planes and the old pillboxes and you wouldn't even know a war was going on. The men have picked up quite a few souvenirs: German rifles, M.G.'s, helmets, insignia, canteens, grenades, shells, magazines, and various other odds and ends. And they have found a few of them booby-trapped, but so far no one has been hurt except one of the pet dogs that has a broken leg.

5 July - The American artillery sounds good in the distance. Don't think I told you but the closest any shell has come was the day we arrived. We were riding down the highway well aware that a war was going on but feeling very secure a good distance back from the front line when w-h-e-e a German 88 whizzed overhead and landed about 100 feet away. We picked up speed and again the whirr and again that one landed about 75 feet away. They kept shelling but we left the place. Up until that time my machine gunner had been half asleep, but afterwards he was as fidgety as a rabbit. My 1st sergeant and the truck driver shook hands and said "Here goes". Me, I had a funny sensation in the middle.

I am still marveling at the tremendous organization and morale of our troops in overcoming the obstacles that they have. The Germans didn't miss a trick in defending this country. They even put poles in the middle of the fields to catch the poor glider pilots. These Normandy fields provide an ideal defensive set-up. Despite the defense, the men are still picking up dead Germans, some filled with maggots. With the amount of German equipment around it is easy enough to gather souvenirs.

The Normandy hedgerows differ quite a bit from the British. Here nothing is pruned & most of the hedges are 50 to 60 ft., elms and ashes with briery underbrush. The whole countryside is lush in vegetation and there are some fine herds grazing. Yesterday I saw quite a few dead untouched beefsteaks turned bottom side up and every other way.

6 July - Everything is fairly quiet and under control. It is going to take some hard driving to move these

---

* LETTERS here and throughout the book are denoted by the indented text prefaced by the vertical dashed lines. Always, the location from which the letters were written is indicated followed by one or more excerpts from one or more dates.

Germans out of here and a lot of good Americans will have to be sacrificed. The French seem to be getting along fairly well and have not suffered too much under German rule. They need clothing and shoes. Most of the women wear black and nearly all the rural citizens wear wooden shoes. The children seem to be fairly well dressed and fed. They look much better physically than the French children in N. Africa. Of course you see the men in G.I. fatigues, caps & field jackets. You occasionally see a boy with a German garrison cap. Even though all seem well fed, they really go for our "C" and "K" rations, especially the candy in them.

There is very little opportunity or occasion to spend money. All French towns have been declared off-limits which is a very wise idea. I don't see why they didn't declare a few English towns off-limits. American money now goes to America and the French don't have to worry about inflation. A lot of the French won't take any money for food they give or washing they do. A farm woman near here is doing a lot of washing for the men and she sets no price.

10 July - This lovely weather, rain, rain, and more rain and temperature isn't conducive to very high morale. I've been wet so long though that I hardly know how it would feel to be totally dry. At any rate wetness is the custom here rather than the exception as in the states. It could be a lot worse and will be.

Yesterday we had Sunday services in the apple orchard. Quite a crowd sat on the ground with their helmets on and weapons slung over their shoulders.

12 July - Three years ago today I came into the Army .... I hope the dear people don't get the impression that these Germans are a pushover. We have green troops against well-seasoned veterans and the farther inland we go the more experienced those Germans are. If the dear people could see American heads with their brains scooped out and good American bodies being piled in trucks and trailers like so many dead hogs, they would increase production instead of lowering it. There is nothing more maddening to our front line fighters and other troops than reading about strikes. Supply is winning the war for us ....

I am having a little trouble keeping as clean as I would like. We have plenty of water and a shower but the air temperature stays at 60 degrees or lower and the water temperature stays lower so I take a so-called spit bath every 2 or 3 days in my foxhole ... the foxhole and bedroll are under a pup tent and I have blackout cloth to close the front. Some fun, huh! I am now sleeping on top of the ground and if anything comes up all I have to do is to roll over once and I'm in my foxhole with bedroll and all. I've slept like

Carentan, France, Bastille Day. WWI veteran with grandchildren; their father is in German POW camp. Many less fortunate French children were in desperate conditions.   *National Archives - 14 July 1944*

Carentan: F1, 46 [The town noted is found, in this case, on the map at the Front of the book/section 1 and also on the map on page 46.]

a log at night but stay rather cold all day .... I'm still doing my scrubbing. Some of the men are having the French women do their laundry, but after seeing them beat it on the rocks with a stick, I've decided to do my own. The women I've seen work like slaves. Nearly all the young men & women have been moved to Germany to work. I've seen very few men younger than 50 & and the few I have seen I thought were Germans in civilian clothes. Incidentally, my German has come in handy in studying captured gadgets & papers.

16 July - 'Tis Sunday afternoon, everything is quiet and peaceful, no artillery fire, no planes, only the group orchestra tooting away disturbing the peace. Jerry stays out of the sky during the day but comes over every night. Most of his planes are reconnaissance with a few bombers thrown in for good measure ... the skies cleared this afternoon so we are having a beautiful evening for a change ... In half an hour we will have a church service under the apple trees. Hope we aren't rained out. We have regular services with organ and hymn books. Occasionally the organ decides to balk but it is better than nothing.

Haut Verney (17-28 July 1944) *[location not found on modern maps]*

17 July - I saw a pathetic sight this morning - a French family with a herd of cows moving down the highway to their old home. The father was pushing two of the children on a bicycle with a flat tire and the eldest daughter was pushing a baby in a carriage while mamma herded the 13 cows along. All three of them wore wooden shoes & their clothing was well-worn. They certainly looked forlorn and dejected. War is hell and you certainly don't have any conception of what it really is until you actually see it.

Carentan, France. Rubble resulted from aerial bombardment and naval gunfire prior to occupation of the city by American troops (one month prior to the arrival of the 51st in the area). *National Archives - 17 June 1944*

21 July - 'Tis raining toad frogs after two sunny days. The mud is ankle deep now and after a little sloshing about, it should be around our knees. Who am I to complain about the weather? I have a pair of hip boots to wade around in; that is something that the poor infantryman doesn't have … up until last night I had slept approximately 10 hours in the last 96. I managed to hit the hay about 2000 and didn't stir until 0700 this morning despite the rain in my tent. I was so sleepy yesterday morning I was actually dizzy … 'tis pretty rough at times but it can always be rougher.

Hedgerow country near **St. Lo.** The 51st Engineers were luckier than these soldiers whose vehicles were destroyed by mines. The road is being swept for more mines. *National Archives - 20 July 1944*

Speaking of miracles I think I have seen a few. An 88 shell landed in a tree the other day with 5 men under it, one in a truck. All of the men were knocked down, the man in the truck blown out of the truck, all helmets were blown off; 2 tents nearby were riddled with shell fragments as well as the truck; not a single one of those men was scratched. Those men picked themselves up & scrambled for foxholes, some of the men dived into a cut in the bank at the foot of a tree. Z-z-bang and a second shell landed at the base of a tree 3 feet from the man in the cut in the bank & again nary a soul was scratched. All of those men prayed a little harder that night. Two men were riding in the cab of a truck when one 20 mm. shell & about 10 or 15 .30 cal bullets came through the windshield & their seats with a lot of glass from the windshield & neither was seriously wounded. Both should be out of the hospital in a couple of weeks.

There's one thing I don't have to worry about any more - and that's my men digging foxholes and dugouts deep enough. Very few of them sleep on top of the ground or in an open foxhole anymore. You can really see American ingenuity at work when they build these underground compartments. My muscles are rather hard from digging, too. Wish you could see Weinstein's or Poronsky's homes. They take no chances whatsoever. All have had more excitement than they ever hoped to have ... all the men are doing a good job. So far, not a single man has done less then I expected of him; most are doing more. (Weinstein was a medical officer, Poronsky a dental officer.)

Pedersen's bedroll and raincoat were cut to shreds the other day about 1730. 'Twas a good thing he wasn't enjoying a catnap at the time. Everyone had a good laugh when they looked at his equipment, but he was as pale as this sheet (of paper). One minute intended Death is around and the next minute everyone is laughing at each other's reactions. The old saying "Here one minute, gone the next" is too shockingly true .... I have one big gripe - the abundance of cows. One stepped into a foxhole the other night and the occupant came out with bayonet flashing.

Chow - pork chops, rice, gravy, spinach, pineapple and white bread - a deluxe meal for wet G.I.'s .... This afternoon and most of the night we are having movies in a deserted French barn; it has walls 2 feet thick. ... The men have a lot of cleaning to do before they can show the film. A dead pig, dead cow and a live jackass claim the place for living quarters. My mail clerk has been using the jackass for mail delivery, what little there is.

23 July - The pictures, of devastation, decimation and starvation we saw made me feel like weeping; but actually seeing them makes me weep. Poor little French kids covered with sores have been begging for food and something to drink all day. We have 24 babies near us too young to eat solid food yet and no milk is available. At least 75 men, women and children have been evacuated to a small group of buildings near us without food, clothing, or bedding.

Our medics are treating them & we are sparing all we possibly can from our kitchen. A few civil affairs officers are with them but so far that organization has not been able to take care of them properly. My men are feeding them better than the civil officers with what they stole - in the army stealing is soldiering. The men now say they will never complain again about "C" rations nor will they waste any food. Those French now know that one group of Americans will give the shirts off their backs if they have to.

The mud is a little more than ankle deep now. And it is still drizzling. I wish the sun would shine for a little while so I could get my washing done. Some of my men look like mud puppies. Night before last the rain drove them out of their underground homes, looking like drowned rats. ... Two days ago it was difficult to see 30 yards ahead on account of the dust and it is now difficult to stay on the road. Three or four of my trucks have slipped into the ditch here in the bivouac area. These mosquitoes seem to like shelter-half cover during the rain.

The news is more encouraging every day. I wouldn't be a bit surprised to be near Paris when this -- I almost forgot that we can't make predictions in letters. At any rate I don't think it will last much longer. The Germans are beaten now [-146]. The German generals know it all too well.

-- Later: I did get letter #110 with pictures of David to brighten the day ... letters 105, 106, 107 & 108 are still missing. The mail is being held up after it crosses the Atlantic, I believe. My men had to travel over a good portion of American occupied France to find this. Whoops, I just evacuated my foxhole after having to enter rather fast. Capt. Huxman was taking a bath in the middle of the orchard as nude as the day he was born; he had to scramble. It didn't take any of these moles long to crawl into their holes .... (The Germans shelled the area.)

24 July - I didn't sleep too well last night because the earth shook most of the night. I can usually sleep through anything but the tremors were a little too strong last night.

25 July - Everything is running smoothly now. The company has just about reached its efficiency peak. Morale is high and everybody is doing his best. Some of my men have worked 48 consecutive hours without a gripe or complaint of any kind. As long as they can see the value of a thing they'll work until they collapse, but if they have to follow orders that can't be explained (security reasons or otherwise) they are rather difficult to handle at times.

26 July - Yesterday afternoon I sent my laundry to a quartermaster laundry outfit and this morning it was returned nice and clean. Scrubbing coveralls, shorts etc. in a 2-gallon bucket isn't much fun especially when you have to haul water 6 or 7 miles. I washed and boiled my shorts and underwear this morning and actually got them clean for a change. It is rather difficult to keep my underwear clean since I have to sleep between blankets that have not been cleaned for 9 months. Blankets get mighty dirty when you sleep on the ground and sometimes on and under them, with shoes and dirty clothes on. I sun my bedding every opportunity. You can't see the blackout curtain I had under my bedroll for the mildew. That is not an exaggeration in the least .... With the water shortage, I have decided to wash from the waist up one day, waist down the next, and my head the next .... Our PX ration is free. We are getting quite a variety of candy - Life Savers, Life Savers and more Life Savers. The French children enjoy them.

27 July - Today I had my first hot shower in Normandy. It felt wonderful .... You should see the assortment of equipment, mostly German, that we have added to our T.E. allowances: German soup kitchens as asphalt mixers; bedposts as tamper handles; glider wheels on cargo trailers; gas mask canisters as toilet article cases; steel cases as candle holders; road tanks as road sprinklers; German gas capes for water proofing mattresses; powder canisters as map cases, etc. We have improvised quite a bit for increased efficiency. For comfort and reading one of my men built a portable latrine for the company that can be disassembled into four parts for easy moving. Nothing is static - new ideas and changes pop up every day. The assistant motor officer just came up with an idea for prolonging the life of our water pumps by many hours that the army is going to put into effect as soon as possible. We make life as comfortable as possible under the conditions. Wish you could have seen the planes pass over the other day. It was a wonderful sight to behold. Not a single German plane came up to challenge them and the ack-ack was silenced after the first 1000 came over. It took 2½ hours for them to pass over and they were "closely packed". [Reference to the 3000 plane bombardment - greatest Allied assault of the war - over or near St. Lo.]

28 July - Everything is quiet and peaceful and running very smoothly. Our dough boys and armor are really rolling along. Our P-47's and P-51's must be having a great day strafing and dive bombing fleeing Nazis. It's a great sight to see our planes shuttling to and fro every daylight hour. A few German planes sneak over during the night. They are more of a nuisance than anything else.

La Chappell-en-Juger (29-31 July)

31 July - The men are picking up pets right and left. We now have cats, dogs, rabbits, a yearling - all we are lacking is a jackass which we did have for a short time. Oh, yes, the mess sergeant had a little pig, but I wouldn't let him bring it along the last time we moved.

In answer to a few questions: There are thousands of those young Nazi SS culprits in this area. I believe they are the first kids in history to be trained for "glorious murder". And those kids are mighty arrogant when captured. The M.P.'s have to keep machine guns pointed at them when they are taken to

From Normandy to the West Wall ... INTO BATTLE

the PW cages .... The trees in the hedgerows are 50-60 feet high and the dirt banks are 2-4 feet thick .... the ditches are 3-4 feet deep. CP here differs considerably from what it was in England. I have a lot more work to do most of the time even though I have the best organization I've ever had ....

Yesterday was the first Sunday we've missed having a service; the Captain was too busy burying the dead to preach .... I studied some French in England and brushed up on my German. We have 6 men in the company who speak French very fluently, so there isn't much trouble in that respect. At least 4 men in the company can speak German, 6 Polish, 2 Italian, 3 Russian.

Le Bourg (1-14 August 1944) *[location not found on modern maps]*

1 August - Somewhere in France: Some reporters have given erroneous impressions if they describe French standing in doorways watching street fights and their standing around nonchalantly while shells are exploding. Most of them are evacuated before a town is ever fought in and 90% of the places you see mentioned in the papers don't have a doorway to stand in. This war is too devastating for that. The French I have encountered dived for the ditches when one of our guns went off. A few Jerries came over one night and they scattered like jack rabbits in all directions. You don't stand in fields very long watching shells explode because 75 mm and up pitch out showers of steel and death from 50 to 300 yards. Even falling flak has killed men. One of our men has been at death's door for 3 weeks with a piece of flak in his intestines. I have seen 10 lb. shell fragments thrown at least 500 yards.

Capt. Scheuber & Sgt. Rankin (killed at Trois Ponts) view some of the nearly total devastation of **St. Lo**, wrought mainly by Allied bombardment prior to Operation Cobra. *Collection of Joseph Milgram - August 1944*

The French population has enough sense not to be curious when things start popping. Many French are going to die through ignorance after peace has descended upon this torn countryside. One Sunday while on a mine hunting and booby trapping expedition, some French kids led us to some German explosives. One of the boys tossed egg grenades and 81 mm mortar shells around like they were pieces of metal. My French speaking mail clerk warned them of the danger in handling grenades, shells and ammunition.

3 August - It doesn't take long to get dirty when you sleep in dirt and dig in it all the time. I am thankful I can dig and sleep in peace. Too many G.I.'s are sleeping in the open forever. Think I will be an active peace crusader when I return .... Fritz Kreisler is plunking away over the radio. Certainly is a pleasure to be able to hear good music occasionally.

Blumenstein, Massoglia, Wong and that crowd (in the 238th Battalion) are less that 1/2 mile from us now. They are getting along fine and doing a magnificent job with very few casualties. Wong has been recommended for the silver star for gallantry. I think his platoon will get a citation .... He is a daredevil with brains and ingenuity. He is one of the best officers, all around, of the old regiment. He spearheaded one of these numerous drives as an infantryman and did such a good job that everybody and his grandma that has come in contact with him is trying to get him in his outfit. He is still somewhat shy and reserved and does very little talking, but his speed in action is something few men have.

Reafsnyder gets more nervous every day. If we ever come under any great pressure, he will crack. Weinstein (an obstetrician) is practically a wreck now. Yates is trying to get him transferred where he can be of greater value and in more peaceful surroundings. All in all, the men are holding up very well, on the whole much better than the officers. Everyone is enthusiastic and eager in his work. Anything that we can do to get home sooner is being done.

4 August - The news certainly is encouraging -- encircle and annihilate; German blitzkrieg tactics in 1940. These small pockets of resistance can be a nuisance just like the German air force. They have been over every night since I have been here. I go to sleep nearly every night with a German plane droning overhead. They don't do much damage and the percentage of them getting back to their fields isn't too high. This rapid warfare leaves the countryside and villages more intact. Only where the Germans decide to resist is there great destruction. It doesn't take long for our artillery to level most anything. As we move along we see more French men, the old and very young.

5 August - The people at home should be somewhat elated over our successes by now. Our armored - infantry - air corps teams really pack a wallop. And that is going on into Germany before Christmas, if the Nazis last that long. And after that is over we'll go home touring through Japan. I hope the European people want to police Germany when they surrender. I can't think of a much more provoking life than acting as occupation troops .... The highways are littered with the wreckage of strafed and bombed German troops .... No one will ever know exactly the number of men we have killed. We must be getting 5 or 6 for one. The blankety-blank Dummkopfs are now getting what they dished out in 1940 and 1941.

We had services in the apple orchard again. There are lots of apple orchards in France and they make nice bivouac areas. No two services so far have been held in the same orchard .... You should see the police detail get busy after each meal around the kitchen and where the men sat. Those 7 ducklings don't leave a crumb on the ground; saves the kitchen force a lot of work. I'll have to watch my men to see that they don't carry the police detail with them when we move. They wanted to make Sunday dinner out of them but my answer was "No." The French need all the food they can get .... I didn't get any mail again yesterday. It is difficult for the A.P.O.'s to keep up with the rapidly advancing forces. Some of our combat teams have moved 50 miles a day.

6 August - In the states we had bed-check; here we have bed-check Charlie who is as regular as the days that roll around. Every night at dusk he drones over, is given a warm reception, and then returns to signal more of them over all night. I think bed-check Charlie is a Ju88. A few days ago one of his playmates grazed the tree tops in C Company's apple orchard and had all the men running for foxholes. Very funny, huh; well I think our new night fighters will destroy our nightly nuisance. They seldom were underground at the time so no one was hurt. Kirkland was last reported at 6 feet and still going deeper, doing the digging himself.

7 August - This certainly is beautiful country, even more beautiful than England. The rolling hills and natural meadows are a pleasant sight to behold from a lofty spot. It's difficult to tell that fighting armies have surged through the areas until you reach the intersections and road junctions where the air corps or tanks caught a few trucks and heavy guns. I have traveled quite a few miles over occupied France and I think the German vehicle losses are 100 to 1 or better, and tank losses are about 10 to 1. Of course that was a very rough estimate.

The weather is nice and sunny again today. Our planes really capitalize on the situation these days. The air corps really had a picnic yesterday afternoon and last night. By now you have heard of the tremendous and enormous German counterattack near and through Mortain. They should have known better by now. If they had any sense they would throw in the towel. They can't retreat fast enough to get out of the way and they aren't strong enough to hold any position long.

11 August - We are having a farewell dinner for Capt. Weinstein today. He is going to a hospital where he can be of much more value to the service as well as to himself. I hate to see him go because he has been one of my closest friends in the battalion. All of the officers are going to chip in to buy him a watch as a little token of our esteem. We'll get a new medic shortly. His medics are certainly in the dumps over his departure.

Carteret, France (F1, 46). Time for R&R at "rest centers" far from the front lines. Women filled vital roles in the war. Here nurses and WACS (Women's Auxiliary), helping form a "Conga Line", find some recreation also. *National Archives - 13 August 1944*

"Dear little Adolph" is purging the army so he can sacrifice the German nation to protect his own neck. I expect to see someone strong enough in Germany overthrow him and his clique shortly*. A rumor is out that Himmler has already been killed ....

---

* The July 20 bomb attempt on Hitler injured him little. His revenge was brutal, including impaling some conspirators on meat hooks. Gen. Rommel, Germany's version of Patton, was at least sympathetic to the conspiracy; but he had served the Reich so brilliantly, he was "allowed" to commit suicide over the matter. While Hitler recuperated, he conceived of the offensive that became the Battle of the Bulge.

12 August - Most of the plants I have seen so far are escapes from cultivation ....This country has been inhabited too long to find many wild plants ....Your dear little husband lost interest in plants when he discovered he was in the middle of a minefield. I don't know whether I told you .... I had trouble keeping Lt. Attardo and Lt. Mueller 15 yards apart walking through that area but not after I started probing around a couple of French antitank mines ....

Symphorien-les Monts (15-18 August 1944) (No Letters)

Desertines (19-25 August 1944)

21 August - Yesterday my men played a little softball and football, much to my delight. That marks the first time in France that they have participated in any athletics ... the chaplain pitched awhile. He eats with us quite frequently and hangs around for bull sessions with the officers and men. Most of his friends are on the battalion staff and in H & S Company, He would gladly leave his present surroundings to live with us, so would Weir and Casey .... A lot of the officers bought 5 or 6 pairs of o.d.'d, pinks, and blouses [uniforms] - none of which they have worn and will not wear. There isn't going to be a letup in our drive until the Germans surrender and then maybe the officers will have them to dress and walk around the woods and fields .... We had dry cereal in individual containers for breakfast a few mornings ago .... Tomorrow I am sending a detail of 3 to pick blackberries for a pie.

The news gets better every day .... The Germans promised us glider bombs on the 8th of August but we have not seen any. The Germans missed their greatest opportunity of damaging us the night before July 25. After our men moved out the Germans bombed the cleared areas.

Broad fields, somewhere in central France "tank country". Free of Norman hedgerows, the Army has a clear path to Germany.   *National Archives - September 1944*

23 August - I am feeling fine but am greatly annoyed and irritated by insect bites, mostly spiders. These yellow jackets are getting more plentiful and "meaner" as the days go by. You have to fight them off every time you eat. The first sergeant had wrapped candy inside his desk drawer and they had opened the wrapper, and started carting it way .... I was using some of the gratis PX brushless shaving soap that is perfumed, when those things smelled it and started chasing me all over the place.

From Normandy to the West Wall ... INTO BATTLE

Northern France Campaign

Maintaining and rebuilding roads; Constructing, repairing, removing bridges; Racing through celebrating Paris; Capturing Germans; Driving many miles to procure gasoline, supplies and mail.

Neufchatel-en-Saoanois (26-28 August 1944)

28 August - [-100] While looking for equipment and lumber, a bunch of us rambled into a German underground city, not completed. The French say that there are 15 miles of tunnels. We rambled through approximately 2 miles of it - prowling into unused quarters with very nice furnishings, inner spring mattresses, and rooms where bombs were stored, the heaviest of which weighed approximately 750 lbs. .... There were a few flying bomb wings, 2 demolished flying bombs, and numerous parts. What the whole thing was to be used for no one has been able to decide. The Germans would not let any French enter the place or the town over the tunnels. (V-1 construction site)

Gas (30 August-3 September 1944)

2 Sept. - I am supposed to take off on a 150 mile trip in a few minutes. I've really been on the go this past week. Have not received any mail in 8 days.

3 Sept. - Guess by now you know we are out of hedgerow country, into the level farming regions of France. There are beautiful wheat fields, cover crops and truck gardens all through this area. There are quite a few forests scattered here and there that seem to be government controlled. There are a few pine forests, but most are oak, beech or poplar.

Perlé (4-9 September 1944)

6 Sept.- In 3 or 4 days we should receive all back mail unless we move a couple hundred miles which is likely to happen as not. At present we are in a beautiful valley with a small stream running through the middle of it. Takes me 20 minutes to walk around the company area ....The Poles in my company enjoy this location because there is a small farm village nearly completely populated by Poles .... My three Polish, Russian, and Slavic cooks ... have bartered for cabbage, cucumbers, carrots, and Irish potatoes for supper to supplement our "K" ration diet.

9 Sept. - I am sitting in my pup tent while the rain pours. The Poles near here say that this is their rainy season. Seems to me as if we've had a continually rainy season since coming overseas. The temperature is dropping every day and it is getting decidedly uncomfortable. The bees or yellow jackets are still with us. One of the men put a piece of fruit bar in his mouth with yellow jackets and now has a swollen tongue.

Had an interesting experience recently: We were breezing along at 40 miles an hour when we came over a rise and into plain view of a Mark IV or V German tank in the middle of the road. My driver tried sliding over the back of his seat. I ordered him to go straight ahead .... We drove into the ditch to get around it and everyone breathed easier when we saw that it had been knocked out! Needless to say, I had a rather sinking feeling in the pit of my stomach for a few seconds. I had 3 of my men with me, all armed with carbines. Popping off at that with .30 caliber ammunition would have been the equivalent of shooting chinaberries at the side of a house with a popgun, hoping to knock the house down.

Desertines, Neufchatel-en-Saoanis, Gas: 46   Perlé: F6

In another place we found a crashed Piper Cub with the right wing damaged and the tops of the prop knocked off. One of my men was playing with the controls when he decided to push the starter button. Much to his surprise she started with the throttle wide open - and he had never been in a plane before. He turned off the ignition and piled out of the place like a frightened jack rabbit. A few minutes after that happened, I saw the pilot sneaking around a hedge with his rifle ready to kill anything that popped up. When the plane started, he was in the truck on the road and it sounded like a German machine gun firing, so he was coming to our rescue .... That will give the group something to tell their grandchildren.

Good Morning! .... It was rumored last night that there were 22 bags of mail at the A.P.O. so the mail clerks took off ....Turned out to be 4 bags of packages. Our mail service should be improving all along unless we start running over Germany like we have France and Belgium.

Rozoy-sur-Serre (10-16 September 1944)

11 Sept. - As we move along we get more and more reports of the Germans hiding out, but the Free French are taking care of most of them. The Boche will surrender to the Americans but I have heard numerous stories of their committing suicide before surrendering to the French .... We have been using the French to guard some bridges ....

12 Sept. - The apple crop is being harvested now - guess most of them will be converted into cider. None of them are fit to eat. Blackberries are just getting ripe .... the few peaches I have seen are still green ... wheat has been harvested .... Fall plowing with 4 to 6 oxen hooked to the plow is well underway. Have not seen a mule

Too late for this bridge, destroyed by retreating Germans at **St. Mihiel**, France (F6) on the Meuse.

National Archives - 10 September 1944

since I have been in France but have seen some sturdy draft horses .... It is getting late and I have a 300 mile trip ahead of me in the morning so I guess I had better get to bed.

14 Sept. - We are sticking to one traveling APO now even though we have to travel 200 miles for mail at times .... We had a very heavy shower last night ... everything is covered with mud ... a beautiful day and rather uneventful as far as the war goes. Oh yes, so far the unit has captured 61 prisoners, wounding 2 and not losing a single one of our men.

From Normandy to the West Wall ... INTO BATTLE

Ardennes Campaign (Belgium)

Repairing and constructing bridges; Maintaining roads; Prescient infantry training; Sawmilling; New leadership.

Martelange (17-30 September 1944)

18 Sept. - [-89] Guess you notice ... that I've changed countries, 2 of them recently .... Belgium reminds me a lot of western North Carolina, especially with the beautiful woods and valleys .... The battalion is capturing Germans right and left and so far none of the Jerries has put up much of a fight. If the present rate continues, I'll have to build a stockade near the bivouac area.

19 Sept. - If a cat tried to come in our area at night, I'm quite sure it would be shot. We would have a lot of fun if some Jerries tried to come in.

20 Sept. - Nothing exciting has happened except for a few Jerry reports. Spent the better part of yesterday following Belgians looking for them without any luck. The ironic part of it was that a Jerry surrendered to one of our men this morning in one of the places we searched yesterday. His company had been annihilated ... he was wounded in the leg ... has been without food for 8 days. Of course he was very weak under the circumstances. There wasn't very much fight left in any of them but some of them will still shoot until the odds are too great.

23 Sept. - Yesterday I met the leader of the Belgian underground or Free Belgian Forces. He is a small, dapper, sharp-eyed colonel who was an aviator before Germany moved in. He must have had $10,000 with him plus a body guard and interpreter. His transportation was a 1940 Ford V-8.

Practically all of the continental cars and trucks were built by Ford .... Practically all the farm machinery is American made .... I visited a tank factory, German, yesterday, looking for engineer materials and we found a lot of material that will help us a great deal. 'Twas a huge place with quite a few tanks on the assembly line ... a real nice setup all above ground with only a small percentage of it destroyed.

We are really getting a change in diet these days ... the mess sergeant turned up with fresh celery, cucumbers, potatoes, cabbage, onions, carrots, turnips, and water cress yesterday. The fresh vegetables help a great deal, but our days of bartering are limited as you can well understand ... insects are not as bad as they were ... but spiders (seem) to be rather plentiful. Think I have found a spider in my helmet every morning ... always shake my shoes and clothes before I don them ....

... You mentioned rest periods in one of your letters. Yep, we've heard of them but haven't had one since we've been in France. It has been work and more work 7 days and nights per week. We were supposed to have had a 2-day rest period a month ago but due to a mix-up in orders the men worked harder those two days than they had previously. No one is complaining about overwork, everyone is doing his best to get this over with as soon as possible.

25 Sept. - We now have stoves in all of the section tents that help quite a bit. The stoves and coal are German, both taken from the huge tank assembly factory. Sounds as though we have our generator working so we should have lights soon.

Martelange: B7

Near **Metz**, France (F6), 50 miles south of the 51st while at Martelange. The type of damage a Teller mine can do: first aid is given to the driver of a jeep which drove over one.   *National Archives - 26 September 1944*

26 Sept. - My morale is lower than a snake's belly this morning - no mail again yesterday. The mail clerk is scouting the countryside for it this morning. He's following one clue that should bring results .... If I had written you 3 letters in one day, I could have put 3 countries on the heading ... this is a really moving army. Bed-check Charlie was slightly annoying last night for the first time in a long time ... he kept going up and down the road. The poor fool was just 3 hours too late as he has been in every case so far. German intelligence must not be what it is cracked up to be. My deer hunters and hog hunters have been trying to add meat to the larder but so far no one has, though every man out has gotten a shot at deer...One of the men came within 20 yards of a wild boar, a sow, and 6 shoats, but since no tree was available, he wouldn't blast away ... they are vicious when wounded.

28 Sept. - Life isn't too bad with mail and sunshine. And tomorrow we get an electric radio. Now all we need is continued sunshine and regular mail service .... Several of my men have been deer hunting but no one has shot one ... though they have fired quite a few rounds at them ... I keep hoping and praying to get home as soon as possible ... my reasoning tells me that it will be at least another year before I get home.

29 Sept. - You should see the Orderly Room now. We have a kitchen fly stretched over wire and poles rigged between a few sturdy trees. We have leaves piled around the bottom to keep out the cold air from the sides; a latrine screen doubled several times over one end; a German front door from a prefabricated hut over part of the front; a piece of plywood and a German shelter half stretched over the other part. From the outside we have a very efficient German stove that doesn't burn more than 2 gallons of coal per day and throws out plenty of heat. We have no less that three elbows in 10 feet of pipe to get

From Normandy to the West Wall ... INTO BATTLE

Timber trestle bridge built by Company A in **Montmedy**, France, 40 miles southwest of Bastogne. Many bridges had to be rebuilt as Allied forces pursued the Germans eastward.   *Corps Files - 27 September 1944*

the smoke out. By the German radio which we acquired yesterday, we have a very nice box, Lundebahnbefeuren, that we use to carry rockets, grenades of every type and ammo in. Along side it we have 50 lbs. of TNT which I am going to remove .... On the latrine screen end I have a huge situation map and on the other side is the mail clerk's desk, the 1st Sgt.'s and mine. We now have electric lights with power furnished by an American generator; the power line is American telephone wire, the light Belgian, the socket French, and the intermediate wires German. We accumulated all this junk in three countries, no four.

The radio certainly is a pleasure ... all the German programs seem to be excellent musicals, classical ... got a kick out of listening to the "Achtungs" when our planes approached the other night ... broadcasts in English from Germany are preposterously funny in their exaggeration. Tomorrow we get paid in Belgian francs ... the men will be very confused in their crap games on account of the different rates of exchange of the franc.

Mont Rigi (1-22 October 1944)

2 Oct. - [-75] Censorship regulations have been eased considerably. So far I've seen Germany, Luxembourg, Belgium, England, France, Morocco, and Algeria. Some of the more interesting cities have been Reims, Paris, Cherbourg, Mortain, Arlon, etc.

4 Oct. - Even though this is an H & S Co., we have been in an "embarrassing spot" once or twice. Engineers are not usually ahead of the infantry and an H & S Co. usually has its line companies for protection, but in one locality the closest any troops were to us was 3 miles, and they happened to be 500-600 Germans with artillery. None of us lost any sleep or even bothered to dig foxholes; just another case in which we felt secure in the trees .... Speaking of bivouac areas, this is the wettest yet and the coldest.

Montmedy: F6   Mont Rigi: B4

6 Oct. - The Belgians are really doing a good job of policing this disputed area. The soldiers are clean, eager, intelligent looking men. The ones guarding a road near our area are provoked because they can't form a battalion and fight the hated Boche. I don't think they have failed to arrest at least one German per day in civilian clothes trying to sneak into Germany.

7 Oct. - This mountain region reminds me a good deal of Western North Carolina. Game reserves and trails dot the area. Further west and at lower elevations most of the forests are beech and oak with occasional pines ... radio is certainly a great boon to morale. We have 3 loud speakers running into various sections of the company. It's turned on at 0730 and off at 2330. Quite a few of the men stay up to hear the World Series results at 2300. This is supposed to be another more or less rest area but we have more work to do now than ever before.

8 Oct. - This has been the most beautiful day we have had in weeks. Apparently the German stronghold nearby has been knocked out because we can't hear any more firing ... your National Geographic map makes a very good situation map. I can now show the Russian front as well as the Western front.

9 Oct. - Last night we had church services in one of the large tents with approximately 1/3 of the company attending. Afterwards most of the men spent their time listening to the World Series direct from St. Louis. The chaplain was sniped at on the way home but no one was hurt. This same sniper took a shot at the mail clerk.

Too many people are unable to appreciate the supply problems involved in a rapid advance or the formidability of the West Wall. After the men run the Jerries out of the pill boxes, they sneak back in. Our men are now welding the steel doors and pushing huge mounds of earth over the embrasures. American ingenuity and guts will get them through o.k. Guess I told you I have a new nickname (Pappy), given me by the men, for some inexplicable reason.

11 Oct. - Rain, fog, and more rain. Well, it will take a lot to dampen the fighting spirit of the American G.I. Additional woolen clothes and a blanket have reduced the number of colds considerably. We are fairly well acclimatized after the outdoor training at Plattsburg - but I'll never like it.

Yesterday afternoon I had my first cleansing hot shower since I've been in Europe, on the continent at least. One of the hospitals in a German school nearby has permitted the men to enjoy the luxury of hot water in a steam heated room. I certainly feel like a new man after soaking most of the dirt out of my hide.

12 Oct. - The weather has changed slightly for the better but skies are still overcast. The men now have overcoats, gloves, and plenty of blankets so there is no complaint from that direction. Instead of mud on the roads we now have soup. And after the muddy bituminous roads are souped it is almost impossible to control a vehicle. We've had to cut our speed considerably; despite that we have wrecked quite a few vehicles, very few men.

14 Oct. - The bombers and fighters really buzz over this area, including a few Germans. The woods are so thick it is almost impossible for them to spot us from the air. As long as their artillery doesn't open up and none of our patrols stumble in, we are perfectly safe. Due to a few incidents lately that have struck home a little more closely, everyone's wrath has considerably increased .... I don't think many of the Nazis are going to escape after this mess is over. We already know exactly whom we want .... In the last two days the British have practically obliterated Kleve and Emmerich [adjacent Rhine River towns about 15 miles SE of Arnhem].

Arnhem: F2

From Normandy to the West Wall ... INTO BATTLE

Just paid a visit to the rows and rows of Dragon teeth*, part of the Siegfried Line. The Jerries wasted thousands of tons of good cement, in my estimation. The German kids smile and wave at you, just like the French and Belgian kids. The older people don't look at you very enthusiastically.

17 Oct. - Weather is still rain, rain, and more rain. One of the men remarked that we would all die of sunstroke if one little ray of sunshine fil-

West Wall near **Roetgen** (124), Germany: 3rd Armored Division, First Army passes through first West Wall defenses.   *National Archives -15 September 1944*

tered through these clouds. The mud is close to knee-deep now. If we stay here much longer, I'll have to build corduroy roads to get around on. Most of the men sleep dry and warm so we can't kick too much.

Night before last one of the guards thought a German patrol was approaching, so he called the Orderly Room for help. The lst Sergeant and I went to investigate. I lost him 20 yards from the Orderly Room door. He tried to walk through a 2½ ton truck. You couldn't see your hand before your face in the woods so I moved to the edge of the road. I was scared to walk in the road because the Germans might open up and if they didn't, the guards might catch me in machine-gun cross fire since they were so jittery. I stuck to the edge of the woods and almost broke my neck trying to cross a couple of logs. Carbine went one way and I the other. I finally got there, calmed the guards' nerves (too vivid imaginations), gave them instructions, and returned to the Orderly Room .... I now have a warning system around the area. Nothing can get within 25-75 yds. of the area without the guards knowing it.

Some of the men were slightly embarrassed yesterday .... A report was out that Germans in American uniforms were operating in the woods. One of the platoon leaders took a couple of squads out, surrounded the hideout and captured one who spoke English very haltingly. He was a White Russian who later lived in France and then the U.S. The fellow had American credentials and said he was from one of our corps that wasn't in this sector at all. They brought him in, stayed around awhile and finally captured the captain. Carver took both to higher headquarters for interrogation. Imagine their embarrassment when they discovered that the captain was head of the counterintelligence corps of the corps mentioned, and were on a special mission in this area. The White Russian spoke six languages, English the worst of all.

Everything is quiet and peaceful. The 1st Sgt. [Samuel Dennis Hall] is busy filing. I've got a very dependable man that I think a mighty lot of. He [Hall] was a very successful farmer in Buncombe Co. (NC) before the army sent him his greetings. He is 31 and very mature. All the men respect him and give him no back talk. He tolerates no foolishness and is big enough to back up anything he says

---

*The West Wall or Siegfried Line had tank traps, barriers, hardened pill boxes, and machine gun nests with crossing fields of fire, etc. The troops in the photo have sped in six weeks from Normandy to a dead end at the German border, at the end of a 600 mile supply line. When the invasion resumed in five months, the 51st would be in the forefront, bridging the Roer and Rhine.

physically and mentally without benefit of rank or company commander ... the company has been running much more smoothly since the Scotch-Irish mountaineer took over.

20 Oct. - I'm getting a day room fixed up for the men with German tables, benches, stove, radio, etc. As soon as I get it completed we should move out. I'll take it with me, even if I have to return for it.

21 Oct. - The bivouac area is looking more like shanty town every day. One section has built a log cabin, another a shack of woven spruce which is very warm and comfortable, and practically all the pup tents are raised off the ground. By tomorrow night I expect to see a house built in the trees. The roar of artillery and planes serenade us to sleep each night and some of the men have had the pleasure of hearing some of the buzzers. If these little things could be better controlled, or more accurately controlled, they would be much more than a nuisance .... The 238th seems to be making quite a reputation for itself. One of their boys had to use a transit while building a bridge under fire and couldn't use a light so he did his alignment by using glow worms that are very common in France and Belgium. I think some of Blumenstein's bunch pushed that German demolition laden train into a city with the bulldozer.

The mud is as deep as ever but the temperature has been a little higher today .... Had a spine-tingling scare last night just after I crawled into bed. One of those little buzzers came over about 200 feet overhead and it sounded like its "motor" was dying. I was beginning to brace myself for the shock but it made its way on over our mountain. One of the men said, "It is quite a sensation to have a ton of TNT floating around with no one knowing where it is going to land."

Champlon Famenne (23 October-5 November 1944)

24 Oct. - [-54] The people of Marche apparently have not seen many soldiers. We stopped at a corner to post a sign and before you could say scat a woman dashed out of the house and gave us a piece of pie and asked if we wanted coffee, but since we can't fraternize I told her no for the whole bunch. It's difficult not to fraternize with friendly people in rear areas but the army knows best. The soil is well drained here and one pasture is actually dry enough for a volleyball net. Played two games today, first time since leaving England ... saw my first robot bomb [V-1] sailing over this morning; have heard at least a dozen but have been unable to see them on account of low hanging clouds.

25 Oct. - We certainly had a freak accident in one of the companies yesterday. One of the men put his rifle on a chain saw* in a truck and somehow the trigger guard was caught on a saw tooth. When the truck lurched, the safety was knocked off; and another lurch set the weapon off. It fired 7 times; 3 slugs ripped through one man's stomach, killing him [Paul Duffalo], and another had the knee of his o.d.'s perforated and a hole through his overcoat without a scratch. The slippery roads have made driving extremely hazardous. One of my men had his trailer slide into another filled with caps and firing devices without setting them off. This army has taught me a great deal about administration and responsibility. So far, I have definitely benefitted by this army career.

27 Oct. - Believe it or not ... the army now furnishes us vitamin tablets that contain half a day's requirements. As the men go through the chow line at night the mess sergeant places one daintily in each man's mouth. We are taking them to increase resistance to colds. All known vitamins are in those pills except "E". Guess the omission was intentional.

28 Oct. - Some of the men picked up a few German SS paratroopers today who are very hard-bitten individuals. Also picked up was one of our tail gunners who parachuted from a disabled plane.

---

* Floyd Wright [2001 Reunion] says an M-1 rifle was set off by the shifting of a bicycle, which had been piled into the back of the truck.
Champlon Famenne: 88

From Normandy to the West Wall ... INTO BATTLE

29 Oct. - We have church services at 1830 tonight and then I'll patiently wait for the mail man who has to travel 100 miles for the mail ... doesn't look as if any mail is going to come in again tonight. It is nearly 2100 so I think I will go to bed.

30 Oct. - The weather has been foggy, damp, and cold all day. It's an ideal day for buzz-bombing and a few have been over but didn't land anywhere close. One of these gadgets plowed into a mountainside near the area we just left and another exploded just on the other side. Two of the men were in a building when one exploded and they said the walls buckled but did not collapse. They don't carry very much explosive but what there is has a terrific blasting effect. Those play things are one of the least of our worries. It's time to take action when you hear the "motor" stop.

None of us have dug foxholes in nearly 2 months even though in one area there was nothing between us and the Germans except space and not much of that. The infantry unit closest to us had log covered holes. "Twas a good thing because Jerry bombed them several times. Of course we have had a multitude of convenient ditches in most areas. Have not slept in a foxhole since the first week in August and hope I never have to sleep in another, especially in this type of weather. Being on top of the ground is bad enough.

Tomorrow is another pay day which means a long cold ride of more that 100 miles .... One of the companies got the Battalion's first German plane this morning. Ran out of gas and came to a safe landing near the bivouac area. The company hasn't managed to round up the Germans yet. Guns and all were fully loaded when the men reached the plane. Some little gal back home will get a silk parachute dress some day ... the plane turned out to be a Stuka dive bomber and the B.F.I. said the Jerries asked some civilians if they were in London; they were informed that they were near Brussels and then the Jerries wanted to know if the Americans had been there; the answer was "No", in hopes that the Jerries would run into our company on their way to Germany. So far they have not been picked up dead or alive. Remarkably enlightened, those birds are.

I've heard of odd and strange associations in bed partners but this one is tops: the mail clerk sleeps with the first sergeant and the first sergeant is complaining because the mail clerk crawls under the cover, sticks the bottom of his feet against the first sergeant's and then proceeds to scratch them with his toenails. The first sergeant is ready to pitch him out and I don't blame him.

Allied planes are certainly battering the daylights out of Cologne. We've heard the bombers going in that direction every night for quite awhile. It's music to our ears but a discordant note in the form of Jerry creeps in occasionally. Jerry's robot counterpart still whizzes overhead as harmless as can be. The Germans are in for a rude awakening one of these days.

Marche (6 November - 17 December 1944)

7 Nov. - [-39] Here I sit with a soft glowing chandelier overhead and with bay windows all around ... the walls are covered with fancy tapestry and over the fireplace is a huge gilt-edged mirror ... the window sills are highly polished marble. This is a $10,000 chateau with 3 dry floors, no mud. The section officers are on the first floor and the men who don't sleep elsewhere are upstairs ... some of my S-4 men are sleeping in the propagation beds in the greenhouse. They say it is a wonderful feeling to watch the rain splatter off instead of on. We have ... well-wooded areas to disperse the trucks in and ponds to get water from. The Germans were thoughtful enough to put barbed wire around the place and two pill boxes in ... so my security problems have been decreased.

Cologne (Köln): F3, 6   **Marche**: 6, 88, B2

8 Nov. - We are having our first snow tonight .... Jerry is taking advantage again of the low ceiling ... launching quite a few buzz bombs .... Nearly all of our deciduous trees are bare so that means our camouflage problems are increased.

9 Nov. - By morning I guess the ground will be thoroughly frozen. It has been almost 2 years since I have had the pleasure of shaking the snow out of my eyes when I opened the pup tent flap.

10 Nov. - As usual, no mail last night. It is high time some of those mail laden ships arrived on this side of the pond. It looks as if the sun is going to come out - I'd like to see what it looks like again.

11 Nov. - We received a directive today that said mail service would be much slower due to less air space for letters .... The men are working harder than ever and establishing a few new records I think. Everyone is having minor troubles galore, though. Capt. Hodges needed horses to haul logs so a Belgian told him he could get 10 if the American government would furnish 10 kilos of oats per horse per day. It is a rather difficult matter for engineers to produce Belgian rationed oats and we don't carry that item in our supply.

12 Nov. - The weather is cloudy and rainy again this morning. We had just as much cloudiness and rain in the USA but the weather didn't make much difference. It is now a determining factor in everything we think or do. The Belgians say they have approximately 5 clear days per month during the winter.

This place sounds like a juke joint this morning with the radio running full blast, everybody talking, section leaders discussing the pros and cons of the generator running, and a ping pong ball being batted all over the place. A few buzz bombs should soar over to increase the confusion. Guess you heard about the German rocket [V-2] that soars 60 or 70 miles into the stratosphere ... quite an achievement for the Germans but militarily valueless. We knew all about it before it was ever fired. The Germans are not pulling anything new on us. Our intelligence men do a pretty good job. [-34]

Zweifall*, Germany (124). Engineers (not the 51st) build a corduroy road. The 51st spent much time here in February 1945. On this day, they were 50 miles southwest; it rained on them as well and snowed very heavily the next day. Five miles south of here the "Battle of Hürtgen Forest" rages, with over 30,000 US casualties, many from trench foot. *National Archives - 13 November 1944*

14 Nov. - Went to bed fairly early ... then one of the section leaders came storming in with the news that 4 of his men were a.w.o.l. Quieted him and found all four of his men minding their own business in

---

* November 13, two miles north of Zweifall, First Army's major assault past captured Aachen toward Cologne to trap German forces west of the Rhine failed in good measure, argues Cooper in ***Death Traps***, because Patton had his way getting fuel-efficient Sherman instead of Pershing tanks -- superior otherwise. From Normandy onwards, Shermans proved death traps (a 600% casualty rate in N. Europe!).

From Normandy to the West Wall ... INTO BATTLE

their tents. Snow or no snow it looks as if we are beginning to throw our Sunday punches at the Boche and it shouldn't be too long before we throw our haymaker, I hope.

I've been overseas a little better than a year now .... Never will forget the day I boarded that Liberty tub. I was the first in the battalion to cross the gangplank and that was at 1517 this month (November 1943). The band played "Over There". I'll never forget my mixed feelings as I watched the states fade into the background. In another year I should be able to see Europe fade into the background.

No snow, no rain, no mail ... but plenty of dampness .... Maj. Yates, Anderson, Barnes, Dave (Henry) and 2 of my enlisted men just received the "Soldiers Medal" for heroism not in actual combat [fighting ammo dump fire at **St. Mère Eglise**: p.46]. They deserved it; I'll tell you the story some day. Of 6 medals received so far in the battalion, H & S has received 4, with a 5th coming up. That does my morale a lot of good.

The area we just vacated must have nearly 3 ft. of snow on the ground by now. Some of the roads have at least 1 foot that we've got to clear. We have some winter pictures of these roads with snow piled 10 to 12 feet high. Our Plattsburg training will come in handy now .... The last war casualty producer is beginning to crop out again, trench foot ... the men are well aware of the dangers of damp, cold feet ... all colds have practically disappeared since we moved inside ... fruit juice and vitamins have helped also.

16 Nov. - Something exciting happened this morning - the sun was out for 3 hours. Something else exciting occurred in the form of a buzz bomb cutting out its "motor" over our bivouac area. It glided safely past, how far we don't know yet ... another shook every window in the house this morning when it passed over. Looks like their line of flight is immediately over our area. Just hope those Jerries don't get our range ... this morning we had our first ice and the coldest day of the year. Temperature must have reached 25 degrees .... Nothing exciting has happened (next morning), everything is quiet and peaceful despite all the hell that is breaking loose over other places. Seems as if a general offensive is well under way all along our line.

20 Nov. - Christmas packages are arriving every day and most are consumed within 2 hours. A couple of sections are saving theirs for a big Christmas party, they hope. We plan to give a party for some of the children in the town if we are here. We are saving all Life Savers and hard candy from our rations. The men always give it away anyway. I expect the situation to be radically changed by that time though. We had a driving rain this afternoon during the ceremony. I would stand braced against the wind and then it would decide to stop and I would almost fall over backwards. So far there have been 4 Soldiers' Medals in the company and I am sure I'll be able to recommend another man for a bronze star shortly. I wore my o.d.'s for the first time since I have been across the channel ... feel much more comfortable in fatigues.

23 Nov. - Rain, rain and more rain. Looks as if the weather would have eased up on Thanksgiving. Tonight we are having turkey, cake and cranberry sauce. We even had a fresh egg for breakfast. We have been getting one per week for the last three weeks. On the whole the food situation is excellent. The laundry service is still good, 24 hours or less but it is still all rough dried. There goes the chow bell .... I've just finished a dinner of braised ham and rice, candied sweet potatoes, carrots and pineapple. 'Twas fairly well prepared and nourishing. (This was obviously lunch).

Later -- we had a nice Thanksgiving supper tonight: roast turkey, mashed potatoes, giblet gravy, glazed yams, peas, carrots, chocolate cake, cranberries, bread and coffee. Everyone had very full stomachs .... We'll have leftovers a couple of days now .... The ping pong table is still being used 16 hours a day. Every

During the assault, lead Shermans stalled trying to power mine flails and plow through mud. Heavier but wider-tread Pershings would have excelled. Of 64 Shermans in this advance on 16 November, 48 were destroyed in 26 minutes. [In fairness to Patton, in August and at other times, his bold initiatives were rejected for various reasons, perhaps letting slip the opportunity for a pre-winter, pre-mud victory.]

free moment the men get, they run to the day room to play a game. It's going to be rough when we have to return to the woods.

26 Nov. - A buzz bomb awakened me this morning as it went over. It exploded nearby, rattled windows, and bounced a piece of shrapnel off the side of the building. The Jerries are improving their aim .... The first sergeant asked one of the guards why he didn't shoot the thing down. Reply, "Hell man, I was too busy praying for the thing to clear the tree and keep going to shoot at it." From reports, it wasn't more than 500 ft. high and descending .... We have not been able to keep up with the news lately since we lost the generator ... now is the time we need the radio with the 3rd, 7th, and French 1st armies on the loose. Hope we are successful in trapping the Germans in the Vosges. 7000 are supposed to be surrounded now.

Hürtgen, Germany. The news doubtless mentioned the endless "Battle of the Forest". The 121st Infantry Regiment, 8th Inf. Div., V Corps, FUSA, perhaps march to their own slaughter past a Sherman tank on guard. The 51st would later be in this area in mud, ice and deep snow.   *National Archives - 30 November 1944*

29 Nov. - The radio is running full blast again. The first sergeant borrowed a "beat-up" generator from ordnance and the medics paid a visit to the scrap pile and now we have a smooth running generator and a radio with 5 speakers.

2 Dec. - One buzz bomb came over at 1800 at which one of my men fired and I caught the devil from some very jittery officers. The man fired at it from at least 1/2 mile away with the bomb going away.

6 Dec. - [-10] Exploded the German demolitions this morning, knocking out two windows a mile away so I am now known as the V-3 originator here. We have a lot of easily frightened officers around here. Some of them were still as white as sheets when I returned 15 minutes after the explosion. Apparently I annoyed the nearby town because in less than 10 minutes 100 Belgians were out, including the fire department. I tried to explain to them it wasn't a German V-1 or V-2. (I had destroyed all of the mines, igniters and booby traps I had been gathering since I landed in Normandy).

7 Dec. - Yesterday was St. Nicholas or Christmas Day for the Belgians. The American soldiers here and in town held a party for 800 children. Some of them showed a couple of movies in the theater and then tried dividing the candy which we had saved. Don't think those kids will ever forget the Americans. They all had a very jolly time. 'Twas the first time most of them had tasted chocolate in years.

8 Dec. - Seems like the Germans are running short of buzz bombs .... This peace and quiet may be broken in the near future, wouldn't surprise me a bit .... The Rhine is going to be a humdinger to cross .... None of my men drew the plans that will be used by army.

Hunningen (B4). GI's shared what they could. Here nurses and doctors fit a Belgian boy with a jacket donated by Belgians. *National Archives - 24 February 1945*

The snow is really pouring down, and the road is getting icy. So far during this skirmish I've had three men banged up in a wreck, hospitalized, and at present I have one nursing a broken collar bone when a vehicle turned bottom side up. My mail clerk and driver luckily came out of that unscathed.

12 Dec. - [-4] Seems as if we are in for a few changes for the better I hope. It takes some people a long time to learn. Everything has been peaceful and quiet the last 2 days. Either the Jerries have run out of V-1's or they are hoarding them for the big blast because none have come over lately. Our bombers and fighters have been roaring over steadily and from all reports are doing a bang-up job.

14 Dec. -[-2] Our new C.O. is a West Pointer only 26 years old and a Lt. Col. He is a real live wire and seems very likable. He knows what he wants even though he has not had much troop experience. He has a lot to learn but I am sure all the officers will be behind him 100%. Reafsnyder is as happy as a lark.

15 Dec. - [-1] Nothing exciting has occurred in the last few days. Only 1 buzz bomb has roared over in the past week. It was a dud and fell intact. Within 24 hours it was stripped for souvenirs. Ice is all over the place and the ground is covered with frost. If we were in the area we just vacated, we would be enjoying 18 inches of snow and a Jerry strafing and bombing every day. About dusk German planes swoop down that stretch of road past the old bivouac area ... now called Jerry boulevard.

The new C.O. really has us stepping. He's bullheaded and impatient but seems to be a very bright boy itching for combat. Yates returned today after more than three months in the hospital. Everyone was glad to see him and he certainly was happy to return. Maybe he will be able to keep this new gent under control. This fellow is having us build a road in the area that will take a much longer time to build than I think we will stay put. He also wants a mess hall with benches that you can't manufacture in a few minutes. He'll be tempered as time marches on. This is the closest he's ever been to combat and at present we are miles behind the front lines. [All hell broke loose on December 16th.]

Timbering somewhere in the Ardennes - late 1944. Not all of the Ardennes was forested. The 51st ranged over and became very intimately knowledgeable about much of the Ardennes region in the weeks prior to the morning of December 16. They had no clue as to what was coming.   *Collection of Floyd Wright - 1944*

Last night we had our first excitement in quite awhile. A Jerry came nosing around and everybody and his grandma threw plenty of lead at him but he buzzed merrily on. After the plane incident, someone started popping way with a carbine or small-bore weapon. Guess some Belgian was feeling his oats at 2 a.m. 'Twas a good way to die suddenly. "Umpteen" men were out looking for him before the echo died. Dave Henry shows me pictures of Mary frequently. He's mighty proud of his wife.

Ciergnon (18-21 December 1944)

18 Dec. - It doesn't seem like I'll have much more time to write now. The Jerries are entertaining us. By now I am sure you have heard of their attack on a 60 mile front. I got about 3 hours of sleep last night with my clothes on. When we break this we should just about have their backs broken.

Ciergnon: B1

A Place in History: The Battle of the Bulge

(16 December 1944 - 3 January 1945)

INTRODUCTION
THE PATTON MYTH
HOLDING THE LINE:
DEFENSE AT TROIS PONTS
BATTLE OF HOTTON

WITH EXCERPTS OF LETTERS WRITTEN FROM THE FIELD
by Captain Albert E. Radford to Laurie S. Radford
December 22, 1944 to January 2, 1945

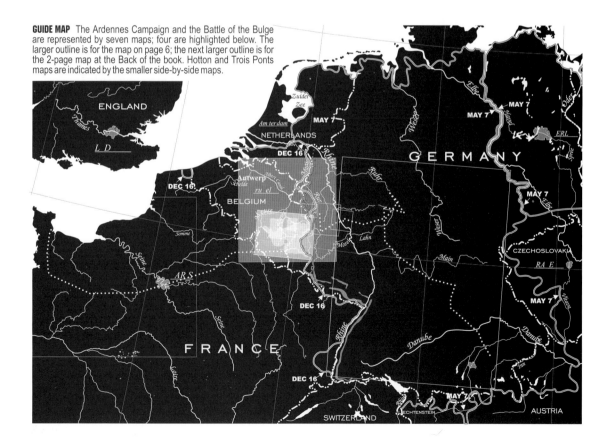

GUIDE MAP The Ardennes Campaign and the Battle of the Bulge are represented by seven maps; four are highlighted below. The larger outline is for the map on page 6; the next larger outline is for the 2-page map at the Back of the book. Hotton and Trois Ponts maps are indicated by the smaller side-by-side maps.

Introduction

By Albert E. Radford

Excerpts from Merriam's **Dark December** and Hechler's account of The 51st Engineer Combat Battalion and the Battle of the Bulge graphically describe the role of First Army Combat Engineers in delaying the German Ardennes Offensive in "The Greatest Single Victory in U.S. Army History." From sleepy false calm to the ensuing nightmare, a miraculous 10-day sequence of events, called "Providential" by General Fraser, unfolded for the 51st Engineer Combat Battalion:

December 13   our overly nervous battalion commander is finally relieved of duty.

December 14   a bright, aggressive regular army officer assumes command.

December 15   our dynamic, dedicated executive officer returns from hospital in England.

December 16   without warning ... a desperate Blitzkrieg of half a million German soldiers, three entire armies, burst through the thin American lines in the Ardennes and the lives of 630 men of the 51st ECB, "saw-milling" in the Ardennes, were dramatically changed in the confusion and shock of the enemy onslaught.

December 17-22   for five sleepless days and nights we established and defended positions against the German Armored Units.

December 23   the ubiquitous 51st, with some men from other units, stop the forward elements of two Armored Divisions, one from the Fifth and the other from the Sixth Panzer Armies. The outstanding performance of the new battalion commander, executive officer and men of the 51st during those sleepless days and nights, became the basis for awarding the Battalion the Presidential Unit Citation and the French Croix de Guerre with Silver Star.

The Battle of the Bulge … A PLACE IN HISTORY

The Patton Myth*

The Patton Myth About The Bulge

"A great, great many people believe the Battle of the Bulge was won by General Patton's Third Army, which did indeed liberate the now consecrated town of Bastogne. Few knew that the major German Forces during the first five days of fighting were attacking northwest against steady, but unspectacular, Hodges' First Army. Fewer realized that the heaviest fighting around Bastogne occurred not when the town was surrounded, but about ten days later when the Germans turned south with sudden fury, after Hitler had abandoned his grandiose scheme for the capture of Brussels and Antwerp." p.226.

"As we now realize, Patton's initial fighting, though important, was conducted against the German Seventh Army composed of four mediocre infantry divisions sent to the south for the express purpose of blocking Patton. Meanwhile, in those nightmarish ten days, both Fifth and Sixth Panzer Armies punched, slugged and battered their way through the First Army to the north getting ever nearer to the Meuse River."pp.226-7

"While Patton was battling the infantry divisions of the German *Seventh Army*, four panzer corps with 1200 tanks and 250,000 men in the Fifth and Sixth Panzer Armies were pounding 60,000 Americans of Hodges' First Army. **Here was the great crisis of the attack**. The Germans continually attempted to turn the flank of the First Army forces who were desperately trying to build up an east-west line. But new American units, the 3rd Armored, 84th and then 2nd Armored, were fed into this brittle Allied line, and they managed always to stay one road ahead of the leading German columns.

"Only on *December 26*, after the crisis in the north had been met and Hitler realized his great dream was going up in smoke, did the Germans turn to the south to attack Bastogne in force. The defenders, by this time greatly reinforced, in a magnificent stand beat off eight German divisions. The crisis had been passed, however, and the Germans were attempting to buy time by capturing Bastogne, which would have given them a more adequate defense line behind which they hoped to sit, and tie down more allied divisions. Patton's army performed well; his glory was as part of a team, directed by Eisenhower, which was flexible enough to rebound from a completely surprising attack." p.227.

"Two Handfuls" of First Army Soldiers at Trois Ponts and Werbomont

"Early in the morning of **December 18**, Peiper [1st SS Panzer Division, Sixth Panzer Army] attacked Stavelot, which was held by a company of armed infantry and a squad of the engineers from Malmedy. Peiper rode roughshod over these troops as he seized this vital Amblève River crossing. Part of his outriders started north toward Spa, and were only turned back by a torrent of 100,000 gallons of gasoline from the southern edge of the great gasoline dumps, which was poured into a steep cut in the narrow road and then ignited. This fire forced Peiper back**, and turned him on his main route to the west. Peiper knew that if he could cross the Salm River at the town of Trois Ponts, some four miles to the west of Stavelot, he would be out in the open, into the better road net, and free for a straight run to the Meuse. Success seemed within his grasp as he started confidently along the Amblève River road which wound toward Trois Ponts.

---

* Quotations from **Dark December** [emphasis added].   ** Later historians note Peiper was unaware of fuel dumps else he would have made them top priority. Also, Hitler forbad deviation from routes under pain of execution; Spa was forbidden to Peiper from the start.
Bastogne: F6, 10, B7   **Stavelot**: 78, B3   **Malmédy**: 10, B4

But he was halted.

> "An engineer company of the 51st Engineer Combat Battalion, which had been operating sawmills in the Ardennes forests had been ordered to Trois Ponts, and had arrived there about midnight on the night Peiper had arrived at Stavelot. Their orders were to blow the bridges at Trois Ponts, if the enemy approached. When Peiper arrived, they were waiting — 140 men, 8 bazookas, 10 machine guns, and an antitank gun which had been commandeered as its crew wandered through the town looking for its organization. This small group halted Peiper's lead tanks with its antitank gun, then retreated across the river and blew the bridges. *'If we could have captured the bridges intact, it would have been a simple matter to drive through to the Meuse River early that day,'* Peiper lamented later. But as speed was of the essence, he again turned to the north, into the steep valley of the Amblève River as it turned north toward Liège. And this was his undoing." pp.143-144.

"All during **December 18**, troops of the 82nd Airborne Division closed into an assembly area at Werbomont, their assembly itself only made possible by the defenders of the bridges of Trois Ponts (primarily 51st ECB) and just to the east of the Werbomont (291st ECB)." p.146.

"Here is the case where the fate of divisions and armies rested for a few brief moments on the shoulders of a handful of men; first at the town of Trois Ponts [primarily 51st ECB], and then, only hours later, with another, smaller, handful of men [291st ECB] at the bridge just to the east of Werbomont. Had either of these small groups failed in their job (and the temptation to run away must have been very great), the probability that Peiper would have got to the Meuse River the next morning, behind Skorzeny's 'Trojan Horse', would have been very high.

"And even though his was a lone panzer Kampfgruppe, such was the confusion at the time, the uncertainties and doubts raised by the German war of nerves, the lack of information at the higher headquarters, that it is most probable that Hodges, or Bradley, or Montgomery might have been thrown into a frenzy which would have led to the forced withdrawal of all American troops behind the Meuse River. And the Germans, standing off with 2 SS Panzer Corps, waiting for just such a break, would have quickly followed through and exploited to the full any hole Peiper would have been able to make.

"But those two handfuls of American soldiers, despite the grave uncertainties as to the whereabouts of either friendly or enemy forces, chose to ride out the German attack. As a result Kampfgruppe Peiper was sacked in the canyons of the Amblève River, and the second major defeat had been dealt to the Germans." pp.147-148.

Another "Handful" of First Army Soldiers at Hotton*

"The Germans [Fifth Panzer Army units on **December 19**] then continued on through the gap between Bastogne and St. Vith, and turned toward the northwest to strike for the Meuse River. Here they collided head-on with the weak reconnaissance forces of the 3rd Armored Division, cautiously moving along the only three parallel roads between the Ourthe River and the Bastogne-Liège road. The resulting collision ended the immediate attack plans of both Germans and Americans, and resulting developments suddenly plunged the XVIII Airborne Corps into a grim fight for very existence. The gap-plugging mission was forgotten.

"With neither force expecting the other, the colliding Germans and Americans were soon completely tangled up. One of three American columns was cut off and, eventually, forced to abandon its equipment, and make its way back to friendly troops on foot. One German column [116th Panzer Division, Fifth Panzer Army] which attempted to seize the vital Ourthe River Bridge at a little town called Hotton, was turned back by another of the unheralded small handfuls of men [primarily 51st ECB, on December 21] so important in the ultimate Allied victory. This fighting between the Bastogne-Liège road and the Ourthe river went on fiercely from ***December 20 to 23***; the weak forces of the 3rd Armored Division were gradually strengthened, first by the Division's combat command which had been on anti-parachute duty at Eupen, and then by small independent units rushed to the crisis zone. The German panzers, 116th Panzer Division, unable to capture Hotton, slipped back, crossed the Ourthe River, and then struck northward again, hoping to get around this new resistance. But this only brought them head-on into the 84th Division, which was assembling just west of the Ourthe river at the town of Marche, the first of the VII Corps divisions to arrive preparatory to the counterattack being planned by Hodges. The 116th Panzer Division was once more frustrated in its ambition to reach the Meuse, again by only a matter of a few hours, as the 84th Division closed into Marche just ahead of the striking panzers." p.165.

The unheralded "handful(s) of American soldiers" were led by these commanders and staff of the 51ECB, themselves mostly college-age young men become leaders with life and death responsibilities. This photo was taken in Germany, April 1945. Major Yates is absent, having been reassigned just prior to the photo being taken.   *Corps Files*

Eupen: 6, 124   **St. Vith**: 6, B4

Holding the Line*
December 1944 - January 1945

During the German breakthrough in the Ardennes, the 51st Engineer Combat Battalion held and delayed the enemy at a number of vital points along the lines of penetration. For four days -- **18 to 21 December** -- Companies A and B held a barrier line from Barvaux to Hotton, south of Marche to Rochefort, blowing up and defending three footbridges while holding a 25-mile front against enemy armored and infantry thrusts. At the same time, Company C was holding Trois Ponts, denying the enemy the use of the vital east-west Highway N23 to Werbomont. Company C stood its ground in Trois Ponts, tricked the enemy into believing it had superior forces and armor, and, after being relieved by a regiment of the 82nd Airborne Division, covered the withdrawal of that regiment from the town after its abortive attack east of the Salm River.[1]

There was nothing in the background of the battalion that was related to these achievements. Since activation as the lst Battalion of the 51st Engineer Combat Regiment on 13 June 1942, this unit had passed a rather uninteresting career. They trained at Camp Bowie [Texas]; shivered through a hard winter at Plattsburg Barracks, New York; did the dirty work on target ranges and road construction at XIII Corps' West Virginia maneuvers of 1943; and acted as demonstration troops for the Engineer School at Fort Belvoir [Virginia].

The battalion landed at Normandy on D-Day plus 21, but life degenerated into dumping crushed rock on Carentan's roads, maintaining a few water points, and sweeping some mines. Two incidents stood out during the routine months on the Continent: quick thinking and heroic action saved many lives and equipment during a Normandy ammunition dump fire, and eight men of the battalion quelled and captured 60 German paratroopers after a brief, sharp firefight in mid-September.[2] The battalion did have one common bond that assisted it during the December fight against overwhelming odds: nearly all of the officers and men were veterans of some two years of service in the battalion; the companies had worked together as a unit; and teamwork was clicking smoothly.[3]

On the eve of the breakthrough, the battalion was operating about 30 sawmills in the vicinity of Marche, Dinant, Rochefort, Ciney, Hotton, and Erezée, thereby contributing materially to the First Army winterization and timber-cutting program. The battalion had cut 2,600,000 board feet since the inauguration of the program in October. The average for the first 17 days of December was 58,717 board feet per day, with a maximum of 86,000 board feet in one day.[4]

At that time, the 158th Engineer Combat Battalion had been charged with the defense of the Marche area.[5] Routine activities in the running of the sawmills were conducted by the 51st on the first day of the German breakthrough, but on 17 December at 1730 the battalion was alerted for ground activity.[6] The alert came from the CO of the 158th Engineer Combat Battalion. The line companies were immediately alerted and a staff meeting was called to make plans for action.[7]

---

* Text in this section is taken whole from *Holding the Line*. Emphasis is added. Notes at the end are condensed from that document.
Barvaux: 88, B2   **Dinant**: 6, B1   **Rochefort**: 88, B2   **Ciney**: B1   **Erezée**: B2

Commanding Officers

The performance of the 51st Engineer Combat Battalion during the following days can better be appreciated by knowing the commanding officer, Lieutenant Colonel Harvey R. Fraser, and his executive officer, Major Robert B. Yates. They were two different personalities who complemented each other in directing the battalion.[8] During the breakthrough, Colonel Fraser was with that portion of his battalion along the Barvaux-Hotton-Rochefort front; Major Yates was at Trois Ponts.

The peculiar angle to the performance of these officers is that they both arrived at the battalion within two days of the start of the breakthrough. Major Yates, a veteran member of the battalion, had been hospitalized in August and returned to his post on 15 December. Colonel Fraser was a newcomer to the Battalion, having assumed command on December 14. Both officers were almost immediately called on to command units and slow the German advance.[9]

When Colonel Fraser arrived, the first thing he did was call the battalion officers together, introduce himself, and outline his policies. He sketched his own past and had an opportunity to talk with each of the officers long enough to find out their background and size them up personally.[10]

Prior to coming to the battalion, Colonel Fraser had a brilliant background, but it was almost entirely confined to staff work. After graduating from the U.S. Military Academy in 1939, he spent a period of close to three years on Oahu [Hawaii] at Schofield Barracks. He was due to return 8 December 1941, but remained by request for nine more months.

The remainder of his pre-breakthrough career was spent as an Engineer Battalion commander working on routine road and airstrip construction, plus doing a few shifts with Communications Zone base sections checking training and allocating troops. At St. Malo [northeast coast of Brittany, southwest of Normandy], with sniper fire still chattering on the day the citadel fell, Colonel Fraser led a reconnaissance party that obtained timely information on harbor, beach, and railroad facilities. But this was as close as this 28-year-old, nervously active, and sharp-minded officer was allowed to come to combat operations.[11]

Irked by this inactivity, Colonel Fraser went to see the First Army Engineer [Carter] on 12 December to ask for a combat assignment. He was so sure he would not return to Brittany Base Section that he took all his equipment to Spa; two days later he was commanding the 51st. "When I saw what they were doing at the sawmills and along the roads," said Colonel Fraser, "I asked whether it really was a combat outfit. I was soon to find out."[12]

When the 158th Engineer Combat Battalion departed to assist in the defense of the Bastogne area, the 51st was left with the responsibility of defending the [Marche] area. Captain John W. Barnes, battalion S-3, states, "Colonel Fraser sat down with a map and decided that the Ourthe River was a natural defense line, and he prepared plans to erect roadblocks and prepare key bridges for demolition. Several days later Group sent down an overlay directing that defenses be established at precisely the same points which Colonel Fraser had selected."[13]

It was not only his organizing ability, but also his leadership that made Colonel Fraser a factor in the success of the battalion. Throughout the defense of the 25-mile front, he was ubiquitous. At times it is impossible to trace his trail because so many men claim that he was with them at widely separated points. During

TROIS PONTS AREA: December 18-25

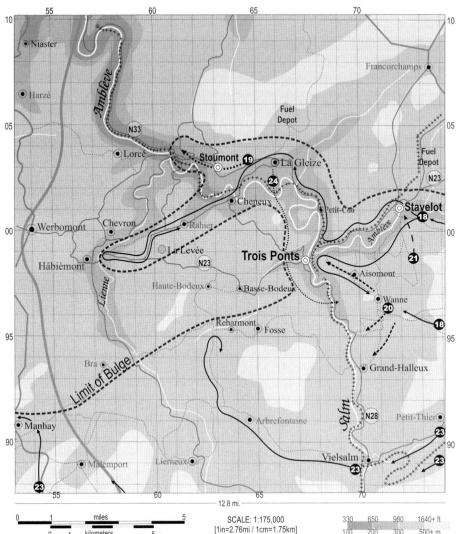

Trapping Hitler's vanguard. Trois Ponts was on the assigned route of Col. Joachim Peiper's Kampfgruppe (battle group) of 4000 men and 75 tanks. To this best hope to reach the Meuse River and more, Hitler had assigned the "decisive role in the offensive".

Late on the 17th, exhausted and sensing a major battle, Peiper paused before Stavelot. The next morning, he sent a contingent via Aisomont. But Stavelot was nearly undefended and his main force soon reached Trois Ponts, the other contingent arriving soon after, just to the south. Too late. Company C of the 51st Engineer Combat Battalion prepared and blew the critical bridges. Peiper was forced down the Amblève. While crossing at Cheneux he was attacked by P-47s, which delayed him for about 2 hours.

At Hâbièmont, the 291st ECB prepared the Lienne Creek bridge with 30 minutes to spare. It was blown as Peiper watched. His tanks were not able to cross the ravines or other weak bridges so Peiper returned to the Amblève. He was blocked west of Stoumont, cut off and surrounded. (The 51st defended Trois Ponts, alone for two days then for two more days with 505th Parachute Reg. of the 82nd Airborne Div.).

At 2am, December 24, Peiper abandoned all equipment and 300 wounded and led the remaining 800 on foot at night. At noon on Christmas Day, 770 reached Wanne. They were frozen and devastated - all that remained of the 4000 SS panzers plus an attached 1800 others.

Thus, Hitler's vanguard was crushed well short of the Meuse. The defense of Trois Ponts had sealed its fate.

Main Roads ——— Dirt tracks ....
Railroads +++++++ (Modern highway ———)

Peiper's Night Marches ....→
(The Amblève was crossed near La Gleize and the Salm was crossed near Trois Ponts. A fairly clear route can be found in *The Devil's Adjutant* by Michael Reynolds.)

GRID lines are from the military maps in *Holding the Line*. Thus, the Salm River bridge (674986) was located at the intersection of lines 674 and 986.

㉓ Dates of German troop movements are from *A Time for Trumpets*. The dashed black line bounds extent of German activity through December 26.

Right. The Salm Bridge, in Trois Ponts, was built in September by the 51st after the retreat of the Germans. On December 18, the 7th Armored Division crossed on its way to defend St. Vith and then the bridge was blown as Kampfgruppe Peiper appeared.

Contours and main roads and features are transposed from *The Times Atlas of the World*, p. 61. German routes are taken from maps found in *A Time for Trumpets*. Other detail is from *Holding the Line*.

the severest test of the battalion -- at Hotton on 21 December -- Colonel Fraser was on the enemy side of the river for a period. He kept the widely separated forces unified.[14]

Major Yates had a different task at Trois Ponts. His problem was more one of deceiving the enemy into thinking that there was a superior force defending Trois Ponts. He also had the job of inspiring confidence in 150 men who after the first day of action had no tank destroyers or antitank guns and were opposed by German armor.[15]

Before the breakthrough, Major Yates had held various staff positions within the battalion for the preceding two years, having been its CO for several months in 1943. His 6-foot, 3-inch, 200-pound figure towered over the scene at Trois Ponts. An affable Texan, easygoing in nature but determined in spirit, Major Yates held together his little company by prodding, cajoling, and encouraging them to resist long after they had reached reasonable limits of human endurance. "I would find them asleep standing up after 94 hours on the job," said Major Yates, "but they were standing up."[16]

Colonel William E. Ekman, CO of the 505th Parachute Infantry Regiment, which entered Trois Ponts on 20 December, paid high tribute to the spirit and courage of Company C of the 51st and singled out Major Yates for his leadership. "He had everything under control," said Colonel Ekman, "and appeared ready and able to hold the town indefinitely. When the 82nd Airborne Division came in, we expected to find this unit decimated and discouraged. Instead, Major Yates approached me and uttered a classic phrase, 'Say, I'll bet you fellows are glad we're here.'"[17]

Adding a note of commendation to the many other tributes for Major Yates, Colonel Fraser observed, "I do not know another officer who could have handled such a difficult situation as admirably as you did."[18]

Defense at Trois Ponts

Company C left Melreux at 2200 on *17 December* and arrived at Trois Ponts at 2330 the same day.[19] The company, commanded by Captain Sam Scheuber, immediately started to establish defensive positions on the west bank of the Amblève [*Salm*]* River, which skirts the east edge of town. Company C's strength at this time was approximately 140 men, about 20 still being absent at the sawmills.[20] The company had eight bazookas, six .50-caliber machine guns, and four .30-caliber machine guns. A 57-mm. antitank [AT] gun from the 526th Armored Infantry Battalion also became available. In personnel, the company was reinforced by a squad each from the 526th Armored Infantry Battalion and Company A of the 291st Engineer Combat Battalion, as well as several stragglers who were picked up coming through Trois Ponts.[21]

Trois Ponts is studded with bridges, underpasses, railroads, rivers, cliffs, and road junctions.[22] The Amblève and Salm rivers join there, as do railroad lines running south to Vielsalm, northwest to Aywaille, and northeast to Stavelot. Highway N23 enters Trois Ponts from Stavelot by under passing the railroad at two points just before it joins north-south Highway N33, merges with N33 south for a few hundred yards, crosses the Amblève River, and then turns west across another bridge over the Salm River and proceeds toward Werbomont. The enemy approached Trois Ponts by this road and was thwarted in its attempts to go west to Werbomont because the 51st had blown up two bridges over the rivers. The enemy then turned its columns north after clearing the railroad underpasses and proceeded toward Stoumont.[23]

---

* [*Salm*] and other notations in brackets are [corrections] to *Holding the Line*. With an accurate mapping of Trois Ponts, as done for this writing, one sees that there are a number of errors in the original or else in the transcribed history.
Vielsalm: 78, B3   **Aywaille**: B3

TROIS PONTS Defense: December 18-21

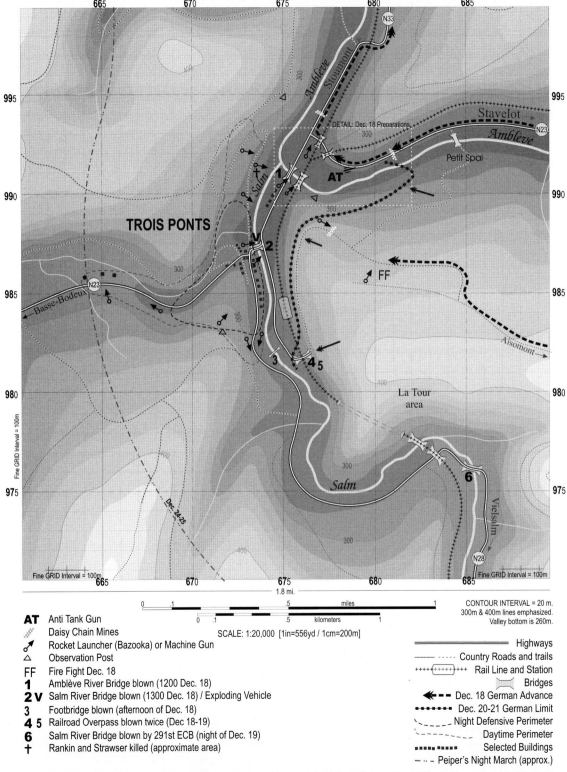

AT	Anti Tank Gun
	Daisy Chain Mines
↗	Rocket Launcher (Bazooka) or Machine Gun
△	Observation Post
FF	Fire Fight Dec. 18
1	Amblève River Bridge blown (1200 Dec. 18)
2 V	Salm River Bridge blown (1300 Dec. 18) / Exploding Vehicle
3	Footbridge blown (afternoon of Dec. 18)
4 5	Railroad Overpass blown twice (Dec 18-19)
6	Salm River Bridge blown by 291st ECB (night of Dec. 19)
✝	Rankin and Strawser killed (approximate area)

CONTOUR INTERVAL = 20 m.
300m & 400m lines emphasized.
Valley bottom is 260m.

SCALE: 1:20,000 [1in=556yd / 1cm=200m]

Highways
Country Roads and trails
Rail Line and Station
Bridges
Dec. 18 German Advance
Dec. 20-21 German Limit
Night Defensive Perimeter
Daytime Perimeter
Selected Buildings
Peiper's Night March (approx.)

Contours and features are from *Carte Topographique de Belgique: Esneux-St. Vith* (1:100,000 - #116). Battle data are from *Holding the Line* - maps, text and inferences.

The Battle of the Bulge ... A PLACE IN HISTORY

Picture Postcard aerial view of **Trois Ponts** in the 1960s. It is much as it was in 1944. The Salm River bridge is easily seen just left of the rail lines; the station is to the right of the picture below the steep slopes.   *Collection of Joseph Milgram*

The 1111th Engineer Combat Group had its CP [command post] in Trois Ponts at the start of the action, and its small staff hurried the preparations for defense before the arrival of Company C of the 51st. Somebody asked Colonel Harry Anderson, CO of the group (and former regimental commander of the 51st), whether he intended to withdraw. His reply was characteristic, "We have come several thousand miles to fight these Nazis -- not to withdraw from them."[24]

On the morning of **18 December**, the columns of the 7th Armored Division were passing through Trois Ponts on their way to stem the enemy attack in the Vielsalm-St.Vith area. The 7th Armored had two accidents in twisting through Trois Ponts, which rebounded to the benefit of the defenders of the town. A half-track with a personnel complement of 12 men, towing a 57-mm. antitank gun, broke down in Trois Ponts. This half-track belonged to Company B of the 526th Armored Infantry Battalion. (The 526th Armored Infantry Battalion was not a part of 7th Armored Division; it was a separate battalion. Company B was on its way to Malmédy). Colonel Anderson directed his S-4, Captain Robert N. Jewett, to take command of the squad and supervise the placing of the gun. Captain Jewett put the gun and crew in position on Highway N23 on the road to Stavelot, about a mile [1/4 mile]* toward Stavelot from the two railroad underpasses.[25]

The second accident benefitted the defenders of Trois Ponts a little less directly. A tracked vehicle (observers do not agree on whether it was an M5 light tank or an M7 105-mm. Self-propelled armored field artillery "Priest") slipped off the road while making a sharp turn at the bridge (674988). The vehicle went over on its side into the river and was abandoned. Later in the day, when the 51st was forced to blow the bridge,

* One full mile maps out very incorrectly. The Hechler report shows "1/4mile" typed jammed together. An editing mark to separate the two was a vertical 1-like mark, much bolder than the faded "1/4" and apparently was mistaken for a "1".

the ensuing fire set off the ammunition in the tank. However, it did not go off all at once but exploded at intervals all afternoon and into the evening of the 18th. Enough time elapsed between explosions to allow for loading an artillery piece, possibly tricking the enemy into thinking that artillery was available to the group defending Trois Ponts.[26]

Little by little, the 51st company picked up a few more reinforcements. Three men from the 341st Engineer Battalion who had originally been in Trois Ponts guarding the bridge at [676991]* were attached to Company C. A soldier in a British uniform drove his truck through town several times before being apprehended and attached to Company C. He had a carbine, a second lieutenant's insignia, and a captain's map case, but the news of Operation GREIF had not yet caused suspicion toward such characters. A GI who said he was from a nearby artillery unit walked up and down the town with a girl on his arm until he too was called in and attached to Company C.[27]

A somewhat larger group was attached during the morning of the 18th. At 0800, Lieutenant Albert J. Walters, a platoon leader in Company A, 291st Engineer Combat Battalion, left his battalion CP at Basse-Bodeux to assist in preparing for demolition of the bridge at [684978], one mile southeast of Trois Ponts. En route, he was intercepted by Lieutenant Colonel James A. Kirkland, executive officer of the 1111th Engineer Combat Group. Col. Kirkland attached Lt. Walters and his squad to Co. C, and they continued to defend the bridge on the south flank of the defenders of Trois Ponts.[28]

The defense of the town initially consisted of one platoon with two bazookas on high ground covering the approach from Aisomont; Captain Jewett's group with the lone antitank gun covering the road from Stavelot; a rear guard covering the N23 approach from Werbomont; and the remainder of the company deployed with bazookas, machine guns, and M1s in the buildings of the town that fronted the Salm and Amblève rivers.[29]

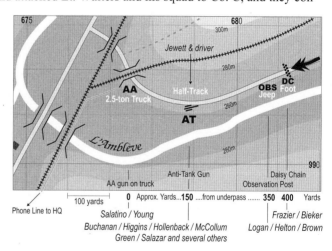

DETAIL: 18 December, 11am ... facing the approach of Peiper (⬅). This shows weapons used by whom and type of transport at each spot.

Captain Jewett sent two of the 526th Armored Infantry men, Corporal Bruce W. Frazier and Private First Class Ralph J. Bieker, 250 yards up the road toward Stavelot with a daisy chain of ten mines and instructions to jerk them across the road when a tank approached and then run back to where the 57-mm. antitank gun was placed. Four 526th Armored Infantry men (McCollum, Hollenback, Buchanan, and Alonzo B. Higgins) were manning the antitank gun. Lieutenant Richard Green, platoon leader of 3rd Platoon, Company C, 51st Engineer Combat Battalion, along with Private First Class Andrew Salazar of the same unit, was immediately behind the gun. The half-track, with its driver from the 526th and with Captain Jewett, was backed into N23 on the opposite side of the road from the antitank gun, ready to pull out in the event of a tank attack that might overrun the position.[30] Several more men from Company C and the 526th were in a ditch along the road back of the antitank gun. Just beyond the underpass on the Stavelot side Staff Sergeant Fred Salatino was manning the .50-caliber antiaircraft gun in a 2½-ton truck,

---

* [675991] bracketed coordinates are [corrections] for apparent errors made in **Holding the Line**. These corrections match the detailed map of Trois Ponts printed in this section. Coordinates not changed appear in simple parentheses, such as (674988).
Basse-Bodeux: 78, B3

along with Technician Fifth Class Jacob Young. A wire was strung from this truck back to the company CP in the Trois Ponts railroad station.[31]

About 200 yards up the Stavelot road beyond the antitank gun, Lieutenant Green posted a combination outpost and getaway consisting of Technicians Fifth Class Robert Logan and Elmer Helton and Private First Class Milbert Brown of Company C. Brown as driver had his jeep; up until that time Helton had been an air compressor operator and Logan a truck driver, but they were pressed into service for reconnaissance. The plan was to have the three watch the men with the daisy chain and then alert the gunners and the rest of the squad if a tank approached.[32]

Firing was heard in the vicinity of Stavelot during the early part of the morning. Shortly before noon, a Tiger Royal tank nosed around the bend toward the AT gun. Frazier and Bieker strung their mines, but could not resist the temptation to take a few shots with their rifles at the heads of enemy tankers that protruded from the lead tank. Several other tanks soon followed the lead tank, which stopped at the daisy chain. Brown, Logan, and Helton say that the tank started firing its machine gun, so they returned with their jeep to Lieutenant Green's position with the simple report, "They're coming!"

Peiper approached **Stavelot** from the SE (upper left). Exhausted and fearing a major battle, he stopped overnight short of the Amblève (one bridge is in center left). The next day and later, the town was repeatedly shelled.
National Archives - 30 December 1944

Lieutenant Green replied, "OK, notify them at the CP in case I can't get them on the telephone, and then come back here with the jeep."[33]

By this time, the squad on and near the gun could see the lead tanks and hear others through the trees. "Now let's be damn sure they're Jerries; let's not mess this thing up," somebody said. Others echoed this thought. Perhaps as a result of this, the enemy tank in third place fired four rounds before the 57-mm. gun could get off a round. One shell, an AP [antipersonnel] tracer, skipped on the river to their backs. Another zipped no more than six inches over their heads. Another hit a tree behind the gun, tipping over the tree and showering fragments in the area. Then the gun crew opened up, and one of their early rounds started the leading enemy tank smoking.[34]

There was some difficulty at first with ammunition for the antitank gun. There were seven rounds for the

Stavelot: 78, B3

gun, and the crew said that if they couldn't repulse the attack with seven rounds that would be all they would ever get a chance to use. It soon became apparent from the strength of the enemy armored attack that more rounds would be needed. Captain Jewett said that he could observe eight tanks coming around the bend toward his position. There were no dismounted infantry accompanying along the road, but about a dozen infantrymen were working their way along the south side of the road[35]. Colonel Anderson, observing from across the river through field glasses, counted a total of 19 tanks that came through the position and later turned right on the road to Stoumont.[36] The little crew of defenders started an ammunition bucket brigade, with Captain Jewett tossing the shells across the road to Lieutenant Green, who forwarded them to Private Salazar, who handed them up to the gun crew.

The morale of the defenders was not raised any when a resounding roar from the town told them that the northern two bridges had been blown, cutting them off from Trois Ponts. The 88-mm. shells hit closer and closer until one hit at the base of the gun, killing all four of the crew and stunning Private Salazar. Realizing the futility of further resistance, the remainder of the crew piled into the half-track and proceeded by their only escape route - toward Stoumont. The 2½-ton truck followed. Lieutenant Green and his survivors from Company C made a wide circle at Petit Coo and returned to Trois Ponts at 1500 by coming in from the west on Highway N23, while Captain Jewett and the survivors of the 526th Armored Infantry Battalion found their way back to the new group CP at Modave.[37]

Almost simultaneous with the battle along the Stavelot road, the 2d Platoon of Company C, commanded by Lieutenant Fred L. Nabors, was also attacked by enemy armor. Lieutenant Nabors' platoon was deployed along the hill on the Aisomont road. One bazooka was firing southeast from the road below at (677988), from which it had perfect field of fire. Another bazooka had a good flanking firing position slightly to the east.

During the morning of 18 December, three enemy tanks approached the 2d Platoon's position, and they were detected approximately ½ mile away. The first tank had reinforced armor plate on the front and was allowed to pass by toward a string of daisy chain mines across the road. The bazooka then engaged the second tank, but did not knock it out. The third tank started to fire its machine guns and forced the 2d Platoon out of position by the intensity of the fire. Thereafter, the 2d Platoon retired to the town side of the river and took up protection of the right (south) flank of the Company line. The defense collapsed because one of the bazookas failed to fire, another was knocked out of the loader's hands with machine gun fire, and the daisy chain was exploded by machine guns. None of the three enemy tanks, however, attempted to follow the 2d Platoon, Company C, into Trois Ponts.

The bridge over the railroad at the junction of N33 with the Aisomont road was blown 18 December, but foot troops could still cross the structure. Lieutenant Nabors' platoon blew it up again the following day. A footbridge across the Salm River at (674982) was also blown on the first day of action.[38] At 1300, the bridge over the Salm River on Highway N23 was demolished. Shortly thereafter, Major Yates arrived in Trois Ponts, unaware of the situation and merely bound for the daily liaison meeting at the 1111th Engineer Combat Group. Colonel Anderson charged him with the defense of the city and under FUSA [First U. S. Army] orders, the group left Trois Ponts for Modave.

Major Yates deployed his men in houses along the river, providing flank and rear guards and good fields of fire for machine guns and bazookas. One enemy tank, which turned left on N33 instead of taking the Stoumont road when it reached the junction of N23 and N33, was surprised with .50-caliber machine gun fire. The crew had dismounted, and five of them were hit by a gun manned by Sergeant Evers Gossard. A sixth member of the crew remounted the tank and started to turn its gun toward the .50-caliber machine gun, whereupon Sergeant Gossard and his crew discretely retired. The enemy tank hovered around for the remainder of the day, firing sporadically. It withdrew on the night of the 18th.

"We kept sniping at them across the river for the next few days," said Major Yates, "but every shot of ours seemed to draw about a thousand in return. So we decided to deceive them as to how great a force we had available."

The company had about six 2½-ton trucks available, and they were kept running in and out of town. After dark, they were run out of Trois Ponts on Highway N23 toward Werbomont without lights and then run back on the same road with their lights on, simulating the arrival of reinforcements. Major Yates hit on the idea of simulating the presence and arrival of armor in Trois Ponts. This was done by putting chains on a single four-ton truck, and it was clanked back and forth repeatedly during the next few days. The closest facsimile to artillery or antitank guns that the company had were the bazookas, and as Major Yates said, "They made a pretty loud noise, so we used to shift them around from place to place after dark and it may have deceived the enemy into thinking we had a couple of light artillery pieces." In addition, he moved small groups of riflemen from place to place and had them fire in such a way as to create the impression of considerable strength in small arms.[39]

Lienne Creek bridge blown by 291st ECB, **Hâbièmont**. Losing this bridge forced Peiper back to the Amblève and entrapment. [*Background to the right* (SE) is the driveway to the DuPont family chateau, where Pvt. Snow was ambushed]. *Corps Files - September 1944*

On the afternoon of the 18th P-47s were observed to take a toll of four or five enemy tanks that were circling north and northwest along N33 toward Stoumont. Enemy armored columns passing along this road were strafed and dive-bombed quite effectively. "But lots of us in Trois Ponts felt pretty helpless with rifles and carbines on our shoulders," said Lieutenant Green.[40]

After the return of Lieutenant Green's group and the withdrawal of Lieutenant Nabors' platoon, the three platoons of the company were consolidated into two -- one group being placed on the river south of town, with its line swinging back to the west on the edge of town. Most of Lieutenant Green's 3rd Platoon was on the north side of Trois Ponts, also swinging its line to the west on the outskirts. Listening posts were established 500 to 600 yards out from the MLR [main line of resistance], and pulled into a tight perimeter defense after dark. (This was done because the small number of men available for listening posts were

Stoumont: 78, B3   **Hâbiémont**: 78, 204, B3

widely separated and would have given the enemy opportunity to infiltrate patrols between them had they not been pulled in about 300 yards from their daytime positions.[41]

At 0900 on **19 December**, Lieutenant Green and Technical Sergeant Matthew R. Carlisle crossed the river, covered by Major Yates and three others, and went up the Stavelot road toward the knocked-out 57-mm. gun. They found nothing in the railroad underpasses but noticed four men in American uniforms around the gun. A little farther up the road was an M8 armored car and a jeep with freshly painted white stars. "Hey, Joe," yelled Sergeant Carlisle, and the men excitedly cried, "Amerikans!" and started to fire. The motors of the M8 and jeep turned over, but Lieutenant Green and Sergeant Carlisle did not wait to see if they were being followed.[42] "After that," said Major Yates, "we did not need any patrols; we could see everything that was happening across the river."[43]

A brief firefight occurred on 19 December when men in Lieutenant Nabors' platoon engaged enemy on the hill just south of the Aisomont road at (680985). When rifle fire was directed at this infantry group, the enemy replied with both small arms and artillery on Trois Ponts. No casualties resulted from this brief scuffle, but it taught Company C to keep better hidden and change positions frequently in order to avoid artillery concentrations.[44]

Civilian casualties of Peiper's ruthless push toward the Meuse; killed by bullet and rifle butt in **Stavelot**, Belgium.   *National Archives (photo taken later) - 22 December 1944*

After the bridges had been blown, Colonels Anderson and Kirkland observed several enemy tanks approach one of the blown bridges. An elderly couple ran out in front of their house and motioned with their arms; it was difficult to tell at first whether they were waving at the tanks or trying to tell them that the bridge was blown. One of the dismounted tank men was observed shooting the woman with his pistol; the man caught her when she fell and then he was also shot. Additional shots were fired into the motionless figures on the ground.[45]

During the engagement, Major Yates observed a Belgian boy of about 12 running toward the river chased by a German rifleman, who was firing after him. Four or five other German soldiers were standing across the river, laughingly watching the performance. Enraged, Major Yates fired several shots at these spectators and dropped one of them before they dispersed, while the boy and his tormentor disappeared behind the buildings[*]. Enemy patrols attempted to probe across the river throughout the period, but were all repulsed by rifle and machine gun fire and grenades. The enemy had no way to bring armor across to Company C's positions without building a bridge. They did not give signs of desiring to build a bridge[**] or make an assault crossing of the river.[46]

On the night of 19 December, Lieutenant Walters' squad from the 291st Engineer Combat Battalion blew the bridge that they were defending at [684978]. Just as enemy infantry coming up from the south started to cross the bridge, Sergeant Jean D. Miller touched off the charge and the squad worked its way back to join Company C in the defense of Trois Ponts.[47]

Another welcome addition to the small force at Trois Ponts arrived at 2000 on 19 December, when a patrol from the 85th Reconnaissance Squadron, consisting of fifteen men and three M8 assault guns, arrived on Highway N23 from Basse-Bodeux. Not realizing that they were friendly troops, Company C's rear guard fired on them, but identification was quickly made. The next day the three guns were set up on the outskirts of town on high ground where the patrol could observe and still keep its guns in defiladed positions. Although the assault guns remained in position outside of Trois Ponts, the patrol never actually engaged the enemy.[48]

On **20 December**, elements of the 505th Parachute Infantry Regiment of the 82nd Airborne Division learned of the presence of the force defending Trois Ponts, and the regimental commander, Colonel William E. Ekman, ordered his 2nd and 3rd Battalions to send three bazooka teams each to the beleaguered town. The rest of the regiment then started to move into Trois Ponts, and the 505th's CP was established at 1300 on 20 December.[49]

Company C had its greatest casualties on 20 December, although this was by no means the day of greatest fighting. From 1930 to 2100, enemy artillery intensified in the entire waterfront area. Private Carl Strawser was killed when a shell hit his .50-caliber machine gun position, and Sergeant Joseph Gyure was seriously wounded at the same time. Staff Sergeant William W. Rankin was killed by a 20-mm. shell while stationed at an OP [observation post].[50]

A platoon of Engineers from the attachments of the 505th Parachute Regiment (307th Airborne Engineer Battalion), assisted by Company C, then repaired the bridges at [676991] and [674987] for a company of the 505th to cross. Later in the night a second company crossed on the repaired bridge, while the defenders of Trois Ponts held their positions in the face of sporadic enemy artillery fire.

At 1100 on **21 December**, reports began coming in that the two companies of the 505th were having difficulty across the river. The enemy launched a strong counterattack and started to surround elements that were defending on the hill overlooking Trois Ponts from the east. At 1500, Major Yates received a message from the 1111th Engineer Combat Group ordering Company C to withdraw. He brushed it aside and characteristically replied that it was impossible to disengage from the enemy, inasmuch as Company C was covering the withdrawal of the 82nd Airborne Division.[51]

Captain Scheuber, Company C's commander, at 1500 ordered that the bridge at [674987] over the Salm River and the bridge at [676991] over the Amblève River be prepared again for imminent demolition.[52] Of these, the timber trestle bridge over the Salm was the most difficult to blow. The task was assigned to Lieutenant Joseph B. Milgram, Jr., and six [enlisted] men -- Sergeant Elvin Goldsmith, Corporal Odis C. Faust, Technician Fifth Class Paul H. Keck, Private Jessie R. Mock, Private Maurice S. Walker, and Private Jose E. Marquez. Knowing that the bridge posts had previously been blown, Lieutenant Milgram decided to use necklace charges for the stringers and to use time fuses and primacord to set off the charges. He ordered his

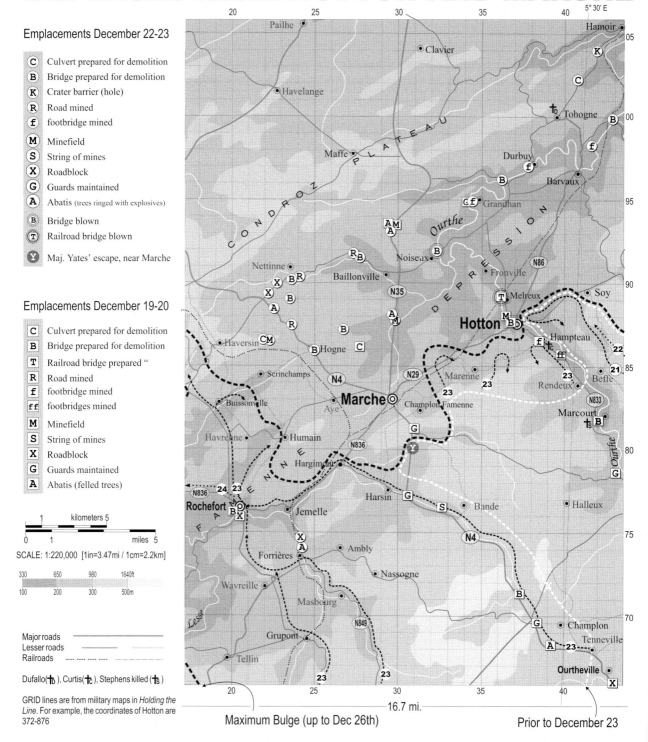

men to make nine necklace charges.

When these were ready, the group proceeded toward the bridge on both sides of the road and were subjected to machine gun and small arms fire along the route. Lieutenant Milgram's plan had been to prepare the stringers on the friendly side of the bridge first by working from the top side of the bridge and placing the charges on the sides of the stringers. However, the removal of the decking would have entailed too much work under fire, so the group crossed the bridge to the enemy side and climbed underneath in order to get the maximum amount of cover from enemy fire.

Their movement was observed, and the fire increased, so Lieutenant Milgram ordered all but Technician Fifth Class Keck to crawl along the enemy side of the river and wade across at a point lower downstream that would give a little more cover. The next job was to secure the primacord on the friendly side of the river at a point where it might be reached to blow up the bridge After this was completed, the entire group waded the river and reported to Captain Scheuber that the bridge was ready for demolition. At 1650, the order was given to blow the bridges.

The Amblève bridge presented no unusual problems, but the Salm bridge was more difficult. Lieutenant Milgram and Technician Fifth Class Keck proceeded to within 60 yards from where the primacord lay. From there Lieutenant Milgram crawled the remainder of the distance, checked the cord, pulled the fuse lighter, and then ran about 50 yards in the fading light but in full view of the enemy until he reached the cover of a building.[53]

Having accomplished his aim and mission of covering the withdrawal of the 505th Regiment's elements from the east of Trois Ponts, Major Yates ordered Company C to begin withdrawing from the town at 1930 on 21 December. The withdrawal was completed by 2000, and the company rejoined the battalion at 2330 at Marche.[54]

The Battle of Hotton

The most bitter and tactically important battle fought by the remainder of the 51st Engineer Combat Battalion was in defense of the vital Ourthe River bridge at Hotton on 21 December.[55]

In the days preceding the battle of Hotton, the two companies in the Marche area feverishly prepared bridges, roadblocks, minefields, demolitions, and abatis along the Ourthe River line from Durbuy to La Roche. They had numerous minor brushes with enemy forces during the period. With the departure of the 158th Engineer Combat Battalion for the Bastogne area, Colonel Fraser was formally charged with the defense of the area at 1930 on **19 December**. He had already prepared and started to execute plans; at 0500 that morning Companies A and B were combat loaded and poised for action near Hargimont and Hogne, respectively.[56]

Confusion reigned in the towns and along the roads. The local gendarmerie unsuccessfully attempted to check evacuations and then tried to keep the roads clear. Parachutists and rumors of parachutists kept everyone in turmoil. Colonel Fraser finally instituted a rigid civilian check system that resulted in the capture and execution of many enemy spies and agents in civilian clothes. The largest such group was apprehended by Company B in Hotton; it consisted of 21 men in civilian clothes whose baggage contained considerable supplies of American cigarettes, rations, and uniforms. The next largest bag was made the following day when eight civilians were picked up by Headquarters and Service Company at Humain after they refused to surrender their arms.⁵⁷

The next problem that faced Colonel Fraser was the stream of stragglers pouring through the area. Some came with units evacuating in an orderly manner, albeit a bit hurriedly to the rear. Others rushed through in batches, with clothes ripped, feet soaked, and morale shattered -- thoroughly beaten men from overrun units. All of them asked the same questions: "Where is my unit? How far have the Germans broken through?" The next most favorite question concerned traffic and road information -- almost invariably regarding the area toward the west. To create a semblance of order out of this Grand Central Station bedlam, Colonel Fraser directed that a clearing point be established where the name and unit of all these birds of passage be recorded. This information proved invaluable as an aid to reuniting the lost, strayed, and straggling.⁵⁸

The 51st earlier coordinated American traffic flow southeast of Marche; here the 84th Division, First Army, MPs now check ID's in **Marche.** Part of Hitler's plan was to send troops in disguise behind our lines to cause confusion and secure bridges; 25 German infiltrators were caught here so far.   *National Archives -30 December 1944*

During the early morning hours of 19 December, the barrier lines were completed. Company B covered the area on the west bank of the Ourthe River from Hotton to Durbuy inclusive. The lst Platoon defended the immediate area of Hotton and Melreux; the 2d Platoon, the area from Melreux to Durbuy; and the 3rd Platoon, the vicinity of Durbuy and the left flank.⁵⁹

At 0400 on 19 December, the 1st Platoon of Company A, under Lieutenant Floyd D. Wright, was ordered to Hampteau to prepare a roadblock and a footbridge for demolition.⁶⁰ Ten minutes later the 2d Platoon, under Lieutenant Paul Curtis, departed for Marcourt on a similar mission regarding a class 10 bridge. At the same time, the 3rd Platoon, under Lieutenant Raymond A. Trafford, was ordered to remain as battalion reserve in the vicinity of Harsin, the battalion CP. Later in the morning, the 2d Platoon reinforced its right flank at (432791) with a strong roadblock consisting of one squad, two bazooka teams, and one .50-caliber machine gun.

More specifically, the following defenses were completed on 19 December:

(368880) - two antitank minefields, 200 yards downstream from the railroad bridge men stationed below.

90

Hargimont, Hogne, Humain, and **Marcourt**: 88, B2   **Hampteau** and **Melreux**: 88, 92, B2

(360890) - railroad bridge prepared for demolition, and a ford beneath mined.

(369879) - highway bridge on N29 prepared for demolition and defended by two 40-mm. guns from the 440th AA. [Antiaircraft Artillery] Weapons Battalion and two .50-caliber machine guns, and two bazookas.

(384867) - footbridge at Hampteau prepared for demolition, defended by two .50- caliber machine guns and one .30-caliber machine gun.

(390865) - refugee and straggler point established in cooperation with local defense officials.

(399859) - two footbridges guarded and prepared for demolition

(421820) - class 1 bridge at Marcourt prepared for destruction, defended by a half-track, bazooka, two .50-caliber machine guns, and one .30-caliber machine gun.

(433790) - road junction defended by one squad, one bazooka, and one .50-caliber machine gun.

(390686) - abatis, 30 mines to be installed after trees blown.

(383698) - intersection defended by platoon of 9th Canadian Forestry Co., 10 men from 158th Engineer Combat Battalion, 13 men from 51st Engineer Combat Battalion, 13 men from 440th AAA Weapons Battalion, one 40-mm. gun, one bazooka and one .50-caliber machine gun.

Enemy air was active over the barrier line on 19 December, strafing Highway N35 north of Marche at Baillonville (295907) and the N4 road junction near Pisson [Pessoux] (180903). Defenses were strengthened on 20 December; by 2400 on that date the following barrier line had been established:

(363961) - bridge prepared for demolition.

(341950) - weak bridge defended by a bazooka and a .30-caliber machine gun.

(362961) - piers of destroyed bridge prepared for demolition; crossing protected by a .50 caliber machine gun and bazooka.

(373717) - masonry bridge prepared for demolition.

(337761) - string of mines.

(306773) - intersection defended by tank retriever with 81-mm. mortar, four railroad cars ready to push across road, and one .50-caliber machine gun.

(310815) - intersection defended by 40-mm. gun, and all men and equipment falling back from road from south and east.

(202762) - roadblock at Rochefort, with bridge prepared for demolition and defended by 40-mm gun, bazooka, one .50-caliber machine gun, and one .30-caliber machine gun.

(300907) - Highway N35: Marche-Aye-Humain-Rochefort blocked to enemy advance from southeast with debris at intersection; at (295936) with abatis and mines prepared for demolition.

(430662) - roadblock on N4. This block was reported complete at 2230, with one squad of Company A in position defending it.

(392721) - contact made with one squad of the 299th Engineer Combat Battalion maintaining a road block on Highway N28. This roadblock and its defenses were then tied in and coordinated with the plan of defense for the intersection of Highways N4 and N28.

Much of the credit for coordinating the scattered defenses between Hotton and Marche is due to Captain Karl G. Pedersen, the modest and diffident-looking CO of Company A. When his roadblocks were established about 0400 on *20 December*, Captain Pedersen cleared with the CO of the 158th Engineer Combat Battalion, which was about two miles south of the junction of N4 and N28*. The CO of the 158th informed Captain Pedersen that there were 15 tanks and an unknown number of infantry approximately five miles south of his position. About 1300 on 20 December, the 158th displaced to the west on another mission, leaving only scattered elements between Captain Pedersen's roadblocks and the enemy's concentration of troops. Although 50 Canadian foresters reinforced Captain Pedersen's unit at 0400 on 21 December, these men were also called away on another mission at 1510 the same day. He was reinforced by an unknown

---

* See Capt. Radford's correction (p. 194) of the recorded disposition of some of Capt. Pedersen's units near Champlon Crossroads.
Harsin and **Baillonville**: 88, B2   **Pessoux**: B1

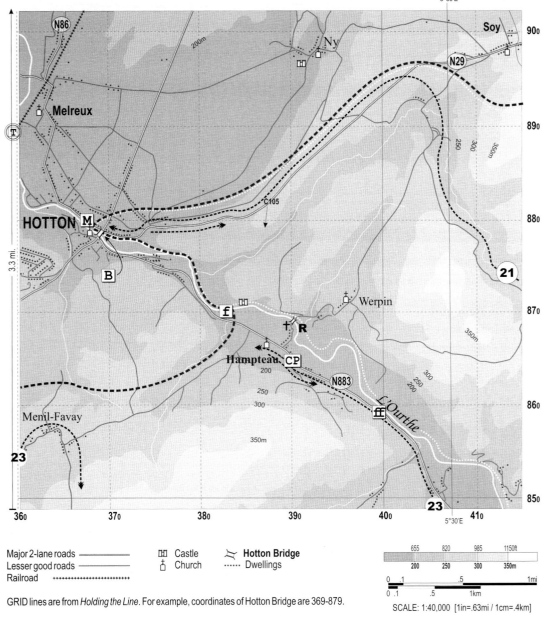

major with a bazooka team, an unknown chief warrant officer with .50-caliber machine gun, and one 40-mm. AA [Antiaircraft] gun from the 440th AAA Battalion.[61]

During the days when these roadblocks were held, they were subjected to numerous minor probings by jeeps and armored vehicles. As with the remainder of the 51st Engineer Combat Battalion, the successful defense of these roadblocks hinged on deception. According to Colonel Fraser, it was due to "deceiving the enemy as to the strength of my small, practically isolated force, in spite of known superiority to my front and known enemy infiltration to my rear." The significance of the defense in the larger picture was that it enabled the 84th Division to reorganize defensive positions around the city of Marche and to keep that city out of enemy hands [emphasis added].[62]

The battle of Hotton occurred on **21 December**. Just before the enemy struck at the Hotton bridge, he attempted to break through the Company A positions and at Hampteau overcame resistance put up by a squad of Company A. The Hampteau defense had been organized by Lieutenant Floyd D. Wright, platoon leader of the 1st Platoon of Company A. About 30 yards northeast of the footbridge across the river, on the road to Soy, a minefield was hastily laid and the position across the river was outposted with Private Stanley A. Driggs and his M1 rifle. Thirty to 40 yards from the footbridge, on the southwest side of the river, a bazooka team of three men and a detonator for the bridge were placed. Along the Hotton - La Roche road, two bazooka teams were placed 700 yards apart, protected by daisy chains of mines. Two .50-caliber, machine guns, half a squad of riflemen, and two tanks were placed west of the Hotton - La Roche road.[63]

Three jeep patrols from the 820th Tank Destroyer Battalion reported that they had received small arms fire in the vicinity of Roche [La Roche], that they had relayed this information to the 2d Platoon of Company A at Marcourt, and that the 2d Platoon had subsequently blown their Marcourt bridge. After attempting unsuccessfully to persuade the 820th to reinforce the 2d Platoon's roadblock at Marcourt, Lieutenant Wright sent his platoon sergeant, Staff Sergeant Donald A. Bonifay with an M8 armored car and one squad (Sergeant Benjamin Ham's) to Marcourt. Task Force Bonifay arrived at the Platoon at 0130 on 21 December, where Lieutenant Paul Curtis, 2d Platoon leader, put them out to assist in the defense of the town. Lieutenant Curtis reported that there had been a brief, brisk firefight between two half-tracks approaching the bridge and his own .50-caliber machine guns. No casualties resulted from this firefight, but through mistaken identity one guard was killed (Cpl. Jerry R. Stephens) and one wounded (T/S Clifton M. Pratt), when they halted an American patrol at Marcourt.

Leaving Sergeant Ham's squad in Marcourt, Sergeant Bonifay returned to Hampteau just in time to get in on the excitement there. At 0510, Private Driggs ran back across the bridge and reported that an armored car was approaching along the secondary road from the northeast. The armored car started shelling the high ground behind and in the village and then started firing its small arms at the bazooka teams. A battalion staff officer, Captain Richard F. Huxman, directed Sergeant Bonifay to blow the bridge; however, this was impossible because the detonator had been removed. The shelling set Hampteau on fire, and by this time the battle of Hotton was commencing and Colonel Fraser ordered Lieutenant Wright to send his men to reinforce Company B at Hotton. Taking a last look at the burning and completely deserted town of Hampteau at 0900, Sergeant Bonifay made his way back to Hotton on foot to join the battle that was in progress there.

The sequel to the Hampteau action is that Lieutenant Paul Curtis, accompanied by Sergeants Joseph H. Ochson and Harry S. Wimberley, returned in the afternoon in an attempt to rewire and blow the bridge.

Soy: 88, 92, B2

Hotton Bridge and Approaches: December 21

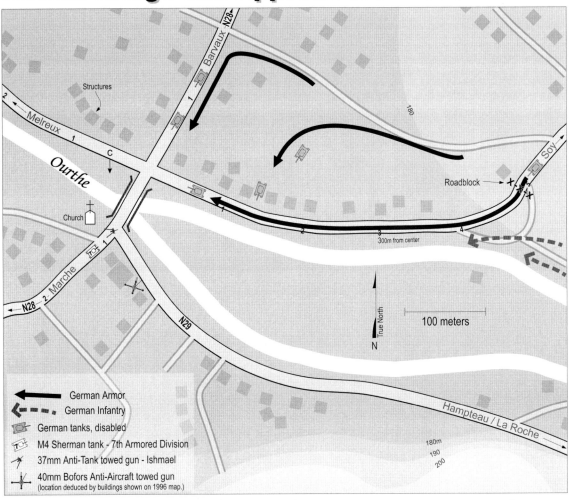

Contours and features are derived from *Carte Topographique , (1:50,000) - Durbuy (#55), National Geographical Institute - Belgium, 1996.* On this modern map, the road numbers are all different and there is no rail line going through Hotton. The number and placement of buildings is modern, though likely very nearly the same as in 1944. Battle placements are from *Holding the Line*.

Bridge over the Ourthe at Hotton. This is looking roughly due south from the German side, probably from the "c" camera position on the road in the map.

Lieutenant Curtis was killed in the unsuccessful attempt.[64]

On 21 December bitter fighting took place at the point (369879) where a vital class 70 bridge spanned the Ourthe River at Hotton (Map 5 [in Hechler's report]). Hotton is at the junction N29 (which runs southeast to La Roche) and N28 (which runs northeast toward Barvaux and southwest toward Marche). The bridge is perpendicular to N29 and connects N28 on both sides of the river. On the east side of the river the road to Soy branches off to the northeast. Along the southern borders of this road are wooded areas and rising ground. Houses line both sides of the river and are closely spaced. The main enemy thrusts at Hotton came from the northeast; from the direction of Soy and Erezee.[65]

The sparkplug of the defense of Hotton was Captain Preston C. Hodges, a veteran graduate of Fort Belvoir's sixth OCS (Officer Candidate School) class, who had commanded or been associated with Company B of the 51st for two years.[66] His leadership held together the miscellaneous elements present at the bridge and inspired them to stand and ward off the enemy attacks. Captain Hodges remained exposed to small arms and artillery fire during the battle in order to coordinate the firing of the various weapons and elements under his command, although slightly wounded by a steel fragment during the battle, Captain Hodges remained at his station until the battle of Hotton had been won and the town was firmly in Allied hands.[67]

The personnel and equipment available to Captain Hodges for the defense of Hotton initially consisted of the following: one squad of the 1st Platoon of Company B, 51st Engineers, commanded by First Lieutenant Bruce W. Jamison; half a squad of men from Company A, 51st Engineers; a squad of Armored Engineers from the 3rd Armored Division, equipped with a 37-mm. antitank gun; two 40-mm. Bofors antiaircraft guns (pressed into service from the 440th AAA Battalion); and a smattering of bazookas and .50-caliber machine guns. Most of this equipment and personnel was on the southwest side of the river bridge. On the northeast side of the bridge were personnel of the 3rd Armored Division trains, supported by what appeared to be a platoon of light tanks and a platoon of medium tanks. A medical unit also was present on the northeast side of the river, lining the Barvaux road. This unit was also part of the 3rd Armored Division.[68]

The Hotton bridge was a two-way timber bridge. Defense from the northeast side of the bridge and river was difficult due to limited observation and the obstruction to movement caused by the buildings of the town. Positions on the west bank could be observed by the enemy but were choicer because they allowed freedom of movement, fields of fire, and better sight of what the enemy was doing. On the night of 19-20 December, Lieutenant Jamison prepared this bridge and the Melreux railroad bridge for demolition. He used 800 pounds of TNT and 300 pounds of satchel charges on the Hotton bridge, preparing one abutment and three piers.[69]

The same night that the bridge had been prepared for demolition, an enemy patrol of 20 men dressed in American uniforms advanced on the bridge, and they came down and started to walk across the bridge. It was never learned what their mission was, but it was supposed that they were to blow the bridge.[70]

One of the most valuable assets that the small group of the 51st Engineer Combat Battalion had available at Hotton was a vehicle from the 7th Armored Division, with a five-man crew.[71] There is disagreement in both oral and written testimony as to whether this was a tank destroyer or an M4 medium tank with a 76-mm. gun. All observers and participants agree it had a 76-mm. gun. They also agree that its crew did a heroic job in the defense of the Hotton bridge, away from their unit. It is unfortunate that none of the

Engineers present at the battle of Hotton have clues to the identity of the tank crew.[72]

Before daylight on the morning of 21 December, Lieutenants Wright and Jamison located this armored vehicle in an ordnance detachment on the outskirts of Hotton. These officers prevailed on the sergeant (tank commander) to get his tank into action to support the detachment defending the Hotton bridge. The tank was employed near the end of the bridge on the west side of the river, close to a protecting house that shielded its hull but allowed it a good field of fire.[73]

Early on the morning of the 21st, Captain Hodges borrowed a 37-mm. antitank gun from the 23rd Armored Engineers of the 3rd Armored Division across the river. The crew, according to all observers, was very hesitant about manning the gun. Private Lee J. Ishmael, driver for Colonel Fraser, volunteered to fire the gun and he manned it throughout the battle.[74]

About 0700 on the morning of 21 December, the enemy commenced shelling Hotton. Shortly thereafter, a firefight developed between elements of the 3rd Armored Division and enemy armor and infantry coming out of the woods on the east side of the river. Captain John W. Barnes, S-3 of the 51st Engineer Combat Battalion, who had just returned from inspecting roadblocks on Highway N4, received the information from Lieutenant Wright that Hampteau had fallen and the group there had been forced back to Hotton, which was being threatened. Captain Barnes asked for volunteers from Headquarters and Service Company to go to Hotton and check the enemy vehicles attempting to break through there. The others in Captain Barnes' group were Warrant Officer Julius J. Horecka, Master Sergeant Edward Colley, Technical Sergeant Kenneth Kelly, Sergeant Arnold Parker, Private Lee J. Ishmael, Private Peter Sirianni, and Private Willis Rackus. Horecka took these men ahead in a 2½-ton truck. When they arrived in Hotton there was a small scale battle in progress between the 3rd Armored and enemy armor.[75]

The 3rd Armored tanks started engaging enemy infantry, which came out of the woods east of Hotton and up the road on the east side of the Ourthe River. A medium and a light tank from the 3rd Armored started down the Soy road toward the enemy infantry, but they were both stopped by a Mark VI tank approaching the bridge from the Soy road. The Mark VI quickly knocked out the light tank; the M4 fired one shot at the enemy Tiger and then backed into a building. The enemy tank crippled the 3rd Armored medium tank, and the crew evacuated. The Tiger tank continued toward the bridge unmolested.[76]

At this point Private Ishmael manned the 37-mm. antitank gun, which the crew from the 23rd Armored Engineer Battalion had hesitated to put into action. Ishmael was a veteran member of the battalion. During late 1942 and 1943, when the battalion had been at Plattsburg Barracks, Private Ishmael had instructed on the 37-mm. He shot approximately 16 rounds in three minutes of rapid firing during which observers noted a few tracers bounce off the Mark VI. Three shots hit the tank's bogie wheels, and the most effective shot wedged between the turret and the hull. This shell apparently prevented the tank's gun from turning around.[77]

Sergeant Kenneth Kelly who assisted Private Ishmael in swinging the 37-mm. gun around, also fired at the tank with a bazooka, which was loaded by Lieutenant Munny Y. M. Lee. Results were not observed because of the smoke and dust, but it is believed that the rounds from the 37-mm. gun knocked the tank out. The crew dispersed, but two were killed and one captured from the group in the tank. Sergeant Kelly also observed a 2½-ton truck, hit by this same German Mark VI, go up in flames.[78]

The Battle of the Bulge ... A PLACE IN HISTORY

About the time that Private Ishmael was dealing with this tank, Colonel Fraser was leaving the battalion CP in the Marche area. He had been close touch with the situations at Hampteau and Hotton until the wire to Hotton went out. Colonel Fraser had appealed to the 84th Division for help to be sent to Hotton. When the 84th (at Marche) scoffed at reports of activity at Hotton, Colonel Fraser put the Hotton telephone close to the Marche line to allow the 84th to hear the sounds of shelling at Hotton.

Mark VI Tiger (right) and Mark IV (left) tanks destroyed in the Battle of Hotton.
National Archives - 26 December 1944

Finally, at about 0830, he went to Hotton himself. In order to coordinate the activities of his battalion with what the 3rd Armored Division was doing on the other side of the river, Colonel Fraser crossed the bridge and was isolated in the enemy territory for much of the morning after the enemy armored spearhead started to advance toward the bridge. He made his way back safely, saw that Captain Hodges had the situation well under control, and then proceeded to Marche to recheck with the 84th Division on reinforcements for Hotton.[79]

Meanwhile, Captain John W. Barnes, battalion S-3, was off on another mission. After Captain Barnes had sent a squad of volunteers from Headquarters and Service Company to Hotton, he went down N4 to the outskirts of Marche, where a Captain Siegal of the 523rd Ordnance Battalion was manning an M10 at one of the 51st's roadblocks. Captain Barnes brought the M10 back through Marche toward Hotton to reinforce the position there. He was stopped by the commanding general of the 84th Division, to whom Captain Barnes explained the situation.

According to Captain Barnes, "General Alexander R. Bolling told me he wanted facts and not rumors or hearsay and he would not allow me to go on with the M10 until he knew more of the situation." General Bolling then dispatched one of his reconnaissance officers in his personal armored car to confirm the seriousness of the situation. When the 84th's troops did arrive, however, it was already 1500 and the battle was over.[80]

Captain Hodges states that the three most decisive actions of the battle of Hotton were the manning of the 37-mm. AT gun by Private Ishmael, the effective firing done by the stray tank of the 7th Armored Division, and the bravery of an unknown, unnamed soldier who volunteered to cross the bridge and flush out several tanks with his bazooka. Captain Hodges and the men from the 51st did not recognize this unknown hero, nor did they have an opportunity in the heat of battle to ask his name, but they were all loud in their praise of his action. After Private Ishmael had knocked out his tank, mortar fire started coming in fairly heavily around the bridge site. Another enemy tank started to edge along the road from Erezée toward the bridge; still another came directly toward the bridge from the northeast. Three shots were fired from the 7th Armored tank. The third one hit the enemy tank approaching from the northeast, knocking it out and killing the crew. On later inspection it was found that the tank was loaded with US GI equipment.

The tank had reached within 75 yards of the bridge when it was knocked out. The other enemy tank approaching from Erezee slid in behind some buildings on the northeast side of the river. It was close enough to the bridge to menace the personnel guarding the bridge. Captain Hodges relates that at this time an unknown soldier approached him at the bridge and said: "Captain, I'll flush out that tank over there." "Well, boy go ahead," Captain Hodges replied.

The unnamed soldier took off alone across the bridge with a bazooka and two rounds of ammunition in his pocket. He was seen ducking into a building on the far right corner of the bridge. Shortly thereafter the personnel at the bridge heard a smash like a bazooka round and the enemy tank pulled up between two buildings so that part of its hull was showing out of an aperture of only two feet between the buildings. The 7th Armored Division tank fired accurately through this two-foot opening, destroying the tank. Expending all but two rounds of its ammunition, the tank remained in position, unscathed, near the bridge. Captain Hodges estimates that it destroyed or maimed at least four enemy tanks and scared away several others.[81]

During the battle, the wiring on the demolition charges on the bridge was shot out by enemy shell fire. Lieutenants Jamison and Wright, without waiting for orders, entered the shoulder-deep water and, under enemy small arms fire, repaired the wiring.[82]

Throughout the morning and during the early afternoon, the tank-infantry battle raged. About 1400, the enemy armor showed signs that it had had about enough and started to withdraw, but the sniper small arms fire was still hot on the northeast side of the bridge. The situation was finally relieved at 1500 with the arrival of a task force of the 3rd Armored Division under command of Brigadier General Maurice Rose*. The relief force of the 84th Division then appeared on the scene from Marche. Most of the elements of the 51st Battalion withdrew toward Marche, having accomplished their mission of holding the bridge. Half of a squad was left at the Hotton bridge to blow it if necessary during the ensuing days.[83] Captain Hodges reports that there were frequent arguments between the commands of the 3rd Armored Division and the 84th Division as to whether the bridge should be blown. In lieu of an agreement between the generals involved, the squad at the bridge took no action and refused to blow the bridge.[84]

Despite the bitter fighting at Hotton on 21 December, only two members of the 51st's force were casualties, both from shell fragments. Captain Hodges received a shell fragment wound in his leg, while Private Ishmael was wounded in the hand. (These casualty figures do not include casualties among the attached personnel who fought with the 51st at Hotton.)[85]

The significance of the defense of the Hotton bridge, which elements of the 51st carried on during the seven hour battle, is that the actions preserved a key link in Allied supply lines to forward units, behind which the 84th Division was organizing and arriving at Marche.[86]

During the next ten days, prior to being relieved by British troops on 3 January, the companies of the 51st continued their mission of maintaining roadblocks and bridge protection along an extended front. On 22 December, a barrier line was installed from Hamoir (423052) to Hotton (369879), along the Ourthe River,

* According to *Citizen Soldiers,* General Rose was "much admired and loved" and also was the only divisional commander in all of the European Theater of Operations to be killed in action, on 28 March 1945 on the southern border of the "Ruhr Pocket".

thence through Marche and southwest to Rochefort. The line consisted of prepared demolitions in culverts; mines in roads at critical intersections, combined with bazooka teams; and 40-mm. AA guns.[87]

At 1500 on *22 December*, Company C, now returned from its defense of Trois Ponts, sent a reconnaissance party along Highway N4 to set up roadblocks. The party consisted of Major Yates, Captain Scheuber, Lieutenant Green, and Lieutenant Nabors. The men approached southeast of Marche and were fired on by the lead vehicles of an enemy armored column at (310805). They stopped their jeep and advanced on foot and were soon cut off by five enemy tanks, two half-tracks filled with enemy personnel, and additional armor that was not actually seen. All officers but Major Yates escaped by taking off through fields and avoiding roads. Major Yates, who had only a few days before returned from the hospital where he had been confined with a foot injury, could not run and hence hid in a bush by the road. After two hours he was discovered, disarmed, and taken prisoner. When the man guarding Yates relaxed his vigil for a moment, Major Yates dived into a stream beside which they stood, worked his way downstream under about three feet of water, and escaped under a hail of small arms fire to return to friendly lines shortly before 2200 the same night.[88]

On 22 December, Company A relieved Company B of the responsibility of the roadblocks in the vicinity of Aye, Humain, and Rochefort; Company B extended its defenses from Durbuy to Hamoir, taking over from the 300th Engineer Combat Battalion.

The following guards and defensive positions were established and maintained by Company B on 22 December:

- (341950) — guard on footbridge;
- (390868) — reconnaissance made of Hampteau bridge (quiet)
- (424001) — bridge mined, up and downstream;
- (415985) — footbridge;
- (377972) — footbridge;
- (360962) — bridge mined;
- (341950) — footbridge mined;
- (322920) — bridge out;
- (360890) — railroad bridge out;
- (369879) — bridge mined;
- (295932) — abatis;
- (407025) — culvert mined;
- (419040) — crater for road and railroad.[89]

At noon on 22 December, a party led by Lieutenant Wright proceeded as far as Jemelle, where it was reported to them that enemy tanks and infantry were in Manogne. Lieutenant Wright was then ordered to prepare abatis in the vicinity of (242741) and to mine the road at (243798). The 3rd Platoon of Company A was ordered to prepare roadblocks on Highway N35 between Jemelle and Marche. Lieutenant Wright's 1st Platoon of Company A then commenced a merry chase that eventually carried them back as far as Givet. After establishing a roadblock at (242745) in the vicinity of Forrières, he successfully moved his platoon to Rochefort, Aye, and Marche. Lieutenant Wright returned to Rochefort at 1900 on 22 December to blow a bridge there, accomplished his mission, and returned to Marche[*]. The following morning, he received orders to repair the Rochefort bridge. While in the town, the platoon was attacked and driven back to Givet along with the 84th Division.

The 2nd and 3rd Platoons of Company A were responsible for the following defenses prepared and/or maintained on 22 December:

    (226883) — abatis;
    (235889) — bridge mined;
    (221894) and (229900) — roadblocks coordinated with elements of 309th ECB
    (236902) — road and bridge mined;
    (264411) — bridge mined; coordinated with elements of 309th ECB
    (278915) — bridge and road mined.

Company C strengthened the defenses of the 51st on 23 December by manning the positions:

    (298878) — abatis with string of mines;
    (267871) — bridge mined;
    (250860) — bridge mined;
    (219866) — culvert mined and minefield on both sides of road;
    (236875) — road mined; and
    (226883) — abatis.

The ensuing days were anticlimactic. Company B was relieved of all duties on the barrier line on the Ourthe River from Hotton to Hamoir, with the exception of the demolition crew in Hotton. The latter was strengthened on 27 December from half a squad to one officer and 10 EM (enlisted men), and the bridge was rewired so it could be demolished from either side. At 0140 on 26 December, the railroad bridge at Melreux was blown. During the remainder of the period before being relieved, Company B maintained a roadblock on Highway N35 south of the junction at N29 and also maintained a roadblock on N35 north of the junction with N29.

Although the enemy had been held off at Hotton, and its advance toward Marche on N4 had been delayed, there was still some enemy activity after 22 December — generally to the east and southeast, and south and southwest of Marche. The enemy appeared to be attempting to encircle Marche and to move to the Meuse River to the west. During the period from 24 December until relieved by elements of the XXX British Corps on 3 January, the battalion was attached to the 84th Division in direct support. The battalion continued to hold a series of roadblocks and bridges against numerous enemy probings, but experienced no serious threats.

Total battalion casualties for the operation were five killed, six wounded. and two missing.

Jemelle: 88, B2   **Manogne**[not on maps, maybe Nassogne?]: B6?   **Forrieres**: 88, B6   **Givet**: 6, B1

NOTES

Sources for the preceding "Battle of the Bulge" text. (Notes condensed from *Holding the Line*, pp 61-66)

AAR/S-3	After-action report and S-3 Journal for 51st ECB
AAR 291st	After-action report for 291st ECB
Hechler PO	Capt. Hechler's personal observations
Co.B, etc.	Histories of Co.B, Co.C, 51st ECB
S-1 Log	S-1 daily Log
Name - h	named individuals interviewed by Capt. Hechler
Name - g	named individuals interviewed by T/4 George

1. AAR/S-3
2. AAR/S-3, 51st
3. Green, Hodges, Wright - *h*
4. AAR/S-3, S-1 Log
5. Fraser - *h*
6. S-1 Log
7. Fraser - *h*
8. Hechler PO, Co.B
9. S-1 Log
10. Fraser - *h*
11. Hechler PO
12. Fraser - *h*
13. Barnes - *g*
14. Hodges, Ishmael - *g, h*
15. Green, Scheuber, Yates - *h*
16. Ibid.
17. Ekman - *h*
18. letter, re. commendation
19. Co.C
20. Yates - *h*
21. Yates - *h*
22. Hechler PO
23. Hechler PO
24. Scheuber - *h*
25. Jewett - *h*
26. Kirkland - *h*
27. Kirkland - *h*
28. AAR 291st
29. Green & Yates - *h*
30. Green, Jewett - *h*
31. Jewett - *h*
32. Green - *h*
33. Green, Jewett - *h*
34. Jewett - *h*
35. Jewett - *h*
36. Kirkland - *h*
37. Green, Jewett - *h*
38. Yates - *h*
39. Yates - *h*
40. Green, Scheuber - *h*
41. Green - *h*
42. Green - *h*
43. Yates - *h*
44. Scheuber - *h*
45. Kirkland - *h*
46. S-1 Log
47. AAR 291st
48. Scheuber - *h*
49. Ekman - *h*
50. S-1 Log
51. AAR/S-3, Yates - *h*
52. Scheuber - *h*
53. Milgram - *h*
54. AAR and S-3
55. Hodges - *h*
56. S-1 Log
57. Fraser - *h*
58. Fraser - *h*
59. AAR/S-3
60. Wright - *h*
61. AAR/S-3, Pedersen - *h*
62. Fraser - *h*
63. Bonifay, Hofmann and Wright - *g*
64. Bonifay, Hofmann - *g*
65. Fraser, Hodges - *h*
66. Fraser, Hodges - *h*
67. Fraser - *h*
68. Fraser, Hodges - *h*
69. Hodges - *h*
70. Bray, Engle, George, Porter - *g*
71. Hodges - *h*
72. Hechler PO
73. S-1 Log
74. Hodges - *h*
75. Barnes, Kelly - *g*
76. Ishmael, Hodges - *h*
77. Ishmael - *g, h*
78. Kelly - *g*
79. Fraser - *h*
80. Barnes - *g*
81. Hodges - *h*
82. Co.B
83. 51st ECB
84. Hodges - *h*
85. S-1 Log
86. Hechler PO
87. AAR/S-3
88. AAR/S-3, Yates - *h*
89. AAR/S-3
90. AAR/S-3
91. S-1 Log

Ranks of interviewed soldiers: **Colonel -** Ekman **Lt. Colonel -** Fraser, Kirkland **Major -** Yates **Captain -** Barnes, Hodges, Jewett, Pedersen **1st Lt. -** Green, Milgram, Wright **S/Sgt. -** Bonifay, Engle, George **Corporal -** Bray, Porter **Private -** Hofmann, Ishmael.

Ardennes Campaign (Letters)
Height of the Bulge; preparing to counter the German attack

Maffe (22-24 December 1944)

24 Dec. - A lot of water has gone over the dam since I last wrote. Last night is the first night I've had a full night's sleep since 17 Dec. I am fairly safe now and so far have not received a scratch. This battalion has really made a name for itself and I am more than proud of my men. For the amount of pounding we have received, casualties have been very light. Censorship regulations will be lifted in another week or so and I'll be able to describe everything in detail. We had a few captured but they got away. 'Tis a great life if you don't weaken.

Clavier (25-29 December 1944)

26 Dec. - With the exception of the roaring artillery everything is peaceful. I am in no immediate danger at present. I have learned to want to kill with vengeance lately. The lowest piece of humanity on earth wouldn't pull some of the things the Germans have lately. I asked one of my men what he wanted to do with a suspicious individual we were overtaking if he turned out to be a German: "Kill the -----." And that is the sentiment of every man in the outfit. So far we've gotten more that 10 Germans for every one we have lost. The situation on the whole is very favorable. And these men have their dander up; they want to scrap.

29 Dec. - I hope you don't believe everything you read and see in the papers. Even our own Stars & Stripes is all wet. The Germans have done plenty of damage but they are catching hell now. I think this is going to turn into one of our greatest victories of the war and I hope it is the last. I had a rather interesting experience a short time ago. I had the mission of contacting the Jerries and finding out where they were. I knew where they had run us out the night before and thought the roadblocks we had blown would hold them awhile, so we went batting around a curve about 25 miles an hour 5 miles from where I thought they should be. Well, we finally stopped 125 yards from the muzzles of 2 Jerry tanks's guns. We had a straight stretch of 400 yards behind us to that curve. We traveled 25-30 miles an hour in reverse zig-zaggings across the road. I could almost feel that shell whistling through that jeep and those machine guns tearing us to shreds. We made it safely and you can thank the Lord for that.

There are three reasons why I think I am not pushing up daisies: the Jerries had just captured a sedan filled with Canadians and the first thing I saw (other than the tanks) was a potato masher sailing over the sedan and another Jerry cocked to throw another one (preoccupation); maybe the Jerries thought we were Jerries because they had been sending a lot of Jerries down that road in American uniforms and in American jeeps; and thirdly our zigging and zagging so fast. As we zigged and zagged rearward I watched the Jerry gunner slink into his turret after he had thrown the potato masher. Incidentally at that time we were 5 miles or more beyond our infantry front lines. P.S.- I didn't have time to get scared. Later 2 of my men and myself went up with a reconnaissance platoon that had three 37 mm guns and after they set up they decided to withdraw. The only time I was really scared was when a buzz bomb landed 200 yards away and I awakened just in time to see the blinding explosion. I am sure at least one of our companies will get a unit citation, possibly the whole battalion. Everyone is proud of the outfit and every man in it. We are one of the few outfits who stemmed the German tide and absolutely stopped it in places. I am sure one of our companies [Co. C] stopped a whole panzer division for 3 days. Everyone has a lot of experiences to relate and I thank God that the greatest percentage are here to relate those

Maffe and **Clavier**: 88, B2

The Battle of the Bulge ... A PLACE IN HISTORY

experiences. All of us feel much freer and easier now that several divisions are where we once were. At present I am comparatively safe and there is nothing to worry about.

Yates had the narrowest escape of those who escaped I guess. If you saw it in the movies, you would say that it was more Hollywood stuff. He and 3 other officers were on a reconnaissance when a Jerry tank opened up on them with machine guns. The other officers ran and escaped but his (Yates') foot was not entirely well, so all he could do was stay there as close to the ground as possible. The Jerries stopped firing and then 15 Tiger tanks and half-tracks rolled past him before he was ever captured. They disarmed him and one Jerry took him back to a tank along side a 6-ft deep stream. Apparently the 2 Jerries were discussing whether to kill him or not when one turned his head and Yates dived into the stream which had risen 2 feet and was filled with debris. He floated down the stream trying to simulate a log as the Jerries emptied their machine pistols all around him. The temperature was 25 degrees and he was nearly frozen, so he crawled out on the bank to get his breath and back into the stream he went. After going about 1/2 mile down stream, he took off across the hills toward home. He arrived 5 hours later nearly frozen, but none the worse for wear. He has what it takes.

Maffe (30 Dec. 1944 - 1 January 1945)

31 Dec.- My c.p. is now in a real nice living room. The people mop the floor, bring us hot water, soup, apples - In other words, they are trying to make us as comfortable as possible. Last night for the first time in 13 months I slept between sheets .... In this building the cattle are next to this pleasant living room and the pigs are next to the kitchen on the other end. The house proper is immaculate. The people take off their wooden shoes before they enter and despite that the floors are mopped every day. "Mama" does all the work while "Papa" sits. They have a good lighting system and running water.

1 Jan. - The colonel had all of the company commanders and staff in last night to toast the New Year in. Our troops celebrated by firing one round of artillery toward German territory from every gun in this sector. The blast almost shook this building to pieces .... We had a nice dinner of ham, raisin sauce, string beans, mashed potatoes, peas, bread and coffee.

Modave (2 Jan. 1945)

2 Jan. - Here I sit in the king of Belgium's sister's home. The guard told me that the oils on my orderly room walls were worth at least $100,000. Some of the chandeliers must be worth $5000 or more. I believe it would take a week to find and count

War sweeps back into a civilized country. Chateau de **Modave**, Belgium. The Command Post for the 1111th ECG was in Modave area in late December, 1944.

Collection of Joseph Milgram (1960's postcard)

Modave: B2

all of these rooms. Each bedroom has a bathroom with tub, wash basin, etc. ... this place was built in 1109, rebuilt in 1836, and remodeled in 1928. I couldn't begin to describe it. It makes everything I've seen in the U.S. look second-rate. Even the House of Rothschild I saw near Paris doesn't compare with this place.

.50 Caliber mobile Anti-Aircraft gun set up near **Soy**, Belgium. *National Archives - 5 January 1945*

Infantry "hit the snow" as a shell whistles overhead near **Krinkelt** (B4) *National Archives - 31 January 1945*

The Battle of the Bulge … A PLACE IN HISTORY

German tanks near **Hotton**. Judging from shadows and terrain, this is afternoon on the road from Soy. Hampteau would be about 2 miles directly ahead (see map p. 92).
National Archives - 13 January 1945

La Roche, Belgium (B2), 7 miles southeast of Hotton: a one-time resort village, devastated by terrific bombardment and shelling by Germans and Allies both.
National Archives - 16 January 1945

Waiting for an attack that never came. 82nd Airborne artillery, having had time to form a defensive line, defend **Werbomont**, Belgium. Because of the 51st and 291st, the 1st SS Panzers never got this far, nor did other Germans later. Soon the Allied counterattack would begin.   *National Archives - 30 December 1944*

Longchamps(B7). About 12 miles south of the 51st, the 42nd Tank Bn, Combat Command A, 11th Armored Div. (on the horizon far center and right) pursue retreating Germans.   *National Archives - 13 January 1945*

Werbomont: 78, B3

Bridges to Victory: The Invasion of Germany

(3 January 1945 - 8 May 1945)

**THE AMERICAN COUNTEROFFENSIVE
GERMANY AND THE ROER (RUR) CROSSING
BRIDGING THE RHINE AND GERMANY AND THE RUHR POCKET
THE RACE SOUTH TO THE DANUBE AND MUNICH**

WITH EXCERPTS OF LETTERS WRITTEN FROM THE FIELD
by Captain Albert E. Radford to Laurie S. Radford
January 5, 1945 to May 8, 1945

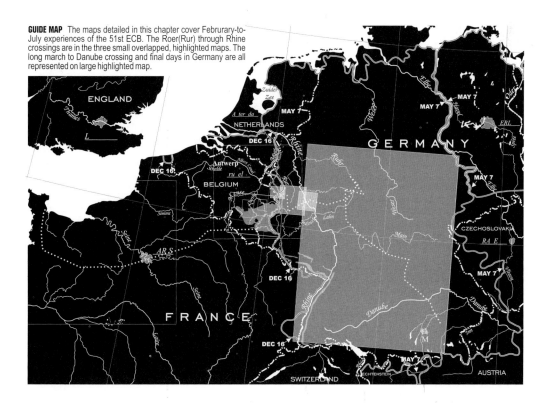

GUIDE MAP The maps detailed in this chapter cover Februrary-to-July experiences of the 51st ECB. The Roer(Rur) through Rhine crossings are in the three small overlapped, highlighted maps. The long march to Danube crossing and final days in Germany are all represented on large highlighted map.

The American Counteroffensive*
From the Ardennes to the Rhine

Introduction

"With our air force pounding the German lines of communication and troop and supply concentrations, as well as supporting the ground troops, the return bout of the Battle of the Bulge began on January 3, nineteen days after the start of the German offensive. While Third Army continued its heavy fighting around Bastogne, First Army began to press from the north, VII Corps leading the attack, accompanied by XVIII Airborne Corps on the east, and the British XXX Corps on the west." p. 205

"Of all the attacks made by Allied forces in western Europe, the conditions under which this was made were, by all odds, the worst. The snow was in many cases waist deep, and even short infantry movements were made under the most trying conditions. The few roads were ice coated, and in many places snow blanketed the ice. Tanks were road bound in nearly all cases, and the Germans, by carefully located anti-tank guns, aided by minefields to the fore, were able continually to halt Allied tank advances until the infantry could move forward to cope with the German strong points. It was unbelievably cold, near zero, and the battle for existence against the elements was at least as difficult as that against the enemy. But as the Third Army beat off the final attacks around Bastogne, First Army troops slowly ground their way forward through the snowbound woods and fields." pp. 205-206.

"On January 12 the bombshell fell which was to disrupt forever German offensive plans on any front. The Russians left their winter quarters and initiated their long-expected winter offensive to the east. This was the final blow to German plans in the west, and when the Russians opened wide holes in the German lines, Hitler ordered release of the entire Sixth Panzer Army to the Eastern Front. This was quickly followed by an order to send east the two Fuhrer brigades and at least three infantry divisions. Now, all the Germans could hope for was an orderly and gradual retreat back to the West Wall from which they had battered their way only a month before." pp. 206-207

"On January 16 patrols from First and Third Armies met in the town of Houffalize, their mutual goal, and the complete tip of the German penetration was eliminated. Both armies wheeled to the east and started operations toward the West Wall. Meanwhile on January 13, V Corps had sprung to the attack and was slowly cutting into the German flank further to the east of Houffalize .... Still fighting the weather as much as the tough German resistance, the two armies relentlessly moved forward and by early February the Germans were back in the West Wall, along nearly the entire length of the Ardennes front." p. 207

"The greatest pitched battle for the Western Front was over. Twenty-nine German and thirty-two Allied divisions participated in the battle which raged for a little over a month. The last great German gamble had ended, not without certain successes, but far short of its ambitious goal. For all practical purposes the war in the west was over. Early in February, the British attacked down the watershed between the Roer and Rhine Rivers." p. 207

"Third Army continued through the Ardennes forests, and through the West Wall toward the Rhine. In the south, the Colmar pocket was eliminated by a Franco-American attack, and back to the north, the First Army seized the vital Roer River dams, which they had been attacking on December 16 when the German attack

---

* Introduction" quotes are from **Dark December**. Otherwise, this chapter is excerpted from **The 51st Again!** and letters from the field. **Houffalize**: 6, B7

began. On February 23, the day after one of our most paralyzing aerial attacks on Germany, in which nearly 10,000 sorties were flown over Nazi rail transportation targets, Ninth Army with First Army support, hopped the Roer River, headed straight for the Rhine, and then in a sudden whirling action, which threw the Germans off their guard, turned to the north to meet the British attack coming down the watershed. First Army continued straight ahead, captured what was left of Bastogne on March 7, and on the same day, in a lucky stroke, seized intact the Rhine River crossing at Remagen, and immediately forced the Germans to revert their few remaining reserves to meet this grave threat to their last defense line." p. 208

82nd Airborne troops advancing toward **Herresbach**, Belgium.
National Archives - 28 January 1945

Support to the Divisions

At the beginning of the new year, the 1111th Engineer Combat Group committed the 51st Engineer Combat Battalion to keeping the Germans from breaking through the Marche - Maffe - Hotton area by maintaining roadblocks and a barrier line. Shortly thereafter, on January 4, 1945, the battalion moved to Modave, Belgium, to begin a long promised rest. The respite lasted just six hours. The group assigned the 51st a new mission, this time, close engineer support to the 82nd Airborne Division. From 5-10 January 1945, the battalion operated in close association with the 307th Engineers of the 82nd Airborne Division, then provided close support to the 275th ECB of the 75th Infantry Division when the 75th relieved the 82nd on line from January 11 to 19.

The battalion's new assignment began on the night of ***January 2***, 1945, while the 1st Platoon, Company A, was guarding a double-double Bailey bridge at Noiseux, Belgium. The bridge had been prepared for demolition. About midnight Colonel Fraser asked if the bridge could support the movement of an armored division. The question could not be answered immediately, a situation which always raised the hackles of the battalion commander when he was looking for an instant answer.

The builders of the bridge had exceeded the recommended length of a double-double Bailey bridge for a class 40 (40-ton) load. They had used good engineering design by constructing a 20-foot pier as a center support, thus creating two connecting short spans, instead of a single long span. However, any load on the bridge caused the lower chord of the bridge to deflect downward until it contacted the pier. In addition, the pier was neither level nor plumb, and many pieces of timber were not properly joined. Had these irregularities not been present, the platoon officer could easily have determined the load capacity of the bridge.

Colmar: F7   Remagen: 132, 136   Herresbach: B4   Noiseux: 88, B2

When he heard all of this, Scrappy ordered, "go out and get a tank and drive it over the bridge to see if it will hold up." The tone of his voice made it very clear that any idiot should have arrived at this solution already. He made it plain that at daybreak an armored division was scheduled to pass over the bridge. Conditions were abominable. The night was pitch black, the temperature below zero, and the roads covered with a thick sheet of ice, built up from several weeks of snow, rain, and freezing weather. We had to find a tank commander, either drunk of crazy, who would drive his tank over a high-level bridge to see if it would support the tank.

Technician Fifth Grade Johnston was a wizard at driving his jeep under such poor road conditions. He and his platoon leader, Lieutenant Wright, headed down the road toward the rear of the division area. Within a few miles they found several tents grouped together that turned out to be a tank field maintenance detachment. About six tanks were parked around the tents. Entering one of the tents, Wright saw that just about everyone was "dog drunk" or well on their way to becoming so. Some of the men were waiting for their tanks to be repaired, while others were waiting for daylight so they could return to their units. A civilian pot-belly stove in the middle of the tent made that small area a "heaven on earth" that few men were willing to vacate. Wright explained his problem to the men present, asking for volunteers to help him out.

After listening to the lieutenant's tale, not one man of the group stepped forward. Finally, after a little more discussion about the pending attack at daybreak and winning the war, a sergeant staggered forward and said, "Let's go, sir." Wright was not encouraged with the sergeant's bravado for he had serious doubts as to his ability to function, considering the adverse conditions of the road, driving at night, and his physical condition. As Wright considered the situation, the driver of the tank, who was cold sober, got up and said that he would go with the sergeant.

With the jeep leading, the group moved off toward the bridge at a snail's pace and under blackout conditions. The tank followed, driven by the sergeant (who insisted on driving), with the regular, but sober, driver in the turret. A short distance down the road the jeep passed a Signal Corps half-ton truck parked on the shoulder of the road. A few seconds later Wright and Johnston heard a loud crunching sound. Johnston stopped the jeep, and Wright hurried back. The tank had completely leveled that half of the truck nearest the roadbed. Fortunately the two linemen with the truck were several hundred yards away looking for a break in the telephone lines. The sergeant quickly decided that the driver should take over and switch places.

It was still pitch dark when the small convoy finally reached the Bailey bridge. Walking out onto the bridge with a flashlight, Wright explained to the sergeant and driver that he would walk in front and guide the tank to the center of the bridge where the driver would stop it. The lieutenant would then inspect the center pier after which the tank would proceed on across the bridge.

This stopping on the center span violated all standard operating procedures (SOPs) for crossing military bridges. At every bridge built by combat engineers, a sign prohibited stopping or changing gears on the bridge because of the increased stress these actions caused. However, on this night, Wright intended to stop the tank in the middle of the bridge so that the center pier could be inspected under load. Additionally, the stopping created more stress on the bridge than could reasonably by expected from moving tanks, thus ensuring the capability of the bridge to stand up under an armored crossing.

After hearing the crossing procedure explained, the sergeant either sobered up or found his senses. He emphatically stated that he would not drive his tank across the bridge. No amount of persuasion was going to change his mind. Finally, the tank driver agreed to drive it across. From that point on the sergeant kept repeating to Wright that he, Wright, would be completely responsible for the tank if anything happened to it.

The sergeant stood on the abutment of the bridge while the tank crossed to the center. There the tank stopped while the center support was examined. Then it completed the crossing. Once across, the tank turned around, recrossed, picked up the sergeant, and vanished into the darkness. Because nobody thought to ask, the names of the sergeant and driver have been lost to posterity.

Wright then told Fraser the bridge would support a tank. About two hours later, at daybreak on January 3, 1945, the 2nd Armored Division raced across the bridge without a hitch. About noon that same day, two officers from a British Army pioneer company arrived at the bridge to relieve the 1st Platoon. Their first question was, "Where is the Officers Mess?" Wright pointed to an open case of C Rations sitting in the corner of the room and invited them to help themselves.

During the first part of the Allied offensive, the 51st ECB kept the division main supply routes open in spite of the snow. It also maintained a barrier line along the Lienne, a river which flowed north into the Amblève near Stoumont. The weather made the battalion's mission all the more difficult, for the winter of 1944-45 proved to be very severe. The extreme cold, accompanied by heavy snow, added greatly to the difficulties and hazards of constructing bridges, removing mines, and clearing snow from roads. Without the engineers to perform these missions, the infantry could not advance.

The 51st and 238th Engineer Combat Battalions, the 501st Engineer Light pontoon Company, the 629th Engineer Light Equipment Company and the 994th Engineer Treadway Bridge Company all joined or rejoined the 1111th Engineer Combat Group, First Army by *January 4*, 1945. It marked the first time that the 51st, 238th, and 1111th operated as a unit since training days in Plattsburg. The 51st and 238th were the original battalions of the 51st Engineer Combat Regiment before reorganization and the activation of the 1111th Engineer Combat Group.

The 300th ECB was already part of the 1111th Group at the time these units were attached. That brought together Lieutenant Colonels Jay P. Dawley, 238th ECB, and Riel S. Crandall, 300th ECB, along with Harvey Fraser, all classmates at the United States Military Academy. Upon graduation from the academy, all three of them had been assigned to the 3rd Engineer Regiment in Hawaii. Bachelors at the time, they were known as "The Three Musketeers."

That same day the 1111th tasked the 51st, now located at Xhoris, Belgium, to provide close engineer support for the 82nd Airborne Division. Company A, also at Xhoris, was to maintain the roads in the Army net within its company area. One platoon was attached to Company B to assist in road maintenance, and one squad, still at Noiseux, continued guarding treadway and Bailey bridges. Company B, located in La Levée, Belgium, maintained 10 roadblocks along the Lienne on highway 432 between N23 and N33. The rest of the company maintained roads in their company area. Company C, located at Niaster, Belgium, maintained the road network within its company area.

Xhoris (3-7 January 1945)

5 Jan. - Things are running more smoothly with us every day. This new C.O. is really on the ball, but is

Stoumont: 80, B3   **Xhoris:** B3   **La Levée:** 78, B3 [2 sites were found; the one near **Rahier** is more likely]   **Niaster:** 80

> still a little young and green in some things. He is teaching us more than we are teaching him. I think we'll have one of the best outfits in the army before long. We've got a good one now that is snapping out of its lethargy.
>
> **6 Jan.** - The snow still covers the ground, the sky is overcast, the bombers are droning overhead. and the radio is blaring away in this one horse schoolhouse. At present nothing exciting is occurring except approximately 50 buzz bombs going almost directly overhead every day. Most of them are landing 2-5 miles away. Some of them come so low that every window in the place vibrates. A standard saying is that as long as you can hear them you are safe - but now I know that they explode with the exhaust wide open. Last night in headquarters one came over low, and as it came closer and closer everything got quieter and quieter and faces became whiter and whiter. They made an interesting psychological study. I have one poor cook's helper who jumps straight out of bed during the night when he hears one and takes off for no place in particular, sans shoes. I think he is now sleeping with them on .... I've heard that the battalion has been recommended for a presidential citation. We have also been recommended for a service award for the work done before this fracas. One of these days I'll give you the whole story.

Probably the most difficult duty for the 51st during the period was removal of the numerous minefields and barriers emplaced by various units, both enemy and friendly, during the recent German breakthrough. Records of the minefields were vague and sometimes did not exist. Even so, it fell to the engineers to find and either mark or remove those minefields and demolitions. The 51st was one of those Engineer units expected to accomplish this job despite snow and extreme cold.

On *January 8* the battalion established a new command post at Stoumont, co-located with Company A. Company B moved to Chevron, and Company C to Lorcé, west of battalion headquarters, and north of Company B. In addition to the maintenance of roads in the new area, Company A also had to clear a minefield near Trois Ponts, construct a culvert in Basse-Bodeux, and maintain and guard a class 10 bridge near Fosse. It completed the culvert the following day at noontime, and finished removal of the minefield at 1900 hours on January 9.

Company B continued its barrier line maintenance, but turned over the northern half of the line to Company C. It then took over the duty of guarding bridges and maintaining roads in its new area. Company C, in addition to its barrier line duties, was assigned the duty of clearing a liaison aircraft landing strip west of La Gleize which it completed the following day. It also began work on a steel culvert at Reharmont, southwest of Basse-Bodeux. The construction of the culvert released two treadway bridges for use on the front lines. The company completed the mission at 2300 hours, January 12.

On January 11 the general mission of the 51st changed from close support of the 307th to the close support of the 275th ECB, 75th Infantry Division. The 51st was to be prepared to build bridges in support of division operations. From January 15 to 18, 1945, the 51st constructed five bridges in the division area around Stoumont.

Stoumont (8-19 January 1945)

> **11 Jan.** - The poor engineers are catching the devil these days, night and day. If they are not fighting, they are removing mines and clearing roads ... the Stars & Stripes irks us showing one place in German hands that has never been in Jerry hands. They are also praising our airborne divisions to the sky but

Chevron: 78, 204, B3   **Lorcé, Fosse, and La Gleize**: 78, B3   **Reharmont**: 80

The Invasion of Germany ... BRIDGES TO VICTORY

never a peep is said about the company that held the Germans until the airborne division could get there and covered their withdrawal after they had been chased out. All in all I hope we don't have to contend with that again.

Dinner at **Stoumont**, Belgium: 1st Platoon, Co A. (Sgt. Benjamin C. Ham, PFC Ervin H. Anderson, PFC Sidney L. Wood, T/5 Raymond Mitchell). *Corps Files - 19 January 1945*

Bridging at Grand-Halleux

One of the five bridges [around Stoumont] was a class 40 double-single Bailey bridge put across the Salm River at Grand-Halleux by the 1st Platoon of Company A. The small village of Grand-Halleux was located about six miles south of Trois Ponts and four miles north of Vielsalm. The platoon moved into Grand-Halleux on ***January 11***, to prepare for the eventual construction of the bridge.

The Salm River, running south to north, essentially divided the village in half. From the river, moving either east or west, the terrain rose gently over snow-covered farmland for about 1,000 feet before turning to heavy forest on the ridge line overlooking the river and the village. Located in the west half of the town was an infantry battalion of the 75th division. One of its rifle companies had crossed the easily fordable river and occupied a line along the eastern edge of the village. From there the infantry could observe across the open farmland to the forested ridge line.

The Germans controlled this ridge line, which gave them direct observation for mortar and artillery fire on the bridge site as well as on the road leading into the village from the west. If more than one truck or jeep

Grand-Halleux: 80, B3

at a time used the road, the Germans shelled it. For this reason the platoon moved into Grand Halleux by infiltrating one vehicle at a time. The infantry battalion command post was in a building located on the north side of the main road about 200 feet from the bridge site. The 1st Platoon moved into a building on the south side of the road about 100 feet from the bridge site.

They brought bridge material in at night one truckload at a time. After each truck was unloaded it went to the rear. This was done as quietly as possible, so as not to attract the attention of the Germans. During this effort to move material into town the 3rd squad truck, driven by Private First Class Ernest F. Minyard, was hit by an 88 shell. Eight pieces of shrapnel tore into the back of the cab and destroyed a tire. Nobody was wounded by the shrapnel, but Minyard's ears were damaged by the concussion. The area was covered with several inches of snow and the soldiers used bed sheets from the empty buildings to cover the bridge material, hiding it from the Germans. By *January 12* all bridge material was at the site, camouflaged, and ready for construction.

Staff Sergeant Bonifay, with the 1st squad, led by Sergeant Benjamin C. Ham, laid out the bridge site. Tracing tape strung from bank to bank established the centerline of the bridge. The ground was leveled from this line to receive plain rollers and four rocking rollers. Shortly after the layout crew left the bridge site, a German mortar shell exploded on the centerline tape on the near shore, breaking the tape. The implication of this deadly accuracy was clear. The Germans had zeroed in on the bridge site. The centerline tape was not reinstalled.

Bridge construction was delayed until the night before the division's scheduled attack. For four forlorn days the platoon waited for the order. The weather was miserable — rain, snow, freezing temperatures, and then snow again. Most of the time the temperature stayed well below freezing. The Company A mess sergeant, Staff Sergeant Robert L. Hardcastle, managed to visit Grand-Halleux once a day so that the 1st Platoon could have at least one hot meal. On one such occasion, German artillery broke up the repast and chased the mess truck out of the valley.

The Germans bombarded the village several times each day. The timing of the shelling was unpredictable. When the shells came in everyone dove for the cellars of buildings. On *January 13*, the third day of the wait, Private First Class Emile B. Doucet, while racing for the cellar during one such shelling, was struck in the left elbow by a piece of shrapnel coming through a window. Doucet was evacuated, eventually receiving a medical discharge from the army. His left arm remained stiff for the rest of his life.

> **13 Jan.** - [Stoumont] I see where Gen. Bradley thinks the Germans made one of the biggest mistakes of this war when they attacked through the Schnee-Eiffel. I believe they did. They are mighty fool-hardy. There are very few supply routes and that high forested ground is covered with snow and firs. They at least removed any ideas of holing up for the winter.
>
> **14 Jan.** - I see where the town of Marche was announced to the world as not being captured as had been previously stated. I wouldn't be writing you today if it had fallen into German hands. The papers state that a division held the place but they don't know who held it for 5 days until that famous division (84th Infantry) arrived and got organized defensively. Every time the men read about that and a few other stories they start howling. We have to toot our own whistle.

On the fourth day the phone call ordering construction of the bridge finally came from the division G-3 at

2200 hours. Fraser was notified immediately. The night was pitch dark and cold, with the temperature some 15 to 20 degrees below zero. The panel crew, consisting of Ham's 1st Squad and Sergeant Charles G. Kroen's 3rd Squad, began work immediately. The transom crew was given to Sergeant John J. Stiftinger's 2nd Squad.

As the first two panels and a stringer were placed on the steel rollers a problem appeared. Three days of rain, snow, and freezing weather had left a layer of ice about an eighth to a quarter of an inch thick on the bridge parts. The ice prevented the assembly of the bridge. Clamps would not reach to hold the stringers in place and bolts and pins could not be placed.

The men used hacksaw blades to scrape the ice at critical points so the bridge could be assembled. It worked well, but it was slow. The bitter cold prevented the men from working more than short periods of time. When their hands became numb they were unable to hold either the hacksaw blades or any other tool. To keep the job going the engineers rotated into the platoon building to warm their hands enough for them to go back to work.

Shortly after construction started, Colonel Fraser arrived. The night was still dark and he wanted to know why he could hear so much scraping. He listened patiently to the explanation then said "get some torches to melt the ice." He felt it was taking too long to scrape it off. Scrappy was told about the 88-mm. shells landing in the village, and about the direct mortar hit on the centerline tape, but he brushed those concerns off. The bridge would not be ready for the 75th when needed.

The men broke out the blow torches and got to work. The first torch had been lit for about one minute when all hell broke loose. German artillery rounds began pouring in. At first the rounds landed well behind the bridge site. Then the Germans began walking them toward the bridge. As they exploded the men hit the ground and tried their best to disappear into holes in the ice and snow. When the shelling was over and all was quiet the men stood up and, without an order being issued, began scraping ice again with hacksaw blades. Miraculously, no one was injured from the shelling.

Construction continued slowly. As the stringers were placed on the lower chord of the panels, the men always rotated the stringer toward the near shore. This way every man knew which way to move the stringer. It also helped reduce the number of smashed fingers.

In the darkness Stiftinger saw that one man was trying to rotate the stringer in the wrong direction. Stiffy, known for his ability to chew out a man when he did something wrong, started in on the errant engineer and warmed the night with his tirade. Not until first light the next morning did Stiftinger learn that the man he had chastised was the battalion commander. During the night Scrappy had noticed that the stringer crew could use another hand, so he stepped in to help in order to speed the construction of the bridge. By first light it was also noticed that the back of Scrappy's field jacket had been torn to shreds by the shelling during the night. Fortunately not one piece of shrapnel touched his skin. Because of the cold, he wore a coat liner, a sweat shirt, a wool shirt, and a wool undershirt under his field jacket.

> **15 Jan.** - [Stoumont] 'Tis a beautiful morning, the sun is rising and the sky is clear ....The air force should be over in strength today. We had a nice ringside view of the proceedings yesterday. Didn't see a single one of our planes knocked down. The ack-ack was very dense in spots but our planes were either above or below it.

At 0800 hours the morning of *January 15*, the division launched the attack with a hail of small arms fire, mortar fire, and artillery. The bridge was ready. The first tank across started down the approach ramp on the far shore and took a direct hit from an 88 shell. The disabled tank effectively blocked the bridge from further use. The follow-on tanks veered to the left, forded the river, and continued the attack. After the assault wave had passed the tank was removed, permitting normal use of the bridge.

Bridge at **Grand Halleux**, Belgium. Built 15 January 1945. *Corps Files*

The platoon had spent five days in Grand-Halleux, built a bridge under adverse conditions, and had only one casualty -- Doucet.

On the day of the attack, Company B began construction of a 60-foot, class 40, double-single Bailey bridge south of Vielsalm on N28 at Salmchateau. The Germans, still on the far shore, harassed the construction crew with artillery, mortar, and small arms fire all during construction. Although there were no casualties, two vehicles were destroyed. The greatest hazard in building the bridge proved to be the weather. Parts coated with ice made assembly difficult and hazardous. But the construction crew worked steadily through the bitter cold and completed it the next morning [*January 16*].

Sherman [75th Division] rolls into **Salmchateau**. *National Archives - 16 January 1945*

Salmchateau: 78, B3

That same day, Company C built a 130-foot, class 40, double-double Bailey bridge at La Tour. Company A constructed another bridge, a class 40, 48-foot treadway, south of Trois Ponts on N28. At Vielsalm, Company B built a 50-foot, class 60 double-single Bailey bridge. A large number of booby traps and mines had to be removed at that location. The extreme cold, along with ice and snow, made conditions extremely difficult for the men.

For the most part the battalion continued its road maintenance, snow clearance, and mine sweeping throughout the rest of the month. Company A started construction of a culvert near Fosse at the class 10 bridge site on January 25 in order to be able to take down another bridge. They completed the culvert the next night.

> **17 Jan.** - [Stoumont] A division chief told the Col. yesterday that the 51st certainly was a fighting outfit. Our luck is still holding. One of the companies has not had a casualty yet. They were pinned down by artillery at least 4 hours - didn't have a man get scratched even though they lost a couple of trucks.

Vielsalm (20-27 January 1945)

> **20 Jan.** - Was in my first vehicle smash-up. Got a nice knot on my head when I tried to dive through the windshield with my helmet on ... also a bruised shin. The Battalion is building a better reputation every day but everyone is getting slightly tired. Every rest period has turned out to be more work than usual. This is the 7th month of work 7 days a week.

> **21 Jan.** - The situation is somewhat quieter, so much so that the hotel owner has returned to his premises. We gave him one room in the cellar with stove for 5 of them. He was happy to get that since he had been living in a cave during the German stay here. The Germans really tore up the place. They ransacked every drawer and threw all the furniture around.
>
> The Russians are really rolling along now. They should be in Berlin in a couple more weeks at the rate they are going now. If we could reach the Rhine in a month we would be lucky. We aren't doing too badly though. Those Krauts are catching plenty of hell every day. I'll be glad when we move out or the gun just behind the house does. Shells whistle overhead all night long and the gun blast rocks the building every time a round is fired. Lately we have not had any Jerry artillery to contend with. Dave ate with Anderson the other day and he said they were just as formal as possible and that they did not say a word to each other during the meal. We slap each other, fight, squabble, and talk like one big family most of the time.

> **22 Jan.** - I've got some men in this company with a lot of guts. One of my tractor operators was out clearing roads sometimes as far as 2 miles ahead of the infantry. A tank dozer was ahead of him for protection and one of the tanks was knocked out. In the afternoon he was by himself when the Jerries threw 88's at him and then the Jerries opened up with machine guns and rifles and he came back. He asked the infantry captain if he hadn't gone too far up the road and the captain told him that he was only 30 yards from the Jerries. The job had to be done so he is still clearing and living. I am trying my best to get armor plate for him but so far I have not succeeded. I think I told you about another one of my men manning a 37mm gun, loading and firing, and knocking out a Tiger Tank even though he had never fired a 37 before. There have been numerous incidents of bravery. The refugees are littering the roads. It is really a pitiful sight to see old women 50 or 60 plodding along with all their possessions on their backs, leading a cow or two. All are very old or very young, no in-betweens. And it is more tragic to watch them rummage through their destroyed homes.

> **23 Jan.** - One of the cooks just remarked that he had seen everything when a civilian walked into the

La Tour: 80   Vielsalm: 78, B3

mess hall, plopped his pack on the floor and sat at one of the tables waiting to be served. The mess hall was once the hotel barroom and dining room. It didn't take the civilian too long to realize his error.

26 Jan. - I wish you could see this orderly room. We've scorched the wall and are using a dresser for a table. Both windows and one door are boarded up. And in the middle of the floor are 35 chickens we are trying to thaw in time of supper.

On *January 27* the 1111th Group asked the battalion to provide close engineer support to the 504th and 508th Regiments, 82nd Airborne Division. That work included clearance of snow and maintenance of mountain trails and firebreaks used as supply routes in the division zone of advance. In performing this mission, the 51st worked side by side with the 307th Engineers.

The snow was so deep that the infantry could only advance behind dozers. Then men had difficulty finding the mines so the dozer operators plowed ahead, often running over mines and disabling their vehicles. For several days the battalion picked up a new dozer every day from the engineer depot. When a dozer was disabled it was reported to the ordnance people, who picked it up for repair when the snow melted. The dozers had been outfitted with armored cabs for protection of the operators. But the men soon learned that when an operator hit a mine he would be blown into the top and either killed or hurt. So they kept the top open. The operator would be blown out of the dozer and land in the snow with only minor injury.

From *January 29 to February 4*, 1945 the 82nd Airborne Division advanced much faster than the unit on its right flank, the 87th Infantry Division. This latter division formed the left flank of Patton's Third Army. The result was an unprotected gap of about 20 miles on First Army's southern flank. The 32nd Cavalry Reconnaissance Squadron had to cover that gap. The 1st Platoon, Company A provided engineering support. That support consisted of removing obstacles and mines so that the 32nd could move forward, make contact with the Germans, and keep that contact until the 87th Infantry Division could move up and close the gap.

82nd Airborne Division mine sweeping in advance of tank movement into **Herresbach**, Belgium. *National Archives - 28 January 1945*

While moving on a trail in a very dense part of the forest, a troop (company) of the 32nd ran into a roadblock defended by several German infantrymen and an antitank gun. The roadblock consisted of log posts and cribs filled with rock and dirt. The obstacle, along with about 10 inches of snow on the ground and dense woods on each side of the trail, effectively blocked any forward movement. Early in the afternoon the squadron commander decided to eliminate the roadblock with the forces at his disposal and not wait for the 87th to move up. He brought up two more troops and the attached platoon of the 51st.

His plan of attack was simple. One of the troops would move by foot through the forest and come in on the right flank of the roadblock. Another troop would do the same on the left flank. The third troop was to be in reserve. The engineer platoon was given the mission of leading the frontal attack, sweeping for mines as it advanced down the trail. In support of the engineer platoon, and ten feet to its rear, was an assault tank which was to fire on the roadblock as the attack progressed. The plan called for the two troops on the flanks to move into position close to the roadblock and report in by radio when in position. If radio contact could not be made, they were to fire a green flare to show they were in position. The engineers put two mine detector crews in front to sweep the trail, one squad in a column in the ditch on each side of the trail, and one squad in reserve behind the assault tank.

With about one hour of daylight left, and a heavy snow falling, the squadron commander, having received neither word nor signal from the two troops on the flanks, decided to launch the attack without them. With darkness closing in, the engineers clamorously opposed the order: they would be leading an exposed frontal assault with no apparent assistance or support from the flanks, and only the assault tank from the 32nd in the rear immediately behind them. This was a no-win situation for the engineers. But, on command from the squadron commander, they shut up and launched the attack.

As they moved down the trail, each man fired his M-1 rifle into the roadblock while the assault tank behind them fired its howitzer and machine guns as rapidly as possible, adding to the firepower directed on the obstacle. The assault tank personnel did not like being out there either.

The assault had advanced about 200 feet when, through the falling snow, several men could be seen standing in front of the roadblock waving their arms back and forth over their heads. The platoon leader gave the order to cease fire and the assault force moved rapidly forward to the roadblock.

St. Vith, Kunnelburg Woods (woods in next photo). Tanks of 7th Armored Division move to aid infantry attack on heights above St. Vith. *National Archives 25 January 1945*

To the complete and happy surprise of all, they found that the Germans had withdrawn and one of the cavalry flank troops had moved into the position. Poor marksmanship must have been the order of the day for no casualties were reported from the fiasco. Once the exposed flank was closed by the 87th, the 1st Platoon rejoined Company A on **February 4**.

During the first week of February, the battalion continued to work with the 82nd in the Ardennes. In that wooded sector northeast of St. Vith, Belgium, and north of the Luxembourg border, there were no paved roads and the task of opening up forest trails, firebreaks, and an unimproved dirt road to take the pounding of division traffic fell to the 51st. The battalion accomplished this task despite many difficulties. In numerous instances, dozer operators took their dozers ahead of the infantry to complete required tasks, leaving themselves open to enemy attack.

Road maintenance and clearance now became harder because of the warm thaw during the first week of February. The thaw, which followed January's unusually heavy freeze, rendered even good roads impassable in some instances. The paved highway from St. Vith to Schoenberg and Manderfeld, on which the 82nd Division had running rights, required concerted maintenance to keep it passable. Company B worked steadily on this road to keep it open the first two days of February. The work included the construction of a 24-inch concrete culvert on the road between Schoenberg and Andler.

On **February 5** the 51st built two culverts, one at Schoenberg, and one at St. Vith. The former was a 40-foot tile culvert with a creek bottom foundation and a two-foot water gap. The latter was a wooden box culvert. It replaced a masonry arch bridge that had been destroyed.

St. Vith, site of intense fighting during December & January. View to the SE, Kunnelburg Woods are at top of photo. *National Archives - 24 January 1945*

St. Vith: 6, B4   **Schoenberg**, **Andler**, and **Manderfeld**: B4

The Invasion of Germany ... BRIDGES TO VICTORY

Möderscheid, Belgium (B4). Icy roads cause a First Army traffic jam. *National Archives - 30 January 1945*

Mourmelon-le-Grand, France (F6). Far to the west of the snow-bound front, supplies pour in. Failure to reach the Rhine in 1944 was partly due to stretched 600-mile supply lines; a reason Germany was rapidly overrun in 1945 was the endless build-up of supplies later. German production at the end of 1944 was at record levels; but they couldn't maintain that or match American production. Only a few hundred of the feared Tiger tanks were built of Germany's 25,000 tanks; nearly 90,000 American tanks, mostly Shermans, went to war. *National Archives - 14 February 1945*

Roetgen, Germany, AA observation post 150ft above the surrounding forests. The Luftwaffe could still be a deadly nuisance but not much of a threat. *National Archives - 23 January 1945*

Brutal and Bitter: 9th Infantrymen, supported by the 51st, advance through the Hürtgen Forest near **Schmidt**, Germany. The 51st endured landscapes brutalized by warfare and winter conditions more bitter than any in 50 years. *National Archives - 3 February 1945*

Roetgen and **Schmidt**: 124   **Hürtgen Forest**: 6, 124

The Invasion of Germany ... BRIDGES TO VICTORY

Germany and the Roer (Rur) Crossing

Excerpts from letters from the "Rhineland Campaign" cover -- Supporting the 82nd, 75th, and 9th Divisions; Removing enemy minefields and booby traps; Sweeping roads for mines; Filling in quagmires and road craters with rubble; Maintaining supply roads; Patrolling supply routes to keep them clear of wreckage caused by bombing, Strafing and accidents; Building an airstrip and digging gun pits for the artillery; Repairing road shoulders and ditching; Practice bridging for the Roer River assault; Bridging the Kall and Roer Rivers; Constructing the 969-foot long pontoon bridge Across the Rhine under small arms, mortar, and artillery fire and air attacks; Smoking the Rhine to camouflage bridge building; Guarding bridges; Capturing German soldiers; Trucking prisoners from the Ruhr Pocket. Then the long move from First Army to Third Army in South Germany.

On February 4 rumors had the battalion making another move. The next day advance information from group indicated that sometime during the night of *February 6-7*, the battalion would leave for an assembly area northeast of Eupen, Belgium. At 1945 hours the battalion, less Company B, left Medendorf, Belgium, and headed to an assembly area west of Kornelimünster, Germany.

At the end of the Corps offensive in the Ardennes, the battalion, still attached to the XVIII Corps and in direct engineer support of the 82nd Airborne, moved with the Corps to the general sector just south of Aachen, Germany. The 51st made the movement under strict security. All shoulder patches and vehicle bumper markings were removed to conceal the identity of the unit, radio silence was imposed, and the movement took place under total blackout conditions. The battalion arrived in the assembly area the following morning at approximately 0400 hours and spent the rest of the day setting up security, and performing maintenance of individual and organizational equipment. Company B followed on February 9.

Schwammenauel Dam outlet.

National archives - 10 February 1945

The 51st would now be involved in the crossing of the Roer River. It was a difficult period of the war for the First Army. There were seven dams located on the Roer and the Allies feared that the Germans might destroy the Urft and Schwammenauel Dams, sending tons of water cascading down river and flooding the Roer valley. The Germans destroyed only the machinery and valves at the Urft Dam rather than the dam itself, resulting in a steady flow of water which created a long-lasting flood in the valley. It also raised the level of the river and prevented use of assault boats and floating footbridges for many days. When the current subsided sufficiently for the construction of footbridges and the use of assault boats,

Medendorf: B4   Kornelimünster: 124   Schwammenauel: 124, 132

ROER (RUR) CROSSING

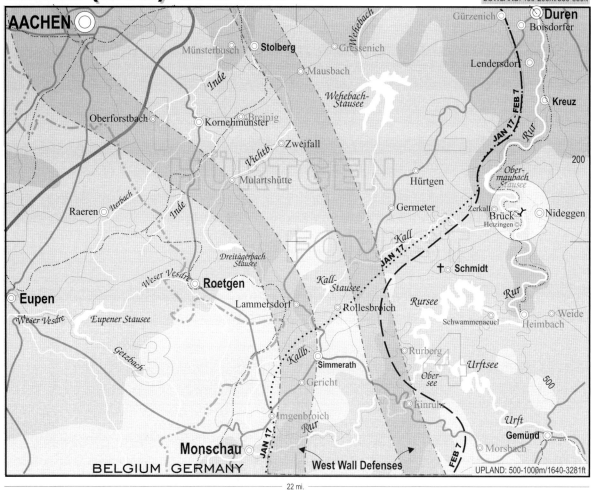

LOWLAND: 100-200m/330-660ft
UPLAND: 500-1000m/1640-3281ft

Scale = 1:220,000
[1cm=2.2km / 1in=3.47mi]

Major Roads (autobahn)
Lesser Roads
Railroads

Brown and Wotton killed (†)

RUR CROSSING
Locations & Dates of Arrival

- Ober Forstbach   7 February
- Langschoss*   15 February
- Rotgen   1 March

*not found on modern maps

Brück crossing. The area of Brück is circled. The Bailey Bridge completed February 28 is at the bottom of photo. German defenders fired down from these heights. Thus the bridge had to be built at night. The straight rail line goes on the left of Brück and over the river, in the distance. This view faces downstream (west).

Contours are transposed from *The Times Atlas of the World*, p. 64. Battle lines and location of the West Wall/Siegfried Line are transposed from the *17 January - 7 February* and the *8 February - 5 March* map sheets of the *West Point Atlas for the Second World War*. All other physical features are representations of recent data transposed from *Geocart Deutschland-Schweiz-Österreich Atlas*, p. 82.

crossing still proved to be hazardous.

With the 51st now just inside Germany, a doctor from the 82nd who was waiting to deliver a baby for a German farm woman came to Doc Maxson for help. Because his unit was moving out he wanted Doc to do the job. Doc agreed and sat with her all night. Finally, about 0900 hours the next morning, she delivered. In limited German, with some sign language tossed in, the father asked Doc his name for he had decided to name the child after Doc. When he found out his name he decided to name it Max if it was a boy and Maxine if a girl. It was a girl. He asked Doc what he could pay him for delivering his child, and together they decided on a bottle of the German's best schnapps. The German then took a pick out into the yard and came back later with a bottle of schnapps. He told Doc that if he had left his schnapps where the German soldiers could have gotten it, they would have drunk it all, so he buried his supply at various locations around the farm. Because it was quite cold, with the ground frozen hard, he had needed a pick to dig up the reward. Headquarters Company sent this account to the Stars and Stripes, stating that this was the first baby in Germany delivered by an American doctor since the war began. The paper subsequently printed Doc's news.

A recent thaw had made roads there almost impassable. The volume of troop and vehicle traffic had literally destroyed the roads. The 1111th ECG appointed the 51st Engineer Combat Battalion to make the roads in the Eupen-Roetgen-Kornelimünster area passable. In response, on **February 10**, Company C installed corduroy on the road between Raeren, Belgium, and Roetgen, Germany.

Ober Forstbach (7-14 February 1945)

> **10 Feb.** - After touring 35-40 miles of Germany I can now understand why these people are called "Krauts". There was a cabbage patch in every garden. German dwellings and factories remind me more of ours than anything I have seen in Belgium or France. As I rode I could better understand why we are having such a time with them. This American "blind superiority complex" is leaving my system. And I realize more and more why we are going to have to show them our best in character and temperament. Most of the German houses I see still have their walls intact, but I don't believe more than 1-5% are undamaged. The Russians are rough but I don't think we are acting like pikers. We should give them more St. Vith medicine. You can see across the whole town standing, on the ground. I believe that place was damaged more than St. Lo. From what I see I am sure most of the common German horde are just as Nazi as any Nazi party member. If looks could kill, a lot of us would be dead. I have to watch some of my men closely.
>
> The other day the first sergeant sent out "big" Indian Chief Bunny (who seldom says anything) after wood. In a few minutes the house sounded like it was falling in. In another few minutes, the Indian came in with the wood and made one remark, dryly, "These furniture made of mighty good wood." Every man in the company is itching for the day when he'll have to blast a house in to get some Jerries out, the first sergeant in particular. He is nursing a bazooka for that purpose.

When the battalion first crossed the Siegfried line and moved into Germany, Captain Pappy Radford of Headquarters Company, decided to organize a deer hunt for a change of menu. Doc Maxson volunteered to help. Radford suggested that Doc get a plain helmet because the red cross on his steel pot (helmet) might cause the deer to jump up and run before they got close enough to shoot them. Even with that wild story, Doc suspected nothing amiss. As the "hunting party" went down the hill to the west of the camp, they found several places where Germans had been sleeping. Doc was impressed with the caution that Pappy used in approaching these areas. All of a sudden, Doc realized that the mission of the hunting party was to secure the camp against retreating German soldiers, not to enhance the diet. Although, in the long run Doc felt the mission was a worthy one, he was angry because he was bamboozled.

On *February 11* at 1800 hours, Company B completed an 80-foot, class 40, double-single Bailey bridge over the Kall River north of Rollesbroich (124), Germany. The 51st had to clear the road of abatis, mines, and booby traps before their trucks could move to the bridge site. That same day the battalion got 425 infantry men from the 48th Armored Infantry Regiment to help with the road work. They were attached to Company A for work on February 12, and to Company C the following day. The men proved willing and cooperative. They accomplished a great amount of work with picks and shovels, clearing the choked ditches along the roads so that standing water could properly drain off.

In preparation for the crossing of the River, Company B began training on constructing assault bridging and foot bridging on a lake near Roetgen on *February 12*. Company A set up a similar program the next day on the Inde River near the autobahn. Both companies put up the triple-treadway expedient assault boat bridge. Although more difficult to construct than other bridges that could span the river, it was much sturdier and stronger. On *February 14* the 1111th loaned the light equipment platoon of the 501st Light pontoon Company to the 51st to assist in the crossing of the Roer River.

In addition to training for the river crossing the 51st continued to maintain the main supply route for the 82nd Airborne Division during the second half of February, when it moved into the Hürtgen Forest south of Zweifall [p.124]. The segment of the route from Lanschoss [not on modern maps] through Germeter [p.124] to Hürtgen was in terrible shape, and every company worked on it full strength for almost the entire two week period. Only constant work from dawn to dusk on the part of all officers and men kept this critical road passable.

During the Battle of the Forest*, the same ground changed hands many times. Both sides suffered terrible casualties. The forest itself, a place of densely planted stately evergreens, had been shattered by the artillery fire of months of close combat. Minefields and trip wires to booby traps were everywhere. Worst of all, these and the ground between the trees had been covered with the tops of trees which had been severed either by air bursts or, as

Out of the snow and into the mud: road maintenance and, of course, road use sometimes came under fire. Camouflage netting helped conceal operations here near **Germeter**, Germany (124). *Corps Files - February 1945*

---

* Given two lines in Eisenhower's military histories, this tragically forgotten battle involved 600,000 US troops over 6 months, cost 30,000 US casualties and 60,000 German dead at a minimum, yielded the largest US surrender ever (10,000 in one day), was of no strategic value, and never should have been fought (according to Gen. Gavin). The Bulge (about 1800 sq. mi.), had it been fought at the intense scale of the Hürtgen (50 sq. mi.), would have involved 21 million American troops with 1.1 million casualties.

some thought, by the use of the new U.S. proximity fuse. It was not really a forest that remained, it was a tangle of stalks where the stench of enemy dead made it even more grim.

Company C had to keep the only road through the forest open so that the infantry and field artillery holding the line on the west bank of the Roer could be supplied, and the buildup for the river crossing could continue. The trucks rolled by incessantly, but every day the bulldozers of Company C pulled increasing numbers of them out of the mire.

It seemed like a losing cause to the men. They had no suitable building materials. Every day the road became muddier as whatever foundation it had continued to sink into the mud. The unit was desperate for a solution. There was only one answer: Schmidt.

The town of Schmidt lay in the middle of the forest. It had already been demolished in earlier battles. The houses of Schmidt had been built of bricks and it was in their rubble that the unit found the answer to keeping that road open. By the time of the Roer crossing, often working under the firing of American artillery -- Milgram says his ears ring to this very day -- the men threw, bulldozed, and trucked just about every brick of the whole town of Schmidt into that quagmire of a road. But the 51st kept it open.

One time while loading rubble from a bombed out building for a road bed, the Chief of Staff of the 9th Infantry Division came out of the cellar hollering. "Hey, you guys are hauling away my CP," Colonel William C. Westmoreland, complained. He later became Chief of Staff of the United States Army. The 51st moved to another rubble pile.

> **13 Feb.** - [Ober Forstbach] The more I see of the new C.O.[Fraser] the more I admire him. He is a little impatient but I would rather have a leader impatient than inert. He is a real soldier in every sense of the word. He is never satisfied with anything. "It can always be better" is his motto. He drives himself a little too much at times. Yates is a good man to keep him tempered. The two of them function like the best oiled machine built. We still have a long hard fight ahead of us but I don't see how it can last into 1946... with the exception of the mud, this is the best setup we have had in a long time. All of the men can eat inside and we have a nice day room. The men write at least 150 letters a day now.

On the *15th*, while Company C was working its stretch of road, one of the men tripped a wire leading to a harmless looking Riegel Mine. It exploded, killing two Americans, Private Gerald C. Brown and Private First Class David L. Wotton, and wounding four, one seriously. The mine had been lying on the surface of the ground in front of a house in which American troops had been living for several days, but no one had bothered with it until then.

On *February 16*, a platoon from Company A constructed a footbridge and assault boat bridge (triple treadway) over the River at the request of Major General James M. Gavin, commanding general of the 82nd Airborne. He wanted his men to practice a real bridge crossing on available equipment before trying to cross the Roer River. The current on the narrow Kall, about six miles an hour, gave the engineers valuable experience in floating bridge construction.

They also gained more experience under fire as German mortar rounds exploded behind them on the training site. On one visit to the site, General Gavin told the engineers that the 82nd was going to cross the Roer even if he had to drive every division vehicle into the river and have his men crawl over the top of them.

During the period, the 307th Engineer Combat Battalion drew up detailed plans for crossing the Roer. The plans called for the 51st to construct footbridges, supply assault boats and the men to paddle them, and build Bailey bridges at specified sites. In anticipation of building a Bailey bridge which might require a "broken back," that is, a bridge not perfectly horizontal, the 51st had obtained parts of the Intermediate Floating Crib, Type A. These included male and female span junction posts, span junction links, span junction bearings, and junction chesses. Training on assembling this junction showed that the "broken-backed" bridge was thoroughly practical and could be used in any situation called for. One would soon be built.

While the 51st planned for the crossing of the Roer, it also completed other tasks. On **February 17** Company A installed an airstrip for the 408th Field Artillery near Schmidt. Company B dug gun pits for the field artillery in the vicinity of Germeter, Germany. Then, on **February 18**, the 51st began providing support to the 9th Infantry Division under III Corps. On **February 21**, a squad of Company C cleared and leveled a field for a 40 by 900-foot pierced steel plank airstrip for the 9th Infantry Division field artillery. It was completed at noon, the 24th.

Respite between snow and more mud and rivers.   *Corps Files - 17 February 1945*

Meanwhile, the crossing of the Roer, originally scheduled for the 16th, was postponed to the 19th, then to the 22nd. Each time the 51st was prepared to cross the river. On the 16th, the assault boats were hidden on the bluffs above the river. That night the men carted the boats down to the river and then struggled to get them back up and hidden before daybreak. On the third attempt, February 22, General Gavin called Fraser and Edwin A. Bedell, the 82nd Division Engineer, together and said: "We are going to get across tonight and if all others fail, Harvey, you and I and Bedell are going across on a log." The third attempt was also aborted. Gavin and Fraser surmised that the First Army plan called for the 1st Division to make the main crossing of the Roer north of the 82nd area, and meant our crossing to be a strong feint to keep the enemy from moving troops to oppose the main crossing. On February 17 the 9th Infantry Division relieved 82nd Airborne, and the 51st was attached to III Corps and placed in direct support of the 9th Division.

Although the general crossing plan did not change under the 9th Infantry Division, changes in the detailed plan did occur. The 9th's plan called for an M-2 steel treadway bridge on pneumatic floats to bridge the Roer. As a result, on February 21, one platoon of Company B began training with the treadway bridge on the Inde River. But once again the date for the crossing was postponed, this time to the 25th.

Germeter: 124

On the night of *February 24*, the 51st was again ready to bridge the Roer. Just southwest of Zerkall, 110 feet of triple-single Bailey bridge stood waiting on trucks. Near Schmidt the battalion had another 110 feet of triple-single Bailey ready to move to Roer-Hetzingen for construction. In an assembly area northeast of Schmidt, trucks loaded with 216 feet of treadway bridge and inflated pontoons were ready to move to a site south of Brück-Hetzingen. A 216-foot footbridge was in Zerkall ready for installation with an equal amount in a draw near Hetzingerhof. Early in the evening III Corps canceled the planned assault crossing. This was the fourth cancellation. At least the men of the 51st did not have to carry the assault boats down to the water this time. The battalion carried the assault boats throughout the entire war, but this was the closest they ever came to using them in action.

Kall R. at **Zerkall**. The 51st passed by here two weeks earlier on the way to the Roer bridge site. **Nideggen** would be on the ridge behind taller tree, about 1.7 miles distant.
National Archives - 9 March 1945

To take the place of the assault crossing, the corps staff planned a hook to the north using the 1st Infantry Division bridgehead. Once the 9th Infantry Division cleared the high ground east of Zerkall and Brück-Hetzingen, the battalion was to be ready to put in any or all of the proposed bridges. Part of the 9th would cross the Roer in the 1st Infantry Division area and attack south in an effort to clear the high ground opposite the 9th Division area.

Lanschoss (15-28 February 1945) *[not found on modern maps]*

> **26 Feb.** - Yesterday afternoon I attended church services in a German Protestant church. The church was simply designed with hard seats that had backs perpendicular to the floor (part of German discipline, I guess). They differed from ours in having pews arranged semicircularly instead of all frontally. We had a nice service and everyone enjoyed hearing a real organ for a change. Since the breakthrough we have not had any musical instruments -- the chaplain's portable organ was lost in the rush some place. Guess the service did me a lot of good because I could have chewed 60-d nails in two beforehand and afterwards only 10-d. I've just been irritable the last few days.
>
> It's a real problem staying out of the mud. I have to watch some of my men when they go after brick and rock for the roads. They are all too eager to blow a good house down - with Germans in it - to get the rubble. We have to maintain some control to show the Germans we practice what we preach. When the Belgians came in here as guards, they immediately started to work on these German people just like

the Germans did on them. That was halted quickly. What a world! It is going to take iron-willed leaders of firm convictions to keep this old planet peaceable.

On the morning of **February 27**, the rest of the 9th Division crossed the Roer River. Company B of the 51st built a 96-foot floating footbridge at Zerkall that afternoon in 30 minutes. Heavy anchors and float cables held the footbridge in place. The downstream end of each float was weighed down by a filled sandbag, elevating the upstream ends and counteracting a tendency for the bridge to overturn in the swift current. The engineers did not have any difficulty in keeping the bridge intact during the crossing of several infantry battalions.

Near **Zerkall:** Company B's footbridge over the Roer. Ninth Infantry crosses under cover of smoke and through a taped-off mine field.   *Corps Files - 27 February 1945*

Company B started a 120-foot class 40 double-single Bailey bridge nearby. Much preliminary work was required in constructing 3x12 foot cribbing to support the bearing plates on both approaches, because the road was only eleven feet wide. The bridge was supported by an intermediate concrete pier, making the 120-foot structure a class 40 double-single bridge. Approach work required the removal of a building so the bridge could be launched, and the widening of road curves in the town of Zerkall, so equipment could be moved on site. The bridge was completed early the next morning.

On the afternoon of the 27th, Capt. Sam Scheuber reconnoitered the site at Brück-Hetzingen for a Roer River bridge. Knowing that the river and the long approach were under enemy observation, Scheuber reluctantly followed orders. He selected First Lieutenant Richard I. Green to assist him. Green, just as reluctant as Scheuber, went with him. Along the way they passed a dug-in infantry unit. The infantry lieutenant tried to dissuade them from going beyond further. But Scheuber had been ordered to make the recon and that was that. With only the two of them crossing the observed area, they felt the Germans would not waste mortar or artillery fire on them. It turned out to be true. They were able to see the blown-out bridge, the middle pier, and the far shore among the shelled buildings from covered positions in the town some one hundred yards away. Scheuber's preliminary reconnaissance of the bridge at Brück-Hetzingen, where a single-span Bailey bridge was planned, called for a bridge whose curvature in a vertical plane might require a two-span, broken-backed Bailey bridge.

Later that night Scheuber and Green came back with dozers and bridging equipment. Company C started construction of the 110-foot double-single Brück-Hetzingen Bailey bridge under cover of darkness. The men constructed and maintained the bridge while under constant artillery and mortar fire and sporadic small arms and automatic weapons fire as well. The high ground opposite Brück-Hetzingen had not been cleared. Fraser and Yates were both at Brück-Hetzingen, and they knew it was hot. They had a radio man with them, and the mortar fire seemed to follow them wherever they went. Yates hollered at the operator to shut off the radio. About the same time, the radio man dove for the prone position and broke the radio, so it was quiet. Yates was sure that the Germans had somehow zeroed in on the radio. Company A provided security for the operation. During construction it turned out that Scheuber had two choices. He would either have to reduce the height of the center pier about one foot and build a heavier bridge, or he would have to reduce the length of the span by one half and get by with a double. Scheuber chose the latter. He used the center pier to support two spans each of which was only half the total length. Double capacity, half the work. What was wrong with that?

Scheuber went to work. The slight curvature of the existing bridge imparted a small angle from the horizontal to each span where the bridge was supported on the far shore intermediate pier. The near shore span was intact, the center span half demolished, and the far shore span completely demolished. To accommodate this small angle, the top panel pin of each of the four panels was extracted and the bridge was strengthened to take shear at the section by the addition of heavy wood uprights between top and bottom panel chords. The intermediate support of the bridge gave it a Class 40 classification, though it was 110 feet in length. They completed the bridge before dawn on the 28th [*February 28*].

Smoke pots conceal daytime crossings from Germans above near **Nideggen**.   *National Archives - 28 February 1945*

Between Roer (Rur) and Rhine

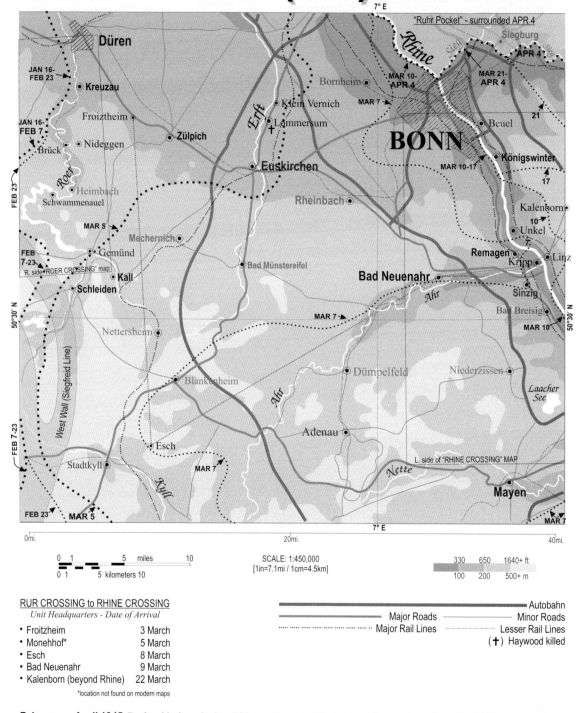

RUR CROSSING to RHINE CROSSING
Unit Headquarters - Date of Arrival

- Froitzheim — 3 March
- Monehhof* — 5 March
- Esch — 8 March
- Bad Neuenahr — 9 March
- Kalenborn (beyond Rhine) — 22 March

*location not found on modern maps

February - April 1945. During this time, the 51st ECB spearheaded critical parts of the front line, mainly in bridging the Roer (Rur) and Rhine Rivers. [Roer(Rur) and Rhine Crossing maps overlap this map.] Otherwise they followed in very close support to units of the FUSA (First US Army). The battlelines February 7, March 5 and April 4 show progress at roughly one month intervals. Dates noted (e.g., **JAN 16 - FEB 7**) show when FUSA forces reached a given point (**JAN 16**) and when further advance was started (**FEB 7**) to the next line.

Background map derived from *The Times Atlas of the World, Comprehensive Edition,* 1983, page 64. Invasion front lines are transposed from the *West Point Atlas for the Second World War: Europe and the Mediterranean,* 1953. Locations of HQ sites for the 51st are from *The 51st Again!*

The Invasion of Germany ... BRIDGES TO VICTORY

The next morning, after an infantry division and its artillery had crossed over the bridge, some staff officer from the 1111th Group came by and noticed one center pin was missing from the upper truss over the center pier. He reported the fact to the battalion commander and to Colonel Anderson. Anderson later chewed out Scheuber and Fraser for poor engineering. But, as Scheuber said, he was only a registered professional engineer in the state of Texas. And after all, a division did cross the bridge without any trouble.

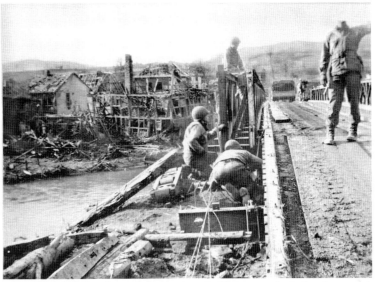

Officer losing his head over "poor engineering"? Apparently the head was accidentally "burned out" in developing the photo. *Corps Files - 28 February 1945*

On **March 1**, 1945, the battalion moved to its new command post at Roetgen, Germany, where it continued its missions of reconnaissance of roads and bridges and of maintenance. On **March 5** Company A constructed a 70-foot, class 40, double-single Bailey bridge across the Erft River in Klein Vernich, completing it at 1800 hours. The next day the battalion came under the control of the 1159th Engineer Combat Group, commanded by Colonel Kenneth E. Fields, but continued its missions of maintaining roads and building bridges in the area.

Froitzheim (3-4 March (1945)

4 Mar. - It has been go, go, and go for more than a week now. Guess I've traveled more than 500 miles during that time, been shot at, and lived through an 8-hour artillery barrage with one dud landing less than 10 feet away. I'm tired tonight and it is past 2300 so I think I'll retire on this concrete floor for the night. In one place a short time ago a few of us were pinned down by machine gun and rifle fire and while there I propped on one elbow and enjoyed watching our shells land on their position. After 30 minutes or so the wind changed and a smoke screen drifted down the valley and we got out. That same night I led an armored bulldozer into town behind a tank dozer. I was walking. A shell landed 50 feet behind the tank dozer, wounding two, and another landed about 50 feet in front of me - no ill effects. That was the beginning of the 8-hour barrage that did not touch our bridge. A little dirt and gravel was kicked on it occasionally but no one was seriously hurt.

At 0630 the next morning we decided to dash out of the place and tried to make it in between bursts. Just as we reached the jeep, so did a Jerry shell 20-30 feet away. Two of the men were showered with dirt and one man had a hole cut in his field jacket but no one hurt. The 51st's luck is still holding. Yates is the man with the charmed life though. He was standing 8-10 feet in front of a tractor when it struck a mine. His only trouble was a sore head as a result of his flying helmet landing back on his head. He picked 1-2" pieces of metal out of a tree next to him .... I heard shells whining for 2 days after that shelling. I never gave death a thought, but the next time I dived into a mudhole, yours truly did a little praying. In one of my dives for the ground, I picked myself out of a manure pile. We are rolling now and the 51st will keep them rolling. The men are combat veterans and are seemingly itching for more at

Roetgen: 124   Klein Vernich, Froitzheim: 132

present. After you've been beyond the front and around the front, you develop a sort of mania for excitement by continually returning. As I've said before, I'm not sticking my neck out any more than I have to. In this past week we've been in everything from pup tents in the snow to this concrete floor in this farmhouse.

The German managers are still here, but their Russian, Polish, Yugoslav, and French labor has taken off. One of the undernourished Frenchmen here who has been beaten rather badly by the SS believes that New York and Paris have been completely demolished. The German manager knew what the score was because we found very accurate situation maps on the walls. When I walked into this place the other day a German fräulein was preparing turkey for supper and when I ran the Germans out of the building they had slices of ham that would cover an ordinary plate. The women wear silk and nylon hosiery. These big shots had no fewer than 4 automobiles. The mistress of the house has no less than thousands of dollars worth of jewelry in the safe (we will not do any looting). One of these days I'll tell you the long, long story .... The infantry doesn't have to work nearly as hard as the combat engineers but they are exposed to more danger. Most infantry say they would not be engineers, and engineers say the same about the infantry. Our citation ribbons are in - Think we will have to have some kind of ceremony before we get them. Have not heard a buzz bomb in three weeks or more.

Company A built a 33-ft Armco steel culvert, 48 inches in diameter on **March 7** in Lommersum. It also assembled a 70-foot, double-single, Bailey bridge at the same location. On the same day the First Platoon, Company A, was clearing what was left of a log crib obstacle in the drainage ditch on the side of the road. The area had been swept and cleared of all metallic mines. However, the mine detector could not detect a wooden box mine buried in the ground. While digging with a pick-mattock, PFC Ray Haywood struck the mine and it exploded, sending mud and stones for fifty feet in all directions. Haywood was fatally wounded. PFCs Earlie Kennedy and Gordon G. Morgan were seriously wounded, but recovered.

Bad Neuenahr. About 8 miles from the Rhine, the 51st headquartered around here, organizing the bridging. [Shown is a cleanup of German panzerfausts by the 2nd ECB, 2nd Division, engineers]   *National Archives - 16 March 1945*

The next day the 51st was relieved of its direct support of the 9th Infantry Division and moved to Esch, Germany. The following day it moved to Neuenahr [Bad Neuenahr], Germany, in preparation for constructing a heavy pontoon bridge across the Rhine River. The Rhine, sometimes called the gateway to Germany, would be the most important river crossing to date for the battalion. The "51st Again" would soon provide one of the first two bridges to span the Rhine River barrier, allowing American troops to pour into Germany weeks earlier than planned.

Lommersum, Esch: 132   **Bad Neuenahr**: 132, 136

The Invasion of Germany ... BRIDGES TO VICTORY

Bombardment of **Schleiden**, Germany, 3.5 miles south of **Gemünd** (132). *National Archives - 14 March 1945*

As the 51st was bridging the Rhine, Patton's Third Army rapidly approached the Rhine and pushed south as well, crossing the Moselle here at **Karden**, Germany (148-1), where Germans have just shelled a pontoon bridge as a wounded soldier on a litter was being carried across. *National Archives - 14 March 1945*

RHINE CROSSING

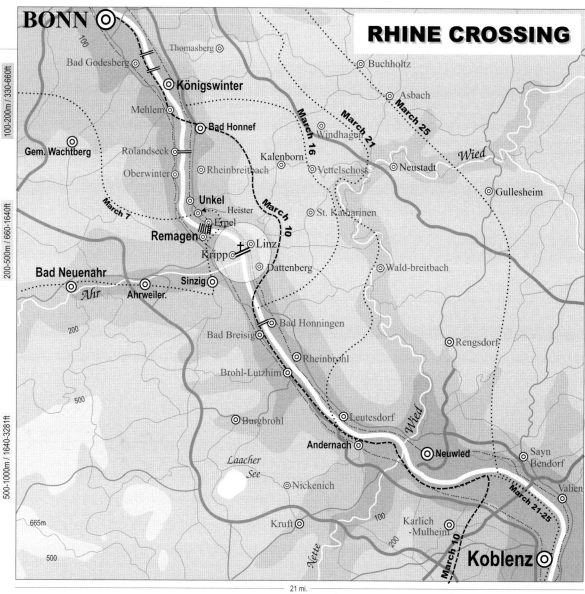

Scale = 1:220,000 [1cm=2.2km / 1in=3.47mi]

```
0       1       miles       5       6.2
0   1           5   kilometers      10
```

Major Roads (autobahn)
Lesser Roads
Railroads, major
Bridges — by the First Army Engineers.

The Ludendorf Railway Bridge ( ) was just north of bridge built by the 51st ( ), circled.

Blackburn, Conley, Mathis, Tillman killed (†)

RHINE CROSSING
Unit Locations - Dates of Arrival

Bad Neuenahr	9 March
Kalenborn	22 March
Gullesheim	27 March

Building site under fire. Engineers survey the possibilities, 10 March 1945. *Corps files.*

Contours are transposed from *The Times Atlas of the World*. Battle lines are transposed from the *6-10 March, 11-21 March* and *21-28 March* map sheets of the *West Point Atlas for the Second World War*. Bridge locations are from *The 51st Again!*. All other physical features are representations of recent data transposed from *Geocart Deutschland-Schweiz-Österreich Atlas*, pp. 83-84.

The Invasion of Germany … BRIDGES TO VICTORY

Bridging the Rhine and Germany and the Ruhr Pocket*

Introduction

"Following the failure of the German Winter Offensive, only the Rhine River stood between the Allies and the heart of Nazi Germany."

On the 7th of March 1945 the 27th Armored Infantry Battalion of the 9th Armored Division found the Ludendorff Railroad Bridge across the Rhine still standing.

The bridge was captured. The soldiers of the 27th were the first invaders since the Napoleonic Era to set foot on German soil east of the Rhine. The Ludendorff was the first bridge used by American troops for crossing the mighty river.

Detonated explosives had damaged the Ludendorff. Wires to other explosives were cut and the demolitions removed from the bridge and piers. Mines were cleared from the east bank. Engineer troops made hasty repairs and traffic was moving across the bridge by midnight of the 7th of March. On the 8th more explosives were removed, more repairs made. The Ludendorff was in danger of collapse.

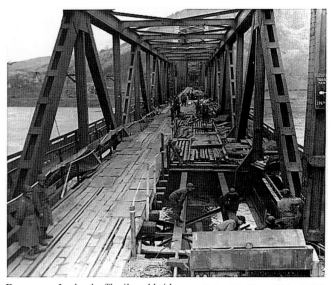

Remagen: Ludendorff railroad bridge.   *National Archives - 9 March 1945*

By 1100 on the 9th of March ferries built by the 86th Engineer Heavy pontoon Battalion and a platoon from the 299th Engineer Combat Battalion were transporting troops across the river.

By 0830 on the 10th of March construction of an M-2 steel treadway bridge was started by the 291st Engineer Combat Battalion and the 998th and the 988th Engineer Treadway Companies, just downstream from the Ludendorff at Remagen.

By 1630 on the same day, the 51st Engineer Combat Battalion and the 181st and 552nd Engineer Heavy pontoon Battalions were building a heavy pontoon bridge, just upstream from the Ludendorff at Kripp.

On the 11th of March the 1032 foot-long treadway bridge was open to traffic at 1700 and the 967 foot-long heavy pontoon bridge was ready at 2200 — in less than 30 hours construction time — for the movement of material and troops east into Germany.

The ferries and two bridges were built under artillery and small arms fire. The bridges survived several air attacks. A limited V-1 rocket assault on the bridges was launched from pads in Holland. Thirty-five casualties occurred at the treadway and six men killed and several wounded at the heavy pontoon sites.

---

* This section prepared by Barry W. Fowle. Quotes are from Chapter VIII of *The 51st Again!*, used with permission of Harvey Fraser.
Remagen: 136   **Kripp**: 132, 136

(Bridges built later in the First Army Area had no enemy interference.)

Upon completion of the bridges Colonel F. Russel Lyons, III Corps Engineer First Army said, "The importance of these bridges is the fact that they are the longest tactical bridges ever constructed and also the first tactical bridges ever built over what was considered to be a major obstacle to the progress of an American Army."

Major General John Milliken, Commanding General III Corps First Army, stated, "I feel that one of the most outstanding accomplishments of the entire operation was the building of the two bridges under artillery and small arms fire — even before we were able to clear the area of small arms fire, which was our first objective. They (the 51st and the 291st) also did a grand job of protecting the bridges and sweeping the river with search lights."

On the 17th of March 1945, the Ludendorff Railroad Bridge collapsed into the Rhine. With its capture and the rapid bridging of the river, the Americans had taken a giant step into the heart of Nazi Germany and opened a window of hope and light to war-weary Allies and Europeans — particularly with the surrender of thousands of Germans in the Ruhr Pocket.

"While Patton's forces in conjunction with our Seventh Army continued to mop up the trapped Germans in the Saar, his infantry forced a surprise crossing of the Rhine River on the 22nd of March, and established a second large bridgehead across the Rhine River. Now the Allies were along the entire length of the Rhine, and across it in two places.

Beginning late on the 23rd of March, Anglo-American forces under Montgomery forced a third crossing of the Rhine River north of the Ruhr Valley, with the aid of a huge airborne drop east of the River. A gigantic pincers around the Ruhr Valley developed from both sides as First and Ninth Army armor raced to meet at the eastern end of the valley, and on April 1 the enveloping forces made contact, pocketing the entire Ruhr industrial area, heart of Germany, and elements of eighteen German divisions." [Quotation is from **Dark December**, p. 208.]

Bridging the Rhine

General Dwight D. Eisenhower ordered General Omar Bradley to put at least five divisions onto the far bank Bradley had already begun exploiting the bridgehead. By the 9th of March an armored command held a lodgment some three miles deep. The 9th and 78th Infantry Divisions quickly supported the 9th Armored Division on the enlarged and strengthened bridgehead, rendering the elimination by the Germans almost impossible.

As a result of the decision to exploit the bridgehead, the engineers made an effort to restore the Ludendorff bridge. By daylight **March 8**, large quantities of heavy equipment were arriving on the west bank of the Rhine. Plans called for additional crossings so the Ludendorff Bridge could be closed for much needed repair. Those plans called for three heavy pontoon ferries, one M-2 steel treadway bridge, and one reinforced heavy pontoon bridge in the bridgehead area near the Ludendorff Bridge.

When Colonel Fraser heard that the Ludendorff Bridge had been captured, he called his friend, Colonel

Stann, and reminded him that the 51st was available to build a bridge across the Rhine. Stann said he thought there would be a job for the 51st, and there was.

Several engineer units were disengaged from their tasks and immediately sent to the proposed crossings. The corps engineer assigned the task of building a M-2 steel treadway bridge downstream from the Ludendorff Bridge to the 291st ECB with support from the 998th and the 988th Engineer Treadway Bridge Companies. It then assigned the 51st, supported by the 181st and 552nd Engineer Heavy pontoon Battalions, the task of building a heavy pontoon bridge across the Rhine at Kripp, upstream from the Ludendorff Bridge.

At 2200 hours, March 8, the 51st, some 40 miles west of Remagen at Esch and five miles south of Lammersdorf, was alerted for the new assignment and attached to the 1159th Engineer Combat Group. It was told, "You are to build a pontoon bridge across the Rhine from Kripp to Linz and are to move to the Kripp area tomorrow." None of the battalion officers had any idea of the tactical situation at that time.

Esch (8 March 1945)

> **8 Mar.** - At present I'm sitting in a school commandant's office writing on his felt-like blotter. We have the nicest houses and hotels in town for our quarters and offices. Most of the men have mattresses to sleep on. Not bad but it won't last long, maybe overnight. We are very much on the move these days and are fast making history if nothing else. That famous river should not be too much of a barrier, not nearly as much so as a lot of people think, now that we have a break. Wish I could tell you the whole story now.

The 552nd and 181st Heavy pontoon Battalions were attached to the 51st ECB and started moving from Zülpich. At 0600 hours, **March 9**, Fraser and his company commanders met with the 1159th Engineer Combat Group (ECG) Commander, Lieutenant Colonel Kenneth E. Fields, at Kripp about 1.5 miles south of Remagen. They looked around for bridge sites, taking into consideration the approaches and the available road net, and found an ideal site with good access to both shores. It also had a good road net to handle the traffic.

Fraser told Companies A and C to construct the pontoons and Company B to prepare the approaches. When the 51st reached the site, it discovered that the high hill across the river northeast of Dattenberg had not been cleared of Germans. They could actually be seen moving around on the hill. The Germans were also sending in a little sniper fire. Colonel Fraser tried to get artillery fire delivered on the Dattenberg area, but his request was refused because there were too many friendly troops in the vicinity.

As a result of the excellent enemy observation on the proposed bridge site, Fraser told Fields that it was not practical to build a bridge there until the German snipers across the river were eliminated. But III Corps directed that the bridge be built regardless, and that construction should begin at 1800 hours, on March 9. Accordingly, Second Lieutenant Hervie Middleton took a dozer and a platoon of Company B across the Ludendorff Bridge and up the river to prepare the far approach. They discovered that the Germans had retreated a few hundred yards to a hill overlooking the bridge site. The engineers were met by small arms fire when they started their task, but took no casualties.

During the afternoon the 51st learned that III Corps had ordered all work on the bridge to stop until further notice. Company B's platoon stopped its preparation of the approach and holed up in the basement of a

Lammersdorf: 124 Zülpich: 132 Dattenberg: 136 Linz: 132, 136, 148-1 warehouse in Linz where the men discovered a large supply of pink champagne.

That night, the platoon set up two .50-caliber machine guns for security at the bridge site on the east shore. After dark, a company of the 78th Infantry Division, supported by two tanks, made a reconnaissance across the river in an effort to clear out the Germans. They started to make good headway, but panzerfausts knocked out both tanks before they reached Dattenberg. Middleton's platoon covered the withdrawal of the American infantry. Captain Hodges suggested to Middleton he should consider retreating. Middleton was appalled. He did not want to "leave all this booze," so the platoon stayed in their warehouse. About midnight the Germans attacked the Company B platoon and Middleton was hit in the arms and hips by a burp gun. Four others in the platoon were wounded, but the German attack was repulsed.

Soon enemy small-arms and mortar fire intensified in the Kripp area driving the .50-caliber machine guns out of their position. By this time, Colonel Fraser demanded artillery fire. "It took two or three hours to get an FO (Forward Observer) up there," he said, "but the artillery laid in several effective barrages."

Bad Neuenahr (9-21 March 1945)

> **10 Mar.** - Everyone is tired of this whole mess, but they are driving and driving onward. This scrapping is more tiring mentally than it is physically. All the men are putting everything they have into the effort .... We are ready to move all 24 hours of the day and during the last two weeks we have moved at least 7 times. In one place recently we were set up at 1800 and at 0515 the next morning we were gone. Think I've had about 3 days in the last 3 weeks for administration at the company during the day. If I had paid all my men personally last pay day, I would have traveled 300 miles in Germany.

On the next day, **March 10**, a task force of the 9th Armored Division pushed down and took Dattenberg. At that time Middleton was evacuated by ambulance. On his way to the hospital he had the ambulance stop at the Company B CP so he could pick up his monthly Class VI ration (a fifth of scotch and a fifth of gin). His part in the war was over, but he fully recovered from his wounds. The platoon sergeant, S/Sgt. Russell E. Watson, took over Middleton's command on the far shore.

Around noon and after on March 10, the men of the 51st ECB would see elements of the 9th Armored Division entering Dattenberg. "We got into a huddle and decided we should get going," said Colonel Fraser. However III Corps had not given the go ahead so Fraser headed for the 1159th ECG headquarters and there found that corps had just ordered the 51st and the pontoon battalions to move to Unkel several miles downstream where the tactical situation was allegedly better suited to building a bridge. Fraser was not happy with this decision. It meant moving 60 heavy pontoon trailers and 50 vehicles through the bumper-to-bumper traffic jam that had formed in an effort to cross the Ludendorff Bridge. In addition the 51st had already staked out the site and had accomplished a considerable amount of approach work at Kripp and Linz.

In light of this new situation Fraser sent a reconnaissance party up to Unkel to survey the proposed site. In the meantime he received Fields' permission to see the corps engineer. He set out for Colonel Lyons' CP near the Ludendorff Bridge. He knew it would be impossible to go by vehicle because of the heavy traffic, so he went on foot. Fraser found Lyons at the 291st ECB treadway bridge site and told him the far shore had been reasonably cleared of Germans and that for obvious reasons, including the heavy traffic problem, they did not want to move. The corps engineer did not know that Dattenberg had been cleared, thus making the Kripp site feasible. When he heard Fraser's plea, Lyons said, "Harvey, if you think you can build the bridge there go ahead." Fraser started back along the river on the dead run but the artillery fire was so intense that he had to "hole-up" several times. It took him an hour to go about a mile and one half despite the fact that he was a fine runner and had lettered in track and cross country at West Point. When he finally arrived at the Kripp site around 1600 hours he said to Major Yates, "let's get going." Yates had everything well organized and was champing at the bit. With approval granted, the men aggressively started work from both shores.

The decision by Fraser to hold to the Kripp to Linz area was significant to the success of the Remagen bridgehead operations. A move to the new site through the traffic jam could have delayed completion of his bridge by two or three days. It might not have been available when the Ludendorff Bridge fell in the Rhine.

Yates was already covering the area with smoke pots. He told Fraser that the S-4, Captain Coats, had "two and one-half tons of smoke pots on a 3/4-ton truck." The wind was perfect for laying smoke and six pots were kept smoking steadily during daylight hours while the bridge was being built. When Company B lit their smoke pots, they received considerable mortar fire in the area, but there were no casualties. The net effect of the smoke, according to Major Yates, was very good.

Enemy bomb burst in **Linz** near final bridge site. *Corps Files - 10 March 1945*

In building the bridge, the abutment was put in first, then the trestle or cross beam approaches. Because of the shallow water on the west side of the river, five trestles were put in on that side and two on the east side or far bank. These trestles were placed fifteen feet apart. Their placement delayed the completion of the bridge for about three hours.

Just as work on the bridge began, six rounds of enemy heavy artillery fire came in. Two landed on the far shore, but three landed on the center line of the bridge site, indicating that the enemy was zeroing in. The possibility of the artillery coming in kept everyone on edge after the first six rounds. The men thought that the enemy might wait until the bridge had been completed, and then open up. Major Yates felt that they had it, but soon friendly forces forced the enemy gun to withdraw.

The speed of the current was also a problem. At the point of construction the current was extremely swift because the Ahr River entered the Rhine just above the bridge site, and because of a bend in the river. Fraser estimated the speed at 10 feet per second, the maximum speed for pontoon anchors to hold.

In spite of those problems, construction progressed rapidly until about 1700 hours when enemy planes began to come over in pairs. The planes did little damage around the heavy pontoon site. They appeared more interested in the Ludendorff Bridge a mile down river.

Interestingly, early in the evening of March 10, civilians in the Kripp area started moving out of town. When questioned they said that the German underground had informed them that Kripp would be leveled that night. That was not encouraging news for the bridge builders. Colonel Fraser contacted the town burgomaster and threatened dire consequences if the exodus did not stop. It stopped!

The bridge was built in parts, with four groups working simultaneously on four-boat rafts, most of which were put together after dark by feel. The parts were together by 0400 hours the next morning. The bridge consisted of 14 four-boat rafts, and 75 feet of trestle. When the rafts were in place, they were reinforced with pneumatic floats between the pontoon boats so the bridge would take the weight of 36-ton Sherman tanks. A total of 60 pontoons and 57 pneumatic rubber floats were used.

As the bridge parts were maneuvered into position with power boats, the river rose and the current became stronger. Maneuvering single-screw power boats was hazardous. If a boat turned crosswise in the stream it would swamp and sink in seconds, even before the engineers could grab their rifles. Although the men were careful, one of these power boats did turn crosswise and sink. Another developed motor trouble. This stymied the operation until additional boats were obtained from one of the neighboring treadway bridge companies that was trying unsuccessfully to operate a ferry. Depot stocks for power boats were exhausted because many had been swamped on the Roer River.

The 51st discovered that the Navy had some landing craft vehicle and personnel (LCVPs) in the area, and called for their assistance. At 1300 hours 10 LCVPs arrived from LCVP Unit No. 1, U.S. Navy, and saved the day for the 51st ECB. By this time, approximately 700 feet of bridge had been constructed on the near side and 200 feet on the far side. Suddenly the anchors began pulling up. The battalion solved that problem by using triple anchors. Shortly thereafter one of the LCVPs on the upstream side of the bridge turned crosswise in the current and was swept down river where it slammed into the 200-foot section of the bridge on the far side of the river. It either broke or pulled up all the anchors, breaking a section loose from the far shore and starting it floating down the river.

Several LCVPs took off downstream after the 200 foot section. They caught up to it, stopped it, and pushed it back upstream

The three LCVPs to the rescue. *Collection of Joseph Milgram - 10 March 1945*

where it was anchored in place again. During that operation the far end of the 700-foot section bent precariously but three other LCVPs moved downstream of the bridge and held it in place until the engineers could strengthen the anchors. The successful maneuvering of the LCVPs kept the bridge from being swept downstream and taking out the treadway bridge under construction by the 291st ECB just below the railroad bridge.

Up to that point, experienced men from the heavy pontoon battalions had been advising the men of the 51st on the technical details. That relationship had led to some confusion as to who was in charge of which projects. Colonel Fraser ordered Major Yates to take full charge of connections, anchors, and the lead section. Fraser, who had overall charge of the construction, took direct control of the abutments on both shores. Now Fraser and Yates were in charge of all aspects of construction, making it easier to construct the bridge now that there were fewer bosses giving orders.

Yates hit on the idea that it would be expedient to anchor the bridge onto a barge tied to the shore on the east bank. They installed more triple anchors, and used ropes to pull the 200-foot section back into place. Construction of the bridge then continued.

After discussions, construction speeds to completion. *Corps Files - 11 March 1945*

Finally, at 1900 hours on **March 11**, 27 hours after starting construction, the 51st completed the 969-foot heavy pontoon bridge except for putting on a few frills like luminous buttons, tread planking, and of course, straightening. The bridge was cleared for Class 12 or lighter loads when completed. Later, with improved rigging and anchorage, it took a Class 24 maximum load. The swiftness of the current would allow none greater. Traffic started at 2300 hours with 1 vehicle crossing every 2 minutes for 7 days. The total traffic during that week amounted to 2,500 vehicles including tanks.

The First Army Engineer, Colonel William C. Carter, arrived during the early morning of **March 12**, and saw immediately that there was trouble with the anchors. Fraser told him that they needed 1,200 feet of one-inch cable. Carter, driving his own pick-up truck, left, and in an hour returned with the cable. The battalion pulled it across the river, anchored it at both ends, and hooked the bridge anchor lines to the cable. The result was a perfectly straight bridge. Carter never revealed where he got the cable.

With the bridge completed, the 51st moved to Bad Neuenhauer for much needed rest and recovery. The 552nd Heavy pontoon Battalion had the task of providing maintenance and security on the bridge and Company C of the 51st was attached to provide security guards on each end. Artillery fire and aerial bombing continued after the bridge had been completed. On March 12 a round hit the bridge, knocking out five pontoons, and puncturing three rubber pneumatic boats. These were yanked out, patched and replaced, by Company C, with the help of the 552nd. Later, one of the booms upstream broke loose and cracked into the bridge, puncturing two pneumatic pontoons. The 552nd got a crane and lifted the boom out. The only delay was a traffic stall for about two hours.

> **12 Mar.** - [Bad Neuenahr] There goes that confound gun again. We have a 240 mm howitzer behind the house that rocks it from one end to the other when it is fired. Artillery doesn't bother me but that heavy gun woke me up several times last night. There are more guns around us than in any one spot that we've been in before - even including Normandy ... this is an SS trooper stronghold. These people had the best and they would quickly cut our throats if they had the opportunity .... Being chased out of their homes is bitter medicine for them to take. They can't understand why the Americans put 5 or 6 families in one cellar while 10 G.I.'s occupy the whole house ... the Americans did take all of the alcohol, cigars, and pickles in town. They also took possession of all SS material for souvenirs. I've got a batch of junk to send home one of these days.
>
> **13 Mar.** - We still have a long drive ahead of us to reach Berlin. The army is soberly optimistic now. We gave them quite a licking between the Roer and the Rhine but they did not lose much equipment. This is the first time the battalion has had a rest period since we landed. Everyone except H & S is getting at least 24 hours rest. Our work will continue daily 'til we are disbanded.
>
> I'm definitely not in a good humor at present. We were supposed to have a show tonight, but so far it hasn't started. Group wouldn't let us have the projector without the operator and the operator kept 100 or more men waiting 30 minutes while he learns to run the machine. One of our operators has the machine running now I think. And to top it off, they brought the wrong film, one everyone had seen twice before .... I would like to know what our special service is good for. This group has been here exactly one month and it looks like they brought the dregs with them. I'm sure we were not that green when we started this mess. It is 9 o'clock now so I think I will go to bed.

During the Rhine River operation, several men were wounded and six were killed. Those killed were: Major William F. Tompkins, Commanding Officer, 552d Heavy pontoon Bridge Battalion; Private First Class George A. Rozich, 181st Heavy pontoon Bridge Battalion; and Private First Class Cecil C. Blackburn, Company C, 51st Engineer Combat Battalion. When the Germans dropped a 500 pound bomb on a barge which Yates had used as an anchor, three men from Company B, 51st ECB were killed: Sergeant L. D. Conley, and Privates First Class Raleigh Tillman and

Taking over the "Watch on the Rhine" - remembering those who gave their lives to build this famous bridge. [Pfc. Elder D. Cannon, Co. A] *Corps Files*

Edgar L. Mathis. Eight or nine additional air attacks followed within twenty minutes. When the barge sank with the anchor ropes still intact, Yates rightfully noted, "A sunken barge is a better anchor than a floating one."

When the bridge was finished Major General John Milliken, CG, III Corps was proud of his engineers. "I feel," he said, "referring to the bridges just completed by the 51st and 291st ECBs, "that one of the most outstanding accomplishments of the entire operation was the building of the two additional bridges under artillery and small arms fire. They [the engineers] started building even before we were able to clear the area of small arms fire which was our first objective. They also did a grand job of protecting the bridges and sweeping the river with search lights." Colonel F. Russel Lyons, III Corps Engineer said, "The importance of these bridges is the fact that they are the longest tactical bridges ever constructed; and also the first tactical bridges ever built over what we have always considered to be a major obstacle to the progress of an American Army."

View of the great Rhine barrier, spanned in 36 hours. *National Archives - March 1945*

When the battalion first moved into the Remagen area, Doc Maxson was in England. Scrappy Fraser had given him a week's leave. On his return he found the aid station in a two-story house on the main street leading down to the pontoon bridge. It was there that he heard his first jet airplane. The noise it made as it flew over was "horrible." Doc was just going out to the bridge to conduct a routine health inspection on a platoon working on the bridge when a German jet came down the river and dropped a bomb. It sailed over the heads of the platoon, exploding downstream about a mile. Obviously

Heavy traffic moving eastward deeper into Germany. *Corps Files - March 1945*

the pilot was short on jet experience, but Doc did not want to give him a second chance. He decided that it was not necessary to go out on the bridge under the circumstances. He penciled in his report, stating that the platoon was okay. It had passed what was commonly called the "graphite" test.

During the building of the bridge, the Germans fired several V-1 rockets at the site from launchers in Holland. That was the only time that the V-1s were ever fired at German soil. On *March 14*, the men of the 51st crossed their own bridge and moved deeper into Germany.

> **15 Mar.** - [Bad Neuenahr] Hope you read today's and tomorrow's columns by Hal Boyle in Associated Press Papers. The old 51st should be sticking out like a sore thumb. I'll send you a copy of the "Stars & Stripes". Guess you are wondering why you don't receive all the S&S's. Due to our rapid movement we are not receiving more than 3 or 4 papers a week.
>
> I read an article about a year ago describing how a man eventually becomes a combat man and overcomes his homesickness as time marches on. That bird didn't know what he was talking about. The number one topic with all the men is home sweet home ...
>
> **16 Mar.** - I hope our story reaches you today. The "51st Again" signs are pretty well known throughout the army now. Today we are dedicating our work to the men who died accomplishing it. Our casualties are climbing but we still have been miraculously lucky .... A short while back we had a nice mess hall in a railroad station with seats for everyone. Everyone was seated comfortably with a mess kit full of spaghetti when a couple of Jerry jets came over strafing and bombing. Those gadgets come in about 500 miles an hour but the spaghetti flew faster when those men heard the machine guns rattle. It was "deadly" funny to watch mass hysteria and the urge for living grip those men. In less than 30 seconds everyone had returned but a quartermaster almost broke his neck sliding on spaghetti when he entered the mess hall. The new men dive for cover every time anything starts shooting. The old combat wise(?) run outside to watch the show. Curiosity gets a lot of people in trouble .... My Roer river experience dampened my curiosity considerably.
>
> **18 Mar.** - The radio just announced the collapse of the Remagen Bridge. I hope we can have everything cleaned out this side of the Rhine very shortly.

Germany and the Ruhr Pocket

Once the bridge over the Rhine was completed, the battalion improved and maintained the approaches to the bridge and guarded the anchorage barges from enemy attempts at destruction. Company A took over the operation of the ferries at site Number 2. Those members of the battalion not directly involved in the operation and repair of roads, bridges, and ferries, turned to the care and maintenance of their individual and organizational equipment.

On *March 21*, 1945, III Corps returned the 51st to the 1111th Engineer Combat Group from the 1159th Group. The 51st then resumed direct support of the 9th Infantry Division on the east side of the Rhine. While the battalion prepared to move, the companies reconnoitered the road network in the new area. On *March 22*, the battalion moved by convoy to the vicinity of Kalenborn, Germany, where it established a new CP. The companies began work on repairing and maintaining the roads in the area, and sweeping the roads and shoulders 20 feet on each side for mines.

The next day the 1111th ECG told the 51st ECB to build a bridge over the Wied River. The battalion S-3 assigned Company B the job of building the bridge, and tasked Company C with repairing the road leading up to the site. Work started on the bridge at 1315 hours, and at 1830 hours Company B completed construction of the 110-foot, class 40, triple-single Bailey bridge.

Kalenborn (22-26 March 1945)

25 Mar. - The artillery shells are roaring overhead like young freight trains, or "sumpin". As long as they continue roaring eastward everything will be o.k. A Jerry plane just came over for us to test our ack-ack guns on. The moon is nearly full and the sky is clear ....You have some interesting questions on recent developments. I thought our story would have been released by now but army censors will not release it. It was the biggest event in the outfit's history. The story should be out one of these days, possibly in the Winston-Salem papers. I'd better get quiet before the censor reads this letter.

I didn't know there was any soap shortage in the states. The GI's here would appreciate it very much if their loved ones at home kept the soap for their personal use. We get plenty in our weekly rations, can't give the stuff away now .... At present we are enjoying life in pup tents on the side of a volcanic peak in oak-beech woods. I think everyone feels better out in the open.

Alloy plant, warehouse and yard seized by First Army at **Kalenborn**, Germany.
National Archives - 18 March 1945

(Later) Our story was released by AP on March 12th ... there have been very few dull moments since the Germans snapped us out of our lethargy in Marche. We've been close enough to the front lines all the time to keep things interesting. A few hours back the Germans sent over some air bursts while men were eating dinner. They sat at the table very much unconcerned. Some turned around to see what was going on. Across the road the infantry dived for foxholes like scared rats. I finally had to disperse my men.

Three days later, on ***March 25***, 1945, Company C began and completed three Bailey bridges within a 24-hour period. Approach work for a bridge near Neustadt, Germany, began at 0500 hours, and actual construction for the 50-foot, class 60 bridge at 0800 hours. Company C completed the first bridge, a double-single Bailey bridge, at 1100 hours. Approach work started for another bridge shortly before 1100 hours. Company C completed this second bridge, a 110- foot class 40, triple-single Bailey bridge at 1745 hours. It began construction on a third bridge, a 50-foot, class 60, double-single bridge, at 1715 hours, completing it in less than three hours.

The 51st ECB moved to a new CP in Gullesheim, Germany, on ***March 27***, and continued repairing and

Neustadt (on the Wied): 136   **Kalenborn**: 132, 136, 138 **Gullesheim**: 136, 148-1

GERMANY: From Rhine to Ruhr to Munich

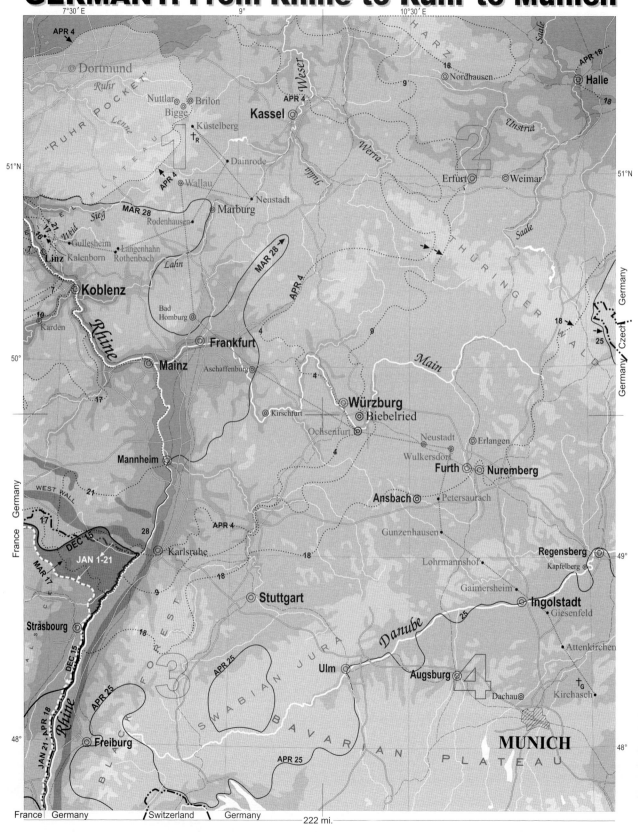

The Invasion of Germany ... BRIDGES TO VICTORY

maintaining roads and guarding bridges. In addition to sweeping for mines, the battalion removed destroyed vehicles and road blocks from the roadways and filled in craters. The next day, the 1111th ECG attached the 998th Treadway Bridge Company to the battalion to remove a treadway bridge. Work began at 0830 hours and ended at 1600 hours. On the 29th, the battalion established a new CP in Langenhahn, Germany, and on the last day of the month moved on to Rodenhausen, Germany.

Neustadt Bailey Bridge assembly on the Weid River. In retreat, the Germans had blown their own massive autobahn bridge. *Collection of Joseph Milgram - 25 March 1945*

Gullesheim (27 March 1945)

27 Mar. - I wish you were with me to enjoy this beautiful country. From some of these peaks you can see 25-30 miles. No wonder the Germans gave us so much trouble at certain points - they could see everything we did on clear days. And as I go farther into Germany, I am amazed at the German's wanton destruction of their own property. If someone doesn't overthrow Hitler pretty soon, Germany will have to rise completely from the ashes. He (Hitler) is systematically seeing to it that all of Germany is ruined before he lets a single high-ranking Nazi die. Of course "Hitler" is used figuratively speaking. They asked for it and we are giving it to them. The town we are in at present is intact with most of the female and kid population still present. Some of the children actually look undernourished but none of the old people do. The children try to

GERMANY: from Rhine to Ruhr to Munich

Scale = 1:2,200,000 1cm=22km 1in=34.7mi

Rail Lines — Autobahn (modern) — Major Roads (modern)
George ($\dagger_G$) / Rich ($\dagger_R$) - where killed

51st ECB LOCATIONS: RHINE TO RHUR TO MUNICH
Locations & Dates of Arrival

• Kalenborn	22 March	• Dainrode	4 April	• Lohrmannshof	26 April
• Gullesheim	27 March	• Kustelberg	7 April	• Gaimersheim	27 April
• Rothenbach(-er Lay)	28 March	• Neustadt	19 April	• Geisenfeld	29 April
• Rodenhausen	31 March	• Petersaurach	21 April	• Attenkirchen	30 April
		• Gunzenhausen	25 April	• Kirchasch	3 May

Background map is derived from *The Times Atlas of the World*, page 62. Invasion front lines are transposed from the *West Point Atlas for the Second World War: Europe and the Mediterranean*. Data for HQ sites for the 51st are from *The 51st Again!*

Langenhahn, Rodenhausen: 148-1   **Neustadt** (on Wied R.): 136 - Note: of over 50 German Neustadt's, three are shown in this book.

barter eggs for "K" rations and candy just like the Belgians and French. We've run several families out of their homes so we could move in; a few were balky. Some of the women went out weeping and wailing. A few of our men reminded them of a few other villages in Germany, France, and Belgium.

'Tis a rough war; this is the easiest part of it for us ... we are getting prisoners by the truck load. Very few letters have been written by anyone. I didn't have time to shave yesterday ... The farther into Germany the more beautiful the country becomes. The land and forests are beautifully kept. I actually believe this country is prettier than England. Most of the rock formations are igneous and irregular. Reminds me of the Brushies in the spring.

Rothen-bacher Lay (28-30 March 1945)

29 Mar. - That citation will be a Presidential one when it comes out in a War Department order soon. About 20 hours after we started that bridge we had only one more raft to put in to complete the structure. While that last raft was being towed into place, a boat got loose, cut the anchor cables and 400 feet of bridge started down the stream. It took 11 hours to get it back in place. That was the brightest spot in battalion history and when the bridge was started some of our machine gunners were still picking Germans off the other bank .... As usual our luck was with us but we had a few men killed, crossing the Rhine. Once when I was in the middle of the bridge, I asked myself, "What in the thunderation are you doing on this bridge? It's bad enough being strafed and bombed but look at this water 27 feet deep flowing 6 miles an hour and you can't swim a lick and you've got a sweet wife and baby." I didn't loiter long.

From *April 1-4* the battalion worked on the III Corps main supply route (MSR) "D" from Burg to Marburg. The condition of the road was excellent, but because of usually heavy traffic, the 51st had to continuously repair the shoulders and drainage ditches. The battalion also maintained a 24-hour patrol along the road to keep it clear of wreckage caused by bombing and strafing and by accidents. The road and an area 20 feet on each side was swept for mines and signs posted indicating the mine-free areas. In maintaining the road, the battalion used 190 cubic yards of crushed rock, 4,650 gallons of gasoline, and 125 gallons of motor oil. Six hundred dump-truck hours were expended during the four-day period.

Rodenhausen Lay (31 March - 3 April 1945)

1 Apr. - A typical Easter Sunday, cloudy, rainy, and cool. The chaplain held services here for the largest group he has ever had from the battalion ... I had to be 30 miles away at the time. The Colonel let the men off work for 2 hours to attend services. Even Major Yates attended ... H & S doesn't build bridges but some of the men are supervising the work, hauling materials to the site, drawing plans, or doing something in connection with the bridge. My job does not ordinarily call for my being anywhere near a bridge site but so far I have managed to get to and into trouble at all of our major crossings. Over the Roer I was the first one in the battalion on the middle of the Roer before operations. That was a foolish situation to be in but there I was. You'll get the whole story later.

I had an interesting experience yesterday. Here goes - Two of my men rambled down the road and zingo they ran into 9 Germans. After a little shooting match my men reported to me in the area. I sent one squad, led by the first sergeant, north along the trail they were taking and I led another detail east to outflank them. While we were moving through the thick brush I lost my whole detail. I rambled on by myself and finally contacted the first sergeant's crew. They were tracking the Germans so I sent them on their way and told the first sergeant I was going to a clearing to gather my straying men and then cut

Rothen-bacher Lay [Rothenbach]: 148-1   **Marburg**: F3, 148-1   **Burg** - not on modern maps

The Invasion of Germany ... BRIDGES TO VICTORY

across country to cut the Jerries off ....

I cut through the brush and bingo I see a big gray blur. I yelled "Hande Hoch!" and the big gray stirred but not fast enough to suit me, so I yelled "Hande Hoch!" again. The Jerries finally got to their feet with their hands up and I told them in German where I wanted them. Apparently the officer didn't understand me or he intentionally tried to run over me. Anyhow after jamming the muzzle of my carbine in his stomach I got the whole crew headed toward the clearing. I knew I couldn't disarm and guard the 9 of them at the same time so I yelled for the first sergeant. Luckily his whole squad heard me and arrived very soon, much to my relief. In the disarming process we got 2 Lugers, 2 P38's, 1 Mauser pistol, and 2 rifles. And none of those birds had discarded their weapons when I lined them up.

51st ECB Bailey Bridge at **Nuttlar**, Germany.   *National Archives - 9 April 1945*

Needless to say your imp was in a rather warm sweat for awhile because he knew he might be able to kill three or four of them but they would eventually get little me. Two officers, and one NCO were in the bag and needless to say I in all probability would have been a dead duck, if those Jerries hadn't seen or heard the first sergeant's squad go by. Well, I have a nice Luger now and a little gift for you. I took my pick of the pistols and passed out the remainder of the captured equipment among the first sergeant's squad. Fear never entered my brain but in the future I'll have another man go with me wherever I go. That's been SOP in the army but I got a little careless. We have been capturing quite a few Germans lately but all have been out on the roads with their hands up.

3 Apr. - Yesterday the first sergeant and first cook went fishing with a pound and a half of TNT. They returned with approximately 150 fish ranging in size from 1/4 lb. to 3 lbs. Company headquarters had a nice little fish fry last night. 'Twas the first fresh fish we have had in a year or more. If we could get the lard, we could have enough for the entire company. That type of fishing is illegal in the US.

Dainrode (4-6 April 1945)

4 Apr. - I slept like a log last night in a feather bed. The German feather mattresses are divided into two sections, one for the lower region and one for the upper. The assembly is comfortable but I don't particularly care to have all the blood in my feet and head concentrated in my stomach. Maybe that is one of the reasons these women are built like Shetland ponies. German beds are built strictly for sleeping purposes or maybe we don't understand Europeans. Who cares? .... In the distance we can hear the thundering of guns again. These remaining Germans and everything that's in Germany is going to catch hell if

> they don't surrender soon. Most of them have nothing to gain by surrendering, so plenty of shooting is in the offing. We are taking no chances with any of these people.
>
> **5 Apr.** - I've got to take a rather fast trip to Aachen, Paris, Liège, and Brussels in the next 10 days. I did not want the assignment but I had no choice in the matter. Should get to see quite a bit and enjoy the change.

On *April 5*, group ordered the battalion into close support of the 9th Infantry Division. The 51st stayed with the 9th for a week, removing vehicles, tanks, and enemy roadblocks from the roads, and maintaining the divisional MSR. At 0800 hours, *April 9*, Company A began a 110- foot, class 40, double-single, Bailey bridge at Nuttlar. They built the bridge over a partially demolished, four-span stone and masonry-arch bridge. The Germans had dropped three of the four spans during their retreat. The intact span and the three stone piers were used to make one complete bridge. Company A completed the work in seven hours.

The next morning, Company A began construction of an 88-foot timber trestle bridge at the site of a demolished two-span stone and masonry-arch bridge near Bigge. It was class 70, one-way, and class 40, two-ways. No part of the wrecked bridge could be used and the parts the enemy had left standing had to be cleared away before actual construction work could begin. Actually only one span of the bridge was partially damaged, but the handrail was bent and interfered with the repair work. Major Yates was in charge of the work and he put a couple of blocks of TNT on the handrail to remove it. When the charge blew, the whole bridge fell down and a small job became a large one. Only odd-sized lumber and timber was available and the engineers of Company A consumed much time in hand-cutting and hand-trimming the material at the bridge site. But they completed the bridge the next night.

The Sorbonne, Paris (France)

> April 8-15: Training at the Sorbonne for the planned post-V-E Day Information and Education Program; Fun; Planning, Organizing & Conducting Educational Program for the Battalion. The Battalion was in Küstelberg.
>
> **8 Apr.** - Here it is the morning of the 8th and I am in Paris. Arrived last night after a 300 mile jeep trip and a 200 mile train ride. I spent the night in Brussels while waiting for the train to leave. Attended the huge Churchill Theater that showed 4 American pictures in French. It was rather interesting to watch peoples' reaction to the 4 different types. Donald Duck had the house roaring while the Harry James Orchestra hardly brought forth a peep. The people there didn't know a war was on. Lights were on at night, civilian cars were scooting all over the place and trolley cars were a dime a dozen. It is a nice clean looking large town. Paris seems just as busy as New York or Philadelphia. Had to do more fighting to get on the subway than I did in New York. They have very efficient fast service though. Those trains must speed along at 60 to 70 miles per hour. I arrived at this place about 10 last night too tired to even wash my dirty face.
>
> This has been the most restful and relaxing day I have spent in months. After dinner I took the Metro downtown to L'Arc de Triomphe, got some money exchanged at the Finance Office, found the PX and the 2M Sales store - both of which were closed, rambled around sight-seeing and then went to the Empire theater and saw the "President". Don't miss it .... I returned to the dormitory, took my first shower in two months and then took a stroll through the city park across the street. It was a real pleasure to watch the children playing in the swings and riding the merry-go-round, the old people sitting on the

The Invasion of Germany ... BRIDGES TO VICTORY

benches, the young couples strolling .... I could feel the pressure removed of not having to be continually on the alert for a Jerry or sniper or civilian taking a shot at me. The people don't know there is a war on except what they read in the papers. Even I feel or have a very detached feeling from war. This is a beautiful place in which I have to spend the next week. It is much nicer than UNC, has a much larger library and more modern buildings. You have heard of it before, I'm sure .... (the Sorbonne). If I get the time tomorrow I'm going to look for the herbarium. It should be intact. War hasn't scratched it.

It really makes me sick to think of what the Germans had us do to Bonn, a beautiful university and resort center. The Rhine valley is beautiful now with apple, pear, and cherry trees in full bloom. The Japanese cherries are in full flower here. Spring is definitely in the air here and about 2 weeks ahead of the last area in which I was billeted. The trees should be fully leafed by the time I return ... 10 days without a letter is a rather long wait. Just hope I can make it back in 12 days. I'll have no way of knowing where they are until I reach the other side of the Rhine. Just hope I can ride a C-47 well into Germany. I'll have no transportation meeting me - will just have to rely on the best way possible.

10 Apr. - Here I am again in the nice quiet library ... wish you could enjoy listening to some of the men we have here. Some are H.R.'s, some are captains but they represent the best of our schools in the states. These instructors preach with a missionary zeal.

11 Apr. - When this war is over I'll have the biggest and most important job of my army career. Wouldn't be a bit surprised if Dave didn't take over the company. Everything will depend on the tactical situation. I will have plenty of educational advancement myself. But no education or anything else will interfere with my return to the USA.

12 Apr. - This is the last day of school. Classes are over at 12:20 and then back to the unit I go. If it doesn't rain I am going to stay overnight and leave bright and early in the morning. There are quite a few places of historical interest that I would like to see inside. Hope I will be lucky enough to get a plane ride back to Bonn. If I have to go by rail it will mean hitch-hiking two-three hundred miles and a couple days on the road. The death of Roosevelt came as a big blow to everyone here*.

14 Apr. - Since I couldn't get a suitable room for tonight and since I had to walk 2 miles to the airfield, I decided to catch the train and bum rides the rest of the way. This is going to be a long tiresome trip in this 3rd class coach, the poorest. If it isn't too crowded I might be able to get a little sleep. It is just about 45 minutes till train time now. I'm resting my weary dogs as I write. I am tired and I will be a happy man when I get back to the old routine.

Saw more this afternoon than at any other time since I've been in Paris. Got a much closer view of the palace, the Invalid's Hospital, and the Army Museum. Some of the flags and tapestries must have been 6-7 hundred years old. They had cannon that ranged from wooden muzzles through 1918 models. I didn't know that there were so many Napoleons until I saw the tombs of Jerome Napoleon I, Jerome Napoleon II, and some other Napoleons. Foch, Tureen, Vander and several other famous Frenchmen were entombed in that shrine. The more I see of Paris the more I have to respect the French: one of these days I hope we can enjoy these sights together. I don't care to see anymore of Paris on foot soon. That concrete is very rough, to express it mildly.

15 Apr. - This is Monday afternoon. The trip was little too long for one day so I stayed overnight at army headquarters and have been riding since. I am at one of my water points now waiting on a truck to take me to the company. I wish it would come on for I am anxious to get my mail .... (Later) Did I hit the jackpot, about 16 letters from you, including the pictures, and 7 or 8 others, also the package with

---

*When Hitler heard that news, he and his staff imagined the war would suddenly turn around for their Nazi cause. Eighteen days later he would take his life as the Soviets seized Berlin at a cost of some 100,000 killed (close to that number of German dead, too). Ambrose in *Citizen Soldiers* notes that the sacrifice was far greater than need be but for Stalin's insane order to fight in the streets.

> the washcloths, cheese, and Ritz crackers! .... Incidentally, one of the men received an article from his hometown paper with that picture in it (headquarters picture) and a write-up on Captain Radford and his 13 commandos. I'll get the name of the paper and you can write for one, if you wish.

On *April 13* the 1111th Engineer Combat Group returned the 51st to maintaining roads and destroying abandoned enemy ammunition in III Corps' rear area. The battalion worked at this assignment for four days. But on April 17 work was suspended because of the sudden collapse of the Ruhr Pocket in the III Corps sector. All available trucks in III Corps were detailed to haul the great number of prisoners taken from the Ruhr to the First Army prisoner of war (POW) enclosure at Brilon. Each line company in the battalion furnished ten 2½-ton trucks with one officer, ten drivers, and ten assistant drivers. H & S Company supplied four 2½-ton trucks, and one weapons carrier with drivers and assistant drivers, one maintenance warrant officer, and two mechanics. The 51st received its orders at 0230 hours, and the battalion detail arrived at Brilon at 0800 hours, ready to haul prisoners.

The 17th of April was indeed a sad day for the 51st Engineer Combat Battalion. Major Robert B. Yates, battalion executive officer, was assigned as commanding officer, 1262 Engineer Combat Battalion. Yates had served the 51st and Scrappy Fraser well, especially through the difficult days of the Ardennes offensive. Fraser assigned Captain Karl G. Pedersen commanding officer, Company A, 51st ECB, as the new executive officer, and appointed First Lieutenant Floyd D. Wright commanding officer of Company A. One other change occurred that day. Captain John W. Barnes, Battalion S-3, was hospitalized and Captain Marino Mussomeli, liaison officer, took his place.

It was at 2230 hours on *April 17th* that Fraser was ordered to the 1111th ECG headquarters regarding a battalion move. There he learned for the first time that the entire III Corps, with all attached units, was to leave First Army for an assembly area in the vicinity of Ochsenfurt, Germany. From there they would move several hundred miles away for an assignment with Lieutenant General George S. Patton's Third Army.

Küstelberg (7-18 April 1945)

> **17 Apr.** - At last I have a man-sized job in this man's army that is going to call for the utmost in tact and skill from your mugwump - planning, organizing, and conducting an educational program for 650 men. Guess I'll soon be losing my job as company commander but I will not mind ... looks like Patton is still getting credit for what others are doing. He is a good man and has one of the best armies in the world but the 1st (Army) was the first to land in Normandy, first to break out of Normandy, first to cross France, first to crack the Siegfried, first to cross the Rhine - but I hope Patton is the first to go home - Yep, I was elected to some kind of society at the Academy but I don't even remember the name.

Neustadt (19 April 1945)   (No letters)

> **19-20 Apr.** - 255-Mile Truck Convoy Trip from Neustadt to Petersarauch: *Transferred From First Army To Third Army*. -- (No letters)

Brilon, Ochsenfurt, Küstelberg, and **Neustadt**(near Marburg): 148-1   **Petersarauch**: 148-4

The Race South to the Danube and Munich*

After the collapse of the Ruhr Pocket, many people thought that Nazi Germany might fall back to a last ditch position in the Alpine region of southern Germany and western Austria, an area called either the Alpine Redoubt or the National Redoubt. The intelligence staff at Supreme Headquarters, Allied Expeditionary Forces, could find no positive evidence of a German plan based on a National Redoubt strategy. However, if the German armored forces did continue to resist, the most logical place would be in the Alps. So it was prudent for the Allied forces to cut off this area.

At this point in the war, III Corps, with six divisions, found itself without an area of operations or an objective. As fate would have it, far to the south in the Third Army Area, VIII Corps, with five divisions, was reassigned to First United States Army. To compensate for its loss, higher headquarters assigned III Corps, with all attached units including the 51st Engineer Combat Battalion, to General Patton's Third Army.

The Long March

As part of this movement, the "51st Again" began its longest motor march of the war at 0200 hours, **April 19**, 1945. It completed the trip of 255 miles to the south at 2200 hours that same day. During those 20 hours the battalion moved from Küstelberg in the Ruhr Valley, to Wulkersdorf, Germany, some 28 miles south of Nuremberg.

The order of march was H & S, A, B, and C Companies, with Colonel Fraser in the lead. The heavy equipment of the battalion followed the companies by 30 minutes. Leaving the initial point at Wallau at 0200 hours, the convoy arrived at the refueling point, Bad Homburg, by 0600 hours that morning. The convoy was intact until it reached a point approximately seven miles from Würzburg. Here, because of a main road intersection at which convoys were converging, control became difficult. Trucks from other units broke into the 51st column, splitting it up. The convoy was delayed at that intersection for approximately four hours.

Private First Class Carleton E. Moore, A's motorcycle driver, remembered the gridlock well. With the convoy unable to move, Colonel Fraser left his jeep short of the intersection and headed for the front of the convoy. Straddling the back of Moore's motorcycle, Fraser directed him to drive forward to find out why the column was stopped. Even on a motorcycle Moore could only get to within 100 feet of the intersection, for all four directions were blocked with halted, bumper to bumper vehicles. Moore could see, but did not hear, the conversation between Fraser and the military police lieutenant who was attempting to straighten out the mess. As the lieutenant braced himself, Moore claimed "that he saw sparks and blue flames gushing from Fraser's mouth." Without further delay, the "51st Again" moved briskly through the intersection. The delay did provide time for the troops to eat lunch. On the outskirts of Würzburg, Fraser halted the convoy to reform it. During that break everyone ate supper.

---

* This section, written by Floyd D. Wright, is taken directly from Chapter IX of ***The 51st Again!***, used with permission of Harvey Fraser. Excerpts of letters written from Albert Radford to his wife Laurie, are spliced in with the text.
Würzburg: F7, 148-2 **Nuremberg:** F8, 148-4 **Wallau, Bad Homburg** 148-1 **Wulkersdorf:** 148-4

Kassel (F3, 148-1), in terrain similar to nearby Ruhr, was heavily bombed because of its specialized war production facilities. By the time of this photo, the streets at least were cleared.
National Archives - 10 May 1945

Kirschfurt (148-1) on the Main River. As the 51st sped across springtime Germany, they crossed the Main on the way to the Danube.
National Archives - 12 July 1945

In the course of the trip, only one major breakdown occurred. A 2½ ton truck broke its steering gear. Lieutenant Henry's battalion motor pool mechanics quickly repaired the truck and had it back in the convoy. Other breakdowns were negligible, mostly flat tires. Colonel Fraser praised the drivers and mechanics for their well-disciplined driving, their efficient repair and maintenance, and for their cooperative spirit during the entire movement. This was an habitual trait of Scrappy Fraser. When the men did something good, he was the first to let them know it loud and clear. This kept esprit de corps high, and gave the soldiers a strong desire to do even better with the next mission.

By 2130 hours, the convoy had cleared Würzburg and headed toward Neustadt. Captain Radford of H & S Company met the convoy there and led it to a bivouac area near Wulkersdorf. Prior to midnight the heavy equipment convoy moved in, completing the battalion move. It was now prepared to work in the United States Army area of operations. By 2200 hours that evening, the unit had been reassigned to its old standby, the 1111th Engineer Combat Group (ECG), commanded by Colonel Anderson.

Assault Crossing of the Danube at Ingolstadt

On *April 19*, the battle for Nuremberg ended when the 3rd Division penetrated its walls and entered the city. The city collapsed on April 20, Hitler's birthday [he killed himself April 30], as did the right wing of the German First Army. A gap opened between the German First and Seventh Armies, and the United States Third Army began its drive to the southeast through this opening. With III Corps freshly assigned, Third Army was ready to exploit the gap in an assault which actually began on April 19.

On *April 21*, the battalion went into close combat support of the 86th or Blackhawk Infantry Division. The battalion's first work included the removal of enemy roadblocks to allow for two-way traffic, the posting of directional signs on the main supply routes, removing destroyed tanks and vehicles that obstructed traffic, sweeping the roads and shoulders out to twenty feet for mines, widening bridges, and filling craters. Five days later, Fraser ordered Company A to build a class 40 treadway bridge across the Danube River in Ingolstadt. At that point the Danube River flows from west to east and is approximately 324 feet wide. That portion of Ingolstadt located on the south side of the river was the original town site dating back to medieval times. Most of a high rock wall encircling the town was still in place. Intelligence reports stated that 300 German Schutzstaffel (SS) Troopers were in buildings on the south side of the river, ready to defend against any crossing at that location.

Everyone knew that the war would end in a couple days, but nobody knew just when. No commander of troops wanted to take an action that would get anyone killed if there was any honorable way to get around it. This applied to all commanders from First Lieutenant Floyd Wright of Company A, 51st ECB, to Major General Harris Melasky, commander of the 86th Infantry Division. Attempts to balance this rationale with a strong desire to end the war as soon as possible caused king-sized headaches for all commanders.

Petersarauch (21-24 April, 1945)

21 Apr. - Until last night I think I'd slept 10 hours in the last 96. Was almost out on my feet day before yesterday .... The capture of the Ruhr was one of the greatest victories of this war in my estimation. We really underestimated the number they had in there .... My men added quite a few prisoners to the total

Neustadt (near the Main R.): 148-4   Ingolstadt: F8, 148-4

while I was gone. A lot of die-hard Nazis are still trying to escape but they are being shot or picked up daily. Three tried to stumble into our area last night but a .50 caliber machine gun put them in reverse. Those Jerries really took off like greased lightning ... doesn't look like this mess can last much longer. We don't have the slightest inkling of what is going to happen.

23 Apr. - This is beautiful country. The woods, fields, & villages look so nice and peaceful and picturesque. The "landscape" is dangerous though. The Wehrmacht surrenders without any trouble but the SS stragglers sometimes turn out as annoying and poisonous as rattlesnakes. It doesn't take any persuasion to give them lead poison About all that is left of the German army is SS .... Men, women and children are working the fields using cows to pull the plows. Occasionally you will see an ox and a horse teamed, or an ox and a cow. Hitler yelled for "lebensraum", but, from the appearance of things, he didn't have enough Germans to occupy and maintain Germany.

I wonder if the German people will ever realize that they have been ruined by the biggest band of criminals in the world. It looks as if Himmler & Company might be sacrificing Hitler in Berlin for the glory of the party and to remove a little of the stain from their necks .... Yesterday we picked up a few Russians and during the course of questioning, the interpreter asked if they had seen any Germans in that immediate vicinity. They said "No, if we had we would have killed them with our bare hands." …. The outfit hasn't worked very hard in more than a month now, but they have covered many miles.

On receiving Fraser's orders, Wright suggested that Company B or C be brought up, because Company A had been the forward company and had completed the last two or three missions assigned to the battalion. But that would take too long. General Melasky had told Fraser that one his regiments had taken Ingolstadt and controlled everything on the near bank (north side) of the Danube. Late in the afternoon of *April 26*, Fraser and Wright went to Ingolstadt to find a suitable site for the bridge. Fraser led with his jeep and Wright followed in his.

After passing through the rock wall around the city and going half the distance between the city and the river, both jeeps came under a hail of rifle and machine gun fire from the buildings on each side of the river. The colonel's driver turned into the first alley he saw, with Wright's jeep close behind. In the relative safety of the alley, a very brief conversation was held which went something like this. "What the hell is going on? We are supposed to have an infantry regiment in this town. Let's get the hell out of here!" By taking the alleys and back streets, the two jeeps got out of town with no injuries to the occupants. Later it was learned that the American regiment was in town, but had occupied the basements of the buildings. The Germans still occupied and controlled everything above ground within Ingolstadt.

The next stop was General Melasky's headquarters. Fraser told him of the situation, advising that the inflated pneumatic floats and other bridge equipment would be destroyed by small arms fire if moved into town under the present situation. That would mean that the bridge could not be built, and the 51st would take numerous casualties trying.

Melasky either did not believe Fraser or did not want to hear what he was being told. He reached for the field phone on his desk and started cranking the handle. As he did so, he stated that he would inform the III Corps commanding general that he had an Engineer battalion commander down here who did not want to carry out his instructions. At this point, Fraser reached over and removed the phone from the hands of the general and informed him, "We'll build your bridge sir!" On this happy note, the two Engineers departed for Company A's CP.

In the Company A command post, Wright sat on a box smoking one cigarette after another while Fraser paced back and forth. They discussed the mission and considered alternate means for bridging the river. After several minutes of this, Colonel Fraser said in effect, "Damn, Floyd, give me a cigarette." At this point Wright learned that Scrappy had decided several weeks before to quit smoking.

Gradually the plan unfolded. During the remaining daylight hours, Company A inflated the pneumatic floats supplied by the 998th Engineer Treadway Bridge Company, commanded by Capt. G. E. Hancock, near the company command post. The men loaded two floats on each bridge truck Although they were a large target, they would greatly speed up construction once the Engineers were on the river bank. Their use would also reduce the amount of heavy equipment required, cutting the noise at the construction site. Noise reduction was essential because the Germans also controlled the south side of the river.

Kapfelberg: (148-4) [not too near the 51st but similar operation]. Pneumatic floats going to the Danube.
National Archives - 26 April 1945

About 2300 hours that night, Company A and the 998th Treadway Bridge Company made a motor march to the edge of town. Here the 1st Platoon became an advance guard on foot to clear any Germans that might be in the buildings on either side of the street leading to the crossing site. Fraser and Wright positioned themselves as the point in front of the advance guard, one on each side of the road. The 2nd Platoon rode shotgun on the bridge trucks. The 3rd Platoon remained motorized and followed the bridge trucks as a rear guard.

The night was still dark when the column reached the bank of the river. Fraser went one way, Wright another, to find a crossing site. Wright was walking on the muddy bank as quietly as he could when someone tapped him on the shoulder from behind and said in a low, but reassuring voice, "I think you can get started now." This scared the daylights out of Wright. He turned around and in spite of the darkness recognized Colonel Anderson, Commanding Officer, 1111th ECG. With the group commander and the battalion commander at the bridge site every soldier knew that somehow everything was going to be OK, even though the Germans still controlled the far bank. The commander's presence at the site of an operation is one of the fibers that holds a unit together and keeps it on track, even when its basic instincts tells it to run like hell. That fiber also converts a good outfit into an outstanding outfit such as the 51st ECB. Scrappy Fraser was always at the scene of the action, continually moving among the troops and gently slapping them on the rump with the same words, "Hurry up, hurry up, hurry up." For the men in Company A he was known as "Hurry-up Harvey", but never in his presence.

Wright deployed one platoon on the bank of the river with .30- and .50-caliber machine guns. They were to place as much fire as they could on the German-occupied barracks and buildings on the far shore. Melasky had furnished the battalion an M-8 armored vehicle with a .50-caliber machine gun and a 37-mm gun, and this was used to good advantage. The orders were not to fire first. The plan called for doing as much as could be done under cover of darkness, and still have the bridge ready when the 86th needed it.

Many aspects of that bridge project were extremely unusual. In the first place, the enemy controlled the far shore. There, the treadway bridge had to be built out into the river from the near shore. A section of the bridge was placed in the water, then pushed out to make room for another section. This was repeated until the first section reached the far bank.

Moreover, there were no power boats to push sections into place. The 998th Treadway Bridge Company's boats had been swamped in the Rhine river crossing and each section had to be pulled into place by hand with ropes. With the bridge extended some 300 or more feet into a river into a current of 7 miles per hour, pulling sections into place by hand was difficult. To encourage men of Company A to move a little faster, Colonel Fraser stationed himself on the lead section of the bridge, and remained there until the bridge was completed.

At the break of day, the lead section of the bridge was about 40 feet from the far bank. German rifles and machine guns opened up from the barracks about 200 feet from the edge of the river. The defensive platoon, now reinforced with two squads from the 86th's 311th ECB immediately laid down a heavy volume of fire. That greatly reduced the fire from the barracks and permitted the bridge building to continue. The M-8 with its 37-mm gun was instrumental in silencing the fire from the round building. As Technician Fifth Class John P. (Kelly) Watson recalled, the M-8 fired its first shot shortly after Fraser broke the silence and yelled back from the lead position, "to give them everything we've got if the burp gun fires again."

About that time, at a distance of about 1,000 feet upstream, assault boats loaded with infantrymen, headed for the far bank, The first thoughts of the men of Company A was, "Damn! This action should have occurred before the bridge was started." Their second thought was that somebody must have reasoned that the bridge, sticking out in the river like a dagger with its point only a few feet from shore, would receive all the attention and fire from the Germans in the barracks. Their third thought was that they were as happy as hell to see the infantry moving over.

In any event, the assault boats reached the far shore without receiving a single shot. Because they were made of plywood, a couple of bullet holes in the side could easily sink any of the boats. As the infantrymen debarked and climbed the ten-foot bank of the river, they formed a skirmish line to advance on the barracks. As the action developed, they received small arms fire from the barracks and began to drop. Those who were able rolled themselves like logs to the bank of the river, and down the slope toward the water, taking advantage of the only cover available. Those unable to roll were dragged to cover near the water's edge by the medics. As if controlled by some magnetic force, these men managed to move toward the treadway bridge. By that time, the leading section of the bridge had reached the far shore.

Once the lead section of the bridge touched the far shore, normal operations were suspended. Ambulances backed across the bridge to pick up the wounded men and get them to an aid station as soon as possible. When the evacuation was complete, the bridge was secured. Steel treadways were then placed between the last floating section and the bearing plates. Finally, bridle lines were moved to the far shore, to be anchored on the bank both upstream and downstream, to hold the bridge in place. The bridge was finished about 0800 hours on *April 27*.

Corporal Lennart A. Fahlander and Private Reno V. Pisano, along with some other men, handled the bridle lines attached to the lead section of the bridge. Pisano was the first man to reach the far shore as he waded through

Bridge at **Ingolstadt**, looking north. *Corps files - 27 April 1945*

knee deep water to haul the bridle lines up the steep bank to anchor the bridge. At this time, with the Blackhawk [86th] infantrymen hugging the ground about 500 feet from the enemy barracks, 400 German soldiers came out of the barracks with white flags and surrendered to Company A. They were immediately moved across the bridge.

While that was going on, Private Pisano walked behind a building and discovered about 35 Germans coming to him in a column of twos. The man in front had both his hands over his head with a white handkerchief in one of them. He was followed by two officers. Although Pisano did not have his rifle, the group surrendered to him. Pisano led them to another group of prisoners who were waiting to cross the bridge. Among the prisoners were many older men and teenagers. At that point Pisano realized "that the war was essentially over."

The prisoners crossed even before friendly forces secured the

Nearing the end. Hundreds of German POWs rounded up and marched north by the 51st over their new bridge at **Ingolstadt**. *Corps files - 27 April 1945*

far shore. The engineers were quick to relieve the Germans of their Luger pistols, bottles of schnapps, cognac, and other goodies. The infantrymen of the 86th began yelling unprintable words at the engineers to the effect that, "Hey! Those are our prisoners, not yours."

After the prisoners had crossed to the American side, the 86th began moving across the bridge in force. With all of that activity, a mud hole began to develop close to the approaches of the bridge. The company put 20 or 30 prisoners to work placing rubble from a nearby rock wall in the holes so the division traffic could continue across the bridge. All elements of the division crossed the Danube and continued their drive to the south. Miraculously, Company A had no casualties during the construction of the bridge.

Ingolstadt, Germany. Troops, tanks and other vehicles move through the streets. *National Archives - 27 April 1945*

Gunzenhausen -   (25 April)

Lohrmannshof -   (26 April)

Gaimersheim -   (27-28 April)

Giesenfeld (29 April, 1945)

> **29 Apr. -** I think I've averaged 75-100 miles per day for the past 3 weeks. We have set up and moved as many as 3 times per day. We are s`till capturing quite a few prisoners. Seems to me that the Germans would run out of men one of these days .... Here's how my day has been running lately: Up at 5 a.m., move at 6, set up by 9, two or three hours for shaking down civilians and mopping up Jerries; go on reconnaissance about 1400; eat supper any time between 1800 and 2200. And in between I take care of

my administration and other duties. At present I could stand a little sleep. It can't last much longer at this rate.

Dachau: 300 corpses of thousands killed here just 10 miles north of Munich.   *National Archives - 25 April 1945*

Horrified American troops came upon many such scenes on the heels of fleeing guards. Dachau was one of a dozen or so major death camps. However, long before and after the "final solution" planned at the secret Wannsee Conference near Berlin 20 January 1942, as many as 15,000 camps and sub-camps were built in Germany and occupied areas from the mid-1930's to 1945 for purposes of detention, slave labor and extermination. Some say the Nazis never would have been allowed conditional surrender, once atrocities were well known. One wonders. Then and later, most Germans professed ignorance of or greatly minimized the scope of death camps. Given very little more time, the Reich could have finished killings and literally buried the evidence. Then, fewer survivor's claims would have been considered an uncomfortable, "wild" exaggeration, perhaps overlooked with the seeming Cold War "necessity" of alliance with fascists to fight communism.

Attenkirchen - (30 April - 2 May, 1945)

1 May - I don't see how this scrap can last much longer. The remainder of the German Army will be fighting outside the homeland before long. The big question is "Where are Hitler, Goering, Goebbels, and Himmler?" Himmler is the bird I would like to see through the sights of my rifle. In my ten months of campaigning, I fired my first 2 rounds day before yesterday. Didn't try to kill the Jerry then, just scared the daylights out of him.

We were the first to bridge the Danube in our sector. 51st luck is still good because no less than 400 Jerries were in a fortress less than 100 yards from the bridge during construction. They did a little shooting and then surrendered. The Danube is by far the fastest flowing stream I've seen since I've been in Europe, faster than the Roer, not the Ruhr.

There certainly has been a lot of work to do in addition to mopping up Jerries and moving every day. Everyone is tired, but everyone will keep driving until the last Jerry is killed or captured ....

Do you remember the captain I mentioned as captured? Anderson got him out of a large prison camp day before yesterday. He has lost a lot of weight and has marched hundreds of miles as a PW. He was once freed by the Russians and then recaptured by the Germans. He has seen most of Europe on foot and on 2 potatoes and a cup of soup a day. Tonight a couple of lieutenants visited us and they ate like wolves. They were so happy they were in a daze - even wanted to kiss the men for feeding them. Gen. Eisenhower now has congressmen and reporters here inspecting the concentration and PW camps so they and we will not be too inclined to be too lenient with the Germans after this war. Gen. Patton rode past here this afternoon to visit this huge prison camp. He was breezing along with his 4 stars covering a large portion of the jeep .... I have had a 10-year education in less than two months. Two thirds of the world doesn't know how the other third lives.

I don't know what to think of my chances of getting home soon. After reading demobilization regulations I am more in the dark than ever. I am quite sure enlisted men will get out much faster than officers, but I believe more officers will return to the states sooner. We should know something definitely in less than a month anyway.

May 1 - (later) Since I've been here, we've spent most of our time mopping up villages. Quite a few have surrendered without any trouble. Some interesting incidents occur while searching these houses. I make it SOP to get all the people in one bunch before I search the house, and when I do, they start pleading because they think we will kill men, women and children. One old German was down on his knees praying and crying like a baby because he thought one of my men was going to kill him .... Hitler has bled the German nation of manpower, which simplifies our job, incidentally. In one truck load we had them from 16 to 46 years old; some had not been in the army more than 2 weeks.

Most of the Germans are donning civilian clothes and are going home to farms because they know they are defeated. You should hear my men when they hear a statement like that. Slave laborers, refugees, and prisoners are really clogging the highways. Most of them are just as happy as can be, but some are wandering aimlessly. They are doing a thorough job of consuming German food stores. Quite a few Germans have been beaten to a pulp. In one of our areas a short while a go, a German factory owner ran after a Pole who had taken an ax from the factory. The Pole started toward him to return it between the eyes. I stopped that in time - threw the Nazi owner in jail. We found a transmitter in his factory and played hide-and-seek with the operator for 2 hours one pitch dark night. He finally surrendered without our having to kill him.

Kirchasch (3-10 May 1945)

4 May - Today is the first day in the past 4 that we have not had any snow. It was bitter cold yesterday during the snow flurries. The weather has been fairly pleasant today .... Sunday I am going to send you a few odds and ends including a German .22 rifle for killing snakes after the war. After firing the pistol a few times I've concluded that I can throw rocks more accurately. I want to keep the pistol for memory's sake though.

Just heard about the surrender of the Germans in NW Germany, Denmark, and Holland - also of the linkup of the 5th and 7th Armies. This thing will be over one of these days. Looks like we will be in on the scrapping until the last German is killed. It can't be much longer. All the men digest the news soberly. I don't think there will be any wild celebrations here. Think I will try to stand on my head that day to see if the world is revolving properly .... The weather turned a little warmer this afternoon but the snow-covered Alps in the distance don't look too inviting. This is "sehr schlecht wetter" to the Germans and sehr, sehr to my not too heavily clad legs. The supply sergeant took all the laundry in today so by 8 a.m. I should be wearing my long drawers. Just hope and pray that he doesn't get ambushed somewhere. Think I told you about liberating two G.I. prisoners who had been ambushed and captured on the 7th Army front. Those birds were certainly happy and thankful to see us. We were looking for SS troublemakers at the time.

5 May - Everything is quiet and peaceful tonight, just hope it remains that way .... We should know where we are going or what we are going to do by the time you receive this. All of the Germans think the war is over and seem very surprised when we start them on their way to the PW cages .... One chap practically got down on his knees pleading to see his wife, especially since he had walked and biked a couple hundred miles ... we picked up several who were traveling with their wives or sweethearts ....

I hope we leave this farm village before the war is over because the whole place reeks of manure. We are in the best houses in the community but the best isn't good enough. Practically or nearly all the men have a bed to sleep in and a stove for cooking and heating, but we have had better. This is the first village we have been in that had a department store. There must be 500-1000 dresses in stock .... The big question still is what are we going to do after V-E Day? There's lots of talk of home. I don't think any of the men are too optimistic but all are hopeful .... The Czechs just announced negotiations with the Germans so the finish should be announced shortly. I predicted May 7th the last time. I don't believe the Japanese will prove as foolhardy as the Germans. They should know they are licked now.

7 May - My morale really soared last night when I received 8 letters from you and one from Ruth .... Everyone is relaxing and taking it easy now that we are out of the war. Doesn't seem possible, but our combat days are over in the European Theater. The question of the future will be solved in a couple of days. If we stay here for a couple of days I hope to take a walk into the snowy Alps in the distance.

Patton and the Third Army are great, but having served in both armies, the First is first in my estimation. The First landed first, was the first to break out of Normandy, the first to enter Belgium, the first to penetrate the Siegfried Line, the first across the Roer, the first across the Rhine, and the fastest beyond the Rhine. And the old 51st spearheaded them across the rivers from the Siegfried on. And the 51st was the first to get the Third Army over the Danube in our sector. In the Third Army it is Patton. In the First Army it is the First Army. It doesn't make any difference anyway, we've got this scrap in the bag and I am very, very thankful that I am still alive and that none of my men were killed in 10 months of campaigning. Quite a few of us visualized the Pearly Gates several times but each time St. Peter told us to return to our business on Terra Firma. Hope and pray we all get home safely or survive the Jap scrap if we have any scrapping to do there.

Tell David Daddy is proud to be his "spittin' image" and inspiration of his tricks. And if Mama can't always understand little boys - Papa will straighten her out when he comes home. How I wish I could see that little rascal, our little independent imp. He's getting better looking as he grows older.

No, Butch, I have not learned much French but I can read enough to get around. I am getting along fairly well with German in handling prisoners and a few civilians. When this is over, I'm going to take time out to really learn the language. Thanks for the money order .... I didn't get paid this month because my voucher was lost .... so that means I'll draw approximately $35 this month. So at present I have $3 plus the money order ....

I explained the purpose of going to school in one of the late April letters. It looks as if I might have a lot to do in shaping the future thoughts of the battalion .... A number of liberated prisoners have visited us lately and they are so happy they are dazed. All of them agreed that the Red Cross was the only thing that kept them alive. We have had quite a few eagerly go Jerry-hunting with us. Most of them are worn out when they return with a handful of Germans. We seldom ever go out without getting a few.

8 May - Das ist alles in Deutschland. I daresay the men here did not celebrate nearly as much as they did in the states. To my knowledge there was not a single man drunk in the company last night. It is a great relief to everyone, but we have been expecting it hourly for several days. Our Corps is or has been out of combat for several days and has already begun its new postwar assignment. Well, V-E Day has arrived on the most beautiful day we've had in a long time. Most of the men have shed their jackets and long underwear and are playing baseball, softball, and volleyball. We beat Group last night in volleyball - the first game in our athletic program. For the first time in almost a year we had breakfast at 0800. The men really appreciated sleeping a little late ....

What we are going to do is still the big question; everyone has a good idea. We'll soon know. We had a real tragedy yesterday: one man was killed on the last day of the war by accident; two others were seriously injured. He was one of the best men in the battalion ... quite a few of the men attended church services the last night of the war in Europe. The chaplain preached a very apropos sermon. He is going to have a larger job than ever now.

The Sharpshooter

Near Munich, while I was trying to convince some huddled Germans with two G.I captives to surrender, an SS lieutenant jumped up and whirled his burp gun toward me. Sergeant Hall fired one shot between his eyes. The remainder of the Germans surrendered. Two freed Americans were deliriously happy. And I am eternally grateful to First Sergeant ***Samuel Dennis Hall.***

Captain Albert E. Radford

Post-War Occupation
Southern Germany

(8 May 1945 - 8 July 1945)

EXCERPTS OF LETTERS WRITTEN FROM THE FIELD
by Captain Albert E. Radford to Laurie S. Radford
May 9, 1945 to July 8, 1945

Biebelried

9 May - Sorry I didn't get a letter off last night or this morning. I had to pay a visit to the hospital for a foot x-ray and I am now on crutches with a badly sprained ankle. A man stepped on my foot while I was pivoting playing volleyball on V-E Day. That's something. This afternoon I baked my ankle in the sun, and the upper half of my body ... so now I have a fairly good tan ... I hit the jackpot again last night. Received 6 letters from you, one from your mother, one from Ruth, and one from Aunt Emma. Certainly helped my morale considerably, but I am still looking for pictures of you .... My foot is much better, and I can put a little pressure on it now. In 4 or 5 days I should be able to hobble around without a crutch or cane. I feel mighty foolish on crutches.

14 May - Do you want a divorce? At the rate I've been writing I guess you are getting a little provoked. I'm busier than ever ... we are getting involved in education now. We will not know whether or not we will initiate the program until we get our mission. Keep your fingers crossed on the CBI. I have enough points for a discharge if 85 is the number required - 46 mos. in the army, 18 overseas, 12 for one child, and 15 for campaign stars - total 91 ... I'm not overly optimistic or pessimistic ....

It is now past 2200 but it looks as though this is the only time I have to write. Organizing this program plus signing 101 different forms for the men that deal with physical exams and potential discharges, censoring more mail than usual, and looking for a new billeting area has kept me pretty busy. Hobbling around does not expedite matters any. I took the supporting tapes off my ankle tonight and much to my pleasant surprise, I can stand on heel and toe - flat-footed. Something feels mighty loose and weak though. Will see the Doc sometime tomorrow for an examination before I start running too much. Wish you could see me now in my shorts and undershirt propped up in this feather bed with my feet on a feather pillow. I have a dresser and wash basin in my private room. Some class after campaigning in every imaginable type of quarters.

The food has improved considerably since V-E Day, B rations every day. We had eggs, ham, and roast beef today. We even have fresh lemons for tomorrow. And mail has been coming in very regularly. I have received 12 letters from you in the last four nights.

16 May - I have a few minutes before the mail goes out. The weather is still beautiful, the sun is shining very brightly and morale is still very good. Worked on the education program until nearly midnight last night. Just completed one report and now the work is really beginning.

Everyone here seems to think more of Truman all the time. I don't know particularly why. Seems as though they are keeping any results of the San Francisco Conference mighty quiet. Seems to me like it has been 5 years since V-E Day, but I guess the waiting before V-E Day accounts for that feeling. I am ashamed to admit it but right now I can't recall the V-E date.

Later - I've just finished a nice bath and rinse-off by showering. Worked up a good sweat pitching a softball. 'Twas the first time I've had my arm "limbered up" since I've been overseas. Certainly was a pleasure to cut loose without my arm hurting. The Colonel ordered me to stay off my foot so I have to sneak in a little pitching occasionally. Guess it will be a month before it will be anywhere near normal, but I can use it about as well as ever without much pain. The Colonel has been hobbling all day after spraining his ankle on the volleyball court yesterday. Dave sprained one of his fingers rather badly

Southern Germany ... POSTWAR OCCUPATION

catching a softball so it seems peace is much more dangerous than war.

We had a big spit and polish inspection this morning. The men are taking this half-garrison life fairly well, but they all want to get home. A few of the men with 85 points or more will soon be leaving. Nothing has come out on the officers yet but I expect the critical score will be much higher. If most of the officers could get a furlough in the states, they would be willing to stay in the army; not I! The battalion is as busy as if not busier than it has ever been. Don't know if we will ever get to use the education program we are working on or not. The deeper I get into it the more involved it gets.

Good Morning! We certainly need a little rain to settle this dust but I wont complain as long as it remains warm. The flies are fairly bad but we should be able to reduce the number as soon as we get the Germans to clean the village. The Germans seem very willing to do any type of work for us. Guess they would rather work for us than some of their former Nazi bosses. We don't threaten them. These people are very industrious. The women are built like draft horses and do more work than the men .... I've been organizing a school, etc. and haven't mentioned my doing any studying. But, if possible, I'm going to study French, German, auto-mechanics, blueprint reading, and possibly surveying. I hope and pray we can institute the program if we stay here any length of time. I don't think I mentioned it before - I actually found one man in the battalion interested in botany as a hobby.

Würzburg was 98% damaged by Allied bombing on March 16. Main River is in the upper left (NW). *National Archives - 11 April 1945*

Würzburg

18 May - I played 5 games of volleyball last night with no ill results. Can't or couldn't pivot as per usual but otherwise the leg and ankle are as good as ever. If I develop my wind and lose about 10 pounds, I'll be in fine fettle.

19 May - This is another lonely Saturday night, no mail .... And here it is Monday morning ....Yesterday morning I had the first organized practice-softball for the men and yesterday afternoon we played B

Würzburg: F7, 148-2

Co., winning 6-2. Needless to say I was rather tired yesterday afternoon so I took a nap. And last night I played volleyball. The Colonel orders us out for athletics. I enjoy playing as much as anybody but I like to or should do a little writing at night. I lost about 5 pounds I believe. Another week and I should be in tiptop shape. Athletics kept me out of church yesterday morning. The officers practiced after the enlisted men so we didn't return in time. The chaplain let me know about it last night .... We are now in Biebelried about 8 miles east of Würzburg. Censorship restrictions have been lifted on geographical locations. We finished the campaign in Kirchasch near Munich. 'Twas a long trip down from the Ruhr pocket where we captured and hauled, mostly hauled, thousands of prisoners. Würzburg is the most demolished town I have ever seen. I've been through the city several times and I have seen only 1/2 of a roof on one building. Nurnburg [Nuremberg] is almost as bad as Würzburg. I've seen enough of Germany; I want to come home to you. I will be happy when we get our mission. This up-in-the-air proposition isn't worth a darn.

On March 19, Hitler ordered Germany's infrastructure entirely destroyed, to offer the Allies a wasteland to conquer. Albert Speer and others, though intimately responsible for the German war machine, raced about Germany to thwart the demolitions. There was damage enough for post-war Germans to recover from, as seen here in **Aschaffenburg** (148-1). Thus ends a people's passion for or complicity in a Reich built on racism, slavery, genocide, aggression, and a dream of Teutonic glory which became humanity's deadliest nightmare.

Corps Files - 1945

21 May - This is a nice quiet evening with the rain pouring steadily .... I signed my official adjusted service rating card yesterday which goes to Corps tomorrow. The highest rated enlisted men in the battalion are already homeward bound but I seriously doubt that any officers will be on their way shortly. I am about 4th in line on points in he battalion. Time will soon tell. I am at least hopeful of a furlough in the next 7 or 8 months. We have our school plan well organized now and would be ready to go within a week's notice. All the men on the staff except the I and E officers have abundant enthusiasm. The men are well "sold" on the programs, are expecting the best when and if the plan goes into effect.

I can't see where Hitler dampened the Catholic spirit any in this community. Seems to me the people are more devout here than in the states. Everyone in the village attended church at least 3 times today. We have had no trouble yet. Quite a few of the civilians start hopping when I walked in. Guess rank and beauty sorta scares them. Don't guess I told you about the officers' mess which doesn't please me too much. We have china, silverware and tablecloths - and wine glasses which are filled two meals a day. You guessed it - I'm not mess officer.

Good Morning dearest! The mail arrived and it took me nearly an hour to digest it all. Received 8 letters from you, one from Mama, one from Aunt Emma, and one from the Red Cross concerning one of my men. Certainly did boost my morale and made me "home-sicker" than ever …. Guess you know which army I am in (Third) and also know that the First Army is on its way to Japan via the U.S. I don't particularly want to go to Japan but I certainly would like to be in the First Army. I mentioned education quite a bit in my last letter. My primary job is to teach teachers how to teach in the battalion classes.

22 May - Everything has been peaceful and quiet today …. German soldiers are walking up and down the road these days, free men. A lot of them are in fields farming. I have seen a lot of happy reunited German couples in the past two weeks. They have plenty of destruction to clear. It is rather difficult for me to see how they can start another war in 20 to 30 years unless the women do the fighting. They are going to have a scrap among themselves getting husbands at the present proportions of sexes.

24 May - Guess you know by now that the German campaign has been broken into three phases which will up my point total to 101. Col. Anderson and the battalion C.O. have declared that no officer in this group will be declared essential if he has the points to go home. That helps, but I don't think there are any prospects of my getting home soon unless the whole outfit returns to the states. Instead of five campaign stars, we will get one silver campaign star.

25 May - (Telegram: "Darling. My love and greetings on Mother's Day. Keep smiling - Albert.").

26 May - There is a real drunkards' brawl going on down the hall. Everyone seems to be in on it …. Hope I don't have to put any of them to bed. I have already thrown 3 into the room where they are all congregated. 'Tis much easier to control them all in one place …. Hope it stays clear all day. We have church services at 11 this morning and a ball game this afternoon with B company At present we are tied for the top of the softball league …. I want to come home. As long as I live there is hope. And I'm thankful I am alive and well.

Ex-Jerry prisoners are really "littering" the highways these days. Some trucks come down the road pulling 4 or 5 trailer loads. It makes some of the men unhappy to see them liberated. It irritates me as long as I see them loose in uniform. I want to get out my pea shooter and start shooting. Don't think I will ever be able to trust another German. As a matter of fact, I wonder if I'll ever feel safe without a weapon in the dear old U.S.A. - at times, anyway ….

I've just finished dinner: Boston baked beans, potatoes, spinach, pineapple, and cocoa. I don't particularly care to see any baked beans in civilian life … for the first time in a year we will have mutton, shoulders mostly. With mines cleared in the Channel, I guess we'll soon be getting fish …. Had the tape removed from my ankle last night and am walking without any support of any kind.

29 May - This is another beautiful day. The sun really beamed yesterday. Took a lot of soreness out of my muscles. The ball teams play good ball when the sun is shining. We had a nice dinner today: spaghetti, beans, potatoes, sirloin steak, and our first ice cream since we left England 11 months ago. We have a German freezer in which we can freeze enough for the company in 15 minutes. It will take us another week to save material for more. From the whooping and yelling I heard at dinner, I guess the effort was worthwhile. Can you buy ice cream at home?

I still don't know what the score is. Third Army is going to the Pacific but that doesn't mean a thing to us. First Army units will retrain at Ft. Jackson, S.C. .... We are a small independent unit and we get our orders independently. All we can do is continue to hope and pray and keep our fingers crossed. I still have a feeling that I'll at least get a leave in the states in 6 months ... volleyball is getting rougher and rougher - two officers were banged up last night - mostly sprained fingers. I have three courts now and I hope to see all of them used at night - that's when most of the men have too much time to think and look at these buxom German girls who look too longingly at some of the men.

30 May - The salutation was as far as I got yesterday. Seems as if everything wrong had to happen at once .... The men are going in more and more for volleyball. Last night we had one court empty and you should have seen these German kids flock there to knock the ball back and forth across the net. Some of them were not any larger than David, I'm sure. I find myself looking at a lot of these 2-year old children these days, trying to picture David's size and physical ability. Wish I could see the little tyke. He needs his Dad around to teach him a few tricks and to show him that this isn't entirely a woman's world .... We are having an indoor swimming pool cleaned up in Würzburg for the Battalion. The pool is 100 meters long, and there are plenty of showers in the locker rooms. As soon as we get it fixed up we'll move - I hope. It will be an interesting diversion for the men and plenty of exercise. We are also establishing a battalion theater for movies. If we can find a 35 mm projector, we'll be sitting pretty.

1 June - I didn't get a letter written yesterday. Received a letter from Bob night before last informing me that Shorty was in Nurnburg [Nuremberg] so I spent the day looking for him without any success [Bob and Shorty were the two brothers of Captain Radford.]. He must have been in some outfit other than a railroad operating battalion because I saw the personnel clerks of the outfit there and he isn't on any of their rosters. Maybe he will write soon and give me some more information on his location. Bob is in Liège now. Much to my disgust I discovered he was in Cambrei when I went through there six weeks ago. Maybe we will get things synchronized one of these days. The only catch is the slow mail. I receive letters from you in less time than I do from Bob or Shorty. Yesterday was payday again. I received $36.45, one month's back pay. I have $65.35 now so I think I will return one of the $20 money orders ....

Haven't heard so much yelling since the battalion was formed. You could hear the 150-200 fans yelling two or three miles away .... We play B Co. tonight ... we are at the top of the league now. It is raining cats and dogs again ... the farmers really need it. All are busy planting cabbages now. Was beginning to wonder if they raise the stuff in this part of Germany.

2 June - By the time you reach 500 (letter 500), I should be some place besides Germany, I hope. We still don't know anything ... don't believe more than half you read in the papers about army movements. When they announce that First Army or Third are both going to the Pacific via the U.S., that doesn't mean much of anything to anybody except army headquarters personnel. Divisions and independent units are assigned and reassigned faster than women want to change their hats.

The educational program will be used by transit troops in staging areas and in the army of occupation.

Southern Germany ... POSTWAR OCCUPATION

Every unit is supposed to have trained education men. The "until I see you coming" attitude is the wisest. Mine is "until I'm on my way". No, I did not get an opportunity to walk into the Alps. The mountains we saw were just south of the Inn River near Munich about 10 miles from us. If I had not injured my ankle I would have hiked there .... I still have the camera and the pistol. The camera isn't much good but the pistol is the only souvenir that I wish to keep.

4 June - Last night ... after I hit the hay guess I stayed awake two hours trying to think of ways and means of maintaining morale. Keep your fingers crossed, I have not had a court - martial in the company in six months and I hope we don't have any more. Maintenance of high morale is definitely our biggest problem at present.

Two years ago today a blue-eyed imp almost gagged me with ether but I tried not to let her know it. We were the proud parents of a little red imp who is rapidly growing into a nice looking chap. It doesn't seem possible that so much could have happened since that happy day in our lives. I'll never forget how sweet our little imp looked and behaved in the Pennsylvania Station, Philadelphia, Oct. 31, 1943. And no one knows but that little imp's mother how much I've missed you since.

7 June - I'm managing the officers' and enlisted men's softball teams and a couple of volleyball teams, so my spare time is well occupied at night ... those cookies certainly are good. They should last a week this time. I have them well-hidden. Have not received mail from you in three days now. My luck should improve tonight.

8 June - I certainly enjoyed your mother's letter ... when your mother-in-law starts dreaming you're home, it's high time something popped .... These people have quite a few gardens but all they have planted are potatoes, lettuce, carrots, and parsnips. We would normally have fresh vegetables if they raised any nearby. But the practice of fertilizing with cow urine sorta kills the desire for anything fresh here. Think I told you that they keep their cows primarily as fertilizer factories. They keep them inside summer and winter, and outside of the barn every farmer has a manure pit which he keeps building summer and winter. They also have underground urine tanks in which they store the drainage. About once a week these people pump the urine from the underground tanks into specially built tanks on wheels. Then they drive the wagons through the fields fertilizing. When the dear people disturb the urine by pumping, they almost gag all the G.I.s in town .... As soon as we get our battalion pool opened, I think I'll try learning to swim. I would like to be able to teach David how to swim one of these days. And as we grow older, we should enjoy the water more.

10 June - This is a nice, quiet Sabbath morning .... I feel wonderful this morning but there is one thing bothering me somewhat - you have been working too hard lately .... First you believe or think one thing then another about my coming home - I feel the same. There is nothing we can do about it except relax, smile and pray. As soon as I get any information you will know. At present we know nothing and what's more the corps we are in doesn't seem to care whether we ever know anything. They have a good reason though, that I can't divulge. I think I'll see you by Christmas .... Dishes and more dishes - don't worry about my ever giving you a set of dishes for Christmas, anniversary, or birthday gift. Those Mt. Neverest dishes, pots, and pans were really irritating at times.

11 June - We have two men flying home today, both of them have more than 100 points. No officers have been returned to the states from this group and I doubt there will be for a mighty long time. We still do not know our status. More and more of our closely related units are getting their status now and are pulling out for various places. One had the job of cleaning Munich to some degree of normalcy. I don't envy them at all, working 10,000 Jerry prisoners .... Another is going straight to the CBI. What we will do is a ? We have to be patient .... P.S. Please send some cookies.

12 June - The rain is still pouring. This is a wet, muddy village today .... It has been officially announced that the 3rd and 7th Armies will be the armies of occupation. That does not affect our status in the least, whatever that might be. When and if they do return to the states, I hope they fly us there. The army is transporting approximately 50,000 a month home by air now - better than three infantry divisions. Certainly would be something for the old 51st to finish this war by flying home.

More wishful thinking. Education manuals for 148 different courses are now available. Next week I am going to give an instructor-training course but at present I can't work up much interest because we don't know our category. I have to have the instructors trained in case we do. All of the men are still busy rebuilding or supervising the rebuilding of this area. It is beyond me how the Germans kept things running as long as they did.

13 June - The sky is overcast with signs of more rain. It is very cool .... This is the morning of the 14th. We've got to move out of these German homes in a few days. Don't know whether we will go into the field or not. Pup tents won't be worth a darn in this kind of weather .... Another day has come and gone and we still don't know what's up. We are changing corps almost as fast as the days roll around. Since this outfit has been activated we've been in the III, V, VI, VII, VIII, X, XIII, XV, XVIII, Corps. Just goes to show you how we get around. We've supported or been attached to the 9th, 75th, 82nd, 86th, 30th and 99th divisions. The 82nd and 9th were by far the best of the lot. Those 82nd boys were not scared of hell or high water. Guess I'd better shut up or the base censor might become irritated.

17 June - Went house-hunting this morning - almost found the ideal place for the entire battalion.

19 June - I have been a little busier the last few days with billeting and court-martials. We have a nice battalion set-up now that I've got to get organized this afternoon. I think everyone will be happier there and if we start an I and E school we will have class space. Looks as if we might move into the city of Würzburg's park area located on the highest hill overlooking the city. It is a beautiful area, but the men will have to sleep in pyramidal tents. They will like that better than these manure piles though. If we stay there this winter, we will winterize by building barracks. We will have a nice mess hall inside where the men can sit to eat. The officers will have room enough in the restaurant to sleep ....

We have had it, dearest! The outfit is in category IV, to be disbanded. Morale is lower than a snake's belly at present. This is the last thing they wanted to happen. It will be up by morning though. The officer's critical score has not been announced, but think it will be 110. How the efficiency rating will fit into the picture I do not know. All this means that the unit will be disbanded in the states after CBI troops have been moved from this theater. Personally, I hope I am lucky enough to remain with the unit until it is disbanded. I do not look forward to joining another unit, that is a dead cinch. Most of the men and officers will be disbanded before that time I guess. I hope and think I will see the states before my birthday. Just keep your fingers crossed and your morale up. It is going to be a long tough row to hoe but we have done it before and we can do it again.

1 June - My morale has gone up several notches if the "Stars and Stripes" is correct. The officers' critical score is 85 which means I should come home with the remnants of the 51st to be a civilian. Civilian, that is a mighty odd sounding word. I really believe I'll be seeing you in the next 6-8 months.

23 June - I am sending the S.& S., with the 85 points story. What that means I do not know. Did you

Southern Germany ... POSTWAR OCCUPATION

"***Würzburg*** *fixer-upper with great view -- suitable for a worthy battalion of engineers*". Double-double Bailey spans center of Ludwigsburg Bridge which retreating Germans blew. pontoons and other materiel in foreground. Fortress Marienberg, in the background, was begun in 1201 and assumed it's present size in 1725. Würzburg seats one of three German archbishops and is a center of Roman Catholic history.
National Archives - 10 April 1945

know that Shorty will be home in September or October? A lot of outfits have their approximate sailing or flying dates. I still think we will be lucky to be together by Christmas .... With the sugar rationing as tight as it is, you should forget about sending me any cookies .... We joined the 3rd Army two days after my return from Paris. The battalion is planning to run off a pictorial journey from England to our present location. We should have it ready in a couple of weeks.

24 June - All is quiet and peaceful tonight in this little farm village ... this is the morning of the 25th. We have the official theater eligibility score for the officers now and it is 85 which makes me feel mighty good. I am ready to return to school when and if I get home.

26 June - Everyone is on the go this morning. We are going up on the mountain top where the air is clean and pure, and the surroundings are more beautiful. There are many wonderful views from the tower down the Main River valley. You can see for miles and miles and look down upon ruined, gutted Würzburg. I still cannot understand how a group of bombers could do such a thorough job in 27 minutes. There must have been a few million dollars damage done every minute. Incendiaries are much more damaging than demolition bombs on the whole ....

We are losing a few volunteer officers now, no more EM's yet. They will hit us hard one of these days and I hope we don't get very many men in return. When we get settled on the mountain top I should have some time for study in a place that is quiet enough for a little work. Doesn't seem like it in some respects, but I have been away from school for four years.

27 June - Our first day in the tents and it has to rain cats and dogs. We are not set up too well yet and this rain has really upset our schedule. By Sunday we should have everything in good shape.

28 June - This is Thursday the 28th and it's still raining. We made a little progress in our building program but not enough to exclaim over. I will have to build myself a bed because me, bed, and all toppled over twice during the middle of the night. Guess you would have gotten a great kick out of seeing me flounder around in my bedroll on the ground. I finally put my springs on the ground and slept there the rest of the night ....

29 June - This is the 29th of June. I am getting along fine but have not had much time for writing. Being busy plus no mail for several days has been no excuse for not writing. I'll do better ... I have not heard a thing on the possibility of getting home.

30 June - No mail again last night; think it has been one week since I received my last letter from you .... I wish you could have been with me last night when I took a walk through this park area. I don't think I've seen many places more beautiful in the states. From one ledge you can see the entire gutted city of Würzburg and mile after mile up and down the Main River. The fields are yellow, green and golden brown with hay and maturing grain crops. The river barges and the demolished bridges all add to the picturesqueness of the scenery. One thing that amazes me is how so many people can find living quarters in a completely ruined city. The city is easily 95% destroyed. And the other 5% of the buildings not destroyed are occupied by American troops. This is payday again. I hope I come out even. Think my pay will be approximately $17.50. I've just paid the men and I came out right on the nose.

1 July - All of the men should be transferred by August 1and I think I'll be home between October 15 and January 15. I doubt that I will be discharged immediately when I get there but I should get a 30-45 day leave .... The battalion softball team is at the top of the group league with four wins and no losses. I like sports, but managing three teams plus running the company and I&E is a little too much ...We are permitted to fraternize with children but since we can't trust most of them, especially boys from 8 to 14, we have to keep them out of the area. Some of the men let them hang around one day, much to their sorrow. The kids carted off most of the men's 2-weeks PX ration, mine included. We now use straps on their rear ends if we catch them in the area.

2 July - Since we've been in tents, I don't think we've had more than three sunny days. It's pouring rain again this morning. The tents are going up today very well despite the rain. If the sun shines tomorrow, all of the men should have their tents framed. By Wednesday noon we should have everything in fine shape .... I am writing tonight in the officers' mess because it's too cold and dark in the tent. Most of the men and officers have gone to the show tonight so all is quiet .... Incidentally, everyone is enjoying this mess set-up. Everyone has a nice clean place to sit and eat. The officers have china and silverware but the men still eat out of mess kits. We even have tablecloths on the tables. The owner of this place is making amends for backing the Nazi party. We kicked him out of here and now have him back washing pots and pans. He seems to be a highly intelligent, influential German, speaks fluent English. His wife acts as waitress in the officers' mess. The old bird brings in vases of roses, asters, and other odds and ends for the enlisted men's and officers' mess.

Guess you have read a great deal about the fraternization in the newspapers. It doesn't seem to bother the men anymore. We have a well disciplined bunch in comparison to most outfits. With the redeployment

Southern Germany … POSTWAR OCCUPATION

transfers, headaches are going to increase. I hope I don't lose my baldheaded first sergeant but I am afraid he is going to be one of the first to go. He is a cool and efficient man that all the men admire and respect. If he ever returns to North Carolina, we'll have to pay him and his wife a visit. Both are great outdoor enthusiasts.

3 July - Rain, rain, and more rain, looks like it will never quit .... This afternoon was the first time I've ever acted as the president of a court-martial. Came through very well I guess. The repercussions will appear later .... Morale certainly went up about an hour ago when the men heard that the army policy was to keep over 70-point men in the unit as long as possible. Two-thirds of the battalion have 70 points or more. Helps my morale considerably also. The breaks seem to be coming our way slowly. We are not going to lose a single enlisted man in corps redeployment.

4 July - This is July 4th, 1945. One year ago today I landed on Omaha Beach amid a maze of shells flying toward German planes. Later that morning as we rode along the beachhead front I had my first taste of German artillery and knew there was a war in progress. Some celebration we had in the Normandy apple orchards. I've really learned a great deal during the past year, most of which I am ready to forget. Where will we be next July 4?

This has been a very quiet Fourth. Had only one drunk that I know of. The rest have been reading, writing, and sleeping. I would like to see your reaction to battlefield odors, if you think those souvenirs smell awful. I don't know anything that smells much worse than man or cow. Believe it or not, my selection of a bivouac area during the Normandy breakthrough was determined almost entirely by a lack of smell. German filth is appallingly smelly. And as I have mentioned before, I've smelled Jerries almost as quickly as I've seen them. That's past history and I don't particularly care about opening that chapter for new adventures .... Someone is celebrating the Fourth with flares, Very pistols, and what-not. There is quite a bit of noise.

5 July - I've just returned from my first USO big time show in 20 months overseas ... Jack Benny, Larry Adler, Ingrid Bergman, and Martha Tilton put on a pretty good show. Jack Benny did a good job but I still don't care for his type of humor. Ingrid Bergman seems to be all that has been written about her .... I feel down in the dumps this morning for some unknown reason. It's not so unknown, I miss you keenly and want to come home. By Monday we will look like a redeployed unit as far as officers are concerned. I am losing all three warrant officers and Dave is going to school in Paris for one week. We've got a lot to be thankful for, but this waiting gets sorta nerve-wracking at times. Received a v-mail from home last night and a letter from you. Looks as if Bob has gone directly to the Pacific .... Barnes is in the States now.

Yates is still with his outfit and I don't know whether he's going home or not. Think he has 142 points. Kirkland is still in a hospital in the States and does not seem to be getting any better. Guess Anderson is still around. No one has heard from him lately or seen him .... The rain has stopped and we are having Jerry PW's busy cleaning the area. PW's or civilians take care of all of our minor details now. I wonder when the Allies are going to turn the prisoners loose. The "Stars and Stripes" said "Bavaria should be independent by fall." I hope so. Oh, yes, the show yesterday was held in front of the Bavarian king's palace which is now a gutted relic. It must have been a beautiful place in its day. Hundreds of warrior statues still adorn the walls. In France it is nude women. Also discovered yesterday that the bridge I've been riding across Main River on into town was built in 707 A.D. [probably the Ludwigsburg Bridge] Only one span was knocked out by war.

7 July - This place is mighty quiet this morning. About one dozen of the old officers left this morning, all over 85 pointers. None of the men are leaving yet! We had a going away party for the bunch last night that went over very successfully. And believe it or not, even though the bunch didn't break up before midnight, there wasn't a single drunk in the place. There were quite a few speeches and much reminiscing. I don't think there was a better battalion C.O. (Fraser) in the whole army. The Colonel almost cried when he left and two of the warrant officers did. I am sure everyone has a dull letdown feeling today. It's pouring cats and dogs again today .... The situation is sad enough as it is without the weather's adding it's 2-cents worth. The irregular mail situation is rather irritating. I haven't heard from you in two days and your latest letter was postmarked the 22nd of June .... Before the Colonel left this morning he told me that I had been recommended for the Croix de Guerre. What it is and what for, I don't know. I doubt that I'll ever get it. Give me an honorable discharge and I'll be happy .... We got our first quota for university attendance today, three enlisted men. If a quota comes down on officers, I am going to try my best to go. Courses are eight weeks duration. All candidates have to have 85 points or more and at the end of the course the students are shipped to a pool and then home.

8 July - Three years ago I became a second lieutenant. I was "sweating out" seeing you just as I am now. Little did I know that two days after I got there, I was being sent to an outfit destined for England .... Reassignment to the old 51st and then sweating out waiting on you. What a happy day it was when I saw you get off that train in Brownwood, Texas.... That fan was certainly a lifesaver in that sultry hotel room. And then our little house behind the hedges. Our little walks down the limestone ridge, our uneventful trip to Brownwood Lake; the only fun we had was sticking our feet in the water ... Plattsburg, David, and now I am waiting on the next chapter of our lives to unfold.

Where they left off. Lieutenant Radford, still with hair under the cap, here hopes for a future beyond 1942 with Laurie and, soon, a baby son he would not see for two years.

Finally safely returned home by the grace of many near-misses and seeming miracles, he and his generation built family and community anew, made up for lost time, and honored the sacrifice and suffering of so many less fortunate or lost.

A Lifetime Later
Recent Reminiscences and Reflections*

Brigadier General Harvey R. Fraser
Major General John W. Barnes
Colonel Floyd D. Wright
Captain Sam C. Scheuber
Captain Albert E. Radford
First Lieutenant Joseph B. Milgram, Jr.
First Lieutenant Fred Nabors
First Sergeant Raymond Millard
T/5 Wilson Roberts
Sergeant Thomas Banks
Corporal Frank Lee

*Ranks indicated are highest ranks earned during military service. All these authors have retired from military service.

Brigadier General Harvey R. Fraser
Lt. Colonel while the Battalion Commander; also a PhD.

Reminiscences and Reflections Forty-Five Years Later:
(Recorded in December 1984)

You have listened to the overall picture from Dr. McDonald and the First Army picture from General Carter. I will discuss a smaller picture but still involving a big area. First, I must recount my good fortune in becoming CO 51st Engineer Bn [Battalion]. In early December I was languishing in Brittany with the communication zone and managed to get ordered to Paris. I took the occasion to visit B. G.[Brig. Gen.] John Hardin, Deputy Engineer ETO [European Theater of Operations]. I told him I was ashamed to draw my pay from sitting out the war and wasting my talent in Brittany. I had been pressuring him for six months to get me into a combat unit. So he said "G.. d..., Harvey, I am going to fix you so you won't be ashamed to earn your pay anymore. You get your gear and report to Col. Bill Carter, Engineer First Army at Spa, Belgium." Carter assigned me to command the 51st ECB, rearmost Engineer Bn in First Army Area. I said "Holy smokes, Col., I wanted to get out of the service of supply." He replied, "You go down there, and do a good job and we may move you forward."

As you have already surmised the Germans saved him from moving me by moving the action to the front door of the 51st CP. On 12 December I reported to Col. H. W. Anderson, Commander of the 1111th Engineer group at Trois Ponts for briefing. On the 14th I reported to the Bn in Marche with the mission of operating 32 sawmills cutting timber for winterization and bridging for the expected Rhine River crossing. Prior to noon on the 16th, I managed a session with the staff and HQ Company and a visit to all line companies and their sawmills. At 1600 the S-4 of the 1111th Group interrupted the Company Commanders' meeting to report that the Germans had broken through the US lines in Schnee-Eifel and were racing for the Meuse River and the port of Antwerp. He said Col. Anderson orders you to send one company to Trois Ponts to defend and prepare the bridges there for destruction and to set up a barrier line along the Ourthe River from Hotton to Bastogne -- only about 20 miles.

Recent Reminiscences and Reflections ... A LIFETIME LATER

I directed my Exec. Maj. Yates, just returned from hospital, to move with Company C to Trois Ponts. Remember that the Bn was scattered all over "Hell's half acre" in more than 32 places. Gathering the troops and combat loads for movement took some time. Yates and Cpt. Scheuber, commanding Co. C, took off and arrived at Trois Ponts at midnight on the 17th.

By now I was, as you can realize, an expert terrain analyst of the area, because I had visited 32 sawmills in the previous three days. The company commanders and staff knew the area well. We looked for road nets, bridges, defiles and towns that were bottlenecks and could be made even more impassable. I can't remember how many barriers were planned but at least 20-30, sometimes 2-3 deep, i.e., blow one and fall back to the next. I will not try to describe them all, but will discuss only three important and effective ones that changed the course of the battle.

You have already heard about the exploits of the 51st at Trois Ponts on 18 December. They faced the spearhead of the 6th Armored Panzer Army and stopped them in their tracks. Maj. Yates and Cpt. Scheuber had 8 bazookas, 10 machine guns, 140 men, one 57 mm antitank gun and lots of guts.

Col. Joachim Peiper, the Commander of the First Panzer Regiment [Kampfgruppe Peiper] of the 1st SS Panzer Division, hit Trois Ponts early on 18 December with 20 tanks and armored infantry. By dint of good planning and a little luck all three bridges in Trois Ponts were blown just in time. Later Peiper said, "We proceeded at top speed towards Trois Ponts in an effort to seize the bridges there. If we had captured them in tact it would have been a simple matter to drive to the Meuse early that day." Score one for the 51st ECB. The Trois Ponts detachments held out until 21 December when they were relieved by the 82 Airborne Division.

Next I will discuss the bridge and battle at Hotton on the Ourthe River. Our map reconnaissance told us this was a very important defile, first because US troops, shell-shocked and scared were retreating across this bridge, and secondly, it was a natural place to effectively delay the Germans and thirdly the bridge and road were absolutely necessary for the US counterattack which we hoped would soon begin.

Hence, we assigned one whole platoon of Company B at this bridge with two tanks, one 90 mm antitank gun, and one 37 mm antitank gun, plus one platoon of a 40 mm antiaircraft Bn who stopped retreating and volunteered to fight with us. There were no other Americans in Hotton when we set up our defense there on the 17th, but late on the 20th the Third Armored Trains moved into this location.

On the 21st we received mortar and small arms fire at Hotton, where 5 or 6 German Tiger tanks appeared followed by motorized armored infantry troops which occupied a hill overlooking the town. It was hot and heavy for several hours. We stood ready with our detonators to blow the bridge, but those 40 mm guns, shooting horizontally, our small arms fire, one 90 mm antitank gun, and our mines kept the Germans off the bridge and held them down all day until combat reserve of the Third Armored moved in late afternoon and the Germans turned tail and started south.

The Sixth Panzer Army had been frustrated at Trois Ponts so the lead passed to the Fifth Panzer Army in the south. Gen. Kreuger ordered his troops to strike while the iron was hot to gain the bridgehead at Hotton, before the US could establish a blocking line. General von Manteuffel, CO of 116th Panzer Division paid tribute to the bravery of the American engineers at Hotton because failure to secure the bridge was decisive for the future of the 58th Panzer Corp. and the Fifth Panzer Army. Both the German Corps and Army commanders praised the feat of arms by a group of embattled engineers.

The corps headed south and the thrust of the Fifth Panzer Army shifted to Ourtheville where the German troops had wrested a bridge from the 158th Combat Bn. The Germans were across in force, but Co. A of the 51st had set up a platoon-sized barrier at a place called Champlon Crossroads just three miles north of Ourtheville. The barrier was probed later on the 21st, but small arms fire and mines turned back the probe and things were relatively quiet all night.

The Germans missed big chances on the 21st, but on the 22nd they moved with determination and power. We held the Champlon Crossroads until the 77th Armored Trains could escape La Roche and head for Marche. We also delayed the Fifth German Army for most of the day until we were driven out. This allowed the 84th Division to prepare to defend the line from Marche to Hotton for a big fight which started the 23rd. The Champlon gang blew other demolition as it withdrew towards Marche, further delaying the Germans for the 84th. The 84th had moved from the Ninth Army Area south to Marche on 21 December and by noon on that day had been ordered to defend line Hotton-Marche. The battle for the 84th started at dawn of the 22nd.

The bulk of our roadblock had been executed by 22 December, but we still had blocking positions in the Celles-Ciney area, but on the 23rd we received the following information from one of our roadblocks, "Tell your old man not to worry anymore, because the Big Deuce is here." -- i.e., the Second Armored Division.

On the 24th with our battle area reinforced by bigger and stronger units, we started to assemble and regroup north of Marche. The 51st had been relieved by the 82nd Airborne Division at Trois Ponts, the Third Armored at Hotton, the 84th and a British Division in the Marche area, and by the Second Armored at Ciney and Celles. This was probably the first and only time in military history that an engineer Bn had been relieved by 5 divisions.

Finally, I would like to make a few general comments.:

First, the only order I ever received from anybody during the entire period was via the S-4 of the 1111th Group on 16 December. We had no intelligence from anybody but ourselves. In fact, we knew more about what was going on in the area between 16-22 December than anybody else. All decisions to blow demolitions, to hold or to withdraw were made by the 51st. There was no interference from higher headquarters.

Second, I want to tell you that the US Army does not retreat in good order. You cannot believe the confusion created by stunned and scared units racing hell bent for election for the Meuse River. The 51st CP was the only stable HQ in the area. We had hordes of visitors night and day demanding information, chow, gasoline, and even counseling. We made every visitor sign in by unit and destination in our log so we could report on those who passed through. We invited all to join us in our efforts and some did!! I remember well Henry V's eve of battle speech, "He who has no stomach for this fight, let him depart now, but he who sheds his blood with me shall forever be my brother, and gentlemen now abed in England shall think themselves accursed they were not here." In addition to the retreating US troops, the roads were clogged with all sorts of frightened civilians in various conveyances and on foot.

Thirdly, I wish to emphasize Stonewall Jackson's remarks: "Don't take counsel of your fears." This doesn't mean that you disregard the dangers of the battlefield. It does mean that you do not worry about all the things that might happen because if fear dominates your thinking the resulting paralysis increases the

Ourtheville, **Champlon** (Crossroads): 88, B6   **Celles**, **Ciney**: B1

hazards. Worry takes blood from the feet to the brain and if you worry long enough you get cold feet. The feet of the 51st Engineer Combat Bn never got cold from fear.

Finally, I'd like to congratulate General Carter on his enlightened decision to send Harvey Fraser to the rearmost battalion. The 51st was a superbly trained, experienced, combat outfit and it was my great privilege to cast my lot with them. We didn't save the First Army front, but we sure as hell helped save its rear.

Major General John W. Barnes
(Reminiscences recorded in 1997)

Battle of the Bulge

I was the S3 (Operations Officer) of the 51st Engineer Combat Battalion in World War II. On December 15, 1944 the battalion was supervising the operation of 32 Belgian sawmills in the Ardennes, producing up to 80,000 board feet of lumber a day for bridge timbers and for winter housing for American troops in Europe. The next day the Germans attacked in overwhelming force in the Ardennes and our mission was changed overnight to combat as infantry.

Major General Barnes

Company C was ordered to the small town of Trois Ponts at the junction of the Salm and Amblève Rivers, where the use of three bridges was critical to the advance to the Meuse River by Kampfgruppe Peiper, spearheading the German Sixth SS Panzer Army. Company C was ordered to blow the bridges and hold the town against the advancing tanks and infantry. Roadblocks were established on the approach routes into the town and the German tank columns were halted temporarily by lead tanks disabled by engineers of the 51st in defiles, allowing the men manning the roadblocks to return to Trois Ponts before the bridges were blown.

For the next three days Company C was able to hold off the Germans by deceiving them into thinking there was a far greater force defending the town. Chains were put on the Company's wheeled vehicles and they and the Company bulldozer were driven continually through the streets of the town behind buildings denying observation by the Germans, leading them to believe that American tanks were reinforcing the defenses of Trois Ponts. The company's wheeled vehicles were also driven blackout without chains out of town at night and then driven back into town with headlights on, simulating motorized reinforcements. Random explosions of ammunition on a burning U.S. weapons carrier, abetted by intentional detonation of individual sticks of dynamite made the Germans believe that artillery had been moved up to reinforce the defenders of Trois Ponts. On December 20th Company C was relieved by the 505th Infantry Regiment of the 82nd Airborne Division.

The result of Company C's defense of the town was to force the German panzer spearhead to detour to the north where it eventually ran out of fuel long before it could achieve its objective of seizing crossings over the Meuse River for the drive on Antwerp to split the Allied Forces.

Meanwhile, Companies A and B had been ordered to defend the Ourthe River from Durbuy to La Roche, a distance of some 20 miles, by defending all river crossings and preparing them for destruction. This involved setting demolition charges on all bridges, mining all fords and preparing obstacles such as abatis, heaps of rubble and daisy chains on the roads and trails leading to the crossings. Each of these sites was also covered by 51st engineer teams and squads with their organic weapons, which included 30- and 50-caliber machine guns, rocket launchers and individual small arms. All of these tasks had been completed by the morning of December 19th.

The major crossing routes in the area were at the town of Hotton, where both civilian refugees and demoralized American troops were streaming in chaos from the shattered front. Our battalion commander, Lt. Col. Harvey Fraser, who had taken over the battalion on December 14th, two days before the Germans attacked, had but little success in convincing any of the retreating American units to join us in our defense of the Hotton bridge and the roads that were critical to the successful withdrawal of American troops. However, there were a few exceptions. Volunteering to join us instead of continuing their pell-mell retreat to the rear were a squad of armored engineers with its 37-mm antitank gun, two Bofors 40-mm AAA guns with their crews, several bazooka teams and one M4 tank with a 76-mm gun. Together with Company B and an attached platoon from Company A, these newly attached squads and crews were hastily organized into an unorthodox but effective combined arms team by Company B's commander [Hodges], who was charged by Col. Fraser to defend the Hotton bridge and its surroundings.

Early in the morning of December 21st probing armored patrols of the 2nd and 116th Panzer Divisions of the German Fifth Panzer Army approached Hotton from the east and were taken under fire by the 51st Engineers. By 0900 Company B and its attached units had put four of the German Mark VI Tiger tanks out of action. Miraculously, the 37-mm gun, a pea shooter by comparison, accounted for one of the German tanks with two lucky shots, the first hitting the sprocket drive wheel and immobilizing the tank and the second hitting the turret ring and freezing it in place. The German crew was killed as they scrambled from the tank. By noon elements of the U.S. 3rd Armored and 84th U.S. Infantry Divisions were arriving in the area and the Germans withdrew.

Throughout the 51st Engineer Combat Battalion area many other teams and squads of Company A and Headquarters and Service Company held the Germans at bay with hastily constructed and defended roadblocks at critical intersections and defiles. When the tide of battle finally turned and the Allies went on the offensive in early January, the 51st Engineer Combat Battalion had been relieved by units of five divisions: the U.S. 2nd and 3rd Armored, 82nd Airborne, and 84th Infantry Divisions and the British 53rd Infantry Division. For its primary role in keeping the German offensive from splitting the Allies and reaching the Meuse River, the 51st Engineers earned the U.S. Presidential Unit Citation and the French Croix de Guerre w/ Silver Star.

Remagen

On 7 March 1945 Brigadier General William M. Hoge's Combat Command B of the 9th Armored Division reached the Rhine River at Remagen and found the Ludendorff Railroad bridge still standing. Acting on his own initiative he seized the bridge and started crossing his command over it to establish a bridgehead on the far shore. His action was flash reported through channels to General Eisenhower, who immediately supported his initiative by ordering the concentration of engineer units and resources in the vicinity to

Ourthe River: 88, B2   **Remagen**: 136

Recent Reminiscences and Reflections ... A LIFETIME LATER

prepare additional crossing sites for a major offensive into Germany.

The 51st Engineer Combat Battalion received orders on 8 March to construct a 25-ton heavy pontoon bridge with equipment provided by the 181st and 552nd Engineer Heavy pontoon Battalions. As the S3 (Operations Officer) of the 51st I was responsible for planning, preparing the orders and instructions to accomplish the task, and staff supervision of the construction activity. The site selected for the bridge was from Kripp to Linz, two small towns opposite each other on the Rhine, about 1½ miles upstream (south) of the Ludendorff Bridge. This was the closest site available with good approach roads on each bank of the Rhine to support concentration of engineer resources and the traffic of major U.S. units which would use the pontoon bridge.

By the morning of 10 March the 51st had moved 40 miles from its previous location to the site and all the resources needed were on hand. Construction began at 1600 with preparation of approach ramps on both shores, interrupted periodically by enemy artillery and sporadic small arms fire until smoke pots were found and used to prevent enemy observation of activity at the site. However, all during construction and until an expanded bridgehead had been established on the far shore, sporadic unobserved enemy artillery fire continued to harass the bridge site. Several engineers were wounded and six were killed during construction of the pontoon bridge, the latter including the commander of the 552nd Heavy pontoon Battalion. The Germans even fired several V-2 rockets from launchers in Holland, the only time they ever fired on German soil. They caused no damage.

Construction continued on into the night and the next day. The bridge was built in parts, with four groups working simultaneously on 4-boat rafts, mostly by feel in the dark. By 0400 the next morning, 11 March, fourteen 4-boat rafts had been completed and were ready to be assembled together as a bridge. When the rafts were in place they were reinforced with pneumatic floats between the steel pontoons so the bridge could take the weight of 36-ton Sherman tanks. A total of 60 pontoons and 57 pneumatic rubber floats were used.

As the 4-boat rafts were maneuvered into position, they constantly extended the bridge from the near shore, increasing the pull on the anchors holding them in place. Triple anchors were then used but as the bridge extended further out into midstream they too started to fail, and the engineer power boats were not strong enough to hold the bridge in place while anchors were being set. At about this time we discovered that they Navy had some LCVPs (Landing Craft, Vehicle and Personnel) in the area and we requested their assistance. Ten LCVPs came to the rescue and were able to hold the bridge against the current until we could install a 1" steel cable across the Rhine immediately upstream of the bridge, to which the anchors for each pontoon were attached. This solved the problem of holding the bridge against the current, estimated to be nearly 10 feet per second. Remaining 4-boat rafts were connected to the anchor cable, eased into position and connected to the ever extending bridge until the far shore was reached.

Finally, at 1900 March 11, 27 hours after starting construction, the 969-ft. heavy pontoon bridge was completed. It was the longest floating bridge ever constructed by the Corps of Engineers under fire. Traffic started at 2300, with one vehicle crossing every two minutes during daylight hours. During the first 7 days, 2,500 vehicles, including tanks, crossed the bridge.

At the same time we were building our bridge, one of the other battalions in the Engineer Combat Group constructed an M2 steel treadway bridge for lighter vehicles immediately downstream from the Ludendorff

Bridge. The two bridges provided two-way traffic across the Rhine, with heavier vehicles crossing our 51st heavy pontoon bridge on the way to the front and returning lighter vehicles crossing the 291st treadway bridge. This enabled closing the Ludendorff Bridge for repairs, which were not completed before it collapsed from fatigue 10 days after its capture.

Colonel Floyd D. Wright
Recipient of Bronze Star for Heroic Achievment

The Battle of Rochefort*

As dawn broke on December 22, the main task for General Bolling's 84th Division was finding the enemy. Major General J. Lawton Collins, commanding VII Corps, feared that the Germans might move in from the south and west, the general direction of Rochefort and Marche, and interfere with the concentration of VII Corps troops. The 51st shared his concern. Major General Matthew B. Ridgeway, CG, XVIII Airborne Corps, dispatched Combat Command A, 3rd Armored Division to set up a screen on the west bank of the Ourthe River between La Roche and St. Hubert. That force ran into the Germans just outside of Marche. The 51st sent Lieutenant Attardo to Rochefort, followed by the 1st Platoon, Company A, under Lieutenant Wright, to blow the bridge in town. That bridge had been prepared for demolition by Company B, but the men had been pulled off and sent on another mission.

2nd Lt. Wright receiving his Bronze Star at **Heister**, Germany
Corps Files - 23 March 1945

Driving from Marche to Rochefort under blackout conditions, the 1st Platoon entered the town of Humain, about halfway between the two cities. There Wright found the 24th Cavalry Squadron. He asked the commanding officer where the Germans were and for support while on his mission to blow the bridge. The commander neither knew the location of the Germans nor honored his request for support, saying he was told to move into the area and wait for further orders.

Wright moved on to Rochefort, not knowing if the Germans were there. He stopped his vehicles on the edge of town and the platoon went in on foot to locate the bridge. No battle noises could be heard, the night was still and very dark. As the men moved quietly through the streets, they knocked on several doors to ask the inhabitants if they had heard or seen any Germans. None had. The platoon moved on to the river and found the bridge.

Wright left his platoon in an alley under cover and with Bonifay [his platoon Sergeant] approached the bridge to set off the demolition. They found the fuse, pulled the fuse lighter, and then "ran like hell" down the cobblestone street, sounding like a "herd of elephants." They had no choice but to make a noisy exit for they did not know how much time it would take before the TNT ignited. Diving into an alley for cover,

---

* Excerpted from *The 51st Again!*, pp. 101-108.
Rochefort: 88, B2   **Heister**: 136

they waited for an explosion. When, after two or three minutes, nothing happened, they realized that something had gone wrong with the fuse. They also realized that after all the noise they had made, if there were Germans in town, they would be waiting for them.

After furtively returning to the bridge, Wright and Bonifay discovered that the fuse lighter had not worked. Wright used his pocketknife to skin back the cover of the time fuse and expose the black powder. Bonifay then lit the fuse with his cigarette lighter as Wright continued to hold it until it started to spit fire. With the fuse burning, Wright laid it down and the two once again ran down the street and dove into the alley. In a few seconds a tremendous explosion shook the ground. Cobblestones rained around the area for several seconds.

Once again the two men returned to the bridge, this time to check their work. Standing on the abutment of the bridge they could see, even though it was dark, that the roadway of the bridge was lying on the river bed. They headed for the edge of town where they had left their vehicles, then returned to Marche a distance of about seven miles.

It was still dark early in the morning of December 23 when Wright arrived at battalion headquarters in Marche. He reported that his mission had been completed; the bridge in Rochefort had been destroyed. Much to his amazement, Wright was ordered to return to Rochefort and rebuild the bridge. Like Trafford with his roadblock, Wright had to undo his work.

Possibly the battalion had gained information about a planned counterattack that would require a bridge in Rochefort. Generals Montgomery and Hodges had agreed on December 22 that VII Corps would counterattack on Sunday the 24th. The 2nd Armored Division would be on the right wing, the 84th Infantry in the center, and the 3rd Armored Division on the left wing, and the 75th Infantry Division in reserve. In actuality the counterattack did not begin until January 3.

Shortly after daybreak on December 23, Wright and his platoon returned to Rochefort. The weather was cold, the sky overcast; it had been like that since the beginning of the Battle of the Bulge. Wright and Bonifay discovered they had done their job very well. They had to measure the span on the completely demolished bridge and obtain Bailey bridge material to replace it. Looking upstream a few hundred feet, Wright was surprised to see a wooden vehicular bridge crossing the L'Homme River. Because of the darkness he had not seen this bridge a few hours earlier when he had destroyed the stone arch bridge. The wooden bridge was unusual in that the wood deck for the roadway was only two or three feet above the water.

Wright and his driver crossed the bridge to reconnoiter the far side. As they drove into the town square of Rochefort, they were amazed to find American soldiers and vehicles on the streets. Wright learned that an infantry battalion headquarters was billeted in the basement of the Grand Hotel de l'Etoile located on one side of the town square. He reported to the commander of the unit, Major Gordon A. Bahe, 3rd Battalion, 335th Infantry Regiment, 84th Infantry Division. Major Bahe had arrived early that morning with two companies to join his Company I, already located there.

The day before, on December 22, the 84th was trying to locate the Germans on their exposed south and southwest flanks, where they feared a possible penetration. General Bolling, after conferring with General Collins, had sent Company I to Rochefort where it arrived late in the afternoon. The 51st was not aware of this action. At the same time Lieutenant Attardo, battalion S-3 section, went to Rochefort to blow the bridge. Late that night when Wright reported in after establishing a roadblock near Jamelle, Attardo had not returned. Wright's platoon was then sent to Rochefort.

Wright asked Bahe if he had heard a loud explosion during the night. He replied that he had but thought it was a German V-2 rocket that had fallen short. Wright then advised Bahe that he had created the noise when he destroyed the L'Homme River bridge to his rear. He also hastened to inform him of the wooden bridge that crossed the river and assured him that he still had a bridge he could use. Wright then promised Bahe that he would replace the one he destroyed as soon as he could get the Bailey material.

When Wright rejoined his platoon at the near shore abutment, a lieutenant from the 300th ECB claimed that he had orders to relieve Wright's platoon in that area. Wright said he would have to receive the orders from the battalion. He was going there to order bridge materials so he invited the lieutenant to follow him. Marche was about a 15-minute drive in daylight.

With Johnston driving and PFC Jordan in the rear of the jeep, Wright set off for Marche. The lieutenant from the 300th led the way in his jeep, sometimes reaching speeds of 50 to 60 MPH. Wright wanted his driver to pass the other jeep because he doubted the lieutenant knew the location of the 51st headquarters. After two attempts, it was plain that it was too risky. Wright fell in behind him.

The two jeeps were soon out of town and into farm country when a German armored vehicle approached from around a curve in the road. It immediately opened fire with machine guns at a range of about 200 feet. It may have been part of the 2nd Panzer Division which was nine miles northwest of Rochefort that night. Enemy fire hit the lead jeep and it stopped in the middle of the road. Johnston turned his jeep into a ditch beside the road. As it hit the ditch the horn started blowing. Wright dove into the ditch, while Johnston and Jordan raced to a nearby farm building for cover. The horn on the jeep continued to blow. The Germans stopped firing and backed out of sight around a curve. Evidently they thought there were other elements following and the horn was a signal.

With the Germans out of sight, Wright got back into his jeep. As he turned the steering wheel the horn stopped blowing. A bullet had struck the steering wheel shaft and shorted the horn wires. Wright's crew went to the lead jeep and carried out the wounded lieutenant and his driver. The radio operator in the back of the jeep was dead. They put the wounded lieutenant and his driver in the jeep and sped back to Rochefort.

Wright told Bonifay to take the wounded men to an aid station. He then sent Sergeant Kroen's third squad south along the west bank of the L'Homme River to a railroad bridge where it was to slow down any German movement from that direction. Sergeant John Stiftinger, 2nd Squad, was put in charge of the platoon. Wright then crossed to the east side of the river to advise Major Bahe that he had German armor to his rear and needed to get some tank destroyers or antitank guns to stop them.

As Kroen and his men approached the railroad bridge to the south, they noticed that the bridge passed over the road that ran parallel to the river on the west bank. He deployed his squad on the bridge in such a fashion that they could arm and drop bazooka ammunition on any German vehicles or tanks that passed under them on the road below. Having lost their bazookas in previous action the men determined to make the best use of the ammunition they were carrying.

In the meantime Bonifay found a medical unit on the Meuse River where he left the wounded men from the 300th ECB. He then tried to return to Rochefort but was turned back by roadblocks manned by the 2nd Armored Division.

At that time American forces in Rochefort consisted of Major Bahe's 3rd Battalion (minus Company L), 335th Infantry [Regiment], a platoon each from the 638th Tank Destroyers Battalion, 309th ECB, and 29th Infantry; and two platoons of the regimental antitank company, besides the platoon of the 51st ECB. By late afternoon on December 23, the Germans had begun to shell Rochefort. A couple of hours after midnight, Panzer Lehr began its main attack from the south.

In just a few minutes the situation deteriorated. Major Bahe could do nothing more than try and hold on in his basement headquarters at the hotel, runners and radio messages from his companies advised that his outpost had been overrun and that the Germans had circled the town. With that news, Wright realized that he could not get out to rejoin his platoon. The platoon already realized it had been cut off and had withdrawn to a pre-arranged assembly point in Givet. The 51st used this procedure so that people would have a known place to assemble.

The infantry wounded were brought into the battalion command post. Major Bahe repeatedly asked regiment on the radio for permission to withdraw. He was told to hold Rochefort. The situation continued to get worse. At one point regiment told him to attack to the north and tie up with friendly forces. He replied ... he could not hold on to what he had and that it was impossible to attack in any direction. He again requested permission to withdraw but was refused.

There was very little food in the basement of the hotel, and supplies could not be brought into town. But a large pile of Irish potatoes and several racks of baked cinnamon rolls were found in the storage bins in the basement which enabled the men to keep their stomachs full.

Throughout the night the rifle companies fought fiercely, but were slowly pushed back toward the square in the center of town. By noon the Germans controlled the streets around the square. From a street-level window of the basement of the hotel Wright could see a .50-caliber machine gun crew force a German tank to back out of sight behind a building. Perhaps the machine gun broke the glass in the driver's peep hole or the fire was so intense that it heated the armor plate so that the driver could not hold his face close to it.

Finally, early on December 24, Major Bahe received permission to leave. Bahe called his company commanders to the basement command post and told them of his intent to withdraw. He noted that there were a few vehicles parked in an alley nearby that the Germans had not reached. They would accommodate only the people in the CP. With the help of smoke grenades and a heavy volume of fire Bahe felt they could run across the street and reach the vehicles. The wounded would have to be left behind with an aid man.

At this point, a soldier sitting in a corner of the room with a bullet hole in his upper lip that was large enough to stick your finger into, got to his feet and in a gurgling voice said, "I'll be damned if you are going to leave me here." Each company was to disengage and withdraw to the west on foot avoiding main roads. Military historian Hugh M. Cole described the situation very well: "Driven back into a small area around the battalion command post where bullet and mortar fire made the streets a 'living inferno', the surrounded garrison made ready for a break."

With smoke and heavy covering fire, Wright and the others dashed across the street one-by-one as bullets ricocheted around them. The wounded who could run did so. Those who could not remained in the basement with the medic. Once in the alley, Wright hopped into a jeep that had a machine gun mounted on it. When the vehicles were loaded, the men drove them out of the alley with all weapons firing as rapidly as possible. The men shot at every door and window in sight. It was like the old Wild West movies when the bandits shot up the town as they made their getaway.

The column headed east then turned south and then west. On this route it did not cross the L'Homme, which loops around the northern part of Rochefort, then joins the Lesse River which flows to the northwest and joins the Meuse River near Dinant. To the complete surprise of the men in the column, after passing the first three or four city blocks, they did not encounter a single German or receive any fire. They did not see any other American forces either. Once in the countryside the men stopped briefly. An elderly lady from a nearby farm house passed out a platter full of fried potatoes as if giving out Christmas gifts. After the men paused to enjoy the food, the column headed for Givet.

That afternoon was unforgettable. It was the first clear sky and sunshine since the Battle of the Bulge began. The sky became even more beautiful as it filled with fighters and bombers headed east to bomb and strafe the German armored columns. By that time, Wright's platoon had the dubious distinction of being shot at by both sides of a pincer movement around Rochefort; to the north en route to Marche by the German 2nd Panzer Division and in Rochefort by Panzer Lehr.

As the column approached the bridge over the Meuse at Givet the men knew they were safe. British tanks in firing positions lined both sides of the road. Major Bahe rounded up several 2½-ton trucks to go back east to find his companies that were coming out on foot. Wright had operated sawmills in the area and knew most of the back roads and logging trails between Givet and Rochefort. He offered to guide Bahe along the roads that his companies would most likely be following.

It was a slow process. They stopped on the top of each hill to look for the soldiers and for Germans: they did not know whom they would encounter first. As late afternoon approached the blue sky changed to gray. It was Christmas Eve, 1944, and still no men in sight. As Bahe and Wright inched their way to the crest of yet another hill and looked to the valley below they saw two columns of U.S. infantrymen, one on each side of the road.

The jeep raced down the hill toward the two columns. The Army 2½-ton truck of W.W.II with its front wheel drive seemed to need two acres to turn around. On this day those trucks turned around on a dime, never leaving the gravel surface of the trail they were on. There was much jubilation from the troops, with cheers and applause, but it quickly ceased for the whereabouts of the German panzer division was unknown. Both columns loaded into the trucks and headed for Givet. Christmas came early for some members of the 3rd Battalion, 335th Infantry Regiment, 84th Infantry Division. Back in Givet Wright found his platoon right where they were supposed to be. It was a joyous reunion.

Several hours after dark on December 24, Wright sent Bonifay and two men back to the chateau near Ciergnon on the Lesse River, where Company A had had its CP on December 17, 1944. All nonessential items of equipment and baggage had been left at the chateau for a week under the guard of Corporal Loyd E. Sweatt. Bonifay's orders were to pick up Sweatt and all the baggage he could and return to Givet. He took the half-track driven by Sergeant Weil and assigned Sergeant Kroen to man the .50-caliber machine gun mounted on it.

Recent Reminiscences and Reflections ... A LIFETIME LATER

Ciergnon lay about 13 miles east of Givet. Having no knowledge of the location of the Germans, Bonifay proceeded cautiously. The night was cold and clear with several inches of snow on the ground. The half-track could be heard for miles. The group passed through Beauraing without incident, then headed northeast toward Ciergnon. There Bonifay was challenged by a small detachment of combat engineers under the command of a lieutenant. After establishing their identity, the lieutenant told Bonifay that the bridge over the Lesse River was prepared for demolition and would be blown shortly. The lieutenant gave Bonifay 30 minutes to cross the bridge, get to the chateau, about a quarter miles from the bridge, and return.

Corporal Sweatt, having been put on guard duty by the Company Commander, Captain Pedersen, was reluctant to leave his post without orders from the captain. Some firm persuasion from Bonifay convinced Sweatt to leave. Loading all the barracks bags and equipment that the half-track could hold, the crew headed for the bridge. Shortly after crossing, a loud explosion was heard as the engineers blew the bridge. Bonifay and his crew returned to Givet less cautiously than when they went to Ciergnon.

The defense of Rochefort had not been too costly: fifteen wounded men, under the care of a volunteer medic, were left in town and another 25 killed or captured. But the Panzer Lehr commander, General Bayerlein, who had fought in both Bastogne and Rochefort, later rated the American defense in Rochefort as comparable in courage and in significance to that of Bastogne.

Captain Sam C. Scheuber
Recipient of Silver Star for Trois Ponts Action

Trois Ponts

Of course the high point in Company C military history was the defense of Trois Ponts. There were other high points as well such as the Roer River bridging, the hard fought Danube crossing at Ingolstadt and our participation in construction of the Rhine River bridge at Kripp-Linz. None of these last mentioned had the over-all strategic importance of denying the German forces, which we faced at Trois Ponts, of their planned route west. While at Trois Ponts, we hardly knew what we were doing (except following specific orders) and the import only comes through in the light of history and the review of our actions at the time. Now it becomes clear why Col. Peiper, leader of the spearhead Kampfgruppe of First SS Panzer Division (that's all we were facing!), as he saw the bridge go up in a shower of dust and debris, banged his knee with a clipboard and said, "Those damned engineers! Those damned engineers!"

Portrait from May 1945. *Corps Files*

I'm not going to go into details of the action at Trois Ponts. You all, first hand or otherwise, know that story. I am going to relate an isolated incidence which none of you know about because all others involved are dead! Except me.

Shortly after the bridge on the highway to Malmédy had been blown (and for all I know Lt. Green was still trying to get over the shock of swimming the icy Amblève River to get back to us) Colonel Anderson arrived in town. He said, "Captain, can you show me those German tanks?" I said "Certainly, Colonel Anderson." We were close by the near side of the blown bridge over the Amblève and from there climbed a steep hill east of us to a ridge of that hill which afforded a view of the Malmédy-Trois Ponts Highway. I had not anticipated a forward movement of the tank column since last viewing them and inadvertently we exposed ourselves while getting to the view point at the ridge. Colonel Anderson had an unknown staff officer along. There we all stood, exposed. Col. was counting "Fourteen, fifteen, sixteen" when an 88 mm tank shell went between us or slightly overhead to explode on the hillside beyond. Now anyone who has had the privilege of hearing an 88 pass close by will never forget the sound or how it will immediately get your attention! When we three finished tumbling off that ridge (there wasn't time to run) Col. Anderson and I ended up in about the same pile! Now remember back about him. Always neat, even prim; always of erect military posture, never perturbed and totally calm. I never ever heard him raise his voice or indulge in profanity ever! Yet when he was in that pile of bushes and people, I found him still on the ground looking at the ground from knee height and softly saying "God Damn! God Damn!" Then he got up, starting to brush himself off and his eyes met mine. "Captain, any man who has been through this once and then asks to come back to it does not have a brain in his head!" (Really, he didn't say those words exactly. He used a much more earthy, and pungent expression as to what might pass for brains.) You see, Col. Anderson had been in WWI!

Anyway, he next asked for a telephone to alert 1st Army in Spa. "Colonel, telephones went out with the bridge." "Then can you lend me a jeep and driver?" "Sure, Colonel." Pvt. Snow, our driver, and the unknown aide departed for Spa. Col. Anderson went back to Group, wherever it was. Pvt. Snow and the unknown Captain died in the roadside ditch near Bra* on their return trip. ["At 1400 hrs. Snow left with Capt. Lundberg 1111th ECG on mission to Army HQ.", according to Millard] We had been surrounded!

Now, let's go on to another high point. I want to tell you how an isolated and under strength Combat Engineer Company might be, can be, and actually was relieved by an entire airborne infantry regiment!

Pvt. Snow and the unknown Captain crossed the Lienne River Bridge on their way back from Spa before meeting German forces. As German forces approached the bridge it was blown by a unit of the 291st. We, in Trois Ponts, were now not only surrounded but cut off. First Army counted us as dead. The 505th Parachute Regiment of 82nd Airborne Division jumped off at Werbomont. (An action only made possible because we, us, you and I were still at Trois Ponts.) They walked for eighteen miles, to meet our western roadblock on the Werbomont Road. Later, in our basement CP, in walked a gaunt, red haired Colonel of Infantry. He said "I'm Ekman, 505th. We have come to relieve you." Instead of cheers of relief after the bad days just passed, Major Yates, without even standing up, said "I'll bet you are sure glad to find us here!" Col. Ekman was, as his commendation shows.

Now, for any and all who have not heard those commendations, here they are paraphrased:

> From HDQ 505th Parachute Infantry -- Commendation:
>
> On Dec. 19, 1944 when this unit advanced to seize Trois Ponts, the Regimental Commander found your unit in complete command of the town and rivers thereby greatly assisting this unit in their mission. Although Co. C had been completely isolated four days and nights, they as-

---

* They were about 4 miles north of Bra. See details in Fred Nabor's "Jeep Driver Incident" account.

Recent Reminiscences and Reflections ... A LIFETIME LATER

sisted in maintaining control for another 48 hours.

1st Endorsement by Major Gen. Jim Gavin 82nd Airborne Div.

2nd Endorsement by Matthew B. Ridgeway, Major Gen. XVIII Airborne Corps.

And I do not want to fail to add the third endorsement of which I am the most proud:

To Commanding Officer, Co. C:

Here read 3rd endorsement by Harvey Fraser:

51st Engr. Combat Bn., APO 230, U.S. Army, 15 January 1945.

TO: Commanding Officer, Co. "O", 51st Engr. Combat Bn., APO 230.

Only a Commanding Officer knows the surge of pride that comes from receiving a letter and endorsements such as this. Superlative phrases of commendation have already been written in the foregoing paragraphs. I heartily concur in every one of them. To them, let me add that the privilege of being in command of troops of such sterling quality and fortitude, such tenacity of purpose and devotion to duty, is the most profound experience that can come to a commanding officer. I know that this performance is another one of a series that will indelibly write the name of the 51st Engineers across the pages of EPO history.

Harvey R. Fraser / Lt. Colonel, CE / Commanding

By God, we are there in the history!

Even a British publication "Battle of the Bulge" (by a British Brigadier, Lieut. Gen. Napier Crooreuden) spends a page, with maps on the action at Trois Ponts.

Besides these references, you are down in history, as Co. C in every other account of the Battle of the Bulge except one, which I will not mention. It says, in essence, that Trois Ponts was saved by the 291st with assist by a squad from 51st Engr. Combat Bn. Such shiii! (Stuff.)

To go on to the greatest accolade of all: from Robert Merriam, of the Dictionary Family, who was a 1st Army historian. Condensed and paraphrased [from ***Dark December***]:

Col. Peiper knew that if he could cross the river at Trois Ponts he would be in the open with a free run to the west. Success seemed within his grasp as he started confidently along the Amblève towards Trois Ponts. But he was halted. Co. C of the 51st ECB had been ordered to Trois Ponts to blow the bridges. This small group halted Peiper's advance with a small anti-tank gun then blew the bridges in his face!

To quote exactly:

Here was a case where the fate of the Divisions and Armies rested for a few brief moments on the shoulders of a handful of men: first at the town of Trois Ponts, and then, only hours later, with a smaller handful of men at the bridge east of Werbomont. Had either of these groups failed in their job (and the temptation to run must have been very great) [He really can't know how great] Peiper's 1st SS Panzers would have gotten through to the Meuse River next morning.

But these two handfuls of American soldiers, despite uncertainties of whereabouts of friendly or enemy soldiers, chose to ride out the German attack. As a result Kampfgruppe Peiper was sacked in the canyons of the Amblève and a second major defeat had been dealt the Germans!

We are in the history and don't need to take a back seat to anyone.

Captain Albert E. Radford
Professor Emeritus of Botany, University of North Carolina - Chapel Hill

Activities of the 51st ECB near Champlon Crossroads -- 21-23 December

A small but important part of the intent of this book is to set the record straight. Herein corrected by the author's well-corroborated personal recollection, is the location of Company A during December 21-23 as the Germans probed the Champlon Crossroads area. Initially sent there by Col. Fraser (hence his recollection that they had *maintained* defenses there?), they soon were nowhere to be seen, having been required for well-reported defensive activities elsewhere.

According to the S-1 Daily Log dated December 21, 1944:
"Company A (2nd and 3rd platoons) contacted enemy on Route N-4 SE of Marche in the vicinity of P 400665 (south of Champlon Crossroads), fire was exchanged and the Co. A men were forced to retire on the blocks and return to Bn. HQ, arriving at 1930."

*According to **Holding the Line**, page 48:* "The 2nd and 3rd Platoons of Company A were responsible for the following defenses prepared and/or maintained on 22 December (226883)--abatis, (235889)--bridge mined, (221894) and (229900)--Roadblocks coordinated with elements of 309th Engineer Combat Battalion, (236902)--Road and bridge mined, (264411)--bridge mined, coordinated with elements of the 309th Engineer Combat Battalion, and (278915) bridge and road mined." These operations were north of Marche, well away from Champlon Crossroads.

According to a conversation with Lt. Henry on July 20, 1997 by the author: "... after Major Yates returned to the CP from his capture by the Germans at 2200 on 22 December Lt. Col. Fraser ordered him along with M/Sgt. Raper to take a 4-ton wrecker to the N4-496 jct. to remove the explosion debris so that the 84th Infantry Division would have a cleared road for its forward movement on 23 December. They successfully accomplished their mission without incident."

*According to **The 51st Again!** by Barry W. Fowle and Floyd D. Wright 1992, pp. 96-98:* "While Company

Champlon Crossroads: 88, B6

B held off the 116th Panzer Division at Hotton, Col. Fraser sent Capt. Radford, H & S Company, with two of his men (Roberts, and Self) to Champlon Crossroads to support Company A and a Canadian Forestry unit (on December 21). When they arrived in the late afternoon, they found the Canadians but no one from Company A. The Canadian unit commander (who had not seen Capt. Pedersen or Company A all day) agreed to deploy in the woods southwest of the crossroads while Radford set up his .50-caliber machine gun in the woods northwest of the crossroads.

"Within a short period of time, a battle could be heard in progress in the southeast toward Ourtheuville. The roar of tanks, bursting shells, small arms fire and the screams of wounded men were easily distinguishable. It did not take long for the Canadian Forestry commander to decide that he had urgent business in the rear; he abandoned Radford and his two men. Fraser then sent Radford seven miles northwest to 496 and N4 to set up a checkpoint" (at a roadblock set up earlier -- Radford stayed at the checkpoint until the railroad cars were pushed across the road the night of the 22nd).

"At the roadblock were the two H & S men, the three 7th AD tank retriever men, and two mechanics and five cooks from Company A 51st ECB. The tank retriever (that night) pushed the cars across the road, effectively blocking it, then took off. TNT was put under the wheels and set off. The explosion tore up the ends of the gravel cars without knocking off the wheels, blocking the road with quite a pile of twisted metal and spilled gravel. The explosion also brought down the power lines along the road and created a spectacular electrical display. If nothing else, perhaps the downed wires would electrocute a few Germans. Radford and his men then headed for Marche."

First Lieutenant Joseph B. Milgram, Jr.
Recipient of Silver Star for Trois Ponts Action & Platoon Leader, Company C

Trois Ponts Plaque Commendation:
Brief remarks of Joseph B. Milgram, Jr. on Saturday May 15, 1993 at Trois Ponts, Belgium, in commemoration of the defense of the town by the 51st Engineer Combat Battalion, Company C

"Mesdames et Messieurs, merci. My apologies; I must speak in English.

"We have a peaceful day in Trois Ponts in the Ardennes. Those of us who were here in 1944 did not find it so at that time. We are today a small group of veterans of the fierce combat that took place here in December 1944 returning to pay a visit, to commemorate events that have since become noteworthy. I shall speak only briefly, and about now ... and about then.

Silver Star awarded by III Corps Engineer, F. Russel Lyons, at **Heister**, Germany - 23 March 1945.
Collection of Joseph Milgram

"Some of us have not come back to Belgium since that time. Others, including myself, have returned several times during the intervening years, not to relive the battles, but rather to visit with the friends we soldiers first made here in Belgium, and to whom we remain close even after these many years have passed.

"I suggest that memories are rarely of violence and death. My own memories are much more of the beautiful country you have, of the peace and quiet I find on visits here, and of the fine families we have come to know and love. My family and I have friendships that began only because I served here in the Ardennes. Our children know each other, we visit each other, especially for weddings. Several of our Belgian friends have come to work and to study in America. Two of my sons learned to speak the French language fluently. (That still does not happen often enough in America today.)

"None of those wonderful things in my life could have happened had I not been here in 1944.

"Because our soldiers had been working and living on the ground in the Ardennes during the fall of the year 1944 before the December counterattack, that knowledge gave us intimate understanding of the terrain, and greatly helped our defense of the area, in which small groups of men of the 51st were able to defend crossroads, bridges and strong points along the line from here to the town of Marche en Famenne, and beyond.

"At that time we knew nothing of the importance of our battle assignment here, but today, after study by the military historians, our successes have come to be known as a vital turning point of the Battle of the Bulge. Yes, Trois Ponts and the two hundred men of C Company of the 51st Engineers are now in all the history books!

"I am pleased to be in the spokesman for Company C of the 51st Engineers, a very small unit of the American Army, that, together with a number of other smaller units in December 1944 defended Trois Ponts.

"And so, forty-nine years later, we are no longer young men, we are no longer so vigorous nor numerous, we return to the battle scene for this short commemoration, and to place a marker on the River Amblève bridge. It is unlikely that together we shall come again.

"Many American soldiers and airmen died or were wounded in Belgium in World War II. I learned that the number of U.S. casualties during the fifty days of the Battle of the Bulge was more than 76,000 killed, missing and wounded. Several were a part of, or assigned to this unit. I can recall the names of at least eight men who died defending Trois Ponts. Still others were wounded or were missing in action.

"It is to them that we dedicate the plaque on the bridge today:

> [526th Armored Infantry: Buchanan, Higgins, Hollenback ,and McCollum. 1111 Engineer Combat Group: Lundberg. 51st Engineer Combat Battalion: Rankin, Snow, Strawser.]

"And, because of the passage of so many years, we sadly include in our dedication the remembrance of the many fellow soldiers of the 51st who have died since then. Thank you."

A few anecdotes that I remember from Trois Ponts *

All during the fall it had been my duty to travel extensively throughout the Ardennes by jeep to visit the

---
* Recorded, 7 May 1988.

many sawmills that our people were supervising. I thought that I knew just about every road, trail and firebreak in the region. It was bitter cold most of the time with snow on and off beginning in September.

Our men regularly encountered suspicious sounds near their encampments at night, saw lights flickering in the trees, found evidence of fires in still warm ashes, and other traces of the enemy.

We regularly reported these findings, but it seemed that we were ignored, nobody cared, nobody inquired further, nobody investigated what we were saying. I was writing many of the reports and wondering if they were even read.

It was nearly midnight on December 17th when the small units -- some were less than squads -- had arrived at Melreux, the Company C Headquarters location having been summoned by messengers from the numerous sawmills where they had been billeted to oversee the cutting of lumber during the past couple of months. We loaded everyone on the trucks and started off toward Trois Ponts. This was the main body of Company C.

We knew the area intimately, having built bridges throughout this region from September onward. But travel that night called for full blackout, so progress was slow. I was in the first truck, and recall that when we finally reached the Manhay crossroads, an MP shone his flashlight into my face and asked in the most incredulous tone of voice, "Just where the hell do you think you're going?"

He had a point because it was at this location that we encountered the most unbelievable stream of traffic heading the other way on the two lane road we were to take to the east. Although it was pitch black, our eyes had grown somewhat used to seeing and it seemed to us that every conceivable kind of vehicle including tanks, tank destroyers, artillery pieces in tow, command cars, jeeps, and trucks was coming the other way, bumper to bumper, sliding off the road and having all sorts of trouble moving. Here we were idiots, heading east.

I replied that we were the 51st Engineers, and that we had orders to be in Trois Ponts by morning, and that we were going ahead, come what may. He waved us on, shaking his head. After the first few miles, our "company" on the other side of the road disappeared, and we settled in to a mighty lonely ride, scared all the way, groping our way along. We made it without incident.

On December 17th or 18th, although they were mined, we held the bridges in the town open before blowing them, to allow a large part of the Seventh Armored Division to pass over them on its way to St. Vith.

At some point, an open top self propelled gun -- perhaps it was a tank destroyer, I am now no longer clear -- slid off the north side of the bridge and into the Salm River. As the last of the convoy of the Seventh Armored passed, the crew abandoned the vehicle and dropped thermite grenades to deny its use to the enemy, should there be a breakthrough. The vehicle burned furiously.

During that day and night and for some days and nights afterward, the ammunition remaining in the hot vehicle exploded sporadically but noisily. That unexpected deception, combined with the noise of our trucks going up and down the hill at night helped considerably, in my opinion, to discourage enemy advances toward the town.

During our stay in Trois Ponts, and before the 505th PI came along, we were frequently fired upon by what was obviously American artillery. They were good, and we came to respect their accuracy, but were thoroughly frustrated that nobody seemed to know that we were there. We spent a lot of time in cellars.

After the joining together of our group with the 505th PI of the 82nd Airborne, their people had found a store of Belgian beer (I still don't understand how we had missed it, but suggest that it must have been that we were awfully busy; at any rate, I believe that we never missed a similar opportunity thereafter!) The beer was contained in thick ceramic bottles of the kind that is closed with a ceramic cap attached to the bottle with wires.

This was our first encounter with the 82nd. We were filled with admiration, even awe, as on the way up the hill to the attack across the Salm, the paratroopers gave us their hand grenades so as to have room in their baggy uniform pockets for the bottles of beer, which were just the right size!

Their engagement on the hill was particularly bloody. There were serious losses in dead and wounded, but the 505th took and held the hill.

Shortly thereafter an order was received from General Montgomery to abandon the hill and return to the west bank and the town of Trois Ponts. There was some delay, during which we supposed that the order was being appealed, but the order held, and down the 505th came.

The paratroopers were, to a man, angry and bitter. Many of their wounded had to be left on the hill. We were told that the 82nd had never before retreated from a position it had taken in an attack.

The 505th did not think well of Montgomery at the time, and I suppose, considering Arnhem, not thereafter as well.

My reading has indicated that Monty decided to "tidy up" the line by removing that salient, as he looked at his map of the front he was newly commanding. (This is the attack referred to on your page 16, I think.)

Letter to my father, from Joe Milgram

Germany, April 30, 1945
"Dear Dad,

"Thanks for the note you wrote on the thirty-first of March, which I just received yesterday. That delay in delivery is due no doubt to the fact that we are now with the Third US Army, and have accordingly changed APO's. Besides that we have moved several hundred miles in the last few weeks.

"The battles for which we received the Presidential Unit Citation were not near Bastogne, but were considerably north and somewhat east of that famous battleground. Earlier in the campaign there was a time when we were in Bastogne for long enough to build a bridge, however. The towns we fought near were Trois Ponts, about 5 miles west of Stavelot and Hotton, about five miles northeast of Marche. I was in Trois Ponts, the town of the three bridges, and a vital road center. If Trois Ponts were held, the enemy would have no route to Liège, for two of the three roads led to the main highway from Bastogne, Houffalize to Aywaille and Liège. During the four days and nights there, we were repeatedly attacked from all sides by the First SS Panzer Division [Kampfgruppe Peiper]. But they never got through. On the fourth night we were contacted by a patrol, from the finest outfit in the army -- the 505th Parachute Infantry

Arnhem: F2

Regiment of the 82nd Airborne Division. The 505th, you will remember, was the one which landed in Normandy long before H Hour on D Day. They also gave an excellent account of themselves at Arnhem. We certainly were glad to see these men, for there weren't many who thought we'd ever get out of Trois Ponts alive, and it was a certainty that we'd never surrender to the SS men, who specialize in not taking prisoners. Afterward we had the pleasure of working with the entire 82nd AB Division, as we engineered them through the Bullion forest east of St. Vith, to allow them to get in position to crack the Siegfried line there, but they never went all the way through it because they were pulled out before they could. There's plenty more I could say if the rules would permit, but at present that's all. There was another time when we worked with the 82nd later on, but I can't tell about that now.

"We're rolling along now, and hoping harder every day that we'll be able to go home before a ride to the Pacific when this part of the war is over, but predict nothing as yet on that subject.

"Time to stop for now. Give my love to Mother and my best wishes to all the people I know but whom I haven't time to write."

First Lieutenant Fred Nabors

Company C 51st Engineer Combat Battalion arrived at Trois Ponts near midnight December 17, 1944, with three line platoons. The Headquarters platoon arrived later. Company Commander Captain Sam Scheuber, a native of San Angelo, Texas, immediately deployed the platoons in a defensive layout to guard the town perimeter. Two bridges were mined with explosives for demolition. Roadblocks were established several hundred meters from the town limits. Lt. Nabors' second platoon had the road to Vielsalm, and the road from the east toward Wanne. No one advised Lt. Nabors that a platoon from the 291st Engineer Bn. had been assigned to mine the bridge across the Salm River on the road to Vielsalm about 2000 meters south of Trois Ponts. Perhaps company headquarters knew it.

England, 1941. *Corps files*

The Town

Trois Ponts is a very small town on the Salm river in the Ardennes Forest of Belgium. The Salm flows into the Amblève on the northern edge of town. Both rivers have cut deep narrow valleys into a low plateau. At the town site the valley is about 100 meters deep. A railway station and rail yard have been carved into the plateau on the right bank (east) side of town so that an almost vertical cliff extends along the rail yard for about 600 meters. The rail line through the station is about 15 to 20 meters above the river level. North of the station the rails cross the Amblève River on a high bridge, and the railroad forks, with one line continuing north and the other turning east. High dirt fills maintain the rails level across the Amblève valley.

Two railway underpasses were built on highway N23 which enters Trois Ponts from the east. Because of the height of the railway fill they actually were short tunnels. Immediately beyond the second underpass, the highway makes an abrupt left turn to cross the Amblève highway bridge into the town. Near the town center N23 turns west, crosses the Salm River bridge and continues towards Werbomont. These above mentioned highway bridges were mined with explosives by Company C for instant demolition. The north-south road from Vielsalm to La Gleize which passes through Trois Ponts merges with N23 for about 300 meters and uses both bridges.

We have learned since the war that Hitler's plan for the Ardennes Offensive plotted five routes to be followed by the tank commanders. Deviation from an assigned route would subject them to possible death by court martial. Two of the routes were through Trois Ponts, or near enough that they were defended by the 51st Company C. Peiper was scheduled to turn north towards La Gleize (which he did). How fortunate for Company C that he was not blocked from following that road.*

Another tank column from the First SS Panzer Division [from Kampfgruppe Peiper] was routed through the little town of Wanne, and west about three kilometers to the cliff overlooking Trois Ponts. The road followed a switch back down the cliff, crossed the railroad by an overpass, and entered Trois Ponts by a street between the river and train station. The overpass was mined but never blown. It remains in use today.

Main street had a row of buildings between it and the river. Entrances were at street level with basements below. Civilians were hard to find, but occasionally a man and woman were in the basement. I don't recall seeing any children. Most buildings were two or three stories high along main street. There was a large church in the center of town. Most buildings were adjoining, but there were a few gaps. At times tracer bullets seemed to fill all the gaps.

First Encounter with the Enemy

Company C was fortunate to get some rest early the morning of December 18. It was almost noon before a jeep arrived in Trois Ponts with the message that a tank was coming down highway N23.

Major Bob Yates gave the order to blow both bridges without delay. The Major had arrived that morning and assumed command. He had been hospitalized with a broken ankle. Upon returning to duty he was rushed to Trois Ponts by the 51st C.O. (then) Lt. Col. Harvey Fraser. Major Yates, a native of Marshall, Texas, was executive Officer of the 51st Engineer Combat Battalion. He was not executive officer of Colonel Wally Anderson's 1111 Engineer Combat Group as some accounts claim.

Colonel Anderson's Headquarters were located in Trois Ponts until about noon on the 18th. He moved the headquarters to Werbomont. The move was so hasty that many men left their barracks bags and Christmas packages behind in a second floor quarters on main street in Trois Ponts. Men of Company C found this amusing. Artillery fire on the 20th ignited the building and it burned to the ground.

The two bridges went off with loud booms, possibly a little prematurely because the chow truck remained at the railway station, a place we were not likely to have chow lines any more. Excitement was high. No one knew what to expect, but they didn't have long to wait.

---

*According to *A Time for Trumpets* (p.162), Peiper was assigned a Wanne-Trois Ponts-Werbomont route. He deviated from plan at **Ligneuville** (B3) then returned to Trois Ponts. Only after the 51st blew the bridges did he divert to La Gleize, a route he knew was more lengthy and problematical; and it indeed proved disastrous. Had the road to La Gleize been been blocked at Trois Ponts, then Peiper's column would have most likely directed its force into Trois Ponts on December 18th, before reinforcements could arrive.

Recent Reminiscences and Reflections … A LIFETIME LATER

57mm Antitank Roadblock

First Lt. Richard I. Green, Commander of the third platoon, a native of Steamboat Rock, Iowa, had a half-track and 57 MM antitank gun for his defense on the north, courtesy of the 7th Armored Division. The four-man gun crew were unable to join their outfit, and volunteered to aid in the defense of Trois Ponts.

Dick Green's first hand account of the initial battle follows: The 57 MM gun was located near the second underpass in a ditch beside the road. Dick and three or four men were there in support of the gun crew. Thirteen shells were laid out on the ground near the gun. When the first Panzer tank appeared at the first underpass exit, the gun crew began firing. Dick said he saw the shells hitting the tank, and bouncing off like tennis balls. One shell broke a track on the first tank. A second tank pulled alongside and, using the first tank as a shield, began firing. The thirteen shells were almost gone and the crew asked Dick to go to the half-track for more. Dick and his men ran through the underpass to the half-track, but before they could return a direct hit destroyed the gun, killing all the crew. Dick withdrew across the river to join the remainder of his platoon.

It was learned later that the tanks were from Task Force Peiper. The tanks were cautious about passing through the second underpass. They sent a captured American armored car and a captured American jeep through, and ran them up to the blown bridge. I watched as men of Lt. Green's third platoon fired their rifles from basement windows at the "American" vehicles. We suspected that their intent was to locate us and gauge our strength. Most of our fire was from basement windows and thus hard to detect.

Staff Sergeant William Rankin, motor sergeant, headquarters platoon was in a building about halfway up the side of the valley. He took a 50 caliber machine gun to the third floor, mounted it in a window and began firing. The Jeep diver was wounded and was aided by his buddies to reenter the underpass. The captured U.S. armored car came out of the underpass and trained it's 37 MM gun on the building where the Sergeant had the 50 Cal. Rankin was killed on the spot. His life and the four antitank crewmen were not in vain because they and others of the Company C Engineers convinced the enemy that Trois Ponts was defended by soldiers who were willing to die for the cause. Perhaps this was the reason 150 men were able to hold Trois Ponts for three days until relieved by the 82nd Airborne Division.

The Minefield Roadblock

Sergeant William S. Cundiff, native of Caddo, Oklahoma, commanded the third squad of the second platoon. He was assigned the task of laying a mine field in the road from Wanne. On the high ground of the plateau, as the road approached the cliff, the forest came close to the sides of the road. At this point a tank could not leave the road. No other vehicle route existed to pass this point so a roadblock here was effective. The mine field was laid out in a pattern to prevent any vehicle from passing through. The mines were placed on top of the pavement. Time did not permit digging them into the road as was normal practice.

The forest had been cleared from a small cultivated field just beyond the mines. This provided an ideal field of fire on anything stopped by the mines. The surrounding forest provided protection from tanks. Hastily dug foxholes would provide some protection for the defenders, but there wasn't time to log roofs for the foxholes. Some of the defenders were dug in on the edge of the cliff with a field of fire down the road over the mines. This field of fire had the disadvantage of facing a tank's thickest armor, but the men were not endangered by tree bursts from the tank's 88 MM cannon.

In the confusion following the blowing of the bridges, and the battle between the underpasses, Lt. Nabors was surprised to see Sergeant Cundiff on the main street of Trois Ponts. When asked why he wasn't guarding the mine field, he said someone in the town had signaled for the squad to come down. That was probably true, but no one admitted to the signal.

In view of the urgency to defend the mine field, and the fact that the entire third squad was not immediately available, Nabors grabbed a bazooka man, Pfc. Eduardo Peralta and rushed up to the mine field. Cundiff was ordered to assemble the remainder of third squad, and return to the roadblock. All was quiet on the road as Nabors and Peralta dug a foxhole alongside the open field a few feet back into the forest and with an excellent view of the road. The rest of the third squad arrived and resumed their former positions. Action followed shortly.

There were no houses along the road so we were surprised to see a baby buggy coming down the road, pushed by a person wearing female garb. Upon nearing the minefield, the buggy turned and went back up the hill towards Wanne. There was a road to the village of Petit-Spai that intersected the road to Wanne about 100 meters from the mine field. That road also connected this road and highway N23. There was a weak bridge over the Amblève River at Petit-Spai. The person pushing the baby buggy passed the road junction and continued up the hill towards Wanne. She (?) soon turned and returned towards the minefield. Cundiff had a rifleman fire a round over the person's head. The baby buggy then turned and went out of sight up the hill at a very rapid pace.

After maybe fifteen minutes, with nothing in sight, a motor was heard to rev up and there was a rattling of tank treads. The tank advanced by short runs, perhaps 100 meters, with only motor sounds between. Finally, after seemingly ages but probably 10 minutes, the tank came into view, and continued advancing by short runs to within 50 meters of the mines.

The tank was a Royal Tiger, 69 ton. It would appear that the tank was being used as a mobile pill box. There were no infantry with it. No doubt the motive was to feel out our strength. Sergeant Cundiff tried to fire a bazooka, and had it knocked from his hands by machine gun fire. Nabors was in perfect range and position to hit the tank in the side with bazooka fire. Peralta was ordered to reload as quickly as possible after firing. It was not to be, as batteries had run down while the bazooka was in storage and the engineers were busy working and not fighting.

The tank began firing its eight MM machine guns at the mines. Occasionally a mine would explode. With no infantry in sight, we could have stayed on defense indefinitely, but we didn't like the idea of the tank exploding all the mines with machine gun fire and coming down the hill behind us. We withdrew into town and joined our main line of defense. It seems the tank was unwilling to cross the mine field, even after most of the mines were destroyed. The roadblock was surprisingly effective. It may have been a different story had the tank been accompanied by infantry.

The battle was not over, however; [Army] Air Force P-47s took charge and bombed and strafed along the road for several minutes. The tank, and possibly other tanks, withdrew. The following morning Major Bob Yates sent Nabors out with a patrol to check the high ground beyond the mine field. The patrol proceeded through the forest alongside the road for a distance of approximately one kilometer. There was no sign of life, neither military nor civilian. It was about eight o'clock, on December 19.

The defense may have seemed stronger than it actually was. Major Yates and Company C had nothing to do with the air strike, but the enemy did not know that. After dark, on the 18th, the Major ordered that trucks be driven through the streets of Trois Ponts all night long. Our largest truck was a four ton which was used to tow the bulldozer. It had a very satisfying exhaust sound, and we kept it busy all night. Who knows whether the enemy was fooled, but something caused him to hold off longer than seemed realistic considering his strength.

The enemy was able to reach highway N23 behind Company C for a very short period on the 18th. The bridge over Lienne Creek was blown by Company A, 291st Engineer Battalion, but the tanks* were able to ford the creek. After some light fighting against 119 Regiment of the 30th Infantry Division beyond the creek, the tanks retired to Cheneux (near La Glieze) before midnight on the 18th. Trois Ponts was never taken. The Bulge stopped there!

The Jeep Driver Incident

Pfc. James M. Snow, Jr. was unquestionably the best Jeep driver in the 51st, and maybe in the whole U.S. Army. A native of Washington, DC, he had some training from his father who was a taxicab driver. He was very blond with flat top haircut. Only 19 years old, in an older outfit, he was loved by all who knew him. He was assigned to the Second Platoon and was considered, by Nabors, its least expendable member. He tangled with a tank on highway N23 behind Trois Ponts and came out second best.

The tank-jeep encounter was later described to members of the 51st Engineers by a Belgian civilian** who lived in a chateau just up the hill from the bridge over Lienne Creek on Highway N23. Company C 51st Engineers, about two months earlier, had been assigned to rebuild the bridge which had been blown by the retreating Germans as the Allies raced across France and Belgium. Company C camped in pup tents alongside the driveway to the chateau occupied by the "Count". Men of the company called him Count because they had trouble pronouncing his name. He may have been a real count. He lived with wife and two young sons on the estate owned by his wife's father, and managed the timber business. The bridge was finished after 48 hours, but the Company stayed on for about 10 days and trained on the estate before getting a new assignment.

The Belgians entertained the Company C Officers with a couple of dinners and a deer hunt. The estate owner, a high government official, and wife attended the deer hunt. The mother-in-law shot a pig and a fox -- the only game. We ate the pig at a formal dinner in the chateau. The older couple asked to ride in the jeep from the deer hunt back to the chateau. James Snow, driver, saw to it that there were plenty of thrills for the riders on the mountain roads.

On December 18, 1944, Jeep driver Snow was loaned to Captain A. P. Lundberg, motor officer of the 1111 Engineer Group. He was to report on the situation in Trois Ponts to First Army Headquarters. They ran into trouble as they returned to Trois Ponts.

The Count described the action as follows: The jeep had crossed the bridge over Lienne Creek and headed up the hill towards the chateau. The Captain told Snow to gun the jeep past some German Solders in the roadside ditch while he opened up with the tommy gun. A Panzer tank was sitting in the driveway to the chateau with the motor running. It was concealed from the jeep by the forest. The tank driver put the tank in gear and rolled up to the entrance on highway N23. The jeep was outgunned and both passengers died.

---

* Only armored cars and half-tracks explored across the Lienne, according to *A Time for Trumpets* (p 430). Few escaped the 119th Regiment. ** The civilian was a Count DuPont, according to Joseph Milgram [personal communication, October 9, 2001].
Cheneux: 78, B3

The Count recognized the jeep as one of the 51st Engineer vehicles by markings painted on the bumper. He did not know the Captain. He was an eye witness, but probably had details filled in by the Germans.

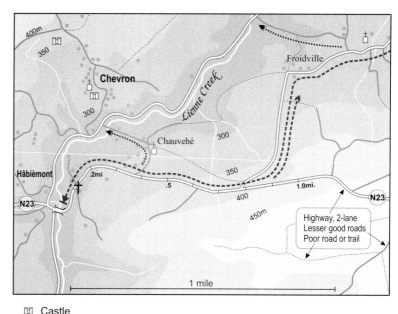

- Castle
- Church
- Dwelling
- Hâbièmont Bridge

Peiper's approach (up to 4:30 pm) ◄------
Panzer reconnaissance (unsuitable bridges) ......↗
Peiper's withdrawal to Stoumont ------►

A few questions remain unanswered*. Why would a motor officer be borrowing a jeep from another company? Why had the Lienne Creek bridge not been blown with the enemy tanks very near on highway N23? Had the 1111 Engineer Gp. Headquarters Company passed along the road without seeing the tanks or the destroyed jeep with its deceased passengers? Why were the tanks delaying before crossing (and capturing) the bridge? Why did the Captain not turn the jeep and rush back across the bridge to safety? Did the Captain have some message from First Army for the commander at Trois Ponts that merited his risking his life to deliver, and what was the message, if such was the case? Were the Germans acquainted with the Count while stationed in Belgium earlier? Why, of all the men in the U.S. Army, did it have to be Nabors' driver?

Private Snow may have been ambushed (†) very near the bridge. The modern basis for this map [*Esneux-St. Vith, #116, Belgian National Geographical Institute*], shows only one possible locale, given the narratives, the photo on page 85 (apparently looking NE), and the single dwelling-with-road shown south of N23. Probaby Private Snow did not see the nearby Germans, shielded by trees. He crossed, made a dash for it and was killed. The bridge must have been blown almost immediately afterwards.

First Platoon Captures a Patrol

Germans were reported to be wearing American uniforms behind the front lines. Therefore, it was not unreasonable for the First Platoon that was guarding the back door to Trois Ponts on highway N23 to challenge a patrol of 505 Regiment soldiers from the 82nd Airborne when they arrived in the early hours of December 19th. The situation was dangerous because the patrol was unaware of the presence of the 51st, and thought they might be Germans in American uniforms. After suspicions were at least partially reduced, Major Yates agreed to the patrol leader's request to send First Lt. John J. Norton, native of Somerville, MA, to inform the Battalion Commander of the situation at Trois Ponts.

En route to the Battalion headquarters Norton became convinced that the patrol were Germans in American uniforms, and that he was in fact a prisoner. As they walked along in blacked out darkness, Norton removed sensitive papers and pictures of his family from his billfold, tore them up and dropped them in the dirt. At the headquarters he met Lt. Col. Benjamin V. Vandervoort and regained enough confidence to tell

---

* According to *A Time for Trumpets* (p. 243), the following occurred at **Lienne Creek** Bridge (78): 3PM - 291st Engineers arrive from Werbomont and start wiring the bridge; 4PM - Col. Anderson and his 1111th ECG headquarters group arrive from Trois Ponts and pass westward; 4:30PM - Peiper's column appears onto N23 from Cheneux; minutes later, in sight of Peiper, the bridge is blown.

Company C Welcomes the 82nd Airborne

him the situation. The headquarters didn't even have a map.

Paratroopers began to arrive in patrols shortly before noon on the 19th. Lt. Col. Vandervoort arrived in the early afternoon and setup Battalion Headquarters in the same building as Company C. He took over command from Major Yates. Men of the 51st Company C breathed a sigh of relief. It was as if the awesome power of the U.S. Army had arrived, and in fact it had. The next two days were to see Company C supporting men of the 505 Parachute Infantry Regiment in some of the hardest fighting of the war.

Nabors was called to the headquarters to report on his patrol earlier that day. After giving the report, he was asked by Vandervoort if he needed anything. He replied that he would like to borrow two or three bazookas since the ones he had were not working. Vandervoort could not lend bazookas, but he would send two bazooka teams to help out with the defense of the south end of town. The teams reported to Nabors and were stationed on the second floor of a three story building. They could not only cover the main street along the road to Vielsalm, but also had a good field of fire across the river along the street that connected with the road to Wanne. They stayed about 24 hours before being recalled to rejoin their units.

Throughout the afternoon some artillery shells landed on the town, and machine gun fire from the top of the cliff made us engineers keep under cover. The paratroopers walked down the center of the streets, defiantly. Sporadic fire continued throughout the night. Some men speculated that the artillery fire came from our own artillery, but on the 20th there was no doubt that it came from the east and was German.

On the 20th, just before noon, the pace picked up until the artillery bursts were continuous. Nabors was visiting with Staff Sergeant Joe South, Platoon Sergeant from Bartlesville, Oklahoma, in front of the building where the 505th Regiment bazooka teams were stationed. The men felt safe since the shells coming over the building were falling quite a distance from the street where they were.

Orders were, that in case of enemy attack across the river, we were to pull out of town and defend the high ground along the west side of the valley. An attack following the heavy artillery fire was a distinct possibility. We realized that the old orders preceded the arrival of Lt. Col. Vandervoort.

Nabors elected to go to the headquarters and get clarification. He took off at a dead run dodging from building to building to foil the continuous machine gun fire.

When he returned, to advise the orders were still in effect, no one was in front of the building. An artillery shell had struck the top front edge of the building and exploded right above where men had been standing just a few minutes before. The cobble stones were chipped with fragments of steel from the shell where several men had been. It was fortunate that when Nabors departed on the run, the men became uneasy and all had ducked for cover. It was several minutes before he found Sgt. South in the basement of the church. The four bazooka men were still in the building. Chalk up another miraculous save for Company C.

The Paratroopers Attack

A messenger told Nabors to release the four men from the 505 Regiment. He ordered them to return to their unit, twice. They remained where they were. After about 15 minutes a Captain, probably their C.O., arrived and asked who was in charge. Nabors admitted to being in charge, and advised him the bazooka teams had been released. The Captain carried a tommy gun and spoke to the men with great urgency, telling them they had work to do that night. Nabors was not sure whether it was "Unit cohesion" or the Captain's tommy gun that convinced them to follow the C. O.

At dusk, the 505 Regiment Company E attacked up the cliff toward the east. They scaled the cliff and were under artillery fire as they did so. Company F followed. The battle raged all night and the next day, until late afternoon. Col. Vandervoort asked for permission to send the reserve company up the hill to insure that they were not pushed off, and to permit withdrawal after dark.

He lost the argument.

Nabors was ordered to place riflemen on the top floors of buildings along the main street and direct fire at the German machine guns along the edge of the cliff as an aid to the withdrawal. He did so, and was directing the fire with his field glasses until ordered to report to headquarters.

Col. Vandervoort inquired about the overpass over the railroad tracks. Nabors advised that the steel beams of the overpass had been cut in two with a cutting torch, but the beams were now supported by a crib of cross ties stacked from the ground to the bottom of the beams. In Nabors opinion the overpass would support tanks.

Vandervoort wanted the overpass mined, but not blown. He said to set the charges and show the igniter to one of his men. Some jeeps remained up the road on the high ground. Installing the explosives would be simple enough if a route to the overpass could be found free of small arms fire. Two teams were to search for a suitable route. Both were to carry the explosives. Nabors headed a team that would try through the railway station. Sgt. South headed a team that would approach from the other direction.

Nabors stopped in a protected area behind the river bank opposite the overpass and visited with some paratroopers who had just come down the hill. They said that the enemy was the hardest charging in attack that they had ever encountered. The enemy had machine gun nests that were backed up by tanks and very difficult to handle. All bazooka teams had been lost trying to attack the tanks. To make matters worse, the enemy had captured a radio early in the battle, and were able to listen in and know what the paratroopers were trying to do.

At this point Sgt. South arrived and reported the overpass had been mined, as planned. All that remained was to get back across the river and report to headquarters, or so we thought. Tracer bullets were everywhere. Finally, after carefully dodging intense machine gun fire, Nabors reported to the Colonel that they were successful. He then ordered Nabors and the second platoon to send one man to pull the igniter and blow the overpass. After careful analysis, Sgt. South and Lt. Nabors chose Pfc. William J. Casale, native of Fairfield, CN, for what might be a suicide mission. There was not the slightest doubt that Casale or any other man in the platoon would make the attempt. After about thirty minutes, Casale reported back to platoon headquarters soaking wet. He said "I almost got killed. I had to jump in the river to escape."

We knew that there was no chance for him to blow the overpass but orders were orders. We were very thankful that he survived.

Lt. Joseph B. Milgram, H/S Platoon, who entered service from Rochester, NY, was charged with blowing the bridge across the Salm River for the second time. The paratroopers had repaired the bridge earlier. That

Recent Reminiscences and Reflections … A LIFETIME LATER

account is covered elsewhere and will not be repeated here, except to mention that he received the Silver Star for completing the task in spite of very heavy small arms fire.

Company C Relieved

Major Yates was ordered to return with Company C to the 51st Engineer Combat Battalion Headquarters in Marche, Belgium. The 505 Parachute Infantry had settled down to defensive positions on the high ground west of the Salm River valley.

Company C departed after dark. An officer from the 505th insisted that Nabors and the second platoon form up and march in step up highway N23 to load into trucks for the trip to Marche. That was to insure that the men of the 505th regiment would know that it was an organized trip and not a bunch of stragglers. Nabors, having gone three days and nights without sleep, slept all the way to Marche. They arrived at 2330 hrs.

Some of the accounts above may vary from other accounts, published and unpublished. All are from firsthand experience, or firsthand accounts from others. The 51st Engineer Combat Battalion and the 7th Armored Division, which fought just down the road from Trois Ponts at St. Vith, each received the Presidential Unit Citation. This may have been the first time and entire Division received that award. It may have been the first time in military history that one Battalion, the 51st ECB, was relieved by five divisions!

Captain Scheuber and Lt. Milgram received Silver Stars, and Major Yates received a Bronze Star. Yates was superb in misleading the enemy at Trois Ponts. He deserves much credit for stopping the armor there with nothing bigger than 50 Cal. for his troops. It is interesting to relate that he also had a hand in stopping an armored column outside Marche, Belgium, on December 22, following his action at Trois Ponts. Here Nabors was also in the thick of battle and had first hand experience.

Yates is captured, but escapes

The 84th Division had relieved the 51st ECB at Marche. Troops were dug-in around the perimeter in strong defensive positions. The Second Platoon, Company C, was assigned to providing security for the Division Headquarters in the town center.

All was quiet on a beautiful sunny afternoon on the 22nd. Major Yates collected Capt. Scheuber and Lts. Green and Nabors in his command car for a ride out to the outskirts of town to check on a bridge or rather a culvert across a very small creek. They were to determine if blowing the culvert would provide a roadblock for the defense against armor.

The road was very familiar to Nabors who had been passing that way every day for a month to check sawmills operated by the second platoon (more about that later). The road was a connecting road to the main highway to Bastogne. The command car was parked at the edge of the valley where the men of the 84th Division were dug-in. No reports of the enemy in the vicinity had been received, and the four officers walked about 300 meters to the culvert over the creek. The creek was not an effective barrier to tanks, and it would take a lot of explosives to blow the culvert.

When they had been there only a few minutes, Nabors saw a head wearing a beret rising above the military crest of the hill. He suggested that British tank crews wore berets. Yates said "lets get off the road to discuss it".

The officers broke for the ditch on the downstream side of the culvert. That was a mistake because the upstream side was forested, but downstream was cleared. The tank fired its 8 MM machine gun into the officers. The bullets passed between Nabors and Green and between Green and Scheuber. One hit Green's binoculars hanging from a strap around his neck. Another bullet passed through Nabors' shirt front. No one was hit, but the command car driver observed what he later described as "tracer bullets passing through the bodies and the officers falling down". He didn't bother to wait, but went immediately to Battalion Headquarters and reported all killed. Chalk up another miracle!

Nabors was the last off the road, and looked up the hill toward the command car. He saw a picket fence of tracer bullets. Without thinking or saying, "Excuse me" he turned and crawled through the culvert which was about one meter square in cross section. It didn't occur to him that such an obvious solution would be missed. He ran a few meters in knee deep water up the creek and then stepped out and ran up the hill through the forest to safety. Green and Scheuber followed Nabors, but amazingly, Yates didn't know where they had gone. He may have had trouble with his formerly broken ankle even if he had known.

The armored column advanced to the culvert. Major Yates was hiding beneath a small pine tree and was captured. The Germans took his side arm and left a grenadier to guard him while the column advanced towards the defensive line of the 84th Division.

When the firing started the dug-in men of the 84th Division radioed for a tank destroyer. There was barely enough time for the tank destroyer to get set in a previously prepared emplacement before the column advanced. The delay to capture Major Yates was just enough to doom the advancing column.

Nabors watched from the forest on the opposite side of the valley as the battle was fought. Five armored vehicles were destroyed in three minutes with no losses for the 84th Division. The Bulge stopped there! Captain Scheuber and Lt. Green and Nabors were able to return to the 51st ECB Headquarters about one hour after dark, but Major Yates took a little longer.

Some engineers upstream from the culvert where Yates was a prisoner blew up a dam and released a torrent of water. The guard left the Major to cross the road and get a better look at the water. The creek was flooded outside its banks. Major Yates escaped by jumping in the flood and swimming under water downstream until out of range.

It was near midnight when Col. Fraser received a call from the Division HQ asking if he knew a Bob Yates. He was glad to get him back, soaking wet and nearly frozen. This is one of General Harvey (Scrappy) Fraser's favorite stories at 51st ECB reunions. Major Yates is no longer with us, and he probably never bragged about stopping the enemy at either Trois Ponts or Marche, but incredibly, neither place ever fell to the Germans.

Company C was able to get a few days rest before joining in the fight to eliminate the Bulge. In this fight they considered themselves lucky to support the 82nd Airborne.

Why was the 51st Again so lucky?

Mature personnel who had a trade or special skill, such as carpenters or contractors, were assigned to engineer units. Company C got more than its fair share of talented recruits. There were many transfers, but the Company seemed to maintain a quality advantage. Training really began in December 1942, with the first trainload of recruits unloading in three feet of snow at Plattsburg Barracks, NY. Nabors' second platoon was lucky to get the first recruits who were mostly from Oklahoma. Many of those recruits stayed throughout the war. Unit cohesion was always strong. Training was long and varied. We could do almost anything in the line of fighting or working.

On December 17, 1944, rumors of the Ardennes Breakthrough were well known to the 51st. Such news spreads fast. Company C was operating sawmills. The second platoon was spread over a wide area with sawmills at six locations. Some were cutting and hauling, others were helping store the lumber. Trucks and equipment were scattered far and wide, It was truly amazing that after a hard days work they could be assembled fully equipped at Company C Headquarters, located at Hotton, and moved as a unit about 50 or 60 kilometers to Trois Ponts by midnight.

Jeep driver Pfc. James Magrutas Snow deserves some credit. He knew where Lt. Nabors was, as always. Every morning Snow and Nabors had been passing along a main street in Marche to check the sawmills. It so happened that a young lady, Susan D., was almost always walking to the milk vendor's to get a jug of milk for her family who lived on the street. The two in the jeep smiled and waved as they passed. After a week or so, Snow was urging Nabors to stop and get acquainted. Some officers at the 51st Battalion Headquarters, which was located in Marche, were planning a dance and inviting local girls. It was time to accept Snow's advice, and get acquainted. The trouble was neither was fluent in the others' language. Nevertheless, the date was arranged.

The dance was a disaster because we Americans failed to realize the class distinctions. Daughters of working parents weren't permitted to associate with daughters of Professionals and Government Employees. Susan was well chaperoned with an older brother, but the dance ended abruptly for the reason mentioned. It turned out that the older brother had a master's degree in languages. Naturally, he and his sister would help Nabors with the French language. The first lesson was scheduled on December 17, 1944, at Susan's house. Nabors arrived about seven (1900 hrs.), and was really learning, when Jimmy Snow knocked on the door. He said, "We're moving out".

It wasn't necessary to ask why. Nabors had always believed in dramatic departures, sealed with a kiss when soldiers were going into battle, or any other excuse. He asked Susan. Her reply was "Fiancé?" Since Nabors was already engaged to his present wife, he missed the kiss. She did give him a picture, and wife Polly has carefully saved the photograph till this day.

First Sergeant Raymond Millard

Company C Morning Report* -- 51st Engineer Combat Battalion
APO 230 - 22 December 1944

SUNDAY 17 December 1944 -- Order to move with demolition equipment fr Melreux to Trois Ponts, at 2000 hrs. Advance section, about 75 men left Melreux at 2200 hrs. and arrived at Trois Ponts 2330 hrs. CP set up in RR station. Began preparation of two bridges for demolition and set up two roadblocks.

* This is a "live report", made very shortly after the battles. Unedited, it retains it's immediacy.

Remainder of Company completed motor march to Trois Ponts early Monday morning. Security organized and set up. Working under orders of 1111th EC Group CO.

MONDAY 18 December 1944 -- By 0800 all members of company present at Trois Ponts except 21 men left as rear detachment. One 57 mm. AT gun fr Co B 526 Armored Inf. attchd and placed on roadblock P680992. Enemy tank sighted approaching fr direction of Stavelot on N23 at 1115 hrs. Tanks approached and fired on roadblock at 1145. First tank immobilized by fire of 57 mm. before 57 mm. was knocked out by fire of two tanks behind lead tank. Four men of gun crew killed. Salazar slightly wounded in leg by shrapnel. Remainder of crew withdrew by way of N35 to Aywaille. First bridge P677982 was blown when enemy tanks were sighted 1115 hrs. Dispositions were made to protect bridge site fr infantry crossings. Three enemy tanks approached roadblock P678988 and were engaged unsuccessfully by AT rocket launcher fire. Roadblock crew withdrew successfully under mg and Arty. fire from tanks. Bridge P674986 blown at about 1300 hrs on order of Col. Anderson. Disposition of entire company made on 500 yd front to prevent infantry crossing at town. OP's sighted approximately 20 enemy armed vehicles proceeding through RR underpass P990678 in direction of Aywaille on W33 at 1330 hrs. Bn Exec officer joined by 1400 hrs and assumed command. Vehicles were engaged by Allied aircraft at 1400 hrs. to 1700 hrs. At 1400 hrs. Snow left with Capt. Lundberg 1111th E C Gp on mission to Army HQ. Both still missing. At 1400 hrs one cal. 50 mg guarding bridge site P676990 opened fire on six members of tanks crew and killed three. Tank was left in tunnel. At 1700 hrs Company was drawn in to give all around protection to town. Sounds of enemy armor activity were heard coming fr underpass P990678 during the night. M-7 TD, destroyed to prevent capture by enemy burned causing arty. ammo within to explode continuously during the night. It is believed that sounds produced deceived enemy so as to strength of holding force. Enemy tank immobilized in under-pass by loss of crew was evacuated by enemy during night.

TUESDAY 19 December 1944 -- Recon patrols to hill P680985 was dispatched and returned with information only of signs of enemy armrd vehicles movement during night. Another recon patrol sent through under-pass P990678 proceeded about 200 yds. from under- pass in direction of Stavelot and encountered enemy troops dressed in American uniforms accompanying US M-8 scout car. Enemy troops fired on patrol which withdrew successfully. Fire was exchanged from hill P675993 with enemy armrd vehicle in under-pass with cal. 50 mg and cal. 30 rifles. Enemy returned fire with arty. and small arms. Movement of armed vehicles was again heard by listening posts during night. About 2000 hrs members of 85th Recon squadron arrived fr direction of Basse Bodeaux and were directed to CP. Until this time, company and attch men were only US occupants of the town.

THURSDAY 21 December 1944 - This morning company held its defensive positions against sporadic arty. shelling. At about 1100 hrs, reports were received that the enemy had counterattacked and were beginning to encircle the 505th elements on the hill. Small arms fire was directed by the enemy on the street and possible defensive positions around the town. Order from CO 1111th ECG to withdraw received 1500. Disengagement from enemy was impossible at this time. The troops who had occupied the hill began withdrawing under cover of small arms fire from members of this company. While this was happening, bridges P674986 and P677982 were prepared for further demolition by this company. This was at about 1600 hrs. The bridge P674986 was blown by order of CO 2nd Bn 505th at 1700 hrs by this company. Members of the 505th reformed on west bank of river in defensive positions. At 1930 hrs this organization began withdrawal from the town, and completed same by 2000 hrs. Left en route to Bn HQ at 1930 hrs. Arrived Bn HQ Marche at 2330 hrs.

Recent Reminiscences and Reflections ... A LIFETIME LATER

T/5 Wilson Roberts
(School Principal - deceased)

Reminiscences

Greeting to all the 51st from South Georgia and North Florida.

When Captain Radford (Pappy, we called him, but we did not address him as such) when he told me that I was to talk for a few minutes on some incident that stands out in my memory of my association with the 51st, I began to rack my brain for something that stood out above other events.

But you know all of that activity in Plattsburg and Europe seems more like a dream than anything else. Specifics have faded, and I can't remember details. But I began attempting to recall. There were so many events popping up in my mind. I first thought about the day Pappy and I went up to help C Co. erect a Bailey across the Roer River while the Germans shelled us all that night. Man I was glad to pull out from that place next morning.

Then I thought of many pleasant things. As soon as we stopped in an apple orchard after landing at Utah, a large number of paratroopers was gathering in from "D" Day. They all needed haircuts. Pappy told me to get my tools and start to work. The beautiful part was that they had captured a German pay wagon and each had a roll of 10p Frank bills that would choke a bull. As I would cut their hair each would peel me off several of these bills. When I finished, I had all pockets bulging. I didn't know if it was good tender or not. I went to Bn headquarters and asked Mr. Marion if it was good. He assured me it was. I bought a money order on the spot.

One happening that stands out in my mind happened at the height of the Bulge while we were at Marche, Belgium. We knew that the German column was approaching. I don't recall the number of that road, but I believe it was from the south or southwest. I went with Pappy and Sgt. Hall, and I don't remember who else, about dark to blow a roadblock. Large trees stood beside the road and on either side of a swollen stream. The trees were ringed with TNT positioned to throw the tree across the road. As you know when the fuse is snatched, you had only a few seconds to reach a safe distance before the explosion. I had blown two trees and when I pulled the third fuse and made a dash for safety, I ran into part of a barbed wire fence that threw me backward to a point near the base of the tree. The explosion went off and I was struck by flying pieces of wood. I lay there for a minute or two and eased my hand to see if I still had both legs. I did but they were pretty banged up. That ended my activity for the night. The bridge was wired to blow and I think finally it was blown.

Next morning, Pappy said to me "Roberts [better known as "Lightning"] I want you and Basic to man a machine gun post that we are setting up at the roadblock." We were instructed to hold the men in the tanks as long as possible, and then scram. Basic and I began to calculate just how long we would last once the tanks spotted us. Later in the day, however, someone, I suppose it was Pappy, thought better of the situation and pulled us in. That was another time I was happy to get away.

Late in the day, a patrol was out that way. When they returned they reported that the Germans got Major Yates. But the Major was too smart for them. About dark the Major showed up ringing wet. He had dived into the swollen stream and made his escape.

There were many comical things that happened both at Plattsburg and Europe. I'm sure it helped to make things more bearable.

In closing, I feel my time with the 51st has been a rich experience. However, I wouldn't care for a rerun. I had the honor of knowing and being associated with a group of the greatest guys in the world: friends and memories that I will treasure throughout my life.

Sergeant Thomas Banks

Some memories of my time with the 51st Engineers Combat Battalion

-- January 5, 1943, train ride to Plattsburg, New York from Fort Dix, New Jersey. The snow building up on the window sills of the train. We didn't see the ground until May ... lining up to get our sulfa pills due to an outbreak of strep throat. Only those with a temperature of 103 or above got in the hospital .... The Fife and Drum pub in town on a pass. I can still hear them playing and singing (*As Time Goes By*).

Banks receiving Soldiers Award from Col. Anderson at Highnam Court, England.
Collection of Thomas Banks - 10 June 1944

I got out of most of the 12 mile marches to Macomb Reservation by driving Lt. Coats (now Lt. Col.) and the supply truck.

Once in a while a humorous event would happen, and we were glad to take advantage of it. Such as Slim (Robert) Watkins coming back from pass into town after a few too many and over jumping his top bunk bed and landing on the floor. He never seemed to get hurt, but caused quite a commotion.

A group of drivers was sent to Ft. Dix, N.J., for new vehicles. We had a convoy going back to Plattsburg and didn't have to stop for a single traffic light going through New York City, sometimes at a high rate of speed. Seems like there was a policeman at every intersection, giving us the speed up signal.

Stopped at Winchester. VA, on our way to Ft. Belvoir. As we passed through town we saw lots of girls and women, so after setting up camp on the edge of town, we lost no time in getting back to town, but much to our dismay we couldn't find any girls. Guess their mother had called them all home.

After Ft. Dix we went to Camp Patrick Henry. After getting prepared for overseas we loaded on a Liberty Ship .... I didn't want to be below deck if there was any action, so I volunteered for a gun crew. I also volunteered to help clean out the ship's refrigerator and freezer. The only two things I ever volunteered for the whole time in the Army.

Passing through the Straight of Gibraltar we could see the rock in the distance. - How nice Oran looked from the harbor but altogether different when we entered .... Hauling guys to and from camp to Oran. I was stopped and written up for speeding. Too many Arabs were walking out in front of vehicles. -- we had a 40 & 8 train ride to Casablanca. Stopped in an orange grove and help ourselves over the owner's objection.

Recent Reminiscences and Reflections ... A LIFETIME LATER

Ship ride in North Atlantic the first part of January. Very rough seas, ship rolling, many seasick. Not allowed on deck. Guys on end of tables in mess hall taking buckets to get coffee and oatmeal, when the ship would roll they would slip and fall, losing the contents of their buckets on floors and walls. It got very slippery.

Arriving in South Wales .... How friendly the people were and they spoke English or Welsh which we could understand. The only way you could tell someone was coming on the sidewalks at night was the clopping of their shoes. Everything was blacked out .... Fish and chips were wrapped in newspaper. We would call them french fries instead of chips. Seemed to be the only plentiful snack food available.

Then we moved to Highnam Court in England. It was really an Englishman's estate. It was there I was presented with the Soldier's Medal in front of several battalions.

Robert Martin and I went to the dock to pick up a D-7 bulldozer and trailer .... In order to break the dozer in a little before going to France, we were sent out to a rock quarry to do some work. The fellow who owned the quarry had a goodly supply of hard cider on hand. After sampling quite a bit of it, Martin said for me to run awhile, he was going to lie down. And that's what started me on a career that stayed with me through a good bit of civilian life.

We had to waterproof the dozer, six ton truck and trailer for LCT trip across the English Channel to Omaha Beach. It rained all night .... Ammunition dump fire and helping to put it out with dozer. Shells and ammunition exploding everywhere. With no cab on the dozer.

Burying dead animals with dozer when we moved into a new bivouac area. The stench was awful and I really puffed on my pipe. Martin had been hurt and sent to the hospital with a broken leg so I had replaced him on the dozer. It was at this time Woodrow Wilson replaced me as truck driver.

One day the sky was full of airplanes, almost wing to wing. They were all bombers and they completely flattened St. Lo.

Lt Henry, Motor Pool Officer, told me to go somewhere and pick up a ten ton roller and take it out on a job and show someone how to run it. I said I don't know how to run it. He said just get on there and act like you had run one all my life. I did but while backing down those steel ramps we carried on the trailer, I slid off into a ditch and had to winch it out with the truck winch. That was a powerful Tulsa winch. One time while snubbed to a large tree I swear that truck stretched several inches while pulling the dozer out of a soft spot.

Buzz bombs flying quite low between Malmédy and Aachen. For some reason I don't remember much about Paris but I do have some pictures taken with some buddies. I do know the champagne flowed freely.

Then there was the time the engine in our truck went bad and we were left at a large chateau while the truck was in ordnance. Wasn't long until we started to hear small arms fire. We learned in a short while the Germans had broken through our lines and the Bulge had started. Our orders were to blow the dozer and trailer and take off in the opposite directions when things got too close. As darkness fell we heard the hiss of air brakes on a large wrecker and we were rescued along with the dozer and trailer by Sgt. Raper and W.O. Horecka.

.... While plowing snow with the dozer in the Hürtgen Forest fire trails I noticed bullets kicking up the ground in front of me. With no cab on the dozer I didn't know what to do. The two guys riding with me were gone without notice. I jumped off balance and tumbled to the ground. I did manage to release the clutch but the engine was still at full throttle. My first thought was to crawl under the dozer but with the engine still running and thinking the plane might return, I ran into the woods looking for a foxhole. I finally found one with a guy in it with blood all over his face. I asked if he had been hit and he said. "No, I ran into a tree." On our way out we counted at least six foxholes we had run past. When we got to the dozer a truck behind me had the tarp over the back shredded by bullets and a jeep that had been coming toward me had three men that were killed. This was only a hundred feet in front of me. Someone higher than any of us must have been riding with me that day.

Those fire trails through the Hürtgen Forest were the scenes of a lot of fighting. I passed tanks that had been hit, some still burning. Some with a man or two that didn't make it out.

Christmas dinner during the Bulge was a can of C-ration hash.

Major Yates, who could forget him. One of those unforgettable persons you ever knew and his driver Travis …. On one fire trail after going quite deep into the forest with the dozer, Major Yates stepped out and after stopping, asked where I was going with that thing. After telling him my orders, he said turn that thing around and get the hell out of here you have already gone too far.

Pulling off another trail to let a convoy of tanks go by and hearing them engage the enemy on the next hill … Plowing snow off a road into a town that had just been taken at dark and plowing into a phosphorus shell that was still smoldering. Then halted on our way out the other side of town to fix the mine detectors that were going ahead of me. Lucky we did for the next intersection was mined.

Anti-aircraft fire over the Rhine River lit up the sky at night. Being strafed while eating in a railway station. After everyone came out from under the tables, there sat Pat Martin still eating as if nothing happened. Earlier Pat had refused a promotion to PFC because he didn't think he could handle the responsibility. We learned later he was an attorney in civilian life.

Quite a few towns along the Rhine started with Bad in their names. We got Bad Godesburg, which hadn't been taken, mixed up with Bad Neuman our destination. All turned out well and we found out Bad means spa.

Crossing the bridge on the Rhine, put there by the 51st.

Meeting Russian soldiers before moving to the 3rd Army section. This was about the time President Roosevelt died. Getting the news the war was over. How we celebrated. I was sent to Camp Phillip Morris at Le Havre with the high point men for 11 day trip home on a stormy ship.

Band playing as we disembarked and the steak meal at Camp Patrick Henry. Discharged from Ft. Meade, MD, October 25, 1945. I didn't get to come home with the guys I went over with which I deeply regret, and I shall always remember the 51st Engineers and my closest buddy (now deceased) Woodrow L. Wilson from Coweta, Oklahoma.

One thing I forgot to mention, along the way I got a leave for R&R and went to Paris to see my girl, who is now my wife. She was in the Army Nurse Corp. As I spotted her in a ward full of G.I.s, you should have heard the response when I embraced her. I could have gotten in trouble, she a 1st Lt. and me [a] Sgt.

Recent Reminiscences and Reflections ... A LIFETIME LATER

Corporal Frank Lee

Recollections of some of my experiences .... Oct. 10, 1998

Arriving in Plattsburg, N.Y. on Dec. 27, 1942, I was assigned to Co. C of the 51st Engineer Combat Regiment, which was under command of Capt. Robert Yates. In March of 1943 I was transferred to H/S Co. of the same regiment. Shortly thereafter the regiment was broken up and H/S Co. and A, B, and C Companies became the 51st ECB. A new H/S Co. was formed and D, E, and F companies became the 238th ECB. I've often wondered what became of them, our sister organization.

We trained hard all winter and spring, under freezing, often sub-zero conditions. We built bridges, laid minefields, installed and removed booby traps, built roads, constructed tank traps and a myriad of other things that combat engineers might be called upon to do, all the while holding to an intense program of physical conditioning and combat training. Each Monday morning we hiked twelve miles out to Macomb Reservation, lived in pup tents all week and hiked back to the barracks on Friday afternoon. It seems that no matter how rough the week had been or the march back in on Fridays, we always had a little left over for the weekend assault on the Fife and Drum, U.S.O. Club, or other favorite meeting place.

In Sept. '43 we moved by rail to Elkins, West Virginia, where we served to support the XIII Corps, the Dixie Division being a part of those forces. While there we built two airfields, one in a town named Davis, and another in a town named Thomas. I'm told they are still there and operating. On Sept. 16, 1943 we moved by convoy to Ft. Belvoir, VA. Our assignment as I understand it was to instruct the O.C.S. candidates in demolitions.

In Oct. '43 we moved again by convoy to Ft. Dix, NJ to prepare for overseas shipment. On Nov. 5, 1943 we left for Camp Patrick Henry, VA for embarkation.

In Dec. '43 our convoy arrived in Oran, North Africa. Evidently for the period of time from Camp Patrick Henry until our departure from Casablanca for Liverpool, England, we were considered C.B.I. troops. My discharge shows that from Nov. 14, 1943 until Jan. 12, 1944 we were C.B.I. troops. Those dates cover that period of time. That was the first of two heavenly blessings the Lord sent our way. If you have to fight a war then it is best to have only one enemy. In Europe we had the Germans, in the C.B.I. they had the Japs and all the other enemies such as malaria, jungle rot, elephantitis and many other unseen enemies which followed them home. There were many other blessings on a daily basis, all of which convinces me that "Somebody up there liked us." In England we underwent rigorous assault training including landing techniques, etc., all the while maintaining a full schedule of physical conditioning. I offer as evidence of such the fact that I thought nothing of hiking into Gloucester to meet a friend and then hiking 12 miles cross country to the town of Stroud because we liked a certain pub and the beer they served there. It was of course another 12 miles hike back.

On June 18, '44 we moved by convoy to Bournemouth, England. On June 19, '44 we loaded on the Liberty Ship Charles D. Paston and moved off shore and lay at anchor near the Isle of Wight. For seven or eight days, there was nothing to do but count the number of German buzz bombs going over on their way inland, all the while praying that they didn't run out of fuel over us.

On June 26, '44 we upped anchor and sailed across the English Channel to Omaha Beach, turned south and sailed to Utah Beach where we lay offshore overnight. Next morning, June 27, 1944, we off-loaded into various landing craft. I can remember stepping on men's hands and having my hands stepped on. If you forgot that the vertical bars of the cargo net were for hands and the horizontal bars were for feet then you would most assuredly pay the price. On occasion we forgot and we paid the price.

As we waded ashore on Utah Beach (up to our armpits in water) I remember having the feeling that now I was on my way "home." All the other moves seemed like I was going farther and farther from home. Now we were going to do the job we had been trained to do and we were ready.

In our first bivouac in an apple orchard, I discovered a cow stuck in the bottom of a huge bomb crater. I enlisted the help of the "wrecker" crew (Gonslo Watts and Dick Tidwell) and together we rigged up a sling and using the wrecker we hoisted her up out of the crater. I then walked her up to what was left of the old farmhouse. The hand pump still worked so I pumped up enough water for her to drink and some I used to wash the mud off of her. Her bag was feverish so I milked her on the ground. I milked her twice a day for three days and then the milk would boil without curdling. From then on for awhile I had my own cow and fresh milk everyday. We made several short moves before the St. Lo breakthrough, and each time I would go back and walk my cow up to our new location. After St. Lo we began moving greater distances each time and I had to abandon "Bessie."

We were bivouacked in about the second or third apple orchard in Normandy, shortly after we landed, when we were subjected to some intense 88 shelling by the Germans. A Company's commanding officer tent received a direct hit. They were in the very next apple orchard to us. Fortunately for Capt. Pedersen, he was not in his tent or he'd have had no more tomorrows. His tent was shredded. The attack produced no casualties, lucky for us. If H/S and A Co. commanders hadn't made an on the spot decision to move out to another area, we may have been all killed while waiting for our Battalion Commander Reafsnyder to dispatch a messenger back to Corps Headquarters to advise him what to do. In my opinion he wouldn't tie his own shoes without first having it OK'd by the Corps.

I remember being strafed between hedgerows in Normandy. We bailed out of the weapons carrier while it was still moving and rolled under the overhang of the hedgerows. Fortunately the hedgerows were wider at the top and narrower at the bottom. I think the roots of the trees and shrubbery must have held the soil at the top while the earth at the bottom eroded away. A cross section would have looked much like a mushroom. Being strafed is the absolute most helpless feeling I've ever endured.

I remember endless streams of civilians filtering back through our lines. They were a most pitiful sight. What worldly possessions they had were strapped on wheelbarrows, crude two-wheel carts, or carried strapped to their backs. They were trying to go home and we knew that in many cases there were no homes to go to.

One of our early combat assignments was trying to extinguish a fire in an ammunition dump that had been bombed. Small arms ammunition was going off all over the place while phosphorus shells were exploding and burning everywhere. The most effective method of extinguishing the fires was to cover them with earth. Bulldozers were pushing up the earth, and when phosphorus fires would break out in one spot, we would borrow earth from another. Often when we would steal dirt from one spot, the fire would resume in the spot we'd just borrowed from. We used our entrenching tools, spent shell casings and in many cases our bare hands. We stuck to the job and succeeded.

We had front row seats for the bombing attack on St. Lo prior to the breakthrough. It was an awesome sight and went on for hours. I yet fail to understand how those planes could fly through such intense flak from the ground. Some didn't, only a very small number, but it was a blessing to us that they were on our side. My hat is still off to the "Fly Boys."

After St. Lo we began to move longer distances, and more frequently. I can remember being commandeered and ordered to help a fighter wing that was involved in bombing and strafing missions in closing the Failaisl Gap. We manually carried gas cans out to the fighter planes on the landing strips. The pilots were refueling their own planes so they could get back in the air and bomb more German vehicles. Later when we moved up through that area all roads in all directions were strewn with burned out military vehicles of every description, lined up bumper to bumper for miles and miles all headed back to Germany. I still feel that was another blessing, for if Hitler had had available to him all the men and equipment he lost in that encounter and subsequently in the Battle of the Bulge, when he assaulted the Siegfried Line, our job there would have been a lot tougher.

We progressed on across France and Belgium building bridges, roads, clearing and widening intersections, laying minefields, clearing minefields, dealing with booby traps and all those other things engineers are called upon to do. We had penetrated into Germany by Sept. when we were ordered back into Belgium to operate sawmills. We sawed lumber until the middle of Dec. when our commander Lt. Col. Reafsnyder was relieved of his assignment and Lt. Col. Harvey Fraser took command. We figured we were in for a long session of "Spit and Polish" soldiering. What else with him being a West Point soldier. As it happened, two days later the German breakthrough occurred, and in short order we were front line troops again. From then on there wasn't time to even spit, never mind about polish.

We made our stand at Trois Pont, Hotton, and all points in between. We held our positions and repelled all attempts to breach our lines when it seemed all others were beating a hasty retreat to the rear. History has written that our action in that area slowed the German advance long enough to give corps, and army "higher ups", time to get a handle on things.

We were subsequently awarded the Presidential Unit Citation for that action. I personally am most proud of that award above all others because it says to all that we stood our ground and got the job done.

During the Battle of the Bulge, I remember living conditions were almost unbearable. Snow, ice, cold rain and mud, mud, and more mud. There was nowhere you could go to get out of it. The roads became like thick, soupy, syrupy rivers. As vehicles progressed they created waves in the mud, just as water produces waves from a passing boat. It would flow from the roadsides into the woods on each side. The best you could hope for is that it wouldn't go over the top of your combat boots. Keeping your feet dry was always the first order of business. At least it was for me. Frozen feet and you were out of business. I remember being posted on guard duty and not being relieved until daylight. Shoot anything that moves was our orders.

In Spa, Belgium, we were fortunate to be housed in a large hotel-like building. The windows were mostly all shot out, but it afforded some protection. It was dry. After the first night we discovered the adjoining stables and about six head of cattle bedded down in clean, dry straw. The next couple of nights I joined the cows and snuggled down in the straw next to a nice warm body. I was comfy cozy, but it didn't last as we moved out to newer digs. However I was on to something and always I would seek out the stables for a nice, warm, cozy sleep whenever possible.

One of the two most horrible jobs I had to do was assist a detail engaged in recovering corpses from a large field. Bodies, both German and American were everywhere. They were frozen in whatever position they were in when they died. They were in trees, foxholes, everywhere strewn across the landscape. I was sick for a week afterwards. Not "Doctor Sick," just emotionally sick.

The second worst experience along those lines, second only because it occurred after the other, was a detail to accompany a photographer assigned to us by Corps Headquarters. He, Sgt. Rackus, I think his name was, was to make a pictorial record of the concentration camp at Dachau. Bodies, in all stages of decomposition, were stacked like firewood in room after room of the camp. On a siding railroad box cars were loaded with bodies just heaved in helter skelter. The smell of death was unbearable; I heaved and wretched for days afterwards. That smell still comes back to haunt me and I'm sure I'll never forget it.

I remember a fun thing that happened to me, at least it was for a boy raised in the Louisiana bayou country. We were bivouacked in the Hürtgen Forest in Germany and during a quiet spell I was C2 on the switchboard in battalion headquarters. The ground began to move just a few feet from me. I couldn't figure out what was going on so I asked one of my "Yankee" buddies if he saw what I saw. He assured me he did and that it was only a mole burrowing underground. I had never seen a mole and decided I would dig him up. It's amazing how fast they can move and change directions. I was soon joined by several cohorts complete with entrenching tools and by the time we finally captured him, we had dug up a sizable portion of Hürtgen Forest. That was the first time I had ever seen a mole.

Our next big assignment was "Bridging the Rhine." As I remember it our battalion headquarters was in Bad Neuenahr, but we had to bridge from Kripp to Linz, two little towns on the Rhine. I think I pulled more guard duty during that period than any other time and it seemed that I was on permanent guard duty. One night in the early hours of the morning I heard a loud explosion and saw a bright flash high upon a large hill or small mountain to our rear. I had heard no plane and ruled out a bomb. It seemed to be too high up and a very unlikely spot for heavy artillery. Also there was no telltale whisper of incoming or outgoing mail. At about that time I heard a telltale whisper of incoming mail and as I listened it followed right to the spot where I had witnessed the loud explosion. The same thing happened a couple more times and I later found out that the Germans had used their new V2 Rocket in our area. It flew faster than sound, and the whisper I had heard was the sound just catching up. Fortunately for us the terrain on the far side of the river was much higher than it was on our side. In order for the Germans to get over the high ground they were overshooting our location.

I still believe we were the first to complete a bridge over the Rhine. However, another battalion was awarded that honor (only by minutes). I truly believe they might have hedged on time when reporting. I can't prove it but I believe it nonetheless.

We went on from there building bridges and repairing roadways and bridges on the Autobahn, until the

Recent Reminiscences and Reflections ... A LIFETIME LATER

First Army was relieved. We were then reassigned to the 3rd Army. We joined them somewhere in the vicinity of Nuremberg. Our assignments continued to take us in a southeasterly direction and included building a bridge across the Danube River, under combat fire. We eventually wound up somewhere not too far from the Austrian border. When war in Europe ended on May 8, 1945 it really was not over for us until about three days later. In our area there were small pockets of German soldiers in isolated patches of woods all around us. They wouldn't accept that the war had ended, and as long as they were firing at us and us at them, it wasn't really over.

In summing up I'd like to say I still feel fortunate to have been a part of the 51st Again Battalion. That brings up another thought or question. How did we come to be known as the "51st AGAIN"? My understanding is that it came about as a result of the Battle of the Bulge. As mentioned earlier we had penetrated even into Germany near Aachen prior to the breakthrough. Our line companies had built bridges all along the way. It became custom to put a sign on each bridge indicating who had constructed each one. "Co. A, B, or C 51st ENGR. C. BN." as the case may be. Well, during the Battle of the Bulge many of the bridges were destroyed in an attempt to slow the German advance. As we began to advance again, and the companies would complete a bridge for the second time, the sign would read whatever company followed by "51st AGAIN." That's the story as I know it. Just thought it should be recorded.

We were the outfit we were (the very best) because we had been well trained by our officers and noncommissioned officers alike. They were all top caliber with only a couple exceptions. We had been tried and proven by all sorts of adverse weather conditions during our training. We were at all times in peak physical condition, this was all proven in combat, especially the Battle of the Bulge. We didn't run! We stood our ground, we fought and won. That's what we had been trained to do.

We became a very cohesive, close knit group. As much a family as is possible under military conditions. We cared about each other, individually and collectively. We were concerned with each other's welfare and safety. And we were and still are proud of our outfit.

These are the many things I still thank God for amongst many others for looking after us as He did.

> For Colonel Anderson and all the hell he put us through.
>
> For changing our orders in North Africa and reassigning us to the E.T.O.
>
> For Major Yates for being the kind of officer he was and at the same time for being one of us.
>
> For sending us Col. Harvey Fraser (Scrappy) when we needed a competent combat commander in the worst kind of way.

I thank you all, collectively and individually, officers and enlisted men alike. I'm still proud of the 51st Again Engineer Combat Battalion and all my buddies that made it what it was.

Honors and Memorials
Awards, Honors and Memorials[*]

PLAQUE PRESENTATION
DISTINCTIVE UNIT CITATION
PRESIDENTIAL UNIT CITATION
CROIX DE GUERRE AVEC ETOILE D'ARGENT
LETTERS OF COMMENDATION
CERTIFICATE OF APPRECIATION
PLAQUES AT TROIS POINTS AND HOTTON
PURPLE HEARTS
INDIVIDUAL AWARDS
1999 GENERAL PATTON AWARD
IN MEMORIAM

Professional military comments on the performance of the 51st Engineer Combat Battalion by the following individuals are found in this chapter or elsewhere in the book on the pages these individuals are cited, as listed in the index.

Major General John W. Barnes, U.S. Army, Retired
Major General Louis A. Craig, Commander, 9th Infantry Division
Major General James M. Gavin, Commander, 82nd Airborne Division
Major General John Milliken, Commander, III Corps, First Army
Major General Clair F. Gill, Commandant, Ft. Leonard Wood, MO
Major General Matthew B. Ridgway, Commander XVIII Corps
Brigadier General Harvey R. Fraser, U.S. Army, Retired
Colonel William E. Ekman, Commander, 505th Parachute Infantry
Colonel F. Russell Lyons, III Corps Engineer, First Army
Colonel Floyd D. Wright, U.S. Army, Retired
Captain Ken E. Hechler, Combat Historian, First Army
Robert E. Merriam, Chief of the Ardennes Section of the Historical Division,
European Theater of Operations

---

[*] Compiled by Albert E. Radford

Plaque Presentation

Distinctive Unit Plaque Presentation Speech
Major General Clair F. Gill, Commandant
Fort Leonard Wood, Missouri
22 September 1995

Brigadier General Harvey Fraser, Members of the 51st Engineer Combat Battalion, Ladies and Gentlemen: Welcome to Fort Leonard Wood. Hope you are enjoying your stay in the Ozarks - Branson's something else, isn't it? Am going down next month.

We're proud to welcome you to our Engineer Museum; I think as you tour it following this ceremony you'll be impressed with what we've pulled together. As combat veterans, I trust you had the opportunity to share some words of wisdom with our soldiers while lunching at our special dining facility.

Today, we continue the Engineer Center's efforts to link yesterday's units and their soldiers to soldiers of today. This is important. For without traditions like this, the Engineers' rich heritage would be lost to future generations.

As I look around this room, I'm deeply moved. You are the Engineers whose courageous exploits have made our Corps of Engineers History. Each of you is a hero in the true sense of the word.

The Battle of the Bulge was the last major German counteroffensive of World War II. They planned to capture Liège and Antwerp, thus dividing the allied Armies. The German assault in the Ardennes began on Dec. 16, 1944, and created a "Bulge" into allied lines. Although suffering about 77,000 casualties, the Allies stopped the German Advance by January 16, 1945. You held the Allied line for four critical days from December 18 to the 21st.

A disproportionate number of battle casualties were engineers. Many, notably those from the 81st Engineer Combat Battalion, were like yourselves operating sawmills or repairing forest roads, of necessity, were called upon to fight as infantry; the 81st Engineers, in defense of St. Vith; you, in defense of Trois Ponts and Hotton. Your unit historian, Captain Ken Hechler, wrote that the 51st Engineer Combat Battalion was not supposed to be on the front line. You were busy operating sawmills to produce the lumber for the First Army's winter quarters.

The 158th Engineer Combat Battalion had left to assist in the defense of the Bastogne area. Your mission was to defend the Marche environs. That mission changed drastically as Peiper's tanks attempted a sweep to the Meuse River. The 51st rapidly created roadblocks, mined and destroyed bridges, and did whatever else it could to stall the German armor and infantry thrusts. As your group commander said, "We have come several thousand miles to fight these Nazis - not to withdraw from them." (Col. Harry Anderson, Commander, 1111th Engineer Group.)

Colonel Fraser determined the Ourthe River was the natural defense line - Group sent you to erect roadblocks and prepare key bridges for demolition, especially on the Amblève and Salm Rivers. By blowing one bridge after an American tank had accidentally gone over its side into the water, you took advantage of the situation and held off the enemy. Since the tank's ordnance went off at intervals all afternoon and into the night - enough time elapsed between explosions, you were able to trick the enemy into thinking you had artillery support.

Major Robert Yates and his men deceived the enemy into thinking there was a superior force defending Trois Ponts by simulating the arrival of reinforcements using deuce and a halves. When the Airborne came into Trois Ponts, it expected to find the unit decimated and discouraged. Instead, Yates approached them, uttering, "I'll bet you fellows are glad we're here."

Charlie Company diverted a German Tank column of Peiper's fast-moving assault tank group at Trois Ponts by blowing the bridges there and defending the village until Airborne troops could reinforce it. Peiper's tanks eventually ran out of fuel well short of this Meuse River objective, and Peiper's men had to abandon them.

Following the War you assumed reconstruction duties -constructing roads, bridges, water and sewer systems, and cleaning debris from the Main River - with the same zeal you had during your successful thrust to the Danube.

What Did It Take To Become Successful? [I] think it stems from solid training especially your winter training near Plattsburg, New York, where you learned to build and dismantle tactical bridges on land and over the Salmon River and Lake Champlain and in night operations and in England as you honed those skills. It also came in strong, solid leadership from men like General Fraser who prior to taking command of the 51st had earned a reputation as a "brilliant" staff officer. His analysis and use of the terrain at Trois Ponts was indeed "brilliant." His "omnipresence" kept widely separated forces united. In your XO, Major Robert Yates whose innovative use of the deuce and a half psyched out the enemy, and in leaders like Captain Preston Hodges and Sam Scheuber, First Lieutenant Joe Milgram and Tech 5 Oliver Connelly - all who received the Silver Star. You maxed out on good leadership. The commitment to others, as seen by the awarding of the Soldiers Medal to seven 51st soldiers: Tech 5 Tom Banks, Captain J.W. Barnes, Pfc. G.M. Cash, First Lieutenant D.H. Henry, Second Lieutenant J.A. Murphy, Master Sergeant Lee N. Raper and Major Yates also played a key role in your success.

In support of the First Army, you demonstrated the ever changing roles and challenges of Engineers - you saw where you were needed and you were there. Although a fairly young unit when it saw action at Trois Ponts - two and a half years old and with no experience in countermobility operations - the 51st is noted for its mastery of combat engineering from the skills of individual soldiers to the unit's endeavors in construction operations and bridge crossings. You demonstrated that strong leadership, teamwork, cohesiveness and courage - in addition to tactical and technical competence - are keys to mission success. I was particularly moved by your historian's account of the deep comradeship, the keen sense of duty, courage and initiative that characterized the 51st soldiers. Your top notch professionalism in the field of combat engineering is to be emulated by today's engineer soldiers.

I know you didn't come here today just to sightsee and reminisce. You came on a most honorable mission - to create a lasting memorial to those who served and to those who gave the ultimate sacrifice.

This plaque is a testimony to your magnificent efforts. We take our Engineer Heritage seriously here, so for your dedication and sacrifice, for fighting to make the world a place where people don't have to fight, for caring enough to carry on the memories of those who served along with you, we are extremely grateful.

I know of no better way to pay tribute to the 51st Engineers than to say that you have truly led the way; you were *"Stopped by Nothing"*!

Thank you. *Essayons*!

THE 51ST ENGINEER COMBAT BATTALION

**✲ 51st ENGINEER BATTALION ✲
LINEAGE**

Activated 13 June 1942 - 51st Engineer Combat Regiment, Camp Bowie, TX

Redesignated 1 April 1943 - 51st Engineer Combat battalion, Plattsburgh Barracks, NY

Inactivated 27 October 1945 - Camp Patrick Henry, VA

Activated 27 November 1951 - 51st Armored Engineer Battalion - Fort Leonard Wood, MO

Inactivated 16 March 1956 - Fort Leonard Wood, MO

Activated 1 October 1967 - 51st Engineer Battalion, Fort Campbell, KY

Inactivated 31 August 1971 - Fort Campbell, KY

"A Distinguished Battalion that participated in the European Theater of Operations during 1944-1945, and was awarded two unit combat decorations.'

By their courageous actions, fortitude and exceptional esprit de corps. the officers and men of the 51st contributed materially to the ultimate defeat of the German Army in Europe. From Utah Beach during the Normandy invasion to Belgium, they cleared mines and obstacles, constructed bridges and maintained vital routes of communication for the movement of soldiers and material for the First U.S. Army.

Functioning as engineers and infantry during the Battle of the Bulge, they stopped German tanks and infantry on a 40-mile front, thus gaining time for the battalion to be relieved ultimately by elements of no fewer than FIVE combat divisions. For their extraordinary heroism, the battalion was awarded a Presidential Unit Citation - the highest award possible for unit action against an armed enemy.

As the war pressed into the heart of Germany, the men of the 51st brought further distinction to their unit by constructing a 967 foot long heavy ponton bridge across the Rhine River near Remagen. Difficult in normal times across a swift flowing river such as the Rhine, this feat was accomplished under sporadic and heavy enemy aerial bombardment, artillery, mortar and small arms fire. Deeper into Germany, the battalion later constructed a 324 foot treadway bridge, again under small arms fire, across the Danube River at Ingolstadt, and captured 400 German prisoners.

Always on the front lines of battle, the hallmark slogan of the elite battalion - "The 51st Again"- greeted thousands of combat and combat support units and soldiers whose operations had been in large measure facilitated by the courageous and tireless efforts of those superb combat engineers. The 51st AGAIN is justifiably proud of its contribution to the United States Army victory in Europe during World War Two, and this plaque is therefore dedicated in remembrance of those who served and especially for those who lost their lives.

**✲ WORLD WAR TWO ✲
COMMANDERS**

Colonel E.P. Ketcham
Colonel H. Wallis Anderson
Captain Robert B. Yates
Lieutenant Colonel Victor J. Reafsnyder
Lieutenant Colonel Harvey R. Fraser

**✲ WORLD WAR TWO ✲
CAMPAIGNS**

Normandy
Northern France
Rhineland
Ardennes-Alsace
Central Europe

**✲ HONORS ✲
AND DECORATIONS**

Presidential Unit Citation (Army),
Streamer embroidered "ARDENNES"

French Croix de Guerre with Silver Star, WW II, Streamer embroidered "ARDENNES"

Distinctive Unit Plaque
Corps of Engineers Regimental Hall
Fort Leonard Wood, Missouri

Presidential Unit Citation*

GENERAL ORDERS
No. 27

WAR DEPARTMENT
Washington, 25, D.C.
10 April 1945

BATTLE HONORS - Citation of Units

Section VII

As authorized by Executive Order No. 9396 (Sec. 1, Bull. 22. WD, 1943), superseding Executive Order No. 9075 (sec. 111, Bul. 11WD, 1942), citation of the following unit in general orders. No. 29, Headquarters First Army, 17 February 1945, as approved by the Commanding General, European Theater of Operations, is confirmed under the provisions of section IV, Circular No. 333. War Department, 1943, in the name of the President of the United States as public evidence of deserved honor and distinction. The citation reads as follows:

"The 51st Engineer Combat Battalion, United States Army, is cited for outstanding performance of duty in action against the enemy from 17 to 22 December 1944, in Belgium. When German forces had penetrated deep into friendly lines on 17 December 1944, and were rolling westward rapidly, the 51st Engineer Combat Battalion was ordered into strong defensive positions in the vicinity of Trois Ponts, Hotton, and Marche, Belgium, with the mission of impeding and containing the enemy advance at strategic points.

"Faced by numerically superior forces in armor, firepower, and manpower, the battalion quickly constructed and stubbornly defended roadblocks, prepared vital bridges for demolition, and served as infantrymen. By their determination and devotion to duty, regardless of the odds, the battalion denied the enemy important avenues of advance, thus permitting strong friendly forces to move into counterattack positions. By skillful use of weapons at hand, excellent terrain appreciation, and the use of ingenious ruses, the enemy was led to believe that strong formations confronted them and that they were rapidly being reinforced. When German tanks attacked repeatedly, fierce fire from rocket launchers destroyed them, infantry attacks supported by intense artillery barrages, were met by a hail of small-arms fire with heavy losses on enemy ranks, when bridges could no longer be held, they were demolished at the last possible moment, denying their use to hostile advancing forces.

"Throughout the 5-day period, the enemy was never able to penetrate the defenses manned by the officers and men of the 51st Engineer Combat Battalion. Their courageous actions and fortitude contributed materially to the ultimate defeat of the German offensive plans in this area and are worthy of high praise."

---

* This is the highest honor the United States government can confer upon a unit for extraordinary heroism in action against an enemy. To receive the award, the unit must have displayed such gallantry, determination, and esprit de corps in accomplishing its mission under extremely difficult and hazardous conditions as to set it apart and above other units participating in the same campaign.

Croix de Guerre Avec Etoile d'Argent
(This is the French Government's highest award to a unit for heroic action)

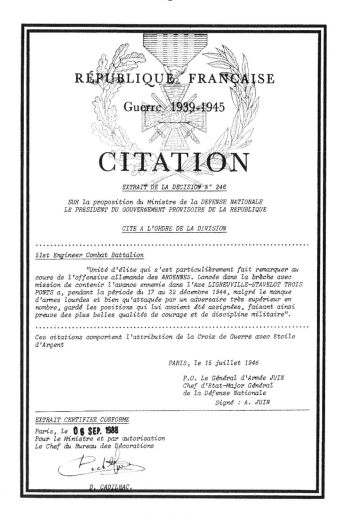

Translation:
Extract of Decision No. 246. Upon the proposal of the Minister for National Defense: The President of the Provisional Government of the Republic Cites

THE 51st ENGINEER COMBAT BATTALION

An elite unit which particularly distinguished itself during the German offensive in the Ardennes. Thrown into the breach with the mission of containing the enemy advance on the LIGNEUVILLE - STAVELOT - TROIS PONTS axis, it, during the period from 17-22 December 1944, despite the lack of heavy weapons and although attacked by an adversary very superior in numbers, held the positions which had been assigned to it, demonstrating proof of admirable qualities of courage and military discipline. … These citations carry the award of the **Croix de Guerre with Silver Star.**

HONORS AND MEMORIALS

Letter of Commendation - Major General Craig

To: Commanding Officer, 51st Engineer Combat Battalion
From: Major General Louis A Craig, Commander
Headquarters, Ninth Infantry Division
Office of the Commanding Officer
APO #9, U. S. Army
25 March, 1945

SUBJECT: Commendation
TO: Commanding Officer, 51st Engineer Battalion. (Thru Channels)

1. I take great pleasure in commending you and your battalion for the smooth and efficient manner in which you have rendered engineer support to the Ninth Infantry Division.

2. Upon the relief of the 82nd Airborne Division by the Ninth Infantry Division at the Roer River in Mid-February, your unit went into support of the divisional engineers. The Roer River was in flood and in itself was a major natural obstacle confronting the division. The velocity of 10-15 m.p.h. was one which challenged the ingenuity and skill of the engineers. Immediately upon the launching of the attack your battalion, with untiring vigor and resourcefulness, bridged the Roer with 2 Bailey Bridges and an assault foot bridge to materially aid the swift advance of the division.

3. Following the crossing of the Roer you again worked in close cooperation with divisional engineers, maintaining supply roads and bridging the Erft River to permit the crossing of supporting armor in the dash to the Rhine.

4. Upon enlargement of the bridgehead and the anticipated crossing of the Wied River, support engineers were again needed by the 9th Infantry Division. The 51st Engineers were assigned that role. On the night 22-23 March an assault crossing was made by the division. The was closely supported by your unit on the morning of the 24th then you constructed a Bailey Bridge across the river thus permitting the crossing of heavy vehicles and supporting armor which could not cross at other points because of an inadequate road net.

5. It is hoped that this association of the 51st Engineer Battalion with the Ninth Infantry Division will be of long standing.

Letter of Commendation - Colonel Ekman

To: Commanding Officer, 51st Engineer Combat Battalion
FROM: Colonel William E. Ekman, Infantry Commander
Headquarters, 505th Parachute Infantry
APO #469, U.S. ARMY
24 December 1944   (*Conveyed through the Commanding General, 82nd Airborne Division*)

1. On 19 December 1944, when this unit advanced to seize critical terrain at Trois Ponts, Belgium, the Regimental Commander found your unit in complete command of the town and bridge across the SALM RIVER at that point, thereby greatly assisting this unit in accomplishing of its mission. Although they had been completely isolated for four days and nights, they continued to assist in maintaining control for another 48 hours.

2. Although isolated, your unit was staying in position and repelling attacks by the Germans including armor. The spirit and courage displayed by your men and officers in this engagement of your small arms against armor was worthy of the highest tradition of the service.

3. Please convey to the officers and men of your unit the thanks of the officers and men of this regiment for their cooperation and support.

First ENDORSEMENT, by Major General James M. Gavin, U. S. Army, Commanding
Headquarters, 82nd Airborne Division / APO #469, U.S. Army
8 January 1945   (*conveyed through Commanding General, XVIII Corps (Airborne), APO #109, U.S. Army*)

It is a pleasure to add my personal recognition of the superior performance of the 51st Engineer Combat Battalion during the initial operations by the 82nd Airborne Division west of the SALM River. I congratulate the officers and men of your command on a job well done under adverse conditions. Please convey to all of them my sincere appreciation for their valiant and skillful accomplishments at a moment when American arms were called upon for the utmost in courage and dogged determination.

Second ENDORSEMENT (201.22 - (AG)) by command of Major General Ridgeway
Headquarters, XVIII Corps (Airborne), APO 109, U.S. Army
11 January 1945

The Corps Commander desires to add his commendation for a difficult task well done.

/ s/ Herbert L. Nelson
Colonel, A.G.D., Adjutant General

HONORS AND MEMORIALS

Certificate of Appreciation*

To

_____

FOR HIS CONTRIBUTION TO THE EXCELLENCE OF THE 51st ENGINEER COMBAT BATTALION IN THE EUROPEAN THEATER OF OPERATION DURING 1944-1945

As your former commander, I am proud to present this outstanding tribute to you. Without your wholehearted effort and unfailing devotion to duty, this fine standard of performance could not have been attained. I extend to you my heartiest congratulations.

Lt. Colonel Harvey R. Fraser, Commander
Brigadier General, US Army, Retired.

To each member of the battalion attending Reunion III at Williamsburg, VA in March 1990, General Fraser awarded a Certificate of Appreciation. Certificates were mailed to those who could not attend. Accompanying each certificate was a copy of the Presidential Unit Citation and the following highlights of the unit's history:

The 51st Engineer Combat Battalion was also awarded the French Croix de Guerre with Silver Star for action in the Ardennes. This is the French Government's highest award to a unit for heroic achievement.

In the confusion following the German breakthrough, many American units were retreating to the rear in great haste and disorder, to avoid entrapment The 51st Engineers, however, stood their ground and courageously held their assigned positions against the German spearhead, thus giving the badly disorganized American forces time to regroup. Finally, the 51st Engineer Combat Battalion was relieved by no fewer than five divisions: the 82nd Airborne at Trois Ponts, the 2nd Armored at Ciney and Celles; the 3rd Armored at Hotton; and the 84th Infantry and the British 53rd Infantry in the Marche area. This was possibly the first time in military history that an engineer battalion had been relieved by five divisions.

The officers and men of the 51st brought further distinction to their battalion by constructing, under fire, a 967 foot long heavy pontoon bridge across the swift Rhine River near Remagen. This was the bridge over which were moved the supplies and materiel so vital to the support of the First Army Drive into the heartland of Germany.

The battalion also built, under small-arms fire, a 440 foot treadway bridge across the Danube at Ingolstadt. This was the first bridge put across the Danube in the III Corps area.

---

* This is the form of the certificate given to members of the Battalion and signed by General Fraser.

Trois Ponts Plaque

Trois Ponts Plaque Dedication Speech
by Brigadier General Harvey R. Fraser, U.S. Army, Retired
Trois Ponts, Belgium, 15 May 1993

M. Le Bourgemestre, Ladies and Gentlemen. We of the 51st Engineer Combat Battalion appreciate your kindness and consideration in inviting us here to dedicate a plaque honoring Company C of our Battalion. Here in Trois Ponts on 18 December, 1944, about 140 men from Company C supported by a squad of soldiers from the 291st Engineer Battalion stopped the spearhead of the Sixth German Panzer Army's drive for the Meuse River and Antwerp during the famed "Battle of the Ardennes". They not only stopped the advance by destroying the bridge over the Amblève and the Salm Rivers but they also successfully defended against repeated enemy attempts to cross the river for four days (18-21 Dec.) until relieved by units from the 82nd Airborne Division of the US Army. This four day delay caused great consternation in the German High Command and resulted in a difficult shift of its main effort from the 6th to the Fifth [Panzer] German Army to the south. On 21 December this 5th German Army was stopped at Hotton and other points on the Ourthe River by other units of the 51st Engineer Combat Battalion.

Of our 130 brave soldiers who valiantly defended this town, only one is here today. Major Robert Yates in overall command here and Capt. Sam Scheuber, Commander of Company C are both deceased. May their souls rest in peace in the soldier's Valhalla. Mr. Joseph Milgram, Jr., one of three officers decorated for valor here is with us today and will describe the sights and sounds of the battle after I read this citation:

"1st Lt. Joseph Milgram, Jr. was awarded the Silver Star for gallantry against the enemy on 21 December 1944 in Trois Ponts, Belgium. He led a crew of five men across the Salm River Bridge under intense enemy fire and directed the installation of the demolition charges. After moving his men to a safe position, he personally set off the charges that destroyed the structure and then crawled to safety." Mr. Milgram made a special effort to be here today and I am proud to introduce a decorated hero of the Battle of Trois Ponts.

Major Robert B. Yates | Captain Sam C. Scheuber | Lt. Joseph B. Milgram, Jr.

HONORS AND MEMORIALS

Hotton Plaque

Hotton Plaque Dedication Speech
by Brigadier General Harvey R. Fraser, U.S. Army, Retired
Hotton, Belgium, 16 May 1993

M. Le Bourgemestre, Ladies and Gentlemen. We of the 51st Engineer Combat Battalion appreciate your kindness in inviting us here to dedicate this plaque. The German breakthrough in the Ardennes on 16 December 1944 sent shock waves through the American units in the area. The 51st Battalion supervising sawmill operations in the Marche area was alerted for ground combat action on 17 December. Company C was ordered to Trois Ponts and during 18-21 December heroically stopped a determined thrust by the Sixth Panzer Army. Companies A and B were assigned to defend the west bank of the Ourthe River from Durbuy on the north through Hotton to La Roche on the south. Company B under Captain Preston Hodges, was assigned Durbuy to Hotton inclusive, and Company A under Capt. Carl Pedersen, from Hotton to La Roche. A number of skirmishes with the Fifth Panzer Army occurred up and down the river at such places as Hampteau, Marcourt and Champlon Crossroads.

Some of the players in these skirmishes are with us today. The most bitter and tactically important battle was fought at the Ourthe River Bridge here in Hotton.

Capt. Preston Hodges was personally in command of the troops at Hotton. Initially he had less than a platoon of Engineers, two 40 mm antiaircraft guns which fired horizontally, and several bazookas and 50 caliber machine guns on the west side of the river. Some elements of the Third Armored Division trains had just arrived on the east side of the Ourthe and were supported by some light tanks. Later a stray 7th Armored Division tank was located and put into service. The actions of this gun and its crew were crucial in the defense of this vital bridge. The German Army arrived in force with tanks and armored Infantry with the mission of capturing the bridge and heading to the Meuse River. The battle started about 6 a.m. on 21 December and lasted until 3 p.m. when the enemy was defeated and headed south on the east side of the river. Mr. Hodges is with us today and will describe the sights and sounds of battle after I read this citation:

"Capt. Preston C. Hodges was awarded the Silver Star for gallantry against the enemy on 21 December 1944, in Hotton, Belgium. Commanding a small force of Engineers, Capt. Hodges successfully defended the vital Ourthe River bridge against a numerically superior force. Although constantly exposed to heavy machine gun and small arms fire, he encouraged his men to direct the fire on hostile targets. Although wounded during the battle, he remained with his men until reinforcements arrived and the enemy was driven from the area."

Capt. Hodges at Macomb Reservation, N.Y. *Corps Files - 1943*

Individual Awards

LEGION of MERIT
Fraser, Lt Col. Harvey R.   Hqrs

SILVER STAR

Connelly, T/5 Oliver M.	Co. A	Scheuber, CPT Sam C.	Co. C
Hodges, CPT Preston C.	Co. B	Yates, MAJ Robert B.	Hqrs
Milgram, 1LT Joseph E, Jr.	Co. C		

BRONZE STAR with OAK LEAF CLUSTER
Fraser, Lt Col. Harvey R.   Hqrs

BRONZE STAR

Bonifay, S/SGT Donald	Co. A	Mack, PFC Jessie R.	Co. C
Chastain, PFC Winford C	MED	Marquez, PFC Jose E.	Co. C
Clark, SGT Fayne B.	Co. C	Morin, CWO Wilfred R.	H & S
Coats, CPT Maurice E.	Hqrs	Mueller, 1LT William R.	Hqrs
Cundiff, SGT William S.	Co. C	Nabors, 1LT Fred L.	Co. C
Goldsmith, SGT Elvin	Co. C	Pederson, CPT Carl G.	Co. A
Gossard, SGT Evers	Co. C	Reynolds, SGT Payton E.	Co. A
Green, 1LT Richard I.	Hqrs	Stiftinger, SGT John J.	Co. A
Hodges, CPT Preston C.	Co. B	Walker, PVT Morris S.	Co. C
Horecka, WOJG Julius J.	H & S	Wright, 1LT Floyd.	Co. A
Ishmael, PVT Lee J.	H & S	Wright, PFC Philip F.	MED
Jamison, 1LT Bruce W.	Co. B	Yates, MAJ Robert B.	Hqrs
Keck, T\5 Paul H.	Co. C		

SOLDIER'S MEDAL

Banks, T/5 Thomas G.	H & S	Murphy, 2LT J. A.	Co. B
Barnes, CPT J.W.	Hqrs	Raper, M/SGT Lee N.	H & S
Cash, PFC G. M.	H & S	Yates, MAJ Robert B.	Hqrs
Henry, 1LT David H.	Hqrs		

CROIX de GUERRE avec ETOILE d'ARGENT (France)

Fraser, LTC Harvey R.	Hqrs	Rankin, S/SGT William W.	Co. C
Radford, CPT Albert E.	H & S		

CROIX de GUERRE avec PALME (Belgium)
ORDRE de LEOPOLD, GRADE de CHEVALIER avec PALME (Belgium)
Radford, CPT Albert E. H & S

HONORS AND MEMORIALS

1999 General Patton Award

Presented to Brigadier General Harvey R. Fraser
November 13, 1999

Joining the select company of Generals Jimmy Doolittle, Wimberley LeMay, Omar Bradley, Matthew Ridgeway, Colin Powell and President Jimmy Carter and others, General Fraser was the choice for 1999 to receive this unique honor from the General Patton Memorial, in recognition for his significant contributions to world peace.

Specifically, General Fraser was recognized for "leadership and bravery with the 51st Engineer Combat Battalion, United States Army, during critical battles to halt the German offensive in the Ardennes, during December 1944; and for your post-military career, remarkable for its concentration on delivering a high quality of educational opportunities to students at the United States Military Academy, West Point, New York; the South Dakota School of Mines and Technology, Rapid city, South Dakota; the Oregon Institute of Technology, Klamath Falls, Oregon; and the California Maritime Academy, Vallejo, California."*

*The excerpt is from the notification letter of 1 August 1999, to General Fraser from Jan Roberts, Board President, General Patton Memorial Museum.

Purple Heart

Abbott, William H.	Co. A	Green, Richard I	Co. C	Ochson, Joseph H.	Co. A
Bailey, Theodore O.	Co. C	Greenwood, Leo O	Co. C	Palmer, Anthony J.	Co. A
Banks, Thomas G.	H & S	Groce, William M.	Co. B	Peale, John B.	Co. A
Barco, Colon A.	Co. C	Gurnsey, Edward B.	Co. C	Pedersen, Karl G	Co. A
Blackburn, Cecil C.	Co. C	Gyure, Joseph	Co. C	Phillips, Charles	Co. A
Booth, Larry C.	Co. B	Harmon, Bill	Co. B	Pickard, Ossie L.	Co. C
Brown, Clyde R.	Co. A	Haywood, Ray	Co. A	Pratt, Clifton M.	Co. A
Brown, Gerald C.	Co. C	Herrin, Mimz C.	Co. C	Preston, Bennett	Co. C
Capps, Glenn L.	Co. B	Highfield, James E.	Co. A	Rankin, William W	Co. C
Carlisle, Matthew R.	H & S	Hindman, Charlie S.	Co. C	Roberts, Wilson	H & S
Carney, Warren K.	Co. B	Hodges, Preston C.	Co. B	Romano, Frank B	Co. C
Carroll, Nelson	Co. A	Houdlette, Clarence	Co. C	Rose, Winston W.	Co. C
Carruth,, John N.	Co. B	Howry, Lamont	Co. B	Salazar, Andrew G.	Co. C
Casados, Casimiro	Co. A	Huehn, Carl L., Jr.	Co. A	Scenna, Frank B.	Co. A
Conley, L. D.	Co. B	Ishmael, Lee J.	Co. B	Sherwood, George	Co. A
Connelly, Oliver M.	Co. A	Jenkins, Edgar L.	Co. B	Smith, Coy D.	Co. A
Conner, Grover C.	Co. C	Joyner, Marvin C.	Co. B	Smith, Harold B.	Co. A
Cowen, Thearndeen	Co. A	Kennedy, Earlie	Co. A	Smith, Philip G.	Co. B
Crews, Charley E.	Co. C	Livermore, Thomas W	Co. B	Snow, James M.	Co. C
Curtis, Paul W.	Co. A	McFarland, Dewey A.	Co. B	Spivy, Radford	Co. C
Cuthberth, Russell R.	Co. C	McFarling, Thadius J.	Co. B	Stephens, Jerry R.	Co. A
Diffenbach, Patrick A	Co. C	McBee, Earl C.	Co. B	Strawser, Carl	Co. C
Donato, Andrew A.	Co. C	Malcolm, Barnett R.	Co. C	Tillman, Raleigh	Co. B
Doucet, Emile J.	Co. A	Maples, Lehn	Co. C	Trafford, Raymond A	Co. A
Dunlap, John G.	Co. A	Marquez, Jose E.	Co. C	Tritt, William D., Jr.	Co. C
Elliott, Frank J.	Co. A	Mathis, Edgar L.	Co. B	Warzechowski, Stanley	Co. B
Evans, William D.	Co. B	Middleton, Hervie L.	Co. B	Wheatley, James T., Jr.	H & S
Fairchild, Houston M.	Co. A	Mims, David C.	Co. B	Williams, Arthur F.	Co. C
Fernandez, Emiliano	Co. A	Montgomery, Edgar	Co. C	Wininger, Marion M.	Co. C
Formby, Doyle, M.	Co. C	Morgan, Gordon G.	Co. A	Wotton, David L.	Co. C
George, Alex	Co. B	Nabors, Fred A.	Co. C	Wright, Floyd D.	Co. A
Gossard, Evers	Co. C	Nelson, Charles	Co. A	Yeates, Buster	Co. B

Roll Call

The following soldiers gave there lives in the line of duty in Europe:

Killed Overseas		Date			Location	Manner of Death
PFC	Cecile Blackburn	Mar.	11,	1945	Rhine River	killed during bridging
Pvt.	Gerald C. Brown	Feb.	15,	1945	Germeter, Germany	tripped Riegel mine near Schmidt
Sgt.	L. D. Conley	Mar.	14,	1945	Rhine River	500 lb. bomb dropped on Rhine bridge
1st Lt.	Paul W. Curtis, Jr.	Dec.	21,	1944	Hampteau, Belgium	machine-gunned while attempting bridge demolition
T/5	Paul Dufallo	Oct.	24,	1944	Tohogne, Belgium	accidental discharge of M-1
S/Sgt.	Alex George	May	07,	1945	Southern Germany	premature explosion during demolition operation
PFC	Ray Haywood	Mar.	04,	1945	Lommersum, Germany	struck box mine while digging with with pick-mattock
PFC	Edgar L. Mathis	Mar.	14,	1945	Rhine River	500 lb. bomb dropped on Rhine bridge
S/Sgt.	William W. Rankin	Dec.	20,	1944	Trois Ponts	killed by 20mm shell while stationed at OP
S/Sgt.	Floyd P. Rich	Apr.	09,	1945	Northern Germany	truck accident
PFC	James M. Shanes	July	25,	1944	Haut Verney, France	buried by rock quarry over-explosion
PFC	James M.Snow	Dec.	18,	1944	Hâbièmont, Belgium	ambushed by tank on N23, near the DuPont chateau
Cpl.	Jerry R. Stephens	Dec.	21,	1944	Marcourt	took friendly fire while on sentry duty
Pvt.	Carl Strawser	Dec.	20,	1944	Trois Ponts	88mm shell hit his 50-cal. machine gun position
PFC	Raleigh Tillman	Mar.	14,	1945	Rhine River	500 lb. bomb dropped on Rhine bridge
PFC	David L. Wotton	Feb.	15,	1945	Germeter, Germany	tripped Riegel mine near Schmidt

Amazingly, only 16 of the 630 men in the 51st Engineer Combat Battalion lost their lives in the line of duty during 10 months of combat in Normandy, Northern France, the Ardennes, the Rhineland and Central Europe Campaigns.

Along with the superior leadership of Lt. Col. Harvey R. Fraser and the ingenuity of Major Bob Yates, a partial explanation for the low casualty rate in the 51st may be found in a letter to Mrs. H. Wallis Anderson from Laurie S. Radford, dated December 19, 1988:

"The more I read about the war and think about all that the men under him (Col. Anderson) accomplished, the more I admire him. He had so much common sense, foresight and anticipation of what sort of hard training they needed to be able to face and endure the drudgery, the misery, the horror of combat - they couldn't realize what was coming, but the Colonel (a veteran of the Mexican War and WWI) knew and prepared them to face it.

"I'm sure they grumbled and complained about all the hard training at Plattsburg, but it paid off. So many of the men said later they never endured anything much worse in combat! So they got excellent training from your husband. And thanks to your husband, in large part, there were very few war widows (or grieving family members) among the 51st ranks, and others he trained."

The following pages are extracted from a list, maintained over the years by Frank Lee, of Battalion members during the European campaigns. The men are grouped by company and the last known location is listed.

COMPANY A

Last	First	MI	City	State
ABBOTT	William	H.	Fort Worth	TX
ALEXANDER	William	D.	Humboldt	TX
AMARAL	Louis		Bristol	RI
ARBOGAST	Jesse	M.		WV
ARMIGO	Fidel			NM
BADDELEY	Alfred		San Jose	CA
BAILEY	Marc	H.	New Orleans	LA
BAILEY	Wesley	G.	Spindale	NC
BELCHER	Frebert	L.	Valliant	OK
BILL	James	H.	Brockton	MA
BLANKENSHIP	Ernest	V.	Adamsville	TN
BOGGS	Alvin	R.	Dothan	AL
BOLHA	Albert			PA
BONIFAY	Donald	A.		TX
BOROWSKI	Edward	W.	S Williamsport	PA
BOWENS	George		Green Cove Spr	FL
BRADFORD	Gordon	L.	Birmingham	AL
BRADLEY	Seward	T.	Ila	GA
BREEN JR.	John	J.	Charlotte	NC
BROWN	Clyde	R.		PA
BRYAN	Julian	C.	Thomaston	GA
BYRD	Roy	B.	Henderson	MN
CANNON	Elder	D.	Tallassee	AL
CARPENTER	Vernon	I.	Durham	NC
CARROLL	Nelson		Liberty County	GA
CASADOS	Casimiro		Chamisal	NM
CLARK	Maynard	A.	Eagle Rock	VA
COMBS	George	E.	Hays	NC
CONNELLY JR.	Oliver	H.	Cornersville	TN
COSTANTINO	Peter	D.	Ontario	CA
COWEN	Thearndeen		Sentinel	OK
CRITSER	W.	C.		KS
CRITSER	Willie	O.		KS
CROMES	Edgar	F.		OH
CURTIS	Paul	W.		
DAVIE	Harold	G.		PA
DAVIS	Isaac	N.		AL
DEO	Ralph	A.	Corona	NY
DILL	Harry	L.	Johnstown	PA
DILLON	Elwood		Dillon	SC
DITCH	Cecil	D.	Joplin	MO
DODA SR.	Milton	L.	Baltimore	MD
DOUCET	Emile	J.		LA
DOVE	Leonard	A.		GA
DRIGGS	Stanley	A.	Manchester	CN
DUDLEY	Harold	D.		FL
DUNLAP	John	G.	Auburn	ME
DURAN	Edumenio		Capulin	CO
EBLEN	Thomas	F.	Kingston	TN
EIKELBERGER	Robert	M.	Chattanooga	TN
ELLIOTT	Frank	J.		AL
FAHLANDER	Lennart	A.	Savannah	GA
FAUSSETT	Loren	H.	Booker	TX
FENT	Roy	G.	Guthrie	OK
FERGUSON	William	H.		TN
FERNANDEZ	Emiliano		Espanola	NM
FINK JR.	Joseph		Vero Beach	FL
FISHMAN	George		Bronx	NY
FLEMING	Leroy		Florala	AL
FOLDEN	Junior			VA
FOREMAN JR.	James	S.	W. Palm Beach	FL
FORMBY	Doyle	M.	Newman	GA
FOX	Eugene		Bartlesville	OK
FUSSELL	James	E.	Center Hill	FL
GARCIA	Samuel	S.	Rincon	NM
GAY	Felix	H.		TN
GIBSON	S.	W.	Roanoke	VA
GOODE	James	B.	Salisbury	NC
GOYET	Raymond	D.	Westbrook	ME
GRAHAM	John	H.	Satsuma	AL
GRISSOM	Louis	F.	New Bern	TN
HAM	Benjamin	C.		FL
HARDCASTLE	Robert	L.	Bakersfield	CA
HAYWOOD	Ray			TN
HEFTER	Leonard	S.	New York	NY
HENDRICKS	Boyce	W.		NC
HENDRIX	John		Rome	GA
HIGHFIELD	James			GA
HIGHTOWER	James			GA
HOFMANN	Wilbur	H.	Binghamton	NY
HUEHN JR.	Carl	L.		FL
HUNTER	Parks	R.	Miami	FL
HUTSON	William	A.		TN
JAMISON	Bruce	W.	Seattle	WA
JAZVINSKI	Teddy	J.	Watervliet	NY
JOHNSTON	Floyd		Anaconda	MT
JORDAN	Clinton	L.	Charlotte	NC
KELLEY	Jay	H.	Washington	DC
KELLY	Herbert	L.	Tampa	FL
KENNEDY	Earlie		Jacksonville	FL
KING	Daniel	T.	Pembroke	VA
KROEN	Charles	G.	Petal	MS
LANE	J.	B.	Atmore	AL
LANKFORD	Herbert	R.	Canon	GA
LEE	Haywood		Fayetteville	NC
LEYVA	Sebastian	D.	El Paso	TX
LINETTY	Sidney	A.	Baltimore	MD
LOTT	Carl	F.	Henderson	TN
LOVINGOOD	Don	W.	Murphy	NC
LYTWAK	Lawrence	P.	Scottsdale	AZ
MABES	James	H.	Spray	NC
MACHADO	Anthony		Isleton	CA
MANLEY	George		Wetumka	OK
MAY	David		Brentwood	NY
MAZUROWSKI	Walter	J.	Newark	NJ
MCCORD	William	R.		MD
MCCOY	Cecil	C.	Bal Harbour	FL
MCLAIN	Eugene		Atmore	AL
MINYARD	Ernest	F.	Boaz	AL
MITCHELL	Raymond	G.	Rockwood	TN
MONEYHEFFER	Paul	E.	Riverdale	GA
MONTGOMERY	Charles	B.	Martin	TN
MOODY	Charles	E.	Euless	TX
MOORE	Carlton	E.		VA
MORGAN	Gordon	G.	Hendersonville	NC
NAGY	Frank	A.	Parma Heights	OH
NELSON	Charles			TX
NOLAN	Leo	F.	Watertown	MA
OCHSON	Joseph	H.	Pittsburgh	PA
ODOM	Johnnie	P.	Wrightsville	GA
OWENS	George	B.	S Jacksonville	FL
PADGETT	Douglas	A.	Vinton	VA
PEALE	John	B.	Eagleville	PA
PEDERSEN	Karl	G.		CA
PERRY	Charles	M.	Portsmouth	VA
PHILLIPS	Charles		Stevenson	AL
PISANO	Reno	V.	Nahant	MA
PRATT	Clifton	M.	Manatee	FL
PULTZ	James	A.	Staunton	VA
PULVER JR.	Arthur	J.	Schenectady	NY
QUINN	Garnett	R.		OK
RACEK	Joseph	F.		PA
RANKIN	Floyd	E.		VA
REYNOLDS	Peyton	E.	Marianna	FL
ROBERTSON	R.	B.	Hollow Rock	TN
ROBINSON	William	E.		PA
RODINE	Alva	L.	El Paso	TX
ROMERO	Roy	J.	Abbeville	LA
ROMEYN	Warren	A.	Amsterdam	NY
RUSON	Carl			LA
RUSSO	Anthony	J.		MD
RYAN	James	M.	Charlestown	MA
SAUNDERS JR.	William	T.	Sparta	NC
SCAFF	Audrey	J.	Hilliard	FL
SCENNA	Frank	B.		PA
SCHULTZ	Walter	T.		PA
SEVERI	Ado		Talmadge	CA
SHELETSKY	John	F.		PA
SHERWOOD	G.	M.	Haddonfield	NJ
SLEMAKER SR.	Charles	I.	Richmond	VA
SMITH	Coy	D.		OK
SMITH	Harold	B.	Shelbyville	TN
SMITHEY	Floyd		Humboldt	TN
SPIVEY	Gaston	F.	Altha	FL
STAMEY	Glenn		Candler	NC
STEVENS	Jerry	R.		
STEWART	Glenn	H.	High Bridge	WI
STIFTINGER	John	J.	Masury	OH
STRAWHACKER	Ralph	A.	Lowgap	AR
SWEATT	Loyd	E.	Amarillo	TX

ROLL CALL

SWEETING	Joseph	R.	Miami	FL
TAYLOR	Horace	G.		TN
TEAGUE	Nolen		Hickory	NC
THOMAS	Roy	L.		NC
TRAFFORD	Raymond	A.	Raymond	ME
VANCE	David	B.		NC
VIGIL	Elfido		Questa	NM
WALCZYK	Felix	L.		WA
WALSINGHAM	Willie	E.	Wausau	FL
WARD	Buron	V.	Montgomery	AL
WATSON	John	P.		MA
WATT	Benjamin	A.		IL
WEIL	Leonard		Nashville	TN
WHITAKER	Archie		Rolla	MO
WHITTAKER	Bennett	H.		FL
WILLIAMS	Warren	G.	Fries	VA
WILLIAMSON	Robert	G.		AL
WIMBERLEY	Harry	S.	Greenbrier	TN
WOOD	Sidney	L.		TN
WOOLARD	Oscar	E.		TN
WORDEN	George	M.		IL
WRIGHT	Floyd	D.	Bonita Springs	FL

COMPANY B

ALARID	Alfonso	N.	Santa Rosa	NM
ANSELL	Willie	T.	Winston Salem	NC
BAIRD	Carl	C.	Pioneer	TN
BARGAR	John	R.		FL
BARTSCHER	Raymond	A.	Salem	SD
BECKER	Marvin	L.	Rockham	SD
BISHOP	Harold	L.		MA
BOHLIN	Harry	W.	Montoursville	PA
BOHON	Calvin	T.		VA
BOULINEAU	Ray	A.	Wadley	GA
BOWMAN	Luther	D.		OK
BRAND	George	H.		GA
BRANNON	Homer	H.	Fairfield	AL
BRAY	George	W.	Winter Garden	FL
BROWN JR.	Preston	L.	Badin	NC
BRUCE	John	A.	Nashville	TN
BULLINGTON	James	L.		TN
CALDWELL	Leazar	M.	Concord	NC
CAPPS	Glen	L.	Oklahoma City	OK
CARNEY	Warren	K.	Oklahoma City	OK
CARRICK	Richard	H.	Erie	PA
CATHERMAN	Floyd	W.	Frostburg	MD
CHILDRESS	Jack	M.		NC
CHIMEL	Anthony	W.	Binghamton	NY
CLARK	Forster		Dayton	TN
CLARK	Troy			TN
CONLEY	L.	O.		OK
COSNER	John	J.	Miami	FL
CROCKER	Norman	R.		TN
DAVIES JR.	John	J.	Erie	PA
DERK	Ivan	W.	Shamokin	PA
DICKERSON	Fay			GA
EDWARDS	Angus	L.	Ponce De'leon	FL
ENGLE	Andrew	B.	Sheridan	PA
EVANS	Charlie	E.		TN
FARLEY	Joseph	E.		NY
FINLEY JR.	William	H.	Philadelphia	PA
FLATER	Don		Jasonville	IN
FOUNTAIN	Fred		Rome	GA
FRANCE	William	R.	Roanoke	VA
FRANKHAUSER	Ray	E.	Clinton	AL
FRYE	Ralph	E.	Hickory	NC
GARZA	Edmundo	R.	Juarez	MX
GASKIN	Ernest		Boaz	AL
GEHR	Ralph	W.	Randleman	NC
GEORGE	Alex			PA
GLADNEY	Luther	L.		GA
GLENN	Olen	T.	Glenville	GA
GREGORY	James	M.	Martinsville	VA
GRIFFITH	Harold	J.	Jefferson	GA
GROCE	Lee	R.	Cycle	NC
GROCE	Raymond			KY
GROCE	William	M.	Advance	NC
GUFFEY	Calvin	L.	Staunton	VA
GURNSEY	Edward	B.		AZ
HANLEY	Louis	V.	Greene	IA
HARMON	Bill		Fairburn	GA
HARRELL	Ernest	F.	Knoxville	TN
HARWOOD	Vincent	J.		PA
HAUDENSCHILD	Edward	L.	Miami	FL
HAWKINS	Claudie	C.	Binger	OK
HAYES	James	R.	Shreveport	LA
HODGES	Preston	C.		VA
HOLLAND	Claude	R.		NC
HONEYCUTT	Horace	L.	Radford	VA
HOROWITZ	Nathan		New York	NY
HOWERTON	Jim	R.	Hot Springs	AZ
HOWRY	Lamont		Geronimo	OK
HUVAL	Paul	M.		LA
INGRAM	Claude	A.		NC
ISHMAEL	Lee	J.	Woodburn	OR
JACKSON	Charlie	E.	Fairburn	GA
JACOBY	William	C.		PA
JAMES	Henry	W.	Lexington	NC
JARRARD	Lee	G.	Dahlonega	GA
JARRELLS	Travis	R.	Oxford	AL
JENKINS	Edgar	L.		VA
JOHNSON	Dullus	J.	Hendersonville	NC
JONES	Ira	E.		VA
JOYNER	Marvin	C.	Jackson	TN
KIDD	Hughel	I.	Kannapolis	NC
KIDD	Willard	L.		OK
KIRKLAND	Loren	C.	Humboldt	TN
KRUER	Arthur	G.	Clarksville	IN
KUYKENDALL	Omer	N.		OK
LANSBERRY	Maurice	R.	Ashton	ID
LAWSON	Rudolph	W.	Mayodan	NC
LENHART	John	J.	Charleroi	PA
LEVY	Joseph	T.	Baltimore	MD
LEYBA	Lorenzo	G.	Bernalillo	NM
LIVERMORE	Thomas	W.	Sharon	PA
LOGAN	John	W.	Brundige	AL
LONG	Ralph	W.		VA
LONG	William	N.	Mckenzie	TN
MATHIS	Edgar	L.		OK
MAUGANS	Joe	C.	Trinity	NC
MCBEE	Earl	C.	Knoxville	TN
MCCAY	John	T.	Plainview	TX
MCCORKEL	Fred	L.	Jacksonville	FL
MCCUE	Albert	E.		VA
MCFARLAND	Dewey	A.	Winslow	AZ
MCFARLING	Thadius	J.	Birmingham	AL
MCLENDON	Joel	T.		NC
MCWHORTER	Marion	G.		AL
MESH	Michael	S.		PA
MIDDLETON	Hervie	L.	Modesto	CA
MILLER	Ralph	W.	Watertown	NY
MIMS	David	C.	Albuquerque	NM
MORA	Esquipula	L.	Cuba	NM
MURPHY JR.	James	A.	New Britain	CT
MURRAY	Leo	L.		MD
NELSON	Leo	E.	Richland Cntr	WI
O'NEILL	Harold		Carlisle	PA
O'NEILL	William	J.	Norristown	PA
ORTEGA	Tomas	G.	El Paso	TX
ORTIZ	David	T.	Chimayo	NM
OVERHOLTZER	Chester	R.	Thurmont	MD
OWENS JR.	William	H.		TN
OZIER	Edward	L.	Buena-Vista	TN
PARKER	Maddie		Charleston	SC
PARRISH	Calvin	C.	Staunton	VA
PARRISH	Otis	B.	Trenton	TN
PAUL	Frank		Ambridge	PA
PEIO	Paul	D.	Bedford	OH
PENDERGRASS	James	A.	Dickson	TN
PETRINI	Nevio		Naples	FL
PIERCE	Raymond	G.	Petersburg	IL
POLLINI	Phillip	C.	New York	NY
PORTER	Loren	H.	Cornville	AZ
PRATER	Mark		Goodwater	OK
PUNTCH	Harold	E.		NC
PURGASON	Allen	R.		NC
QUENTIN	Robert	C.	Bronx	NY
RAMOS III	Frank			LA
RANDOLPH	Lloyd	D.	Havre	MT
RICH	Floyd	P.		NY

ROTAN	Delton	B.	Oklahoma City	OK
ROUTH	Roscoe	C.	Idabel	OK
RUDISILL	Earl	H.		PA
SANDERS	Ray		Crestview	FL
SANDLIN	John	S.	Wetumka	OK
SCHENKER	William	S.	Farrell	PA
SCHLOSSER	Harold	E.		PA
SCHLOSSER	James	A.		PA
SCLAFANI	Carmelo			NY
SEBASTIAN	John	A.	Reddies River	NC
SHARBER	Frank	L.	Rockvale	TN
SMITH	Anthony			WI
SMITH	Perry		Lewisburg	TN
SMITH	Phillip	G.	Sharon	PA
SMITH	Thomas	W.	Elkmont	AL
SPEARS	Troy	L.	Crossville	AL
STEELE	Willie		Newnan	GA
STILLITANO	Carmen		Monongahela	PA
STRATTON JR.	Herbert		Philadelphia	PA
STRINGFELLOW	Robert	L.		LA
STULGIS	Peter		Scranton	PA
TACKKETT	George	W.		KS
TAYLOR	Arnold			AL
TILLMAN	Raleigh			
ULBIG	Elmer	F.	Baltimore	MD
VAN HOOSER	Sterling	V.	Nashville	TN
VERRALL	George	M.	Phildelphia	PA
WARZECHOWSKI	Stanley			PA
WATKINS	George	N.		VA
WATSON	Russell	E.	Las Cruces	NM
WILKERSON JR.	Jessie	O.		TN
WILSON	Albert	H.	Dry Creek	LA
WILSON	George	W.	Miami	FL
WILSON	Marvin	D.	Gleason	TN
WINESETT	John	L.		VA
WINNIECKI JR.	Roman	P.	Mercer	PA
WOGGON	Leroy	F.	Toledo	OH
WOGGON	Lewis	C.	Toledo	OH
WOLFORD	Floyd	E.	Detroit	MI
YEATES	Buster		Okeechobee	FL
YOUNG	Lucien			

COMPANY C

ALLEN	Charlie	R.	Alta Vista	VA
ANDREWS	Leroy			GA
ANSLEM	Merrick	J.	Opelousas	LA
ARMSTRONG	William	C.	Collingswood	NJ
BAILEY	Theodore	O.	Fairfax	VA
BALL SR.	James	E.		MD
BARNES	Reese		Opp	AL
BARR	Meade	J.		PA
BEALE JR.	William	B.	Norfolk	VA
BEAM	Howard	B.	Charlotte	NC
BECKLER JR.	Frederick	C.		LA
BEGLEY	Carl		Blackey	KY
BENOIT	Donat	A.	Central Falls	RI
BLOUIN	Lorenzo	A.		LA
BONER	Webb	P.		NC
BORKOWSKI	Joseph	J.		PA
BOYETT	John	W.	Grovehill	AL
BLACKBURN	Cecile	C.		VA
BRADLEY	Euel	D.	Fort Gibson	OK
BREEDEN	William	C.	Knoxville	TN
BREHM	Clifton	C.	San Antonio	TX
BROWN	Gerald	C.		
BROWN JR.	Milbert	W.		VA
BURKETT	Roy	S.	Wellington	KS
BURNETT	William	B.		NC
BURT	Claude	P.	Jacksonville	FL
BYRD	Charlie	A.	Ronda	NC
CARNEY	Jeff	E.	Oklahoma City	OK
CARTER	Clinton		Andalusia	AL
CASALE	William	J.		CN
CASTLEMAN	Joseph	P.	Palmetto	FL
CHANDLER	Boyd	W.	Binger	OK
CLARK	Fayne	B.	El Paso	TX
COBB	Clarence	A.	Atlanta	GA
CONNOR	Grover	C.	Uree	NC
COOPER	J.	T.	Kenton	TN

COOPER	Thomas	F.	Newton	NC
CRAWFORD	James	M.	Spindale	NC
CREWS	Charley	E.	Tampa	FL
CUNDIFF	William	S.		OK
CUTHBERTH	Russel	R.	Memphis	TN
CYR	Eugene	A.		CN
DEGROOT	Oscar	W.		NM
DELGADO	Pablo		Smelter Town	TX
DEMASTUS	Robert	E.	Orlando	FL
DIEFFENBACH	Patrick	A.	Seattle	WA
DONATO	Andrew	A.		MA
DUFFALO	Paul			
EDWARDS	Julian			GA
ELLER	Osmond		Atlanta	GA
ESSARY	Rollen	O.		TN
EVERS	Sylvester	C.	Loretto	TN
FAUST	Odis	C.	Robeline	LA
FINCHER	George	W.	Charlotte	NC
FORRISTER	Orville		Oklahoma City	OK
FRANKLIN	Charles	A.		TX
FROST	Earl	H.	Galax	VA
GARGANO	Alphonse	J.	Kingston	NY
GARRETT	Dennis		Lavergne	TN
GIBBS	Meyler	W.	Logan	NM
GLASGOW	James	B.		PA
GLASS	Lester	H.	No. Wilksboro	NC
GLOVER	Lonnie	V.		OK
GOLDSMITH	Elvin			PA
GOODEN	Charles	W.	Talldega	AL
GOODSON	Floyd	L.	Dodson	TX
GOSSARD	Evers		Salisbury	MD
GOWER	Otto	J.	Keywest	FL
GREEN	James	R.	Mineral Spr.	PA
GREEN	Richard	I.		IA
GREENWOOD	Leo	C.	Eunice	NM
GYURE	Joseph		Daisytown	PA
HADDAWAY	Thomas	E.		MD
HAMPSHIRE	Raymond	F.	Stratford	CT
HATCHER	Lather	M.	Reidsville	NC
HELTON	Elmer	H.	Myrtle Grove	FL
HERALD	Samuel	R.	West Graham	VA
HERRIN	Mimz	C.	Mcadenville	NC
HUGHES	William	A.	Franklin	TN
JACKSON	Alton		Opp	AL
JACKSON	William	J.	Philadelphia	PA
JANICZEK	Joseph	F.	Nanticoke	PA
JOHNSON	Willie	L.	Jacksonville	FL
JUSTISS	Bennie	J.	Titus	AL
KECK	Paul	H.	Gibsonville	NC
KELLEHAN	Heyward	L.		SC
KIRK	John	H.		TN
KLINK	Carl	M.	Bala Cynwyd	PA
KOVAL	Stephen	A.		PA
KUPCHELLA	William		Barnesboro	PA
LADO	Nich			PA
LANHAM	Junior	W.	Covington	KY
LAPOKA	George			PA
LARRIMORE	Samuel	W.	Tampa	FL
LATHAM	Royal	E.	Bemis	TN
LEONARD	Grover	P.		NC
LUGAR	John		Johnstown	PA
MALCOLM	Barnett	R.	Lakeland	FL
MAPLES	Lehn		Muskogee	OK
MARCHANT	Glenn	I.	Palm Harbor	FL
MARQUEZ SR.	Jose	E.	Fairview	NM
MCCALL	Lee	R.		NC
MCNEALIS	John	V.		PA
MEARES	George	M.		FL
MECKLEY	Glen	E.	Watsontown	PA
MIDDLETON JR.	Ralph	K.	Norfolk	VA
MIKUCKI	John		Brooklyn	NY
MILGRAM JR.	Joseph	B.	Cleveland Hgts	OH
MILLARD	Raymond		West Point	MS
MOCK	Jessie	R.	Varnville	SC
MONTGOMERY	Frank	E.	Bassett	VA
MORGAN	Carl	E.		NC
NABORS	Fred	L.	College Sta.	TX
NIERA	Joe	A.	Amalia	NM
NORTON JR.	John	J.	Somerville	MA
OGLESBY	Carl		Millen	GA
OHLER	Raymond	E.		PA

ROLL CALL

OLIVER	John	T.	Philadelphia	PA
OWENS	William	J.	Knoxville	TN
PARM	William	G.	Daytona Beach	FL
PARRISH	George	W.		FL
PASTELAK	George		Sewickley	PA
PEDIGO	Danzel	C.	Nashville	TN
PETERS	Himmel	L.	Graceville	FL
PICKARD	Ossie	L.	Durham	NC
PRESTON	Bennett		Fort Myers	FL
PREVATT	George	W.	Lawtey	FL
QUALEY	Miner	L.		MN
RANKIN	William	W.		
ROBERTS	John		Providence	RI
ROBINSON	Flavil	H.		TN
ROMANO	Frank	B.	Miami	FL
ROSE	Winston	W.	Virginia Beach	VA
SALATINO	Fred	T.	Los Angeles	CA
SALAZAR	Andrew	G.		NM
SANTORO	Vincent	N.	Cohoes	NY
SHANES	James	M.		
SCHEUBER	Sam	C.	San Angelo	TX
SCHLOSSER	Clyde	E.	Mineral Point	PA
SCHROFF	Clifford	P.	Middlestown	OH
SHELTON	Morris	R.		TX
SHORTRIDGE	Thomas	N.	Cadmus	KY
SIMMONS	Jessie	J.	Allen	OK
SNOW	James	M.		
SOUTH	Joe	W.		OK
SPIVY	Radford		Hartsville	TN
STEGER	Daniel	D.		FL
STEPHENS	Elmer	G.		FL
STEPHENSON	Walter		Quinton	AL
STEPP	Joseph	C.	Fort Myers	FL
STRAUSS	John		Nanticoke	PA
STRAWSER	Carl			
SUIRE	Edwin			LA
SULLINS	Grady			FL
TANNER	Nim		Cedartown	GA
TITUS	Ira	A.	Bristow	OK
TOTH	Joseph			PA
TRITT JR.	William	D.	Tampa	FL
VIA JR.	Rufus	L.	Church Hill	TN
WADSWORTH	Chester	M.	Lockhaven	PA
WALKER	Charles	E.	Fullerton	MD
WALKER	Morris	S.	Lawton	OK
WALSTON	John	T.	Farmville	NC
WILBURN	John	R.	Prospect	TN
WININGER	Marion	M.	Scottsboro	AL
WISE	G.	W.		FL
YATES	William	H.	Winston Salem	NC
YONLEY	Joseph	E.	Bellaire	OH
YOUNG	Coy	P.	Hickory	NC
YOUNG	Jacob		Cottondale	FL

H & S COMPANY

ALKIRE	Thomas	W.	Carolina	WV
ANTOL	Zoltan	M.	Cooper City	FL
ATTARDO	Charles	J.	Holiday	FL
BABIN	Cyven	J.		LA
BAIRD	Earle	O.		WA
BAKER	James	W.		TN
BALDWIN	Elmer	G.	Salem	OR
BANKS	Thomas	G.	Karns City	PA
BARGAR	Roger	M.		FL
BARNES	John	W.	Santa Babara	CA
BEASLEY	Edward	W.	Fort Valley	GA
BELL	Elzie	B.	Malone	FL
BEST	Charles	W.		VT
BLANTON	Burrel	V.	Shelby	NC
BLOOMER	Ora	E.	Fairview Beach	VA
BRADSHAW	Earl	R.	Hobart	OK
BRESLIN	John	T.	Allentown	PA
BUNNY	James			OK
CARLISLE	Matthew	R.	Columbus	GA
CARMICHAEL	Duncan		Hamlet	NC
CARVER	Arnold	H.	Sacramento	CA
CARVILLE	Richard	O.	Wilmington	DE
CASH	Garland	M.	Albert	OK
CHRISTIAN	Frederick	J.	Baltimore	MD
CLARK	James	W.	Memphis	TN
CLAVAN	Bernard	P.	Philadelphia	PA
CLIFF	William	L.		PA
COATS	Maurice	E.	Virginia Beach	VA
COLLEY	Edward	B.	Highland Park	MI
CONNELL	James	J.		VT
CONNER	William	B.		FL
COSGROVE	Joseph	E.	Jersey City	NJ
COSTA	Vangel	I.	Worcester	MA
CROOM	Willie	R.	Panama City	FL
DRAPEAU	Arthur	E.	Everett	MA
EDISON	Edward	L.	Salina	OK
EVANS	Billy	C.	Lawton	OK
FAIL	Harvey	J.		AL
FAIRCHILD	Huston	M.	Gonzales	LA
FERREL	Claude	S.		TX
FINN	Henry	A.	Bronx	NY
FISCHBEIN	George		Scottsdale	AZ
FITZSIMMONS	Clair			PA
FOWLE	Barry		Stafford	VA
FRASER	Harvey	R.	Louisville	CO
FREDERICK	Benny		Cleveland	OH
FRICKE	Henry	A.		TX
FUQUA	Cress			FL
GARDNER JR.	Homer		Dayton Beach	FL
GRIFFIS	Jay	W.	Roslyn	NY
HALL	Samuel	D.		NC
HARRIS	Lloyd	A.	Pembroke Pines	FL
HARRISON	James	W.		TN
HENCHIR	Emil		Pittsburg	PA
HENRY	David	H.	Iowa Falls	IA
HORECKA	Julius	J.		TX
HOWIE	Carl	E.	Johnstown	PA
ICZKOWSKI	Frank		Pasadena	MD
JONES	Peter	F.	New Orleans	LA
KELLY	Kenneth		Babylon	NY
KERLICK	George		Sharpsville	PA
KIMBLE	Herman	L.	Rosa	LA
KOCH	Albert	C.		PA
KOEBRICK JR.	Arthur	H.	Toledo	OH
LANGSTON	J.	C.	Clanton	AL
LAPE	Claude	N.		PA
LEE	Frank	H.	Annapolis	MD
LEE	Munny	M.	Honolulu	HI
LEE	Verne	A.	Hallowell	ME
LOCKE	Walter			PA
LOWERY	John	D.	Decatur	GA
MADISON	Daniel	H.		PA
MADISON	Frank	F.	Marysville	WA
MARTIN	Patrick	J.	New York	NY
MAXSON	Reed	T.	Warrensburg	MO
MCCOLLAM	A.	B.	Foresthill	CA
MCCRACKEN	John	T.	Lubbock	TX
MILGROM	Harry			
MORIN	Wilfred	G.	Fitchburg	MA
MOSES	Francis	M.	Pensacola	FL
MUELLER	William	R.		AZ
MUSSOMELI	Marino		Sun City	AZ
MYER	Robert	H.	Hunlock Creek	PA
NEWCOMER	Chester	M.		PA
OVERSTREET	Franklin	H.		GA
PARKER	Arnold	G.	Jacksonville	FL
PERKINS	Myron	T.	Davenport	IA
PORONSKY	John	A.		IL
PORTER	Alden	M.	Niceville	FL
POULTON	Oscar	R.	Belle Valley	OH
POWELL	Lawrence	W.		NC
PRINGLE	Francis	M.		FL
PUGH	Paris	H.		VA
RACKUS	Willis	R.	Los Angeles	CA
RADFORD	Albert	E.	Chapel Hill	NC
RAMBEAU	Wayne	P.	Raleigh	NC
RAPER	Lee	N.	Denver	CO
REED	Apton			LA
ROBBINS	Donald	E.	Elizabethtown	PA
ROBERTS	Clay	E.	Tulsa	OK
ROBERTS	Wilson			GA
RUDIN	Melvin	K.	Brooklyn	NY
SELF	Harold	L.		VA
SENGER	Lawrence		Erie	PA
SHOVER	Frank		Albuquerque	NM

SIMMONS	Delbert	H.	Odessa	TX
SIRIANNI	Peter	A.	Sharpsville	PA
SLAUGHTER	Scott		Grants	NM
SMITH	George			TN
SPEDDEN	James	W.	Cambridge	MD
SPURRIER	James	D.	Broken Arrow	OK
STEINAGEL	Harlan	G.		WI
STINSON	Donald	L.	Owensboro	KY
SWINDLE	John	E.	Carbon Hill	AL
SZALAY	Stephen			OH
TAYLOR	Chester	B.	York	PA
TAYLOR	Eugene	J.	Blackshear	GA
THOMAS	Paul	E.		TN
TIDWELL	Dick			TN
TRAVIS	Cecil	A.		NC
TREW	Charles	J.		PA
TURNER	George	T.	St. Petersburg	FL
VENABLE	Wallace	J.	Latwell	LA
VOLPE	Paul	T.	Poughkeepsie	NY
WALKER	Eldridge		Camden	TN
WARD	William	L.	Dozier	AL
WATKINS	Robert	G.		PA
WATTS	Gonslo		Brockford	NC
WEBB	Robert	W.	Nashville	TN
WEBER	Harry	M.		MD
WHEATLY JR.	James	T.	Jacksonville	FL
WHEELER	William	H.		CN
WILKES	Edward			GA
WILSON	Woodrow	L.		OK
WOMBOCKER	John	D.	Scranton	PA
WOTTON	David	L.		
YATES	Robert	B.		TX
ZIMONT	R.	D.	Three Rivers	MI

MEDICAL

ANDERSON	Erwin	W.	Simi Valley	CA
BEEMAN	Virgil	I.		TN
CHASTAIN	Winford	C.	Edmond	OK
CLEAVER	Walter	J.	Edmond	OK
GRAY	Isaac	S.		TN
HARRIS	Herman	W.		TN
PACE	John	W.		TN
PARKER	W.	J.		TN
ROBERTSON	William	L.	Tyler	TX
SPAIN	Conrad		Huntingdon	TN
SPAIN	John	V.		TN
TAYLOR	Elmer	S.		TN
THORNTON	Buford	W.		TN
WRIGHT	Phillip	F.	Cambridge	MA

GP STAFF

ANDERSON	Wallis	J.		PA
BARZILAY	Ira		Los Angeles	CA
GRAY	John	W.	Puiyallup	WA
KIRKLAND	James	A.	Tyler	TX
MASSOGLIA	Martin		Chapel Hill	NC
TRANSOE	Ray	W.	Rural Hall	NC
WILLIAMS	Thomas	JC	Virginia Beach	VA
WITTWER	Glade	W.	Alexandria	VA

UNKNOWN (on list but unit not recorded)

CARNAHAN	Bill			PA
CASEY	Gerald	J.		IL
MELTON	Ann		Ringold	GA
PERALTA	Eduardo		Polvadera	NM
SHANDOR	Paul			PA
DUBOIS	Dana		Poway	CA

Appendices

Bibliography

[Editors's note: ***Unbroken Line*** is a partial unit history/memoir and not a comprehensive work of history, even of the 51st ECB, unless perhaps combined with ***The 51st Again!*** As such the following bibliography is more eclectic and far shorter than most World War II bibliographies. Of hundreds if not thousands of works on World War II, these selected few include the source materials quoted in this book and a few others. Editing this material has been a long evolutionary process. Part of that process included the books listed below, which provided many hours of absorbing reading while enlarging the perspective and filling in much detail. All are highly recommended.]

SPECIFIC 51ST SOURCES AND OTHER MAIN SOURCES:
Barry W. Fowle and Floyd D. Wright. ***The 51st Again!*** *An Engineer Combat Battalion in World War II*. 1992. White Mane Publishing Company, Inc., Shippensburg, PA. This is an essential companion to ***Unbroken Line***, or *vice versa*. It contains much detail that is not repeated herein. The maps were unfortunately poorly printed.

Ken Hechler. ***Holding the Line***: *The 51st Engineer Combat Battalion and the Battle of the Bulge, December 1944-January 1945*. (1945). Studies in Military Engineering, Number 4. 1988. Office of History, United States Army Corps of Engineers, Fort Belvoir, VA. The original narrative by Ken Hechler, combat historian and Infantry Captain at the time, was based primarily on interviews of participants taken very shortly after action by Capt. Hechler and T/4 Harvey R. George. The manuscript lay in the files for 40 years, and some effort was required to make it publishable — which effort Barry W. Fowle supervised. Kathy Richardson and Connie Potter edited and proofed the manuscript, and Robert R. Weekes prepared all the graphic art. Diane Arms, editor for the Office of History, assisted with the cartographic research and verification of the place names mentioned in the text.

Charles B. MacDonald. ***A Time for Trumpets***: *the Untold Story of the Battle of the Bulge*. 1985. Quill/William Morrow, New York, NY. Perhaps the definitive source on the Battle of the Bulge, this classic is highly readable as it captures the drama and makes sense of the confusion of the Bulge - a must read.

Robert E. Merriam. ***Dark December***. 1947. Ziff-Davis, Chicago, IL. (Current edition: *The Battle of the Bulge*, Bantam Books). Sadly out of print and hard to find even in the cheap paperback version, this is an inspiring, forceful early chronicle of the Bulge, written when memories were still powerfully fresh.

MAPPING SOURCES:
John E. Williams, Editor. ***Prentice-Hall World Atlas***, *Second Edition. 1963. Prentice-Hall, I*nc., Englewood Cliffs, NJ. This is a long out-of-date Atlas but beautifully rendered and a favorite of the editor.

Thomas E. Greiss, Series Editor, the West Point Military History Series. ***West Point Atlas for The Second World War: Europe and the Mediterranean.*** 1980. Avery Publishing Group, Inc., Wayne, NJ. Originally published by West Point's Department of History in 1980. These copyright-free, government maps are also available as good resolution, color downloads on the Internet (http://www.dean.usma.edu/history/...). Indispensable.

The Times Atlas of the World, *Comprehensive Edition*. 1983. Times Books / New York Times Book Co, Inc., New York, NY. This atlas (and subsequent editions) is justifiably called the "Rolls-Royce of atlases".

Geocart Atlas of Germany *(1:250,000)*. 1998. Ravenstein Verlag GmBH, Bad Soden/Ts. If it's in Germany, it's on these richly detailed maps, with very rare exceptions that MAPQUEST claimed to find (sort of).

OMNI RESOURCES, Burlington, NC (www.omnimap.com). Huge inventory of European and other topographic maps, including those used in this book from the *National Geographical Institute - Brussels*.

MAPQUEST (www.mapquest.com). If one had a dollar for every use of this site, one would be wealthy.

WEAPONS, MILITARY INFORMATION AND MISCELLANEOUS SOURCES:
Martin C. Windrow, General Editor. ***Aircraft in Profile***, Vols 1, 2, and 4. 1968. Doubleday and Company, Inc., NY. Richly and concisely detailed; full-color drawings from several perspectives; jumbled organization. A far better organized, more readable, more graphically interesting though less comprehensive work is the one-volume ***The Encyclopedia of 20th Century Air Warfare***. Chris Bishop (Ed.). 2001. Barnes and Noble Books, Inc., NY.

Bernard Fitzsimons, Ed. ***Tanks and Weapons of World War II***: *Beekman History of the World Wars Library*. 1973. Beekman House, NY. Treasure store of drawings and descriptions of many of the weapons used.

Dr. F. M. Von Senger und Etterlin. ***German tanks of World War II***: *The Complete Illustrated History of German Armoured Fighting Vehicles, 1926-1945*. 1974 (translator: J. Lucas; editor: Peter Chamberlain and Chris Ellis). A&W Visual Library. Sketches, specs, and fine organization and detail. Best source found on the subject.

SPECIFIC BACKGROUND SOURCES AND THE WIDER PERSPECTIVE:
Bevin Alexander. ***How Hitler Could Have Won World War II***: *the fatal errors that lead to Nazi defeat*. 2000. Crown Publishers, NY. An eye-opener that paints a broad picture of German expansion and later collapse and pinpoints where history could so easily have taken a much darker path. Basically, Hitler's ego contained seeds of both Nazi success and ultimate failure. Makes sense of major puzzles and the larger shape of the whole conflict.

Stephen E. Ambrose. ***Citizen Soldiers***: *the U. S. Army from the Normandy Beaches to the Bulge to the surrender of Germany*. 1997. Simon & Schuster, Inc., Rockefeller Center, 1230 Avenue of the Americas, New York, NY. This is a highly readable and intimately involving, detailed story of the life of our citizen-soldiers.

Belton Y. Cooper. ***Death Traps:*** *the survival of an American Armored Division in World War II*. 1998. Presidio Press, Novato, CA. Dramatic, first-hand account of the astounding, war-altering job of Army mechanics' salvaging and repairing armor; details terrible vulnerability of Sherman tanks. Field officers in the Nov. 1944 push toward Cologne felt the Bulge may have been thwarted had they Pershings, not inadequate Shermans.

Michael and Gladys Green. ***Patton: Operation Cobra and Beyond***. 1998. MBI Publishing Company, Oscceola, WI. Overflowing with photographs; book gives a fairly straightforward recounting of Patton in Northern Europe.

Williamson Murray and Allan R. Millettt. ***A War to be Won:*** *fighting the Second World War*. 2000. The Belknap Press of Harvard University Press, Cambridge, MA. Highly praised; perhaps the best single-volume history of the war, offering sometimes shocking, fascinating perspectives along with excellent summaries of the campaigns.

Michael Frank Reynolds. ***The Devil's Adjutant:*** *Jochen Peiper, Panzer Leader*. 1995. Sarpedon Press, NY. A fine, fascinating resource for learning more about Peiper; rich with detail and clear maps.[Ja, "Jochen", he says.]

Charles Whiting. ***The Battle of Hurtgen Forest***: *the untold story of a disastrous campaign*. 1989. Orion Books, a division of Crown Publishers, Inc. 225 Park Avenue South, New York, N.Y. A haunting and gripping story of a long-buried battle that preceded and accompanied the Bulge but is virtually unknown, perhaps by tacit design of generals shamed by failure. As the author notes, lessons not learned in the Hürtgen were repeated in Vietnam.

APPENDICES

About the Maps and Photographs

MAPS. Every map in this book is 100% digital, consisting of "bezier" curves controlled by "nodes", placed manually one by one wherever such curves change direction. For example, the "Battle Lines" map has over 15,000 nodes to define contours, streams, battle lines, etc. Such detail yields maps somewhat comparable to the beautiful atlas and topographic background base maps. Since adequate military field maps of the time were not found, all the maps created used post-WWII sources. To make each map, a base map would be extracted from an atlas sheet or topographic map. Then other maps were fit onto that unchanging base by means of tilting, sizing, and skewing. References on the overlay (major cities, streams) were thus matched up to the same points on the base and then the associated battle lines or other desired features were transferred to the base map and the rest of the overlay was discarded. Some adjustment was always needed to be ensure that lines were correctly placed relative to streams or towns.

Mismatching was the rule from map to map, due to differences in *projection*, *scale, resolution,* and *quality*. Piecing together the West Wall was an example of this, with the quality of source maps ranging from fine to medium to coarse detail. The various *West Point Atlas* maps even varied significantly in placement and size. The "Battle of the Bulge" map (p.10) shows the West Wall at something like it's true size along the right edge of the bulge (developed from detail in *A Time for Trumpets*) and elsewhere shows the feature at about twice that size. Even a very high quality source, *The Times Atlas*, was inconsistent from one map sheet to an adjacent one, as one learned when trying to match topographic lines between the two so as to splice a small section from one page to the previous page. The same contours from the two different pages proved to be too misaligned to be logically reconciled - perhaps an inherent problem with projections.

At any rate, the maps created for this book accurately give a *relative* sense of the terrain and the related activities of World War II and are intended to be clear, instructive and interesting.

PHOTOGRAPHS. Photographs of the 51st ECB come from the Corps of Engineers Office of History, Alexandria, VA (prints are from the National Archives and elsewhere) and from collections of Floyd Wright and Joseph Milgram with a few other photographs of the 51st from sources noted. At College Park, MD, the National Archives Still Photography collection of wartime Signal Corps photos was searched to fill in the balance of the photography represented herein. This wonderful, though inadequately indexed, resource of millions of photographs contains occasional Ansel Adams quality gems. However, coverage is extremely irregular. Since Signal Corps photography didn't take much notice of the 51st or places they had served, until after the Battle of the Bulge, many non-51st photos were used to show some of what was going on in the same areas and at about the same time that the 51st were present. Obviously missing are images from the heat of battle in Trois Ponts and Hotton areas. Apparently fighting for one's life supercedes photojournalism (and letter writing).

The images, while enhancing the text, nevertheless give only the barest set of reference points to the reality of war experienced by this one Battalion of some 630 soldiers.

Notes on Personnel Changes

<u>51st ECB Staff and Company Officers, 18 March 1943:</u>[1]   The new assignment of staff officers on this date for the 51st ECB was: Executive Officer and Acting Battalion Commander in the absence of Captain Yates (on detached service), 1st Lt. Clifford P. Schroff; S-1, 2nd Lt. Raymond L. Bailey; S-2, 2nd Lt. Arnold H. Carver; S-3, 1st Lt. James H. Ross; S-4, 2nd Lt. Maurice E. Coats; Personnel Officer, 2nd Lt. William R. Mueller; and Motor Officer, 2nd Lt. David H. Henry. Company strengths and officer assignments were: <u>H & S Company</u>, 130 men with 2nd Lt. Albert E. Radford commanding, 2nd Lts. Elmer C. Baldwin and Richard Kelso; <u>Company A</u>, 230 men with 1st Lt. Karl G. Pedersen commanding, 2nd Lts. William G. Garrity, Floyd D. Wright, Elmo F. Johnson, Lyle C. Baugh, Harry W. Fossett, and Edward J. Matish; <u>Company B</u>, 220 men with 2nd Lt. Preston B. Hodges commanding, 2nd Lts. Harold O'Neill, Vincent J. Harwood, Fredrick L. Brucker, Wesley E. Fuller, and George Levitus; <u>Company C</u>, 235 men with 1st Lt. John W. Barnes commanding, 2nd Lts. Richard L. Green, Fred L. Nabors, Robert S. Conklin, Durward C. Hulce, and Nevio Petrini. The First Sergeants were: Harry Milgrom, H & S; Anthony Machado, <u>A</u>; Jack Little (acting), B; and Edward Mills, C. The medical detachment consisted of a battalion Surgeon, Captain Weinstein, and a battalion Dental Surgeon, 1st Lt. John A. Poronsky.

<u>51st ECB Staff and Company Officers at Overseas Staging, 12 November 1943:</u>[1]   The battalion officers at the final staging were: Commanding Officer, Major Reafsnyder; Executive Officer, Major Yates; S-1, Lt. Mueller; Assistant S-1, CWO Morin; S-2, Captain Carver; Assistant S-2, Lt. Senger; Reconnaissance Officer, Lt. Trafford; S-3, Captain Schroff; Assistant S-3, Lt. Norton; S-4, Lt. Coats; Assistant S-4, WOJG Keesing; Motor Officer, Lt. Henry; Assistant Motor Officer, WOJG Horecka; <u>H & S Company</u>, Captain Radford; <u>Company A</u>, Captain Pedersen, Lts. Wright, Baldwin, Boies and Bailey; <u>Company B</u>, Captain Hodges, Lts. Harwood, Scheuber, O'Neill, and Jamison; <u>Company C</u>, Captain Barnes, Lts. Green, Nabors, Nolan, and Attardo.

<u>Additional Personnel Changes in 51st ECB in England:</u>[1]   On 10 April 1944, Captain [Thomas J.C.] Williams of 1111th Group became acting commander of H & S Company and Captain Radford acting commander of Company C. On 17 April Captain Radford returned to H & S Company and Captain Williams returned to 1111th Group. 1st Lt. Scheuber was transferred from Company B to Company C as commander on 17 April. Company changes in this period involved Lt. Jamison from Company B to A to C to B; Lt. Nolan, Company C to B; and Lt. Senger, assistant S-2 to A to B to a medical detachment.

New officers joined the battalion and were assigned as follows: 2nd Lts. Jay M. Kelley and Joseph B. Milgram, Jr. to Company A and Company C respectively on 29 May; 1st Lt. William L. McGarrey to Company B on 24 May and 2nd Lt. James A. Murphy to Assistant S-2 on 1 June 1944.

Captain Schroff was transferred to the 296th Engineer Combat Battalion on 23 April; Lt. Baldwin to the 296th Engineers 17 February; Lt. Bailey to 1111th Engineer Combat Group 23 April and T/4 Salovey to 1111th Group 17 April [neither are listed in "Roll Call" since both left the 51st for 1111th Group].

A cadre of S/Sgt. Hugney, Sgt. Colson, T/5's Anderson and J. M. Johnson, and Pvt. R. O. Lawrence was sent to the 1277th Engineer Combat Battalion 26 February. The 51st received as replacements during this period the following: T/5's Evans, Carroll, Murphy, and Wollard; Pfc's. Flater and Lintner, and Pvt's. Armstrong, Bishop, Costa, Crace, Cyr, D'Napoli, Fahlander, Fischbein, Frankhauser, Hampshire, Horowitz, Larrimore, McFarland, Parm, Raymond, Slade, Tribels, Van Hooser, and Wombocker.

T/Sgt. Oldham returned to <u>Company A</u> and Pvts. Crawford and Larrimore to <u>Company C</u> from North Africa. Individuals placed on medical detachment while in England who had not returned to their units before the overseas

APPENDICES

shipment were 1st/Sgts. Abbot and Middleton; S/Sgt. Simmons; Sgt. Weil; T/5's Barkley, Guisewhite, and Stevens; Pfc's. Rose and Ward; and Pvt's. Bartholomew, Hall, and Scoggins.

The gains through replacements and returning medical detachments were not offset by the transfers, cadre shipment, and lost medical detachments - 623 enlisted men were ready for overseas movement. Officer and warrant officer gains and losses remained at approximate authorized T/O strength for the unit (29 officers and 3 warrant officers).

<u>Letter from Col. Louis P. Leone concerning Company B and Captain Hodges prior to Channel Crossing:</u>

1. Co B of the 51st Engineer Combat Battalion, 1st U.S. Army, has been attached to this command as a training organization for the training of replacement soldiers during the period of 21 February 1944 to date (2 Apr 44). The mission assigned the company was the organizing of training teams to instruct and train replacements, both soldiers and officers, of the several branches of the service represented here.

2. This company has fulfilled its responsibilities here and has accomplished its assigned mission in a superior manner while operating under difficult field conditions and lacking many training aids and facilities.

3. The pride of the individual soldier and officer in the unit's appearance, discipline and conduct is outstanding. The individual and collective enthusiasm of these soldiers integrated in the unit's discharge of its duties, together with their untiring effort and application of initiative and ingenuity in the improvisation of training aids, and the construction of field training facilities reflects the highest credit upon the company. There is no doubt this unit has obtained in its training a superior degree of technical and tactical proficiency and preparedness.

4. It is desired to commend each officer and enlisted man in the unit not only for their individual and collective soldierly accomplishments, but for the unit' high contribution to the training of replacement officers and soldiers. It is also desired to especially mention and commend the commanding officer of this company, Captain Preston C. Hodges, 0110139. Without doubt the unit's high standards have been reached through Captain Hodges' untiring efforts and his outstanding and exemplary leadership. [To this splendid tribute were added similar commendations by endorsements from the Commanding General, First U.S. Army, the Commanding Officer, 1111 Engr Combat Group, and Major Reafsnyder.]

<u>51st Staff and Company Officers, Channel Crossings, 18 June and 2 July 1944</u>:[1]   Commanding Officer, Major Reafsnyder; Executive Officer, Major Yates; S-1, Lt. Mueller; Assistant S-1, CWO Morin; S-2, Captain Carver; Assistant S-2, Lt. Murphy; Reconnaissance Officer, Lt. Trafford; S-3, Captain Huxman; Assistant S-3, Lt. Attardo; Assistant Division Engineer, Captain Barnes; S-4, Captain Coats; Assistant S-4, WOJG Pugh; Motor Officer, Lt. Henry; Assistant Motor Officer, WOJG Horecka; <u>H & S Company</u>, Captain Radford; <u>Company A</u>: Captain Pedersen, Lts. Wright, O'Neill, Boies, Kelley; <u>Company B</u>: Captain Hodges, Lts. Harwood, Jamison, Nolan, McGarrey; <u>Company C</u>: Captain Scheuber, Lts. Green, Nabors, Norton, Milgram; Medical Officer, Captain Weinstein; and Dental Officer, Captain Poronsky.

NOTE: A number of the men mentioned in the above section are not listed in "Roll Call". These include some who were transferred, sent back after early injury or were "booted out" (only two). They include the following: James H. Ross, Richard Kelso, William G. Garrity, Elmo(?) F. Johnson, Lyle C. Baugh, Harry W. Fossett, Edward J. Matish, Fredrick L. Brucker, Wesley E. Fuller, George Levitus, Robert S. Conklin, Durward C. Hulce, Harry Milgrom, Jack Little, Edward Mills, Keesing, (?) Evans, Wollard, Lintner, Crace, Oldham, D'Napoli, Raymond, Slade, Tribels, Boies, McGarrey.

Technical Notes

COMPUTER: Gateway G6-350, PII / 350Mhz, 13GB, 256MB RAM. Visioneer Paperport 6100 scanner.

PRINTER: GCC Technologies, Elite 12/1200N. This is a true 1200 dpi, superior quality laser printer vital for proofing. The book could not have been done without it. The company provides excellent and very personal service as well.

GRAPHICS: CorelDraw V.9 and Corel PhotoPaint V.9. Corel has been the editor's "killer app." since 1991. All the maps and graphics were done in Draw. All the considerable photo editing was done in Paint.

DTP: Corel Ventura Publisher V.8 was the DTP application used for layout. When it worked well, it was wonderful. When it didn't … well, let's not go there. Suffice it to say, I'd rather have been fighting the Bulge! Or at least parts of it.

APPENDICES

Selected Weaponry

NOTE: A vast array of equipment from earlier conflicts and developed during this war shows man's fascination with power, speed, and/or self-preservation. Inventors, both sane and mad, devised tools of all manner of horror. The following pages are not even the tip of the iceberg of man-made destructiveness.

Most military books only mention equipment by name. What in the world is a "half-track", an "88"? How big were the German tanks? What's the difference between a howitzer and artillery gun, etc.? The following is a sketchy rendering of some main weapons mentioned. References used in making these original drawings are listed in the Bibliography. A quick glance at those books reveals a wealth of detail which one is not trying to render here. As with the maps, all these sketches are entirely digital, for better or for worse.

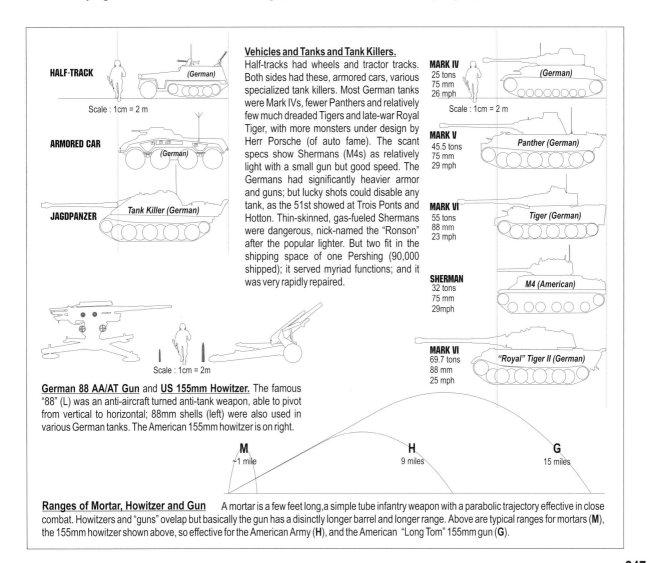

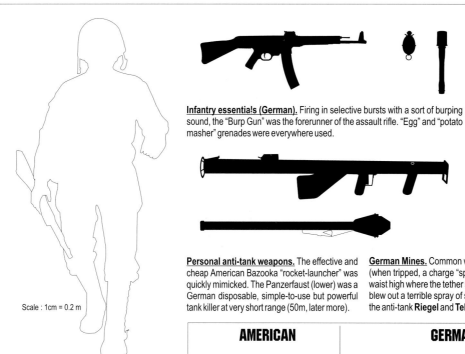

Infantry essentia!s (German). Firing in selective bursts with a sort of burping sound, the "Burp Gun" was the forerunner of the assault rifle. "Egg" and "potato masher" grenades were everywhere used.

Personal anti-tank weapons. The effective and cheap American Bazooka "rocket-launcher" was quickly mimicked. The Panzerfaust (lower) was a German disposable, simple-to-use but powerful tank killer at very short range (50m, later more).

German Mines. Common were **S**-mine "Sprengmine" (when tripped, a charge "sprung" a tethered cannister waist high where the tether set off a main charge which blew out a terrible spray of shrapnel or steel balls) and the anti-tank **Riegel** and **Teller** mines.

Scale : 1cm = 0.2 m

Aerial warfare. Of many craft used on all sides (there was even a Royal Bulgarian Air Force in the war!), four are outlined plus two of the best known German "wonder weapons". The Luftwaffe made its name with screaming Stukas (had a shrill whistle) in the Blitzkrieg that swept western Europe into the Nazi domain with such alarming speed. However, it was an over-rated craft as was the Luftwaffe itself. The American domination of the air over Europe came about with the likes of the fine fighters shown here and briefly mentioned in the text. The German Junkers 88 proved very versatile, especially against the Soviets.

Wonder weapons. Buzz bombs (V-1) proved terrifying as pilotless flying bombs with 1-ton warheads. After D-Day, 9,521 targeted southern England, killing about one person for each of the 4621 that got through; 1.5 million terrified Londoners fled in 6 weeks before the RAF countered the V-1, including use of their first "jet". The much more awesome but less effective V-2 began its arcs into space and back in late 1944. Hitler mistakenly exclaimed, again, that this wonder weapon would "win the war". About 1 50 German wonder weapon projects were still-born in the end. Long before that, they had given up on the Atomic Bomb, which, horribly, may have been used on them had they not been defeated in May 1945.

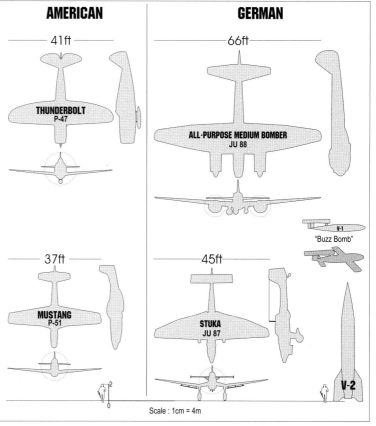

Scale : 1cm = 4m

Index*

A

Abatis 89, 91, 99-100, 126, 184
Aberdeen, Maryland 32
Ahr River, Germany 141
Aircraft, American
    C-47 153
    P-47 fighter-bombers 52, 85, 202
    P-51 Mustangs 52
Aircraft, German
    Jet airplane 145-146
    Ju88 55
    Stuka Dive Bomber 65
Algeria 18, 61
    Fleurus 17, 37
    Oran 17, 35-36, 212, 215
Amblève River, Belgium 73-74, 79, 82, 85, 87, 111, 183, 192-193, 196, 199, 202, 222, 230
American Army 13, 244
    1111th Engineer Combat Group 14, 28, 33, 39-42, 81-82, 84, 87, 109, 111, 118, 125-126, 133, 147, 149, 154, 157, 159, 180, 182, 192, 203, 210, 222, 244
    1128th Engineer Combat Group 38
    1159th Engineer Combat Group 39, 133, 139-140, 146
    1262nd Engineer Combat Battalion 154
    158th Engineer Combat Battalion 76-77, 89, 91, 182, 222
    163rd Engineer Combat Battalion 31
    181st Engineer Heavy Ponton Battalion 137, 139, 144, 185
    1st Infantry Division 129
    22nd Armored Division 34
    238th Engineer Combat Battalion 18, 28, 64, 111, 215
        Blumenthal, Massoglia, Wong 54
    24th Cavalry Squadron 186
    27th Armored Infantry Battalion 137
    291st Engineer Combat Battalion 7, 42, 74, 79, 82, 85, 87, 101, 137-140, 143, 145, 186, 192-193, 199, 203, 230
    299th Engineer Combat Battalion 91, 137
    29th Infantry Regiment 189
    2nd Armored Division 12, 21, 73, 111, 182, 184, 187, 189, 229
    300th Engineer Combat Battalion 111, 188-189
    309th Engineer Combat Battalion 100, 189, 194
    30th Infantry Division, 119th Regiment 203
    32nd Cavalry Reconnaissance Squadron 118-119
    341st Engineer Combat Battalion 82
    3rd Armored Division 12, 21, 73-75, 95-98, 182, 184, 186-187, 229
    3rd Division 157
    408th Field Artillery 128
    440th AAA Weapons Battalion 91, 93, 95
    505th Parachute Infantry Regiment 14, 79, 87, 89, 183, 192, 197, 199, 204-205, 207, 210, 228
    51st ECB, Company A 19, 32-33, 35-36, 38, 76, 79, 82, 89-91, 93, 95, 99, 109, 111-114, 117-118, 120, 126-128, 131, 133-134, 139, 146, 152, 155, 157, 159-161, 182, 184, 186, 190, 194-195, 215-216, 219, 231
    51st ECB, Company B 18-19, 31-33, 38, 41-42, 76, 81, 89, 93, 95, 99-100, 111-112, 116-117, 120, 123, 126, 128, 130, 139-141, 144, 147, 155, 158, 169, 171-172, 181, 184, 186, 194-195, 215, 219, 231
    51st ECB, Company C 14, 18-19, 31-33, 35, 38, 41, 55, 76, 79, 82, 84, 86-87, 89, 99-100, 111-112, 117, 125-128, 130, 139, 143, 147, 155, 158, 181, 183, 191-193, 195-197, 199-201, 203, 205, 207-209, 211, 215, 219, 230-231
    51st ECB, Company H & S 18-19, 32-33, 38, 40, 42, 56, 61, 67, 90, 97, 144, 150, 154-155, 157, 195, 215-216, 244-245
    51st ECB, Units Assigned To 174
    51st Engineer Combat Battalion, Unit History 18
    523rd Ordnance Battalion 97
    525nd Engineer Heavy Ponton Battalion 139, 144, 185
    526th Armored Infantry Battalion 79, 81-82, 84
    552nd Engineer Heavy Ponton Battalion 137
    638th Tank Destroyers Battalion 189
    75th Infantry Division 12, 15, 113, 115-116, 123, 174, 187
    75th Infantry Division, 275th ECB 109, 112
    78th Infantry Division 138, 140
    7th Armored Division 81, 95, 97, 195, 197, 201, 207, 231
    820th Tank Destroyer Battalion 93
    82nd Airborne Division 12, 14, 21, 74, 76, 87, 109, 118, 120, 123, 125-127, 174, 182-184, 192, 198-199, 201, 204, 228-230
    82nd Airborne Division, 307th ECB 109, 112, 118,

---

* **LOCALES** are grouped under **country name**. Also, refer to the map guide on page 8.

128
82nd Airborne Division, 504th Parachute Infantry Regiment 118
82nd Airborne Division, 508th Parachute Infantry Regiment 118
84th Infantry Division 12, 22, 73, 75, 90, 93, 97-98, 100, 114, 182, 184, 186-187, 189, 194, 207-208, 229
84th Infantry Division, 335th Infantry Regiment 190
86th Infantry Division 157, 160-162, 174
86th Infantry Division, 311th ECB 160
87th Infantry Division 118-120
998th Treadway Bridge Company 149, 159-160
9th Armored Division 137-138, 140, 184
9th Infantry Division 12, 15, 122-123, 127-130, 134, 138, 146, 152, 174, 227
Fifth Army 165
First Army 38, 72-74, 76, 108, 111, 118, 123, 128, 138, 143, 154, 165, 171-172, 180, 183, 192, 203-204, 219, 222-223, 225, 229
III Corps, First Army 128-129, 138-139, 145-146, 150, 154-155, 157-158, 229
Ninth Army 109, 138, 182
Rhine Crossing, Engineer Battalions 137
Seventh Army 68, 138, 165, 174
Third Army 68, 73, 108, 118, 123, 138, 154-155, 157, 165, 172, 174-175, 214, 219
VII Corps 75, 108, 186-187
VIII Corps 155
XIII Corps 17-18, 31-33, 76, 215
XVIII Airborne Corps 75, 108, 123, 186, 193, 228
Ammunition Dump Fire 67, 76, 216
Anderson, Col. H. Wallis 13, 18-19, 21-22, 28, 33, 39, 42-43, 67, 81, 84, 86, 117, 133, 157, 159, 164, 171, 177, 180, 192, 200, 210, 219, 222, 235
Anderson, PFC Ervin H. 113
Ardennes 5, 7, 11-13, 15, 21, 59, 72, 74, 76, 102, 108, 120, 123, 154, 183, 195-197, 199-200, 209, 222, 226, 229-231, 233
Arnhem, Netherlands 62, 198-199
Attardo, 2nd Lt. (later Col.) Charles J. 31, 38-39, 43, 56, 186, 188, 244-245
Awards, Individual 232
  Purple Heart 234
Awards, training in England 41
Awards, Unit
  Croix de Guerre with Silver Star 12, 72, 178, 184, 226, 229, 232
  Presidential Unit Citation 5, 12, 72, 112, 150, 184, 198, 207, 217, 225, 229

B

Bahe, Maj. Gordon A. 187-190
Bailey, 2nd Lt. (later 1st Lt.) Raymond L. 34, 244
Baldwin, 2nd Lt. (later 1st Lt.) Elmer G. 32, 244
Banks, T/5 (later Sgt.) Thomas G. 42, 212, 223, 232
Barnes, 2nd Lt. (later Maj. Gen.) John W. 11, 18-19, 27, 34, 36, 38, 41-42, 67, 77, 96-97, 101, 154, 177, 183, 223, 244-245
Baugh, 2nd Lt. Lyle C. 31
Bayerlein, Generalleutnant Fritz 191
Bedell, Lt. Col. Edwin A. 128
Belgium
  Aisomont 82, 84, 86
  Andler 120
  Antwerp 5, 73, 180, 222, 230
  Aye 91, 99
  Aywaille 79, 198, 210
  Baillonville 91
  Barvaux 76-77, 95
  Basse-Bodeux 82, 87, 112
  Bastogne 73-74, 77, 89, 108-109, 180, 191, 198, 207, 222
  Bra 192
  Brussels 73, 152
  Celles 182, 229
  Champlon 194, 231
  Champlon Famenne 64
  Cheneux 203
  Chevron 112
  Ciergnon 70, 190-191
  Ciney 76, 182, 229
  Clavier 102
  Dinant 76, 190
  Durbuy 89-90, 99, 184, 231
  Erezée 76, 95, 98
  Eupen 75, 123, 125
  Forrières 99
  Fosse 112, 117
  Givet 99, 189-191
  Grand-Halleux 113-114, 116
  Hâbièmont 85, 235
  Hamoir 98-100
  Hampteau 90, 93, 96-97, 99, 231, 235
  Hargimont 90
  Harsin 90
  Herresbach 109

INDEX

Hogne 90
Hotton 7, 12, 74, 76-77, 79, 89, 93, 95, 97-98, 100, 105, 109, 180-182, 184, 195, 198, 209, 217, 222, 225, 229-231
Houffalize 108, 198
Humain 91, 99, 186
Jemelle 99, 188
La Gleize 112, 200
La Levée 111
La Roche 89, 95, 105, 184, 186
La Tour 117
Liège 74, 152, 172, 198, 222
Ligneuville 226
Lorcé 112
Maffe 102-103, 109
Malmédy 81, 192, 213
Manderfeld 120
Manhay 197
Manogne 99
Marche 12, 14, 64-65, 75-77, 89-91, 93, 95, 97-100, 109, 114, 147, 180, 182, 186-188, 190, 194-196, 198, 207-211, 222, 225, 229, 231
Marcourt 90, 93, 231, 235
Martelange 59
Melreux 79, 90, 95, 100, 197, 209
Mendendorf 123
Modave 84, 103, 109
Mont Rigi 61
Niaster 111
Noiseux 109, 111
Ourtheville 182
Pessoux 91
Petit Coo 84
Petit-Spai 202
Raeren 125
Reharmont 112
Rochefort 12, 76-77, 91, 99-100, 186-191
Salmchateau 116
Schoenberg 120
Soy 95-96, 104
Spa 73, 77, 180, 192, 218
St. Hubert 186
St. Vith 74, 120, 125, 197, 199, 207, 222
Stavelot 73-74, 79, 81-84, 86, 198, 210, 226
Stoumont 79, 84-85, 111-112, 114-115, 117
Tohogne 235
Trois Ponts 7, 12-13, 73, 76, 84, 112-113, 117, 180-183, 191-193, 195-204, 207-209, 217, 222-223, 225-226, 229-231, 235
Vielsalm 79, 81, 113, 116-117, 199-200, 205
Wanne 199-202, 205
Werbomont 7, 14, 74, 76, 79, 85, 106, 192, 194, 200
Xhoris 111, 188
Bieker, PFC Ralph J. 82-83
Blackburn, PFC Cecil C. 144, 235
Boies, 2nd Lt. Jack E. 34, 36, 39, 244-245
Bolling, Brig. Gen Alexander R. 97, 186-187
Bonifay, S/Sgt. Donald A. 93, 101, 114, 186-191, 232
Bradley, Lt. Gen. Omar N. 18, 38, 74, 114, 138, 233
Bray, Cpl. George W. 101
Bridges
    Bailey 30, 32-33, 39, 109-111, 113, 116, 126, 128-130, 133-134, 147, 151-152, 187, 211, 227
    Footbridges 30, 127, 130
    H-10 portable 29, 32
    Pontoon 12, 15, 28-29, 32, 129, 134, 137-139, 141-143, 145, 185, 229
    Timber trestle 30, 152
British Army
    53rd Infantry Division 12, 22, 184, 229
    XXX Corps 100, 108
Brown, PFC Milbert W., Jr. 83
Brown, PVT Gerald C. 127
Brucker, 2nd Lt. Frederic L. 31
Bunny, James "Indian Chief" 125

C

Camp Bowie, Texas 11, 17, 19, 21-22, 76, 178
Camp Patrick Henry, Virginia 17, 34-35, 212, 214-215
Camp Van Dorn, Mississippi 31
Canadian Army
    9th Canadian Forestry Company 91, 195
Captive Labor 49, 134
Carlisle, T/Sgt. (later 2nd Lt.) Matthew R. 86
Carter, Col. (later Maj. Gen.) William A. 2, 77, 143, 180, 183
Carver, 2nd Lt. (later Capt.) Arnold H. 31, 34, 39, 63, 244-245
Casale, PFC William J. 206
Casey, Gerald J. 56
Cash, Pfc. G.M. 223
Casualties 7, 12, 98, 100, 102, 137, 222
Central Europe 7
Civilians, Belgian 69

Civilians, French 37, 48-49, 51-54, 57, 63, 216
Coats, 2nd Lt. (later Lt. Col.) Maurice E. 32, 39, 41, 141, 212, 232, 244-245
Colley, M/S Edward B. 96
Collins, Maj. Gen. J. Lawton 186-187
Colmar Pocket, France 108
Conklin, 2nd Lt. Robert S. 31
Conley, Sgt. L. D. 144
Craig, Maj. Gen. Louis A. 227
Cundiff, Sgt. William S. 201-202, 232
Curtis, 1st Lt. Paul W., Jr. 90, 93, 95

D

d'Antuono, WOJG 34
Danube River, Germany 11-12, 30, 155, 157-159, 162, 165, 191, 219, 223, 229
Dawley, Lt. Col. Jay P. 111
D-Day 42
Demolitions 12, 24-25, 39, 41, 64, 68, 77, 82, 87, 89-91, 95, 98-99, 109, 112, 137, 182, 184, 186, 191, 199, 209-210, 215, 222, 225, 230
Doucet, PFC Emile J. 114, 116
Driggs, Pvt. Stanley A. 93
Duffalo, T/5 Paul 64

E

Eisenhower, Gen. Dwight D. 73, 138, 164, 184
Ekman, Col. William E. 14, 79, 87, 101, 192, 228
England 37-38, 215
England, Bournemouth/Southampton 17-18, 42, 216
England, Highnam Court 17, 38-39, 41-42, 53, 64
England, voyage to 37
Engle, S/Sgt. Andrew B. 101
Erft River, Germany 133, 227

F

Fahlander, Cpl. Lennart A. 161, 244
Faust, Cpl. Odis C. 87
Fields, Col. Kenneth E. 39, 133, 139
First Army (US) 2
Food 56-60, 64, 67, 103, 154, 168, 171, 216
Fort Belvoir, Virginia 17, 19, 32-34, 76, 95, 212, 215
Fort Dix, New Jersey 17, 33-34, 37-38, 212, 215
Fossett, 2nd Lt. Harry W. 31
France
   Arlon 61
   Carentan 49, 76
   Carteret 55
   Cherbourg 61
   Desertines 56
   Gas 57
   Haut Verney 49, 235
   Hébert 47
   La Chappell-en-Juger 52
   Le Bourg 53
   Metz 60
   Montmedy 61
   Mortain 55, 61
   Neufchatel-en-Saoanois 57
   Paris 61, 104, 134, 152, 213-214
   Perlé 57
   Reims 61
   Rozoy-sur-Serre 58
   St. Lo 50, 52-53, 125, 213, 216-217
   St. Mihiel 58
   Symphorien-les-Monts 56
Fraser 2
Fraser, Lt. Col. (later Brig. Gen.) Harvey R. 2, 11, 18, 22, 69, 72, 77, 79, 89-90, 93, 96-97, 101, 109, 111, 115, 127-128, 131, 133, 138-143, 145, 154-155, 157-160, 178, 180, 183-184, 193-195, 200, 208, 217, 219, 222, 229-233, 235
Frazier, Cpl. Bruce W. 82-83
French Army
   First Army 68

G

Garrity, 2nd Lt. William F. 31
Gavin, Maj. Gen. James M. 127-128, 193, 228
George, S/Sgt. Alex 101
German Army
   116th Panzer Division 12, 75, 181, 184, 195
   1st SS Panzer Division 12, 73, 194
   2nd SS Panzer Division 184, 188, 190
   58th Panzer Corps 181
   Fifth Panzer Army 12, 72-75, 181-182, 184, 230-231
   First Army 157
   Kampfgruppe Peiper 5, 73-74, 86, 181, 183, 191, 193, 198, 200-201, 222-223
   Panzer Lehr Division 189-191
   Seventh Army 73, 157
   Sixth Panzer Army 12, 72-73, 108, 181, 183, 230-231
German SS Troopers 52, 64, 134, 144, 157-158, 165, 199

INDEX

Germany
- Aachen 123, 152, 213, 219
- Antwerp 183
- Attenkirchen 163
- Bad Neuenahr 134, 140, 143-144, 218
- Berlin 117, 144, 158
- Biebelried 168, 170
- Bigge 152
- Bonn 153
- Brilon 154
- Brück 129-130
- Burg 150
- Cologne 65
- Dachau 218
- Dainrode 151
- Dattenberg 139-140
- Esch 134, 139
- Eupen 75, 123
- Froitzheim 133
- Gaimersheim 162
- Germeter 126, 128, 235
- Giesenfeld 162
- Gullesheim 149
- Gunzenhausen 162
- Heister 186
- Herresbach 118
- Hetzingerhof 129
- Hürtgen 126
- Ingolstadt 12, 157-158, 191, 229
- Kalenborn 146-147
- Kassel 156
- Kirchasch 164, 170
- Klein Vernich 133
- Kornelimünster 123, 125
- Kripp 137, 139-142, 185, 191, 218
- Küstelberg 154-155
- Lammersdorf 139
- Langenhahn 149
- Lanschoss 126, 129
- Linz 139-141, 185, 191, 218
- Lohrmannshof 162
- Lommersum 134, 235
- Marburg 150
- Munich 5, 170, 173
- Neustadt (near Main R.) 157
- Neustadt (near Marburg) 154
- Neustadt (on Wied R.) 147, 149
- Nuremberg 155, 157, 170, 172, 219
- Nuttlar 151-152
- Ober Forstbach 125, 127
- Ochsenfurt 154
- Petersarauch 154, 157
- Remagen 12, 39, 109, 139, 141, 145-146, 184
- Rodenhausen 149-150
- Roetgen 63, 125-126, 133
- Rollesbroich 126
- Rothen-bacher Lay 150
- Schmidt 122, 127-129, 235
- Unkel 140
- Wallau 155
- Wulkersdorf 155, 157
- Würzburg 155, 169, 172, 174-175
- Zerkall 129-130
- Zülpich 139
- Zweifall 66, 126

Gill, Maj. Gen. Clair F. 222
Goldsmith, Sgt. Elvin 87
Gossard, Sgt. Evers 85, 232
Green, 1st Lt. Richard L. 14, 31, 82-86, 99, 101, 130, 192, 201, 207-208, 232, 244-245
GREIF (Skorzeny's "Trojan Horse") 74, 82
Gyure, Sgt. Joseph 87

H

Hall, 1st Sgt. Samuel Dennis 63, 166, 211
Ham, Sgt. Benjamin C. 93, 96, 114
Hampton Roads, Virginia 17, 35
Hancock, Capt. G. E. 159
Hardcastle, S/Sgt. Robert L. 114
Harwood, Lt. Vincent J. 31, 39, 244-245
Haywood, PFC Ray 134
Helton, T/5 Elmer H. 83
Henry, 2nd Lt. (later 1st Lt.) David H. 31, 33, 67, 70, 117, 153, 157, 168, 177, 194, 213, 223, 232, 244-245
Hitler, Adolph 5, 7, 73, 108, 149, 157-158, 163-164, 171, 200, 217
Hodges, 2nd Lt. (later Capt.) Preston C. 18, 31, 33-34, 41, 43, 66, 95-98, 101, 140, 223, 231-232, 244-245
Hodges, Lt. Gen. Courtney H. 73-75, 187
Hofmann, Pvt. Wilbut H. 101
Hoge, Brig. Gen. William M. 184
Horecka, WOJG Julius J. 34, 96, 213, 232, 244-245
Hulce, 2nd Lt. Durwood C. 31
Hürtgen Forest, Battle of 126

Hürtgen Forest, Germany 122, 126, 213, 218
Huxman, Capt. Richard F. 32, 36, 38, 51, 93, 245

I

Inde River, Germany 126, 128
Insects and Pests 51-52, 56-57, 59, 169
Ishmael, Pvt. Lee J. 96-98, 101, 232

J

Jamison, 2nd Lt. (later 1st Lt.) Bruce W. 31, 41, 95, 98, 232, 244-245
Jewett, Capt. Robert N. 81-82, 84, 101
Johnson, 2nd Lt. Elmo F. 31
Johnston, T/5 Floyd 110, 188
Jordan, PFC Clinton L. 188

K

Kall River, Germany 123, 126-127
Keck, T/5 Paul H. 87
Keesing, WOJG (later CWO) Walter J. 34, 41, 244
Kelly, T/S Kenneth 96
Kelso, 2nd Lt. Richard W. 31
Kennedy, PFC Earlie 134
Ketchum, Col. E. F. 18-19
Kirkland, Maj. (later Col.) James H. 18, 82, 86, 101, 177
Kroen, Sgt. Charles G. 115, 188, 190

L

Lake Champlain 15, 23, 28-29, 223
Landscape Descriptions 22, 40, 56-57, 62, 66, 122, 126, 147, 149-150, 153, 158, 165, 173, 175-176
Lee, Lt. Munny Y. M. 96
Lee, Pvt. (later Cpl.) Frank H. 24-26, 215, 235
Leone, Col. Louis P. 41
Lesse River, Belgium 190-191
Levitus, 2nd Lt. George I. 31
L'Homme River, Belgium 187-188, 190
Lienne Creek, Belgium 85, 111, 192, 203
Llanelly, Wales 17
Logan, T/5 Robert 83
Lost to Posterity
    A Volunteer and A Bazooka 98
    Tank Driver and Sgt. 111
Lowery, Sgt. John D. 33
Ludendorff Railroad Bridge 137-142, 184-185
Lundberg, Capt. A. P. 203
Lyons, Col. F. Russel, First Army 138, 140, 145

M

Macomb Reservation, New York 15, 22-23, 30-32, 212, 215
Main River, Germany 175-177, 223
Marquez, Pvt. Jose E. 87
Martin, Pvt. Patrick J. 214
Martin, Robert 213
Massoglia, 1st Lt. Martin F. 18-19, 21, 28, 43, 54
Mathis, PFC Edgar L. 145
Matish, 2nd Lt. Edward 19, 244
Maxson, Doctor Reed T. 125, 145
McCollam, Capt. Albert B. 19
McDonald, Dr. Charles B. (author) 180
Melasky, Maj. Gen. Harris 157-158, 160
Meuse River, Belgium 5, 73-74, 100, 180-184, 189-190, 194, 222-223, 230-231
Middleton, 2nd Lt. Hervie L. 139-140, 234
Middleton, Sgt. Ralph K. 31, 245
Milgram, Lt. Joseph B., Jr. 87, 89, 101, 127, 195, 206-207, 223, 230, 232, 244-245
Millard, Sgt. Raymond 209
Miller, Sgt. Jean D. 87
Milliken, Maj. Gen. John 138, 145
Mine detection and removal 12, 15, 24, 31, 39, 42, 47, 54, 56, 69, 76, 111-112, 117-118, 123, 126-127, 133-134, 137, 146, 149-150, 157, 214, 217, 235
Mine emplacement 82-84, 89-90, 93, 99, 181, 194, 197, 199-202, 206, 215, 217, 222
Minyard, PFC Ernest F. 114
Mitchell, T/5 Raymond 113
Mock, Pvt. Jessie R. 87
Montgomery, Field Marshal Sir Bernard L. 74, 138, 187, 198
Moore, PFC Carleton E. 155
Morgan, PFC Gordan G. 134
Morin, WOJG (later CWO) Wilfred G. 34, 232, 244-245
Morocco
    Casablanca 17, 37, 212, 215
Mueller, 2nd Lt. (later 1st Lt.) William R. 32, 41, 56, 232, 244-245
Murphy, 2nd Lt. J.A. 223
Mussomeli, Capt. Marino 154

N

Nabors, 2nd Lt. (later 1st Lt.) Fred L. 14, 31, 84, 99, 199, 202-203, 205-209, 232, 244-245

INDEX

Nazi Loyalists 52, 125, 164, 176

Nolan, 2nd Lt. Leo 36, 41, 244-245

Normandy 5, 11-12, 42, 47, 76, 144, 154, 165, 177, 199, 216

Normandy, Landing 216

Norton, 1st Lt. John J. 38-39, 41, 204, 244-245

O

Ochson, Sgt. Joseph H. 93

O'Neill, 2nd Lt. (later 1st Lt.) Harold L. 32, 36, 39, 244-245

Ourthe River, Belgium 5, 7, 74, 77, 89, 95-96, 98, 100, 180-181, 184, 186, 222, 230-231

P

Parker, Sgt. Arnold G. 96

Patton, Lt. Gen. George S. 73, 118, 138, 154-155, 164-165

Pedersen, 2nd Lt. (later Capt.) Karl G. 27, 51, 91, 101, 154, 191, 195, 216, 231, 244-245

Peralta, Pfc. Eduardo 202

Petrini, 2nd Nevio (Pete) 31

Pets 34, 47, 52, 54, 216

Pisano, Pvt. Reno V. 161

Plattsburg, New York 11, 15, 17, 22-24, 28, 33, 36, 62, 67, 76, 96, 178, 209, 211-212, 223

Poronsky, Dr. 1st Lt. (later Capt.) John A. 41, 51, 244-245

Porter, Cpl. Loren H. 101

Pratt, T/S Clifton M. 93

Pugh, S/Sgt. Paris 39, 41, 245

Pulawski, 2nd Lt. Richard 31, 34

R

Rackus, Pvt. (later Sgt.) Willis R. 96, 218

Radford, 2nd Lt. (later Capt.) Albert E. 21, 29, 31, 34-35, 40, 43, 62, 125, 154, 157, 166, 194-195, 211, 232, 244-245

Radford, David 51, 165, 172-173, 178

Radford, Laurie S. 45, 71, 107, 167, 235

Radford, Letters from Relatives to 165, 168, 171-173, 175, 177

Rankin, S/SGT William W. 87, 196, 201, 232

Raper, M/Sgt. Lee N. 194, 213, 223, 232

Reafsnyder, Maj. (later Lt. Col.) Victor J. 18, 31, 33, 35-37, 41-42, 54, 69, 216-217, 244-245

Reinhardt, Col. G. C. 39

Rhine River, Germany 11-12, 15, 30, 69, 108, 117, 123, 134, 137-139, 141, 144, 146, 150, 153-154, 160, 165, 180, 184-186, 191, 214, 218, 227, 229, 235

Rhineland 235

Ridgeway, Maj. Gen. (later Gen.) Matthew B. 186, 193, 228, 233

Road building 24, 31-33, 39, 41, 57, 59, 63, 70, 76-77, 111-112, 117, 120, 125-127, 129-130, 133, 146-147, 149, 154, 215, 217-218, 223, 227

Road clearing 47, 111-112, 117, 120, 127, 150, 194

Roadblock preparation 89-91, 93, 96-100, 102, 109, 111, 182-184, 188, 194-195, 199, 201, 209, 211, 222, 225

Roadblock removal 152, 157

Roberts, T/5 Wilson 195, 211

Roer (Rur) River, Germany 11, 30, 108-109, 123, 126-130, 142, 144, 146, 150, 164-165, 191, 211, 227

Rommel, Gen. Erwin 55

Roosevelt, President Franklin D. 153, 214

Rose, Maj. Gen. Maurice 98

Rozich, PFC George A. 144

Ruhr Pocket, Germany 123, 137-138, 146, 154-155, 157, 170

Ruhr River, Germany 138, 164

S

Saar Region, France 138

Salatino, S/Sgt. Fred T. 82

Salazar, PFC Andrew G. 82, 84, 210

Salm River, Belgium 13, 73, 76, 79, 84, 87, 113, 183, 197-199, 206-207, 222, 228, 230

Salmon River, New York 15, 29, 223

Sawmilling operations 72, 74, 76-77, 79, 180, 183, 190, 197, 207, 209, 217

Scheuber, 1st Lt. (later Capt.) Sam C. 14, 18, 31, 79, 87, 89, 99, 130-131, 133, 181, 191, 199, 207-208, 223, 230, 232, 244-245

Schnee-Eiffel, Germany 114, 180

Schroff, 2nd Lt. (later Capt.) Clifford P. 18-19, 27, 32, 36, 244

Schwammenaeul Dam, Germany 123

Self, T/5 Harold 195

Senger, 2nd Lt. Lawrence 31, 244

Siegfried Line (see West Wall) 56

Sirianni, Pvt. Peter A. 96

Snow, PFC. James M., Jr. 192, 196, 203, 209-210

South, S/Sgt. Joe W. 205-206, 211

Soviets 5, 62, 108, 117, 125, 158, 164

Spedden, T/5 James W. 42

Spurrier, 2nd Lt. James D. 18-19

Stann, Lt. Col. Eugene J. 139
Stephens, Cpl. Jerry R. 93
Stiftinger, Sgt. John J. 115, 188, 232
Strawser, PFC Carl 87, 196
Sweatt, Cpl. Loyd E.Sweatt 190-191

T

Tillman, PFC Raleigh 144
Tompkins, Maj. William F., CO 552nd 144
Trafford, 2nd Lt. (later 1st Lt.) Raymond L. 34, 36, 39, 41, 90, 187, 244-245
Transport Ships
    HMT Andes 37, 213
    SS Calvin Coolidge 35, 38
    SS Richard Rush 35

U

Urft Dam, Germany 123

V

V-1 Rocket ("Buzz Bomb") 57, 64-69, 102, 112, 134, 137, 146, 213, 216, 247
V-2 Rocket 66, 185, 188, 218, 247
Vandervoort, Lt. Col. Benjamin V. 204, 206
Vosges Mountains, France 68

W

Wales, Llanelly 38, 213
Walker, Pvt. Maurice S. 87
Walters, Lt. Albert J. 82, 87
Watkins, Robert G. 212
Watson, S/Sgt. Russell B. 42, 140
Watson, T/5 John P. (Kelly) 160
Weaponry, American 247
    Bofors 40-mm AAA gun 184
    M4 Sherman Tank 95, 116, 142, 184-185
Weaponry, German 247
    88mm shells 47, 50, 114, 116-117, 192, 201, 216
    Grenades 47, 54
    Mark IV Tank 57, 97
    Mark V Tank (Panther) 57
    Mark VI Tank (King or Royal Tiger) 202
    Mark VI Tank (Tiger) 83, 96-97, 184
Weil, Sgt. Leonard 190, 245
Weinstein, Capt. Seymour 38, 51, 54-55, 244-245
West Virginia 17, 32-33, 36, 76, 215
West Wall 63, 108, 125, 154, 165, 199, 217

Westmoreland, Col. William C. 127
Wied River, Germany 147, 227
Williams, Capt. Thomas J. C. 244
Wilson, Woodrow L. 213-214
Wimberley, Sgt. Harry S. 93
Wittwer, 2nd Lt. Glade S. 19
Wood, PFC Sidney L. 113
Wotton, PFC David L. 127
Wright, 2nd Lt. (later Col.) Floyd B. 11, 18, 31, 36, 39, 90, 93, 96, 98-99, 101, 110-111, 154, 157-159, 186-190, 194, 232, 244-245

Y

Yates, Capt. (later Maj.) Robert B. 13-14, 18, 27-28, 31, 35, 39, 54, 67, 70, 77, 79, 84-87, 89, 99, 101, 103, 127, 131, 133, 141, 143, 145, 150, 152, 154, 177, 181, 192, 194, 200, 202, 204-205, 207-208, 211, 214-215, 219, 223, 230, 232, 235, 244-245
Yingst, Capt. Parke O. 27
Young, T/5 Jacob 83

BATTLE OF THE BULGE - ARDENNES OFFENSIVES

EXTENT OF GE[RMAN ADVANCE]

FIRST U.S. ARMY
Courtney Hodges

THIRD U.S. ARMY
George Patton

Area of penetrations after 2 days is **shaded**. The dashed white line roughly bounds German advances through December 22. The bold black dashed line bounds all German movement. American December offenses were few. Full-scale counterattack in 1945 is represented by January 9, 16, and 24 front lines.

60 miles

26 | 26-24 | 23 | 22 | 21 | 20 | 19-18 | 17

ADVANCES FROM 16 DECEMBER TO 26 DECEMBER 1944

SIXTH SS PANZER ARMY — Sepp Dietrich

FIFTH SS PANZER ARMY — Hasso Manteuffel

SEVENTH ARMY — Erich Brandenberger

THUNDER BEFORE DAWN: The few Americans watching the East long before dawn, 5:30am Saturday, Dec. 16, saw thousands of flickering, silent pinpoints of light along most of the 60-mile Ardennes frontier. Seconds passed. Then came an unceasing thunder of one of the fiercest German barrages of the war. Twenty-eight divisions of 500,000 troops waited in the forests of the Schnee Eifel to execute Hitler's gamble, so unexpected that late into the second day some American commanders still saw only "spoiling attacks".

MASSED ASSAULT: As artillery fell silent, with Panzer forces anxious to follow, tens of thousands of German infantry moved to breach American defenses. They were exhorted to sometimes fanatic courage by "Your great hour has arrived" and "We gamble everything!" [These first thrusts went few miles if any, with varying success, and are represented by the dozens of December 16 lines on the map.]

"TO THE SOUND OF TRUMPETS": As *A Time for Trumpets* dramatically details, individual company, platoon, squad and American soldier stood where attacked, giving no ground easily. Communications mostly cut, world gone crazy, reinforcement in doubt, these thinly deployed forces faced an incredible German strength. But their tenacity and accurate artillery foiled most German hopes for the first day.

FACING THE BREAKTHROUGH: Two SS Panzer Armies were assigned offensive roles, roughly bounded on the map by two dividing lines. Two regular armies were to protect the flanks; Fifteenth Army (north of map), made no advances and is not shown. The lead went to Peiper's 1st SS Panzer Kampfgruppe, to race to Huy on the Meuse. [In the shaded December 17 region, one sees his rapid advance to Stavelot.] On Dec. 18, Peiper hit the 51st ECB defenses and was forced into a death trap. [Trois Ponts area, lightly outlined, is mapped on page 78.]

RUNNING OUT OF TIME: At critical points, American resistance tore into the Germans. This plus severe supply bottlenecks and the difficult terrain, initial blessing, ultimate curse, weakened German columns. Increasingly off-schedule, when opportunities arose they lacked strength to forge on. Major delays where advances stall or stop: Elsenborn, where repeated German assault never claimed the ridge and its crucial roads; St. Vith, which set back the time-table most of a week; Clervaux and Wiltz early on; Bastogne, where the race to secure this transportation hub was barely lost, etc.

THE CENTER STOPPED: The Germans wanted a Marche road hub, similar to Bastogne, & Condroz "tank country". Probing Hotton-Rochefort defenses, they met timely, fierce resistance from the 51st and others and turned aside. [Lightly outlined area defended by the 51st is mapped on page 88.]

BASTOGNE AND BEYOND: Failing to beat American reinforcements into Bastogne, the Germans at first bypassed it. But resisting American teams in outlying areas delayed their bypass. Taking Bastogne became a sort of consolation prize and, later, a strategic goal as the main Ardennes offensive fell further behind plan into total failure. German penetration literally ran out of gas and time and bad weather. By December 26, though some such as Gen. Montgomery, looking over the shoulder of the First Army, feared a renewed SS Panzer thrust to gain the Condroz Plateau and beyond, the threat was only on paper and, now, paper thin.

COUNTERATTACK: In January, a methodical American counterattack forced back a likewise methodical, at times fanatical, German withdrawal. The "Bulge" was erased. By early February the battered Germans were back to their December 16 start. Six weeks later the Allies crossed the Rhine in force; in another six weeks, the thousand year "Third Reich" was dead.

NOTES: The December 25 battle line mapped in *West Point Atlas for the Second World War* was used to draw the southern maximum penetration boundary, the December 26 line on this map. Contours, major roads, streams and features are transposed from *The Times Atlas of the World, 1983 Edition* (freeway-size roads are post-war). *Holding the Line* is the source for smaller and earthen roads shown in the Hotton and Trois Ponts boxed areas. Militarily more important towns are generally emphasized. German route lines are based on maps and text in *A Time for Trumpets*, used by permission of HarperCollins Publishers, Inc.